D0754583

# Representation and Recognition in Vision

# Representation and Recognition in Vision

Shimon Edelman

A Bradford Book
The MIT Press
Cambridge, Massachusetts
London, England

This book was set in Sabon by Windfall Software using ZzTEX and was printed and bound in the United States of America.

Library of Congress Cataloging-in-Publication Data

Edelman, Shimon
Representation and recognition in vision / Shimon Edelman.
p. cm.
"A Bradford book."
Includes bibliographical references and index.
ISBN 0-262-05057-9 (hc : alk. paper)
1. Visual perception. 2. Mental representation.
3. Visualization. 4. Recognition (Psychology) 5. Categorization
(Psychology) 6. Cognitive science. I. Title.
BF241.E28 1999
152.14—dc21 98-39260
CIP

*To my parents—*
*—Shlöm Edelman, MD, and Salomé Edelman, MD*

# Contents

# Acknowledgments

During the preparation of this book, I benefited from discussions with A. Aertsen, M. Bar, S. Barash, I. Biederman, E. Bienenstock, H. H. Bülthoff, P. Dayan, M. Dill, G. Geiger, S. Geman, R. Goldstone, S. Harnad, G. Hinton, Y. Hel-Or, J. Hummel, N. Linial, R. Malach, J. Mayhew, D. Mumford, W. T. Newsome, A. J. O'Toole, T. Poggio, D. Roth, T. Sejnowski, R. Shepard, G. Schechtman, K. Tanaka, S. Ullman, V. Vapnik, Y. Weiss, and D. Weinshall. I have also presented my views on representation and recognition at various seminars and colloquia. I wish, therefore, to thank the Santa Fe Institute, MIT, Harvard, Boston University, Oxford, Stanford, Tohwa University, RIKEN Institute, University of Texas at Dallas, Durham University, the Salk Institute, University of South California, the Technion at Haifa, Hebrew University, ATR Laboratories, Max Planck Institute for Biological Cybernetics, the Royal Society, and the University of Sussex at Brighton. In all these places, I was asked penetrating questions, some of which caused me to re-think certain aspects of my theory, and, occasionally, go back to the drawing board (invariably to my own good).

I owe special thanks to the two places that provided me with the peace and quiet I desperately needed to write this book: the Center for Biological and Computational Learning at MIT (directed by Tommy Poggio), and the School of Cognitive and Computing Sciences at the University of Sussex in Brighton. I hope that my colleagues at CBCL and at COGS will now understand why I was so seldom seen in the common room, and why, when I did appear, I was prone to ask them questions concerning such esoteric issues as the veridicality of object representation.

Much of the original data and computer simulations described here resulted from collaborations with graduate students: Florin Cutzu, Sharon Duvdevani-Bar, Kalanit Grill-Spector, and Tadashi Sugihara. I thank them for everything—not least for the courage shown in accompanying me in research projects whose outcome could not have been foreseen, and for the perseverance required for seeing those projects through.

Throughout the last nine years, I had the extreme fortune of collaborating with Nathan Intrator of Tel Aviv University. Nathan's friendship and scholarly advice were, and still are, indispensable to me. Without his encouragement and intellectual support, this project would have been abandoned long ago. For all that, I am very grateful.

I thank Moshe Bar, Elise Breen, Kalanit Grill-Spector, Dan Hansen, and Tadashi Sugihara for reading various drafts of the book, and for providing invaluable comments. I did my best to follow their suggestions for improving the text. My only consolation for failing to get it right in the end is the observation paraphrasing Paul Valéry, that books are never finished, only abandoned.

Last, I thank my editor, Michael P. Rutter, whose patience, advice, and encouragement at the right moments were of great help. I am also happy and proud to acknowledge my debt to Harry B. Stanton, late of MIT Press, who, together with Elizabeth Stanton, was responsible for the Bradford Books imprint—a series that was and is a great source of inspiration, stimulating ideas, and precisely the kind of fun cognitive science is supposed to be about. The three people whose very presence in my life ensures that this aspect of science is not lost on me are, of course, Esti, Ira, and Itamar.

# Introduction

It is no exaggeration to state that the classic culture of Tlön comprises only one discipline: psychology. All others are subordinated to it. . . .
The geometry of Tlön comprises two somewhat different disciplines: the visual and the tactile. The visual geometry . . . declares that man in his movement modifies the forms that surround him. The basis of its arithmetic is the notion of indefinite numbers. . . . The fact that several individuals who count the same quantity should obtain the same result is, for the psychologists, an example of association of ideas or of a good exercise of memory. . . .
Among the doctrines of Tlön, none has merited the scandalous reception accorded to materialism.

—Jorge Luis Borges
*Ficciones*—1956

In the beginning of the first part of *Beyond Good and Evil*, Nietzsche remarks: "There is a point in every philosophy when the philosopher's 'conviction' appears on the stage—or to use the language of an ancient Mystery: *adventavit asinus, pulcher et fortissimus*."[1] My initial involvement with the twin problems of shape representation and recognition was also motivated by a kind of philosophical 'conviction': a foolhardy yet nonetheless unshakeable belief in the basic veridicality of our perception of the world of shapes.[2] My other prejudice, of an engineering kind, entered the play in the second act in the guise of a firm optimism regarding the plausibility of a particular formal theory of veridicality and the feasibility of its application to visual recognition.

My long-range goal in raising the issue of veridicality and attempting to treat it formally is to help reinstate it as a *comme il faut* concept—a status which it appears to have lost between Locke's *Essay*[3] and Berkeley's

*Treatise.*[4] For ages, veridicality has been a charged term, one whose mention may make some of my more philosophically minded readers try to ambush me at every turn of the road. Because I would prefer them to ride with me (at least until the dust of theory starts to settle in chapter 5 or so), I will begin with a couple of philosophical (or rather, meta-philosophical) disclaimers. First, I would try to lay down a formal groundwork for a discussion of veridicality in shape perception, rather than argue about *a priori* objections to such an enterprise, which are, as a rule, tinged by solipsism. My hope is that once the foundations are in place, the objections may lose their appeal. Second, I would rather investigate the computational underpinnings of perception (conceived as the process whereby things that are "out there" give rise to their representations) than ponder whether or not a causal link between the appearance of an object and its memory trace is metaphysically licit. My premises, which correspond roughly to what Putnam calls "realism with a small 'r' " (in contradistinction to Metaphysical Realism), are that the world of shapes is "out there" for anyone to see, and that internal states causally related to it can be maintained by a visual system (used for all kinds of practical purposes of which object recognition is but one).

The manner in which these internal states can represent the shapes of distal objects veridically, and the computational constraints imposed by veridicality are the central topics to which chapters 1 through 3 are devoted. A representation of the world of shapes maintained by a visual system can be veridical in a number of distinct senses. One possibility is for the representation to be like an internal "library" of geometrical models (much like the data sets manipulated by computer-aided design software), one per object. Veridicality in this case would mean simply that the geometry of each object is faithfully reflected in the internal record maintained for it by the system. The geometry of objects is not, however, immediately and explicitly available in the images that are registered in the eye or in the camera. Consequently, putting together such a library of representations requires a solution to the general problem of vision as it was posed in the now classic book by Marr (1982): starting with a set of images depicting a scene, reconstruct the scene in the fullest possible geometrical detail.

To some, this "reconstructionist" approach to representation seems to be the most logical one, and therefore *a priori* preferable. What could be more logical than to let object shapes be represented by their geometries? This logic, however, is at odds with many state of the art theories and practical results in computer vision (surveyed in chapter 2), as well as with many findings in biological vision research (discussed later, in chapter 6). In particular, those computational theories of representation that forgo reconstruction lead to simpler and more effective recognition systems, and produce more credible working models of human recognition performance.

The persistent difficulties (both theoretical and practical) with the attempt to base recognition on geometrically reconstructed representations of distal objects give rise to a great temptation to cut through the Gordian knot of reconstruction. Any approach to the problem of representation that sidesteps the reconstructionist dogma must, however, come up with an alternative principle that would (1) state exactly what, if not reconstruction, representation is, and (2) in what sense, if not geometric, it can be veridical. One such principle, proposed and discussed in chapter 3, states that *representation is representation of similarities*, or, more generally, of relational qualities. The intuition behind this idea is illustrated in figure I.1.

The attribution of representational primacy to relational qualities may seem like an odd choice in view of my overall goal of explaining the veridicality of representation. In the philosophy of psychology, in particular, professing primacy of (let alone ontological commitment to) similarity is a sure way to get the sheriff's attention, and very probably also to get kicked out of the saloon.[5] Some psychologists (notably, Hannes Eisler) claim that the very concept of veridical representation of similarity—that is, of the internally represented or subjective similarity mirroring the external or objective similarity—is ill-defined, because there is no such thing as objective similarity. In other sources, ranging from C. S. Peirce to S. Watanabe and spanning a century, one finds proofs that similarity can be anything you like—unless a system of observer-imposed biases intervenes to remove the uncertainty.

A close parallel can be drawn between this notion and Berkeley's famous dictum, *esse est percepi*:[6] those who would subjectivize geometric

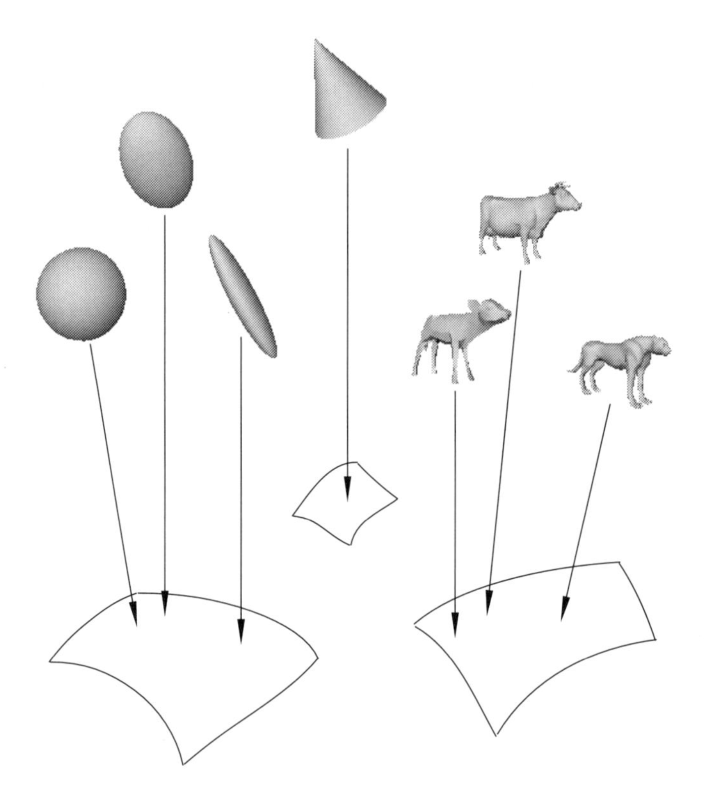

**Figure I.1**
Representation as representation of similarities. Objects with comparable shapes are mapped into the same neighborhood of an internal shape space. In this illustration, there are three such neighborhoods, occupied by ellipsoids, cones, and quadruped animal shapes. If proximities in such a neighborhood are made to reflect geometric similarities among the objects, the resulting representation will be formally veridical, and will be capable of supporting categorization-related tasks. Here, in the quadruped neighborhood, the representations of a calf and a cow are closer to each other than to the representation of a cheetah, reflecting the intuitively proper similarity relationships among these shapes. A theoretical framework for this approach to representation, a computational model, its implementation, testing, and examination in the light of neurobiological and psychophysical data, are described in chapters 3 through 6.

similarity claim that an ellipsoid (for example) is more similar to a sphere than to a cube only as long as somebody sufficiently like us is watching it. On the one hand, this analogy alone suffices to make radical subjectivism about similarity look suspect. In figure I.1 the ellipsoid, not the cube, is more similar to the sphere, and if a theory has it otherwise, too bad for the theory. On the other hand, radical objectivism about similarity is equally untenable.

A way out of this dilemma is suggested by an analogy between similarity, which can be construed as proximity in some kind of a *shape space* in which shapes correspond to points, and geographical proximity. On the one hand, relative travel times between geographical locations (say, Boston, New York and San Francisco) can be anything at all;[7] on the other hand, the great-circle distances between the same points are objective (up to the choice of measurement unit, of course). Their ratio would appear the same to any sentient being (on earth, if not on Tlön). The analogy between geographical space and shape space plays a central role in chapter 3. In that chapter, I describe a shape-space formalism borrowed from mathematical statistics, which allows geometric similarity between middle-sized objects embedded in Newtonian space to be defined rigorously (in certain cases uniquely) and independently of any observer bias.[8] By adding to the shape-space formalism a similarity-preserving mapping that leads to another shape space, one that can be internal to an observer, I then construct a theory of veridical representation of similarities.

Embedding represented objects in a shape space facilitates the formalization of various recognition-related tasks and the development of computational mechanisms that can support them. Intuitively, both the former and the latter can then be based on a navigation metaphor, introduced in chapter 4. According to this metaphor, objects are treated as points that reside in a shape-space "landscape." This allows both categorization (determining the rough location of the stimulus within the terrain) and identification (pinpointing the location of the stimulus) to be approached as navigation in a real terrain, by taking the bearings of the stimulus with respect to a set of *landmarks*. In practical terms, it is frequently more convenient to measure not bearings (directions), but proximities between the stimulus and the landmarks. Moreover, a quantity monotonically related to proximity can be equally useful for localization (as it is in the data analysis technique known as nonmetric multidimensional scaling). This suggests that a mechanism suitable for implementing shape-space localization can be as simple as a tuned unit or module that responds optimally to some shape (a landmark) and progressively less to progressively less similar shapes.

The representational framework based on the outputs of tuned mechanisms is put to the test in chapter 5. I first choose a particular architecture for implementing the tuned module: a radial basis function approximation network. Given several views of a shape, such a network can be trained to produce a roughly constant response to other views of the same object. As a byproduct of training, its response will also decrease monotonically for shapes that are progressively more different from the original one—precisely what is required for the module to function as an active landmark. A system composed of ten such prototype modules, each trained on a different reference object, is then tested on a small database containing several dozen additional objects (smoothly shaded 3D models of quadruped animals, cars, figures, aircraft, etc).

Computer vision systems are normally geared for and tested primarily on the recognition of familiar objects; those for which there is a model stored in the system's library. In comparison, the present system (called *Chorus of Prototypes*[9]), is shown capable also of categorizing novel objects and distinguishing among views of such objects. Furthermore, insofar as the novel object resembles some of the familiar ones, the system is capable of estimating its orientation or guessing its appearance from a novel viewpoint, given only a single "training" view of the object. The computational basis for these capabilities is the representation of all objects as points in a common shape space. Within categories, this space, spanned by similarities to reference or prototype objects, is smooth enough to support interpolation among objects, and to facilitate analogy-like tasks that require generalization from a single view.

The tuned prototype module used to implement the Chorus system bears a strong resemblance to mechanisms found in the brain area in primates which specializes in object shape processing and recognition: the inferotemporal (IT) cortex. For many years, reports of IT cells tuned to views of specific objects, or to object categories, were dismissed by the consensus opinion in neurobiology which considered the predominant theoretical account of these reports—the "grandmother cell" idea—as conceptually and computationally absurd. The main assumption behind that view was that if cells were so narrowly specialized as to respond only to very specific objects, too many of them would be required to represent a sizeable collection of potential stimuli.

The detailed functional characteristics of object-tuned units, described recently by a number of research groups and surveyed in the first part of chapter 6, do not, however, fit the traditional notion of a grandmother cell. Instead of exhibiting high selectivity (i.e., a very narrow response profile in the shape space), IT cells respond to a wide variety of shapes, with various efficacies. In this respect, they seem to behave exactly as required by the Chorus model, in which the shape representation space is spanned by the outputs of a set of functional modules that are broadly tuned to specific objects.

Both in theory and in practice then (as far as one can judge from the published neurobiological data), the mechanisms that span the shape representation space are tuned. At the level of the internal structure of an individual object module, the tuning is to a certain *range of views* of an object; entire modules are each tuned to a certain *range of shapes*. This realization leads to a series of predictions concerning the performance of the primate visual system in object recognition tasks. The two main effects predicted by the Chorus model are, for any but the most familiar objects, the dependence of recognition performance on viewpoint; and, for novel objects, the dependence of performance in generalization tasks on the degree of their similarity to some familiar category. Additional predictions are the effect of similarity on the degree of viewpoint dependence in discrimination (i.e., in telling apart several objects), and the faithful representation of similarities among objects with comparable shapes. All these issues are discussed in the second part of chapter 6, which reviews the relevant psychophysical findings and concludes with a summary of neurobiological and behavioral support for the shape space idea in general, and for the Chorus model in particular.

As I warned the reader from the outset, this book, being philosophically motivated, has raw intuition as its starting point. Things get down to earth pretty quickly after that. Over the course of six chapters, the intuition is translated into a theory, instantiated by a model, implemented in a working system, tested on a range of objects and tasks, and compared with data on recognition in biological systems. To a patient reader, principled veridical representation of shapes will then seem less elusive, whereby my initial intuition will have been vindicated. Naturally, along the way some computational operations will have been taken for granted, a few tasks declared outside the scope of the present treatment, and certain findings concerning biological systems will remain unaccounted for. In chapter 7, these residual pockets of resistance are placed under siege; plans for overrunning them are being made even as I write these words.

## Notes

1. *The ass arrived, beautiful and most brave.*

2. Perception is called veridical if the report of the senses is true to the physical world. Hume's term for this is "veracity," as in this passage from the *Enquiry* (7:120): "To have recourse to the veracity of the Supreme Being, in order to prove the veracity of our senses, is surely making a very unexpected circuit."

3. " . . . I should only show (as I hope I shall in the following parts of this Discourse) how men, barely by the use of their natural faculties, may attain to all the knowledge they have, without the help of any innate impressions; and may arrive at *certainty*, without any such original notions or principles" (Locke, 1690),1 (my emphasis).

4. "As for our senses, by them we have the knowledge only of our sensations, ideas, or those things that are immediately perceived by sense, call them what you will: but they do not inform us that things exist without the mind, or unperceived, like to those which are perceived" (Berkeley, 1710),18.

5. There are a few exceptions to this rule; Austen Clark's (1993) work is a prominent example, which will be mentioned in chapter 6.

6. *To be is to be perceived.* The discoverer of the Encyclopaedia of Tlön in the story by Borges recounts how "Hume noted for all time that Berkeley's arguments did not admit the slightest refutation nor did they cause the slightest conviction. This dictum is entirely correct in its application to the earth, but entirely false in Tlön" (Borges, 1956),23.

7. Imagine a law that for some reason (e.g., energy saving) would prohibit one from flying between Boston and New York, but not between the East and West coasts of the United States.

8. Of course, observers are still free to impose their bias on top of the fundamental geometric similarity. Likewise, a traveler may choose voluntarily to drive between Boston and New York, and to fly between Boston and San Francisco, in which case the latter trip will actually take less time.

9. In memory of Oliver Selfridge's *Pandemonium*, a method for object recognition developed in 1959.

# Representation and Recognition in Vision

# 1

# The Problem of Representation

. . . Consider the nature of signs the mind makes use of for the understanding of things, or conveying its knowledge to others. For, since the things the mind contemplates are none of them, besides itself, present to the understanding, it is necessary that something else, as a sign or representation of the thing it considers, should be present to it.

—John Locke
*Essay Concerning Human Understanding*—1690

## 1.1 A Vision of Representation

What is it that our brain is doing when we see a cat on a mat? What do the brains of two people seeing a cat have in common? If we ever succeed to devise a machine capable of seeing and recognizing cats, what, if anything, need its state have in common with that of the brain of a human observer when both see a cat? Questions of this kind go a long way back in the philosophy of mind (Cummins, 1989). As most philosophers will agree, the answers to the three questions stated above hinge on a single concept, the most important one ever invoked in explaining the mind: *representation*. Very likely, the rest of the explanation—what is the nature of visual representations, how are they related to perception, how can they support action—will differ widely among schools. The consensus stops here.

The consensus, however, is not immutable, and that time during which it is liable to change is the most interesting one to live in. As far as the natural philosophy of representation is concerned, now is such a time. Because of the advances in the understanding of biological vision, and because object recognition by machine seems these days less remote than during most of the history of the study of mind, philosophers now can borrow from knowledge accumulated in an entire range of disciplines of cognitive science to debate the possible answers to the questions posed above. This book, having been written by a non-philosopher, takes the complementary approach: it attempts to build on foundations laid down by students of computer vision, psychology and neurobiology, and aims to meet the philosophers (at least the more empirically minded of them) halfway down the road. The goal, in both cases, is to understand visual representations harbored by sophisticated cognitive systems such as human observers, and the manner in which these representations are used to support "high-level" visual functions: recognition and categorization.[1]

Working out a framework for the understanding of visual processing that would be both comprehensive and as succinctly posed as the concept of representation itself was the central aim of David Marr's *Vision*, published posthumously in 1982. Marr's ideas constituted daring theorizing, and they were put forward at a time when the field was fragmented enough to call for a good theory. Early attempts at object recognition and scene understanding in the 1970s all relied on the extraction of line-like primitives ("edges") from intensity images, and on subsequent combination of these lines into progressively more complex constructs, using explicitly stated rules. The primitive detection stage used to be so unreliable that a typical system only dealt with inputs pre-segmented into lines and corners. The high-level, rule-guided interpretation algorithms did not fare much better. The systems of Waltz, Guzman, and others (surveyed in Mackworth, 1972) could fully label certain classes of line drawings, but did not support categorization of shapes or recognition of familiar objects in any regular sense. Altogether, computer vision methods were limited in so many ways that practical applications in object recognition seemed to be quite remote.

Attempts undertaken in the 1970s to bring data from the study of biological vision to bear on theoretical issues did not fare better. The findings of Hubel and Wiesel, who characterized the functional architecture of early mammalian vision in terms of arrays of orientation-selective cells responding preferentially to short line segments, were routinely compared to the contemporary computer vision methods. This was rather unfortunate, both because alternative explanations for the biological findings existed, and because the computer vision algorithms for turning raw images into line drawings—the would-be theoretical basis for Hubel and Wiesel's view of the primary visual cortex—were never reliable (they tended to lose true edges and to signal plenty of nonexistent ones). Beyond the primary visual area stretched a poorly understood, if not uncharted, territory. Cells in the extrastriate cortex seemed to like strange stimuli such as stars or rosettes. Reports of higher-level cells in the monkey brain responding preferentially to entire face or hand images were puzzled at, or dismissed as unreliable.

A major contribution to the resolution of these conundra was the methodological framework that emerged from the joint work of Marr and Poggio in the mid-1970s. They insisted on understanding the goal of vision before trying to understand its details. The aim of the Marr/Poggio program may have been merely the introduction of this sound engineering approach, good for any information processing task, into the study of vision. In practice, however, the impact of the new "computational" approach was much more profound, because a common goal was postulated for all visual tasks, leading to an essentially monolithic meta-theory of vision.

If visual behavior is to be considered a monolithic theoretical notion, how should one treat the multitude of visual tasks that confront even a simple visual system? To subsume under the same rubric such tasks as judging the ripeness of a fruit by its color, blinking at the sight of a moving object that suddenly looms in the field of view, and recognizing a familiar face in a crowd, one needs a grand unified theory of vision. In such a theory, all the diverse tasks would share the same conceptual core, and, even better, the same kind of underlying processes and data structures.

Marr's work did offer such a theory. According to this theory, the common conceptual core for the various visual tasks was postulated to be representation, and the common processing goal—the recovery of the distal qualities from the visual stimulus and their incorporation into the representation. The intuitive basis for unification provided by this framework is clear: if the visual system recovers the proper qualities of the world—the spectral reflectance of the surface of a banana, or the direction and speed of motion of a baseball, or the structural information that is characteristic of our friend's face—it comes to possess a representation that must enable it to carry out all conceivable vision-related tasks.

## 1.2 Reconstruction

The bulk of Marr's book is devoted to demonstrating how one could attempt to extract such a representation—reconstructing the visual world internally—from a variety of cues. Because the formation of a unified representation was taken to be the ultimate aim of purely visual processing (leading up to categorization or to some other decision mechanism), vision was postulated to be by and large a sequential undertaking, culminating in as complete a reconstruction as possible, given the information available in the stimulus.

This postulate did not remain unchallenged. The discontent with the concept of vision as a hierarchical single-track process dates back to the same decade that saw the emergence of Marr's doctrine. One contributing factor here was the steadily accumulating evidence from psychophysical and neurobiological studies, which made the single-track hypothesis less tenable. At the time of the writing of *Vision*, only a handful of studies had probed the psychology of higher-level visual function in primates. The knowledge of the anatomy and the functional organization of the higher visual areas was also very scarce. As more new data became available, the "big picture" grew invariably more complicated, and resembled a single-track processing hierarchy less and less.

The new findings, such as the realization that object recognition is not quite invariant under stimulus transformations, as the reconstructionists would have it, had to work against the considerable intuitive appeal of reconstruction. The latter stemmed in part from reconstruction's distinguished position as a jack-of-all-trades in the spectrum of possible approaches to representation. In principle, a representation that is in some sense a replica of the thing being represented must be considered adequate for any visual task. If it were not, the visual world itself, being merely an external version of the internal representation, would fail to support visual behavior. Nonetheless, scrutiny reveals representation by reconstruction to be a poor explanatory device for understanding vision, for several reasons.

The first argument against reconstruction centers around its implications for the nature of further processing, e.g., recognition or categorization. To put it bluntly, if the visual world were reconstructed internally, the system would need a homunculus to make sense of it (Pylyshyn, 1973). An appeal to the possibility of various formats which the reconstructed representation can take does not help. Indeed, forming an image, a little 3D model, or even a list of the locations of important features of the stimulus—in other words, any "analog" (Palmer, 1978, 295) representation of the stimulus geometry—does not amount to its recognition or categorization (figure 1.1). Of all possible approaches to scene interpretation, the one that involves reconstruction is the most roundabout, because reconstruction per se contributes nothing towards interpretation.

The second, rather prosaic reason to doubt the adequacy of representation by reconstruction is its scarcity in real life. This pertains both to computer vision, where experience of the last decades shows that such representations are notoriously difficult to recover from raw images, and to biological vision, where many findings support alternative theories of representation (more on these issues in subsequent chapters).

The third problem with the reconstruction doctrine is conceptual. The source of the problem lies in the theoretically universal applicability of reconstruction to any conceivable representational task. Leaving aside for the moment the feasibility of putting together a reconstructed replica of the world or its subsequent manipulation, one may ask whether or not having a universal representation is desirable. It seems that a default answer to this latter question should be negative: the best representation is the representation best suited to the task.

In theories of information processing, the importance of choosing the right representation for a given computational problem is widely acknowledged. This point has been most forcefully made by Marr himself (1982) (although it had been taught long before to software engineers, who used to be told that the choice of the proper data structure is a crucial step towards solving a programming problem; see Wirth, 1976). It seems thus even more amazing that a generation of vision researchers, starting with Marr, ignored the possibility that the best representation of

**Figure 1.1**
An epistemological joke, after L. Wittgenstein (1973) and L. Henderson (1984). The duck/rabbit is Jastrow's famous ambiguous figure, used by Wittgenstein in *Philosophical Investigations* to point out that an uninterpreted image falls short of being a useful representation of a stimulus.

the visual world for a variety of tasks—including recognition—may not be the same as the visual world reconstructed in full three-dimensional detail.[2]

## 1.3 Representation without Reconstruction

The roots of an alternative approach to representation that will be presented in this book can be traced back to Locke's *Essay Concerning Hu-*

*man Understanding*. In the part that addressed what now would be called the semantics of mental representations, Locke suggested that an idea represents a thing in the world if it is naturally and predictably evoked by that thing, and not necessarily, as the Aristotelians would have it, if the idea resembles the thing in any sense.[3] According to this view, and using a standard terminology of vision research, the activity of a sufficiently reliable feature detector constitutes a representation of the presence of a certain feature out there in the visual world.[4] Representations of entire objects and scenes can then be built out of the available primitives, if the repertoire of features is sufficiently rich.

### 1.3.1 The Feature Detector Redux

In theories of natural computation, the original concept of a feature hierarchy developed under the influence of the discovery of "bug detectors" in the frog retina (Lettvin et al., 1959). Recent developments in computer vision and in computational neuroscience indicate that a modified version of the old hypothesis of representation by feature hierarchy may be a viable alternative to the reconstructionist doctrine. The current notion of feature detection differs from the classical one in two respects. First, it is now clear that the representational power of an ensemble of feature detectors may far exceed that of any of its constituents alone. Second, many theoreticians have realized that "symbolic" or combinatorial composition is not the only way to put various features together.

Consider as an example the problem of specifying a representation for spatial discrimination tasks such as vernier acuity. In a typical instance of this task, human subjects routinely discriminate between left and right offsets of two abutting vertical line segments, even when the size of the offset is much smaller than the spacing of the photoreceptors in the fovea centralis (Westheimer, 1981). Early computational accounts of the hyperacuity phenomenon postulated that the visual input is reconstructed, with "subpixel" precision, at a certain stage of cortical processing, making it then possible to determine the sense of an offset smaller than the "pixel" size (Barlow, 1979; Crick et al., 1981). The proponents of the reconstructionist program did not seem to believe in the possibility of implementing any visual function of interest using feature detectors as building blocks (see Marr, 1982, ch.7). The main objection leveled by Marr (ibid., 341) was that "the world is just too complex to yield to the types of analysis suggested by the feature detector idea." This statement is more likely to be challenged now than ten years ago. Regarding hyperacuity, in particular, it is now known that the activity pattern of a set of overlapping receptive fields that cover a vernier stimulus represents all the information necessary for determining the direction of its offset (Poggio et al., 1992; Snippe and Koenderink, 1992), without, however, allowing its reconstruction.

As the next example, consider the perception of coherent motion, a visual task intensively studied on all levels, including that of neurobiological implementation (e.g., Yuille and Grzywacz, 1988; Stoner et al., 1990; Newsome and Paré, 1988). In the middle temporal (MT) cortical area of the monkey, one can find cells with receptive fields tuned to coherent motion in a particular direction. The ensemble of activities of these cells may be regarded as representing the motion of the visual field seen by the animal, in the distributed nonreconstructionist sense defined above. To see that, note that the activity of a given MT cell co-occurs with a certain well-defined motion in the visual field, i.e., the cell fires, *ceteris paribus*, if and only if the motion occurs (Newsome and Paré, 1988). Furthermore, artificial stimulation of the cell causes a behavioral response similar to the one precipitated by a real moving stimulus (Salzman et al., 1990). Consequently, the cell's firing, for all practical purposes, represents the motion event as far as the monkey is concerned. (For a philosophical perspective on this issue, see Albright, 1991.) The visual motion, however, can hardly be considered as reconstructed in the activity of an MT cell. Moreover, it is not clear whether the pattern of activity of an ensemble of MT cells (or of cells in areas that precede MT in the motion pathway) can or need carry out such reconstruction.

The above arguments suggest a re-evaluation of the basic assumptions behind the abstract (in Marr's terminology, computational or information-processing) nature of the tasks that the visual system confronts. Recall that a computational-level description of a task constitutes a specification of its input and output representations (the understanding of the task involves a further specification of the input-output mapping, and of the possible implementations of this mapping in various computing media). One may argue that for a low-level task such as binocular stereopsis, both the input and the output are indisputable: a system capable of stereo vision must accept two disparate images of the same scene, and must produce a representation that *makes explicit* (another coinage of Marr) the depth information inherent in the pair of input images. However, even in such tasks, reconstruction turns out not to be strictly necessary. In stereopsis, for example, qualitative information such as the ordering of the viewed surfaces in depth is behaviorally useful, is relatively easy to compute (Weinshall, 1990; Hel-Or and Edelman, 1994), and may be closer to what the human visual system actually recovers in certain situations (Mitchison and Westheimer, 1990).

### 1.3.2 The Challenge

In higher-level tasks the choice of representation is even less clear. To be sure, a system capable of recognition must accept images of the object or the scene that is to be recognized, but what should be the representation that underlies actual recognition? The simplest and most obvious alternative to the reconstruction of the distal qualities—storing and comparing raw images of objects and scenes—will not do. As pointed out repeatedly by many researchers, the way things look depends on the direction from which they are seen, on the illumination, and on the presence and disposition of other objects. The appearance of an object depends, of course, also on its shape. Can we just recover the geometry of an object from its appearance, then, and use that as its representation? We saw earlier that this will not do either, for a number of reasons rooted both in theoretical and in pragmatic issues surrounding representation.

The quest for a viable theory of representation faces, therefore, a dilemma. On the one hand, full reconstruction seems to be unsatisfactory for a number of reasons. On the other hand, representing objects by their raw images is out of the question. The shortcomings of these obvious alternatives do not mean, however, that the entire theoretical framework based on the concept of representation is mistaken. Rather, these shortcomings call for a revision of the basic assumptions behind the invocation of this concept in explaining vision. This task is taken up in the next chapter, which discusses certain meta-theoretical options concerning representations, and surveys some of the current theories.

## Notes

1. Recognition and categorization here refer to the corresponding commonsensical concepts; definitions of these and other visual tasks will be given later.

2. For some examples of computer vision systems that carry out recognition without reconstruction, see (Schiele and Crowley, 1996; Mel, 1997; Edelman and Duvdevani-Bar, 1997a).

3. Although this notion of *representation by covariance* may fall short of supplying a formal basis for the semantics of mental representations, it seems to do so only insofar as the semanticists strive for the unreachable, such as a definition of the necessary and sufficient conditions under which a mental state represents a thing (for a discussion, and an opposite conclusion, see Cummins, 1989). For my present purpose, it is more important that the Lockean concept of covariance be made to lead to an intuition regarding a possible alternative to the reconstructionist approach to representation.

4. This may be compared with the philosophical notion of the meaning of a representation being in the world, not in the head (Putnam, 1988; Millikan, 1995); see chapter 7 for a further discussion of this point.

# 2

# Theories of Representation and Object Recognition

Let any one try to account for this operation of the mind upon any of the received systems of philosophy, and he will be sensible of the difficulty. For my part, I shall think it sufficient, if the present hints excite the curiosity of philosophers, and make them sensible how defective all common theories are in treating of such curious and such sublime subjects.

—David Hume
*An Enquiry Concerning Human Understanding*—1748

## 2.1 Recognition-Related Tasks That Require Representation

Recognition implies a match between two entities, one of which is normally an internalized version of the present stimulus, and the other a memory trace laid down by some stimulus or stimuli at an earlier time.[1] I shall refer to both entities participating in the process of recognition as "representations." Any theory of recognition must specify both the form of those representations and the details of the matching process. Different theories are compared on the basis of the representations they postulate and the kind of matching these representations require. These factors, in turn, lead to considerations of memory (capacity, structure) and processing ability expected of the system that is being modeled.

Because the issues of representation and matching are closely intertwined, and because different recognition tasks necessitate different kinds of matches between the stored representation and that of the stimulus, theories of representation must be discussed in the context of the various classes of tasks.[2] This chapter will concentrate on the dependence of representation on the *level* of the task (i.e., the level of categorization that

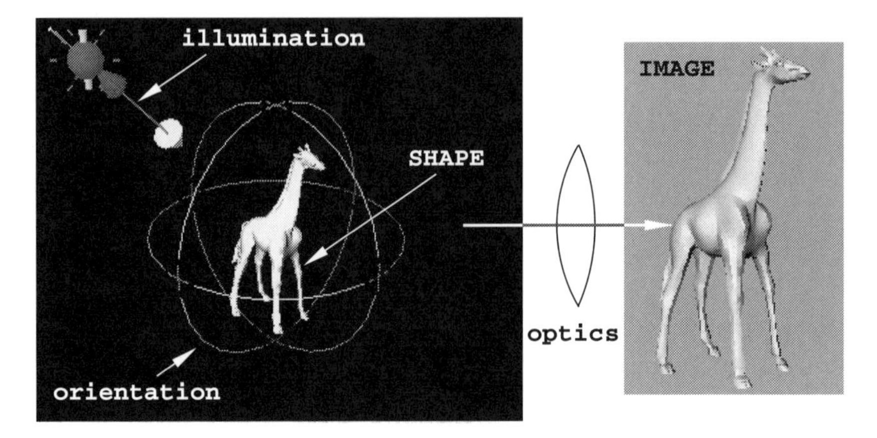


Figure 2.1
The imaging process. Shape (intrinsic geometry), and extrinsic factors such as orientation and illumination all affect the appearance of an object, as captured by an imaging system such as the eye. In this illustration, the extrinsic factors are depicted as a spotlight icon and a set of three mutually orthogonal "handles," a computer graphics device that allows rotating an object on the screen using the mouse. A recognition system must discount the effects of object orientation and of illumination, to be able to process and act upon shape information. It should be noted that real-life scenes may include more than one object of interest, a background from which objects must be separated, and interactions among objects, such as occlusion, interreflections, and the ubiquitous measurement noise; see (Mumford, 1994).

must be performed), and will aim at identifying properties common to all representations capable of supporting it.

To set up a framework for this treatment, let us consider a typical recognition situation that a visual system may confront (figure 2.1). An external object gives rise to an image, which is formed on the photosensitive array of a camera, or on the retina of an eye. This image contains shape information which is intrinsic to the object. Throughout this book, I shall assume that the goal of the recognition process is to discriminate among objects on the basis of their shape. Although this may seem as a simplification, it actually makes recognition more difficult, by leaving out potentially informative cues such as color and texture of the object surfaces. Thus, a system that discriminates well among "bare" shapes is likely to perform even better with colorful textured objects.[3]

In addition to shape, the stimulus image is also influenced by the prevailing illumination conditions, by the object's orientation with respect to the viewer, and by the scene in which the object is embedded.[4] Countering the effects of these extrinsic factors is the main concern in the first kind of task to be discussed.

### 2.1.1 Identification and Generalization

In the identification task, the (rigid) object's shape is assumed to be fixed, leading to the expectation of a precise match in the case of a successful recognition (figure 2.2A). To obtain such a match, the recognition system must discount the effects of the extrinsic factors (figure 2.2B). In principle, this can be done by maintaining representations that are invariant to these factors, or by employing a matching procedure that counters their effects. As we shall see in section 2.3, the current computational theories of recognition all postulate some combination of these techniques.

Discussions of object recognition in the literature tend to stress the difficulties stemming from the influence of the factors extrinsic to shape. In particular, the problem of recognition is commonly introduced by pointing out that objects can look very different from different viewpoints (cf. Ullman, 1996, figure 1.1). It seems to me that this problem is of secondary importance, for two reasons. First, state of the art computer vision algorithms (surveyed in section 2.3) can overcome the variability in object appearance, provided that sufficient information about the object's shape is available in the stored representations. Unlike reconstruction-based approaches, which require a 3D model of the object for that purpose, these so-called multiple-view algorithms need to store only a few views per object.[5] Second, in most everyday tasks changes of the object's shape, and not merely its appearance, must be dealt with. This may happen because the task itself calls for lumping together in the same class objects of different shapes, as in categorization (or because the objects are flexible or articulated). Thus, the most challenging theoretical problems in recognition arise in generalization from a single view (when the multiple-view algorithms cannot operate), and in categorization.[6] The tasks that give rise to these problems are discussed next.

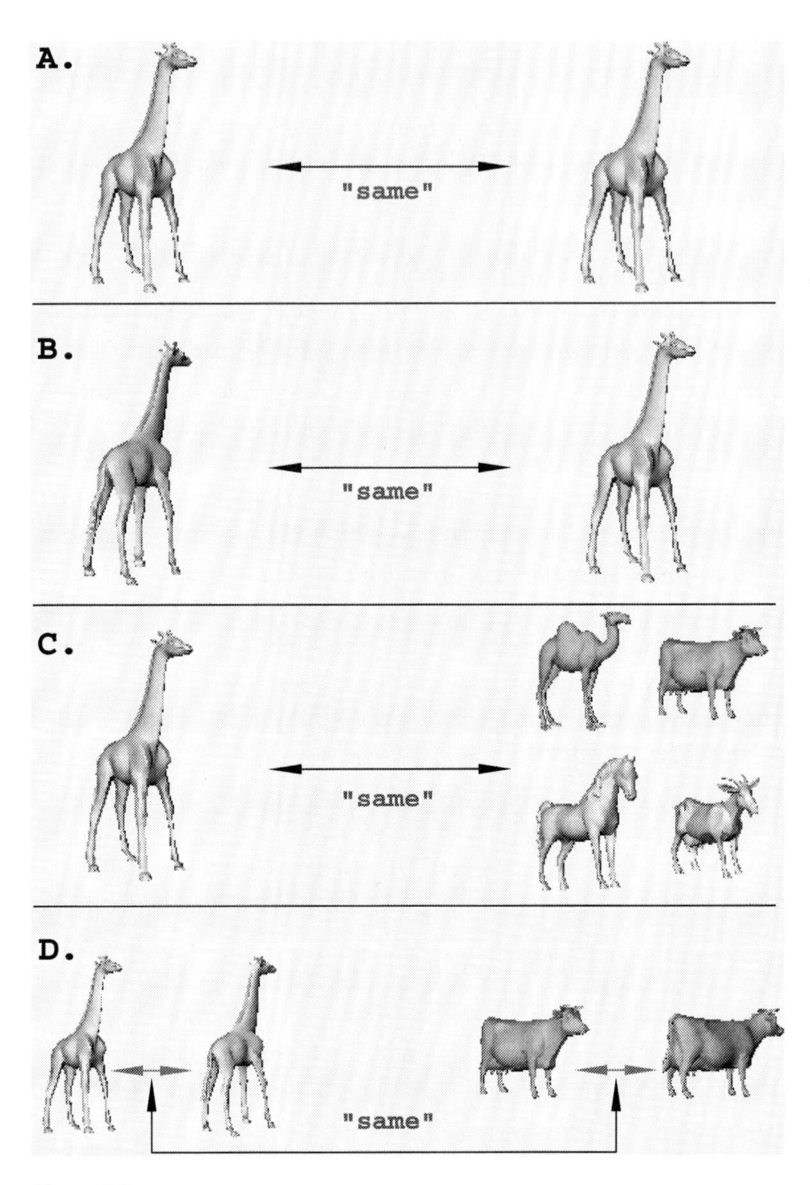


**Figure 2.2**
Four recognition tasks. *(A)* Identification (recognition of a previously seen view of an object). *(B)* Generalization (recognition of an object despite a change in its appearance due to some transformation). *(C)* Categorization (attribution of the object to a class of similarly shaped objects). *(D)* Analogy (drawing a parallel between transformations of distinct objects). See sections 2.1.1 through 2.1.3.

### 2.1.2 Categorization

A basic characteristic of the identification task is the assumption that the system has had prior experience with any object it will ever have to identify. Although this assumption may hold in some circumstances (e.g., in industrial applications of computer vision), it seems to be generally void in the context of everyday visual behavior. For people, the need for identification is confined to a handful of object classes (mostly human faces[7]). More frequently, the observer's goal is to determine the category to which the object belongs, rather than to find out whether or not that particular object has been seen before (figure 2.2C).

#### The Basic Category Level

The primary status of categorization (as opposed to identification) in human behavior has been long discussed in cognitive science. An extensive overview of perceptual tasks in which humans operate by default on a level of object classes rather than that of individual objects can be found in works of Rosch and her collaborators (Rosch et al., 1976; Rosch, 1978). Experimental studies reviewed by Rosch show that among the different levels on which a given object may be categorized (e.g., animal, cat, Siamese, George), names belonging to one particular level (in this example, cat) have a special status. Names at this level consistently emerge as the first to be learned by children, the ones spontaneously produced in response to a visual stimulus, the fastest to be confirmed if true of a stimulus, etc. Because of the converging evidence regarding the central role of this level in categorization, it has been termed *basic*.

In theories of visual recognition, the "entry point" (Jolicoeur et al., 1984) or the "primal access" (Biederman, 1987) to stored representations of objects is believed to occur at the basic level.[8] This characteristic of human vision seems particularly important in view of the possibility of defining the basic level independently of recognition by an observer, in terms of objective (e.g., geometric) similarities between objects. It turns out that the basic level is the least specific one at which various members of the same category still resemble each other visually (all Siamese cats, as well as all cats in general, look pretty much alike; not so all animals).

**Representations That Can Support Categorization**

The main challenge in devising a representation suitable for supporting categorization is the need for abstraction (note that generalization over stimulus transformations also involves abstraction of a sort). Because the system may be called upon to categorize a stimulus the first time it is encountered, the matching of representations must be able to ignore differences in geometric details in favor of similarities among less specific features. Note that omitting details from the representations themselves is only allowed if separate representations are to be maintained for separate levels of categorization. While this option may be exercised by some systems, a representational scheme that allows the "resolution" of the matching process and not of the representation itself to be tuned according to the requirements of the task would be more theoretically satisfying.[9]

Theories of representation that treat categorization as a *sui generis* problem and not as an appendix to identification, usually start from the notion of *prototype*—the most typical member of a class of previously encountered stimuli, or perhaps an abstraction that serves as a surrogate member and is charged with representing the class. A novel stimulus is normally assigned to the nearest class, as determined, e.g., by its similarity to the representations of class prototypes (Basri, 1996). Although this approach may be satisfactory for stimuli that are in fact exemplars drawn from the familiar classes, it is unsuitable for "radically novel" objects, which do not quite fit into any of the known classes.

One may note that problems analogous with the need to deal with such stimuli arise in syntactic analysis, where systems are expected to exhibit productivity and compositionality. The former notion refers to the ability of speakers to produce novel morphological and syntactic structures, and the corresponding ability of listeners to make sense of neologisms and of sentences never encountered before. The latter notion, that of compositionality, states that the meaning of composite linguistic structures (including, of course, novel ones) is derived from the meaning of their components (see Schiffer, 1987, 2). Indeed, some prominent theories that do mention the problem of radically novel stimuli (Biederman, 1987; Bienenstock and Geman, 1995) are explicitly motivated by analogies with language. A major goal of this book is to explore the possibility of an alternative approach to the representation of structure of shapes, which would support compositionality and productivity without relying on explicit syntactic analysis or manipulation.[10]

### 2.1.3 Analogy

One other family of recognition-related tasks to be discussed here combines elements of generalization and of categorization, and is, therefore, the most demanding in the constraints it imposes on representation. Consider a situation in which a system familiar with a number of object classes is confronted with a novel stimulus, and is subsequently required to determine whether another stimulus is a transformed version of the first one (figure 2.2D). In a more concrete example, an observer encounters an unfamiliar face (which is seen only once, from some fixed viewpoint), and then another one. Because of the need to deal with unfamiliar stimuli, the task of deciding whether or not these images are of the same person is related to categorization. It is also clearly an instance of generalization (across viewpoints). In fact, it is the most difficult kind of generalization, because it must operate from a single example.

The only possible basis for generalization in this task is similarity of transformations, or *analogy*.[11] If the stimulus happens to be similar to one of the familiar objects, one assumes that it will also transform similarly. For example, what looks like an unfamiliar human head seen face-on is expected to reveal an ear as it turns around its vertical axis. If this expectation is broken, there is nobody to blame: after all, the only reason to expect an ear in a side view is prior experience with head-shaped objects, and there is no guarantee that the unfamiliar object *is* a head until it has been seen from many viewpoints. This example illustrates the fallibility of generalization by analogy (figure 2.3).

Analogy is central to three related visual abilities that are very desirable from a behavioral standpoint. The first of these is the ability to recognize shapes previously seen from a very limited range of viewpoints, as was discussed above. The second is the ability to recognize familiar transformations of a novel object, e.g., to determine the orientation of a stranger's head. (Note that an amorphous object *has* no orientation as such, and that novel objects only possess well-defined orientations insofar as they resemble familiar objects for which the association between appearance

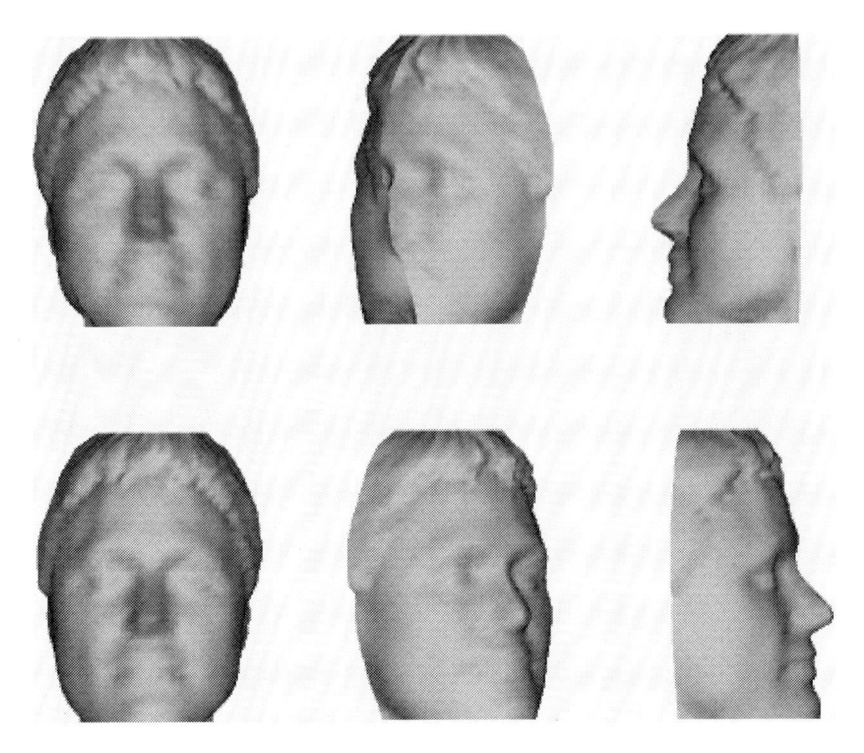

**Figure 2.3**
Failure of the geometry of an object to meet the observer's expectations can give rise to misperceptions. The top three images correspond to a sequence of views of an object circumnavigated by a camera, which starts moving to the left. The object, which looks initially like the head of a sculpture (top left image), appears strange in the next snapshot (top middle image). The top right image dispels the illusion: after some thinking, we realize that the object is a hollow mask, initially seen from its concave side. The bottom row shows the convex side of the same mask, from the same three vantage points. This time, our expectations are met, and the images look normal. This illusion is much more compelling when seen in motion. In visual arts, it is called anamorphosis, and may be found, for example, in the works of Markus Raetz, which explore variations on the theme of the Penrose Triangle.

and orientation is known.) The third is the ability to categorize familiar deformations of a novel object, or, to detect a smile on an unfamiliar face. Because of the importance of these tasks, visual systems are expected to rely on analogy despite its fallibility.

## 2.2 A Formalization of the Notion of Representation

Now that we have on record a list of tasks that require external objects to be represented internally, let us turn to discuss the possible nature of internal representations as such. Following Cummins (1989), I distinguish between two problems of mental representation. The first of these, the problem of *representations* (plural), is basically empirical. Two instances of this problem are the characterization of representations employed by natural visual systems, and the design of the representational substrate for computer vision. The second problem is called, by Cummins, the Problem of *Representation* (singular). Here, the central question is: how, in principle, can an internal state of a system refer to anything at all in the external world.

### 2.2.1 The Problem of Representation

As noted in chapter 1, to some theorists the Problem of Representation appears to have a simple and straightforward solution, in which the internal representation of the shape of an object is its geometrical replica—a kind of scale model, reconstructed from image data using the appropriate computations and kept in memory for future reference. Having discussed the tasks which require access to internal representations, one may note that there is nothing in principle to prevent the replica approach from working. If a visual system has at its disposal a reconstructed replica of a stimulus, it can be rotated until its appearance matches that of one of the stored object models, thus addressing the problem of identification and generalization (cf. section 2.3.3). Furthermore, its shape details can be abstracted until categorization (a high-level match to the description of a class of objects) becomes possible. Finally, knowledge of replica models similar to the stimulus model can allow the system to carry out analogical tasks of the kind mentioned in section 2.1.3.

In the past (e.g., in Marr's work), this idea has been elevated to the status of a meta-theory, not the least because of the intuitive appeal of the unified approach to representation that it embodies. However, even if the persistent difficulties that accompany attempts to reconstruct the geometry of the world do not prove insurmountable, reconstruction may still be only a *sufficient* answer to the Problem of Representation, not a *necessary* one. The possibility that other approaches may turn out to be both sufficiently powerful and tractable is a good reason for opening the Problem of Representation to discussion.

This undertaking—putting Representation on a principled basis that does not presuppose reconstruction—is a challenging philosophical and computational problem. Returning to the example discussed in Cummins (1989), let us consider a situation in which an observer recalls a previously encountered scene that contained, say, a cat. If the representational story is at all true (and the basic assumption throughout this book is that it is, *pace* J. J. Gibson),[12] the observer harbors an internal representation of the cat (or, as it may be, of the class of cat-like objects).

The first question that suggests itself in this context is, what (if not geometrical reconstruction) can it be about the internal state of the observer recalling[13] a cat that makes it refer to the shape of the cat? Note that the question is abstract, as it deals with a *possible* mode of representation, and not with representational means actually employed by this or that particular system. An answer to this question is suggested in section 2.2.2.

The second question that may be raised is, what structure, if any, must the representations of some distal objects possess to support the necessary variety of decisions and actions on the part of the observer? This question is addressed in section 2.2.3.

### 2.2.2 Representation as a Mapping

On the most general possible account, both the representations and their targets are treated formally as sets. Within this framework, representation becomes a *mapping* (Palmer, 1978; Dretske, 1995; Cummins, 1996). This mapping establishes correspondence between the members of the set of distal objects (things "out there" in the world) and the members of the set of proximal entities (things "in here" inside the head), usually referred to as the representations of distal objects. This correspondence, in turn, makes particular representations refer to particular targets, providing an answer to the first question raised above. Under this scheme, the representations need not have any internal structure (that is, they can be symbols[14]), nor, in general, is any structure imposed on their set.

### 2.2.3 First- and Second-Order Isomorphism

Different kinds of distal to proximal mappings are liable to result in representations of varying usefulness. The best situation one can hope for is an *isomorphism* between the domain and the range of the mapping, in which case it must be, formally, "one-to-one" and "onto" (Palmer, 1978). Mappings that are many-to-one—those that put many distal objects into correspondence with the same proximal symbol—are called *homomorphisms*. Such mappings give rise to metameries, or partitions of the set of distal objects that are assigned to the same equivalence class[15] proximally and are therefore indistinguishable to the system (Ratliff and Sirovich, 1978; Weiss and Edelman, 1995). This situation may seem to resemble categorization, where some of the features of the stimulus are ignored to allow it to be lumped together with other stimuli with which it shares more important characteristics. This resemblance is, however, superficial. As pointed out by Shepard (1987), categorization in psychology is normally a matter of choice, not of necessity; the distinctive features of individual objects are ignored, but are available for processing in a task that requires a finer discrimination among the stimuli. Thus, many-to-one mappings are, in general, undesirable, although they are probably unavoidable because of the infeasibility of representing *all* physical distinctions between the stimuli, down to the finest detail, in a finite-resource system. In comparison, mappings that are one-to-many—pairing the same object with more than one symbol—cannot be tolerated at all, because of the ambiguity they introduce into the representational system. Finally, mappings that are not "onto"—those that leave some objects unrepresented or some symbols unused—are also to be avoided.

#### Representation of Relations

The idea of isomorphism as the principle underlying representation dictates the nature of the distal to proximal mapping, but constrains neither the nature of the individual representations (which can be featureless symbols), nor their relations (apart from the obligatory distinctness of each symbol from all others). The need to constrain these aspects of representation arises when the system must represent *relations* among the distal objects. The distal-proximal isomorphism by itself allows the system to decide whether or not two distal stimuli are identical (by comparing their internal symbols), but not, for example, whether two of the stimuli are, in some sense, more similar to each other than to another stimulus.

Whereas the concept of representation as a mapping seems to be acceptable to theorists who accept the notion of representation in the first place, the approaches to the representation of relations differ widely among different theories. These can be subsumed under two general headings, according to whether they impart structure to the individual representations[16] (which, consequently, cease to be mere symbols), or purport to reflect directly those relations among the distal objects that need to be represented.

Let us consider now some of the relations among distal objects that a visual system may need to capture and represent internally. The first kind of relation among stimuli that suggests itself is *common origin*. As we saw earlier in this chapter, the appearance of objects changes with viewing conditions, necessitating an explicit action on the part of the visual system aimed to achieve object constancy. Once this action has been performed for a certain object, it may be advantageous to record its outcome (i.e., commit it to long-term memory). This can be done by forming separate internal representations for the various views of the object encountered by the system, each of which by itself can be a mere symbol (as argued above), and by tagging these representations with a common label, representing the identity (not the shape!) of the object.

In reality, different views of a given object are likely to be encountered in succession (that is, in "runs" or sequences of views), rather than randomly interspersed with views of other objects. The reasons for that are the cohesiveness of objects and the smoothness of the physical transformations that objects undergo with time,[17] which can be used by a representational system (Edelman and Weinshall, 1991; Zemel and Hinton, 1991; Stone, 1996a). Thus, the second kind of relation among visual stimuli that may be considered worth representing is relatedness through transformation, to which I shall refer in short as *transformation* (note that it subsumes the common-origin relation).

The third relation to be considered differs from the first two in that it is defined, generally, over different objects rather than over different aspects of the same object. This relation is *similarity* among objects. Formally, similarity can be defined over pairs or over triplets of objects. In the first case, it amounts to the statement that the two members of the pair are similar to each other (without specifying the units of measurement, or comparing similarities defined over different pairs of objects). The second version takes three objects as arguments, and specifies which two of them are more similar to each other than to the third. This version of similarity is especially useful in tasks such as categorization, because, unlike the two-argument similarity, it provides a basis for clustering or grouping some objects together while keeping others in separate groups (Nicod, 1930; Clark, 1993).

The fourth relation worth mentioning is a *composition of transformation and similarity*. In a representation that preserves such a relation, similarities among the elements change in a prescribed fashion (e.g., in such a manner that their ratios remain invariant) as the corresponding distal objects undergo transformations or deformations. This can be illustrated by considering one of the analogy tasks described in section 2.1.3. Let $v_1^{(1)}$, $v_2^{(1)}$, and $v_3^{(1)}$ be views of three objects obeying a similarity relation $s(v_1^{(1)}, v_2^{(1)}, v_3^{(1)})$. This is to be interpreted as an indication that an analogous situation prevails in the world: $S(\mathcal{O}_1, \mathcal{O}_2, \mathcal{O}_3)$ (that is, $\mathcal{O}_1$ is more similar to $\mathcal{O}_2$ than to $\mathcal{O}_3$; the relations $s$ and $S$ are, respectively, the proximal and the distal similarities). For a representation to preserve the composition of transformation and similarity relations, the same must hold for another set of views: $s(v_1^{(2)}, v_2^{(2)}, v_3^{(2)})$, provided that all the views in that set are related to those in the first set by the same transformation $T$: $v_i^{(2)} = T(v_i^{(1)})$.

### First-Order Isomorphism

One way to capture and manipulate relations such as transformation or similarity among distal objects internally is to incorporate the information necessary for verifying or inferring the relevant relations into the proximal representations of the objects. For example, the assertion that two visual stimuli are images of the same object related by rotation can be verified by recovering the 3D geometry of the object underlying each of the two images, and by attempting to establish congruence between the two proximal geometrical descriptions. The same idea may be applied to the estimation of similarity. First recover the geometry of each of the objects involved in a comparison, then compute the similarities, as one would do with a compass, a ruler, and a set of solid models.

This is, of course, the familiar reconstructionist theory, which seems to have been around ever since Aristotle. Echoes of its central dogma can be found in present-day sources: "Representation of something is an image, model, or reproduction of that thing" (Suppes et al., 1994). One problem raised by this notion of representation is the obligatory involvement of an observer: cartoon cats resemble real cats *to us*; the two kinds share no properties other than perceptual (Cummins, 1989). If taken literally, this stance gives rise to the need for a homunculus and the infinite explanatory regress associated with it (Pylyshyn, 1973; Shepard, 1984). Another problem is the inability of representations of this type to deal with abstraction: echoing Berkeley, one may argue that having an image of a striped cat does not qualify as a representation of a calico cat. Because of these and other considerations, in the philosophy of mind the equation of representations to images has been discredited so thoroughly as to inspire a rare consensus (Cummins, 1989).

Very few people these days believe that a representation of a cat in an observer's brain is cat-shaped or striped, or fluffy. Instead of little pictures in the head, a representation is seen as a set of measurements which collectively encode the geometry and other visual qualities of its target.[18] Nevertheless, the philosophical foundation of the current theories of shape representation is still isomorphism of the kind discussed above. Typically, it is assumed that structural (Biederman, 1987) or metric (Ullman, 1989) information stored in the brain reflects corresponding properties of shapes in the world, *on a one to one basis*. Anticipating the notation to be introduced in the following section, I shall refer to this approach as "first-order structural isomorphism" (Shepard, 1968b), or $\mathcal{F}$-isomorphism, between the representation and its target object.

**Second-Order Isomorphism**

Barring direct one-to-one resemblance between the object and the entity that stands for it internally, what relationship can qualify as representation of something by something else? R. N. Shepard (1968) suggests "second-order" isomorphism:

> (T)he isomorphism should be sought—not in the first-order relation between *(a)* an individual object, and *(b)* its corresponding internal representation—but in the second-order relation between *(a)* the relations among alternative external objects, and *(b)* the relations among their corresponding internal representations. Thus, although the internal representation for a square need not itself be square, it should (whatever it is) at least have a closer functional relation to the internal representation for a rectangle than to that, say, for a green flash or the taste of a persimmon (Shepard and Chipman, 1970, 2).

More recently, the idea of representation by second-order or $\mathcal{S}$-isomorphism has been advanced, under various guises, in a number of fields in cognitive science. Typically, the researchers in these fields take for granted the implausibility of representation by similarity, that is, by $\mathcal{F}$-isomorphism. Consequently, the theories mention merely "isomorphism," it being implied that the isomorphism holds between structures (and is, therefore, "second-order," in Shepard's terms), and not between individual entities (cf. figure 2.4).

A particularly lucid exposition of this point can be found in Gallistel (1990), where the example of numerical representation of physical quantities such as mass is discussed. On p.24 he points out that "(t)he statement that the number ten is isomorphic to some particular mass is meaningless. It is the system of numbers that is isomorphic to the system of masses." Gallistel then proceeds to defend the view that cognitive systems represent space and time by harboring structures that are isomorphic to corresponding structures in the world, subject to the above qualification regarding the importance of entire structures (that is, elements plus relations), as opposed to individual elements. A related version of representation by $\mathcal{S}$-isomorphism has been discussed in (Cummins, 1996).[19] Importantly, Cummins echoes Gallistel in pointing out that constituents of a structure are meaningful only in the context of some structure or other.

A related proposal, albeit in the context of representation of conceptual rather than perceptual spaces, can be found in Holland et al. (1986).

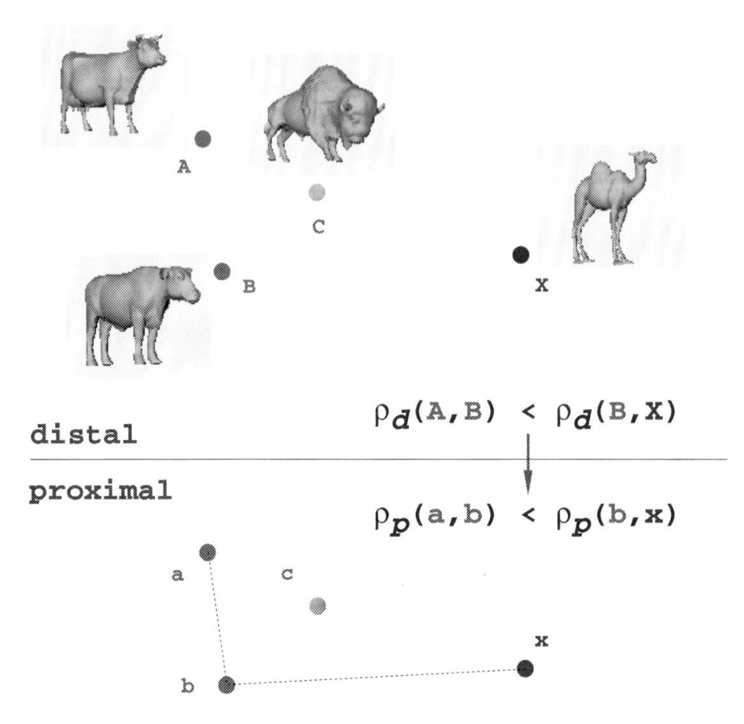


**Figure 2.4**
A representation that fulfills the requirement of second-order isomorphism. Here, it is the isomorphism between distance ranks in the two spaces; $\rho_d$ and $\rho_p$ are the distal and the proximal distance functions. Note that the constituents of the representation are mere symbols, which refer to the distal objects, but do not represent them on an individual basis, except as parts of the entire structure of distances (Gallistel, 1990; Cummins, 1996).

Here, the theory of representation is couched explicitly in terms of a homomorphism between a set of states and possible transitions between states in the world, and the corresponding states and transitions in the internal representation. To use an example from vision, the represented structure may be the natural succession of views of an object rotating in front of the observer, and the representing structure a string of internal states (which here can be symbols), each of which corresponds to at least one view of the object. (That is, the world-to-representation mapping can be many-to-one; the inverse mapping must be one-to-one.) In another example, the represented structure may be a triplet of objects obeying a certain similarity relation, and the representing structure the same relation that holds true of three symbols, each corresponding to one of the three objects. The major difference between the framework developed by Holland et al. (1986) and the one proposed here is their stress on the representation of state transitions instead of, say, similarity relationships. Whereas the present work is concerned with recognition/categorization, theirs deals with prediction and learning of causal relationships.

To summarize, in the context of visual object representation, the idea of second-order isomorphism translates into the notion that only certain relations between the objects—not the shapes of the individual objects themselves—need to be represented. The examples of such relations discussed above have to do with transformation and with similarity. The latter can be similarity of objects (as in Shepard's example stated in the preceding section), or similarity of object transformations or deformations (as in the analogy tasks described in section 2.1.3). Accordingly, in contradistinction to the first-order isomorphism or representation *by* similarity, this approach can be termed "representation *of* similarity."

## 2.3 Computational Theories of Recognition

### 2.3.1 Reconstructionist Theories: A Brief Historical Perspective

The central thesis of the "computational" approach to representation is that a discussion of theories of visual representation and recognition should be detached from the specific disciplines (psychology, neurobiology, or computer science) within which the theories are developed (Marr and Poggio, 1977). The explicit formulation of this principle by Marr and Poggio, and its reiteration by Marr (1981, 1982), led to the advent of a *de facto* standard theory, which called for a hierarchical reconstruction of the geometry of viewed objects.

The meta-theoretical part of Marr's work did not question this fundamental computational choice. Although the prevailing methods in the study of vision were criticized by Marr as "unashamedly empirical," the prevailing standard theory remained unscathed on the strength of the assumption that its empirical details would work out:

> Marr and Nishihara's 3-D representation theory . . . would be little more than speculation unless it could also be shown that such a (3-D) description may be computed from an image and can be manipulated in the required way (Marr, 1981, 133).

According to the standard theory, a 3D description of a scene is the common ultimate representation, which, in recognition tasks, is compared to a library of stored representations of the same kind (Brooks, 1981; Grimson, 1990). Thus, ultimate representation is closely related to the notion of an *intrinsic image*—a description of the true properties of the scene (geometry and layout of the object surfaces, and their color and texture), from which the influence of extraneous factors such as illumination and pose has been removed (Barrow and Tenenbaum, 1978; Barrow and Tenenbaum, 1981; Tenenbaum et al., 1981; Witkin, 1981).

The expected difficulties with the idea of "3-D" representation[20] were widely regarded as a challenge to be met rather than as a sign that something may be fundamentally wrong with the theory. As a result, during the 1980s many of the theoretical efforts in vision were concentrated on problems that arose from the need to reconstruct the visual world, as required by the standard theory (Grimson, 1981; Pentland, 1986; Blake and Zisserman, 1988; Aloimonos and Shulman, 1989; Fischler and Firschein, 1987). As things stand now, there are serious doubts regarding the feasibility of the reconstructionist approach (Pizlo et al., 1997; Edelman and Weinshall, 1998). These are echoed in a recent retrospective by two of the originators of the concept of intrinsic images (Barrow and Tenenbaum, 1993):

> Ten years after the publication of *Barrow and Tenenbaum (1981)*, many issues remain open. Perhaps the most direct issue is, simply, can the recovery process be made to work either for line drawings or for real world images [p.75]?
> It may also be the case that we have placed too much emphasis on analytical recovery models and exact recovery [p.77].

Indeed, of the three approaches underlying state of the art computational theories of recognition—structural decomposition, geometric constraints, and multidimensional feature spaces—only the first propounds anything remotely like the reconstruction of intrinsic images. Theories that adhere to these approaches, along with their limitations, are discussed next; an alternative theory is introduced in the following chapter.

### 2.3.2 Structural Decomposition Theories

In any structural decomposition model, the shape of an object is described in terms of relatively few generic components or parts, joined by spatial relationships that are chosen from an equally small fixed set. Under the classification scheme proposed in section 2.2.3, the structural decomposition theories construe representation as $\mathfrak{F}$-isomorphism. Distal shapes are assigned structural geometrical descriptions, which, in turn, can be manipulated by the system according to the task (e.g., similarities among such descriptions can be computed).

A crucial characteristic of the structural approach is the standardization of the primitives (the parts and their relationships), which allows novel objects to be treated on par with familiar ones, as required, for example, in categorization tasks. In this, structural approaches in visual recognition are related to structural theories of language processing, with objects corresponding to sentences, and object parts to words.[21] Following up on this parallel, the computation of a structural description of an object from image data can be viewed as parsing a sentence. The subsequent comparison between structural descriptions of objects amounts mathematically to labeled graph matching, a difficult combinatorial problem that is asymptotically intractable (Garey and Johnson, 1979).[22] This means that the amount of computation required to reach a solution depends exponentially on the size of the problem (e.g., the number of parts in the objects that are to be matched). This need not present an insurmountable difficulty in situations that involve simple objects or admit suboptimal solutions. Nevertheless, this limitation, which is inherent to the formulation of the structural matching problem and not to any particular algorithm for its solution, must be kept in mind when evaluating the merit of the theory.

#### Recognition by Components

A typical structural theory, Biederman's (1987) Recognition by Components (RBC), postulates a set of thirty or so primitive shapes (geons), claimed to be easily detectable in images due to their *nonaccidental* properties. The latter are 2D image features that can be used to make inferences about 3D object structure because of the low likelihood of the former to arise by chance (Lowe and Binford, 1985). A representative example of such a feature is a pair of parallel lines; because a chance image alignment of two segments that are in fact not parallel in 3D is unlikely, two parallel lines in the image are a good indicator of the presence of a 3D geon such as a cylinder "out there" in the scene.[23]

The use of nonaccidental features to infer the presence of geons, and the distributed computation of the graph structure of the input object are the cornerstones of the implementation of RBC described in Hummel and Biederman (1992). This work demonstrated the ability of a carefully engineered multilayer neural network[24] to derive structural representations from labeled line drawings. In many respects, however, it also served to highlight the shortcomings of RBC (figure 2.5), three of which are discussed below (see also Kurbat, 1994).

### Computational Problems of Structural Decomposition

**The Need for Metric Information** Although RBC is, in principle, capable of representing novel shapes (via their structural decomposition), this ability comes at the expense of ignoring fine (metric, or quantitative, as opposed to structural, or qualitative) distinctions among shapes. This shortcoming was recognized and amended by Stankiewicz and Hummel (1996), who augmented RBC by quantitative variables, encoding, for instance, the lengths of the various parts of an object, in addition to their qualitative characteristics such as convexity or the shape of their cross-sections.

**Difficulties with the Recovery of Parts** A more severe problem faced by the structural approaches is the need for reliable detection of parts in images. One aspect of the detection problem—inferring 3D structure from a 2D projection—is essentially addressed by the use of nonaccidental features. Nevertheless, the difficulty of finding in the image those lines and junctions whose nonaccidental relationships are to be used to infer the presence of geons has so far precluded RBC from being applied to the recognition of objects in gray-level images. The model described in Hummel and Biederman (1992) worked from hand-segmented line drawings; attempts to apply Recognition by Components to images of real objects invariably involve highly simplified shapes consisting of two to three clearly distinguishable parts, and are likely to use range data instead of photometric images.

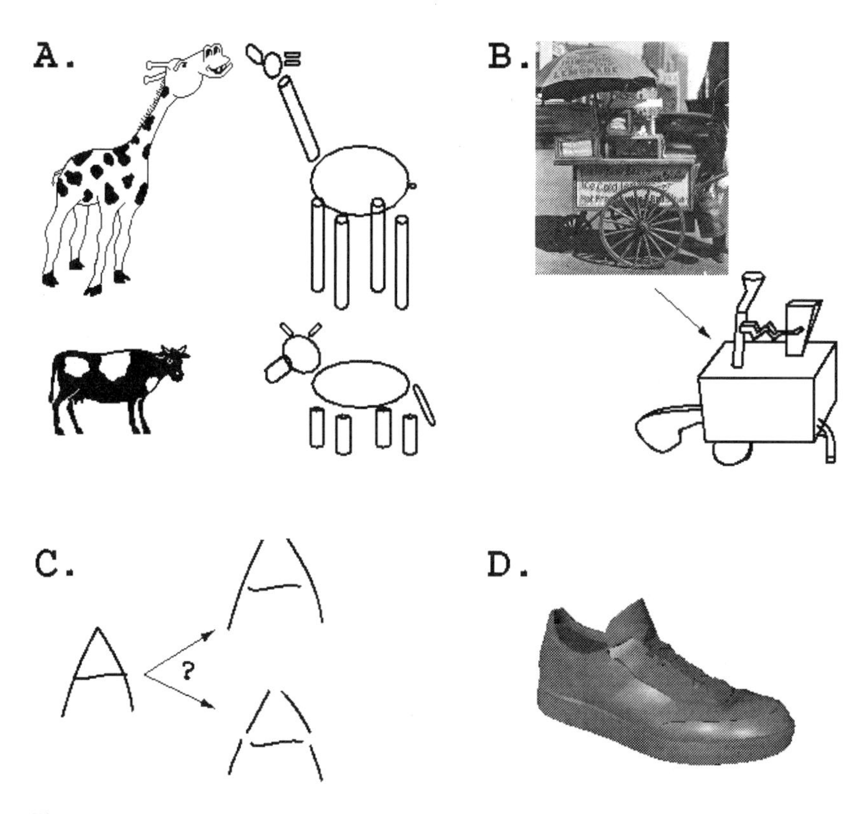


**Figure 2.5**
Computational problems with structural representations. *(A)* Structural descriptions must be accompanied by metric information, to represent differences among commonly encountered categories. The inclusion of metric details reduces the ability of structural methods to deal with novel objects. *(B)* A picture of a New York City street-corner hot dog cart, and a stylized object, which, as Biederman (1987) suggests, may be described as such following a structural decomposition in the visual system. At present, there is no reliable method for mapping a gray-level image into a collection of (labeled) primitives (lines, corners, etc.) from which RBC's geons are constructed. Thus, although a carefully engineered system such as that described in Hummel and Biederman (1992) can form a structural description of the line drawing of a cart-like object, the goal of deriving such a description directly from an image remains elusive. *(C)* Even in simpler tasks (e.g., in character recognition, where the figure is readily separable from the ground), the derivation of a structural description is problematic. The difficulty here stems from the possibility of assigning multiple structural descriptions to the same image. *(D)* In some tasks, coming up even with one structural description is problematic; how does one represent a shoe in terms of RBC's geons (Ullman, 1989)?

**Instability of Description in Terms of Parts** Even if the input to a structural decomposition system is given in the form of a collection of labeled lines, its interpretation in all but the most artificial examples is problematic because of an inherent instability that affects all structural approaches. The instability stems from the possibility of decomposing any shape in a number of ways, depending on the primitives that are assumed to exist. For example, a hand-printed letter A can be decomposed into either three or into five approximately straight lines, depending on whether the sides of the A are represented as single long lines or concatenations of two shorter segments each. If the stored representation of an A and the structural description of the current input have a different number of parts, a mismatch will occur during recognition.

It should be realized that the same problem arises in any combinatorially structured domain. For example, the problem of basis pursuit in signal processing (Chen and Donoho, 1994) consists of choosing a subset of basis functions, whose weighted sum best approximates a given signal. The difficulty here stems from the possibility of decomposing the signal in many different ways, depending on the choice of basis functions and on the optimization criterion. Likewise, in latent-variable analysis in statistics (Jöreskog and Wold, 1982) one is faced with the problem of selecting (or rather, postulating) the set of variables, and of estimating their contributions to the observables.

It has been suggested that the instability problem may be alleviated by imposing a prior expectation (in the Bayesian sense) on each possible solution at a number of levels of a structural hierarchy, as in pixel—edge element—curve (Geman, 1996; Bienenstock et al., 1997). This *compositional* approach attempts to combat instability by *regularization*[25] of the solution, and by using top-down expectations descending from the higher levels of the hierarchy to help disambiguate the interpretations at the lower levels.

Because structural interpretation guided by these principles has not been attempted for unconstrained object classes or for "raw" gray-level images, it is difficult to estimate the effectiveness of the compositional approach in overcoming the instability problem, or the sheer combinatorics of representing moderately complex objects as structural hierarchies (cf. Brooks, 1983; Connell, 1985). Experience with large-scale projects that adopted the structural approach has not been encouraging. A representative example of such a project was the MIT Vision Machine program (Little et al., 1988), which explored bottom-up solutions to low-level visual tasks, intended to culminate in a structural symbolic representation of the input. This project confronted computational difficulties along the way, and eventually ran into a representational dead end. On the one hand, its recovery of shape from various low-level cues proved to be unreliable. On the other hand, nobody seemed to have any use for the recovered shape even when the low-level computations did work. The general abandonment of similar projects in the early 1990s suggests that the current attempts at reviving the structural interpretation methods (Geman, 1996; Bienenstock et al., 1997) are about to face severe difficulties, both computational and conceptual.

### 2.3.3 Theories Based on Geometric Constraints

Whereas structural methods ignore much of the quantitative information inherent in the image locations of object features, geometric methods such as alignment (Ullman, 1989) use this information to identify the object and to compute its pose with respect to the observer. Geometry-based theories posit lists of coordinates of prominent (i.e., easily detectable) features associated with objects as their representations. Thus, the representation of a rectangle (in two dimensions) would be a list of eight numbers—the $(x, y)$ coordinates of the four vertices. According to the nomenclature of section 2.2.3, the geometric approach to representation therefore qualifies as Shepard's $\mathcal{F}$-isomorphism of the abstract variety.

To detect the presence of an object in a given image, methods derived from the geometric theories rely on the following *viewpoint consistency constraint*: the establishment of correspondence[26] between localized features of the object and of the image constrains the relative placement of the object features, and, therefore, the object's geometry (Bolles and Cain, 1982; Lowe, 1987b). Some of the practical approaches to the utilization of this constraint are described below.

#### Varieties of Alignment

Given a library of object models, each accompanied by a set of fiducial geometric features,[27] and a corresponding set of features in the images, one can compute the hypothetical viewing position of each candidate object, and verify the hypothesis of its presence in the image by transforming the model (aligning it to the image) and evaluating the goodness of the resulting match. Algorithms based on this insight have been proposed by Lowe (1987) and by Ullman (1989, 1996), who proved that the locations of as few as three features in the image suffice, under certain conditions, for unique alignment (that is, for hypothesizing the model to image transformation, which is then tested by actually transforming the model and evaluating the goodness of its match to the image). The robustness of the method can be improved by using more features, or anchor points, than strictly necessary (Ullman, 1989; Lamdan and Wolfson, 1988).

The full version of alignment described in Ullman (1989) requires that the representations of known objects maintained by the system contain 3D coordinate information, to allow the alignment process to compensate for transformations such as rotation in depth. Ullman pointed out, however, that a small collection of the object's views could suffice in certain cases. Shortly afterwards, Ullman and Basri (1991) proved that storing a few views per object (with full correspondence) obviates the need for maintaining 3D models of objects. This work prompted the development of a variety of algebraic methods for view-based recognition (Shashua, 1995), all based on the observation that views (i.e., vectors of image coordinates of a set of fiducial points) of a rigid object reside in a low-dimensional subspace of views of all possible objects. (Under orthographic projection, this subspace is linear.)

### Computational Problems with Alignment

**Need for Feature Correspondence** Because the establishment of correspondence is an absolute prerequisite for all the above methods, poor performance of the feature extraction and correspondence stage can completely disrupt subsequent recognition. Given the difficulty of detecting features [either points (Lowe, 1987a; Ullman, 1989) or regions (Basri and Jacobs, 1996)] reliably in a bottom-up fashion, it seems that alignment is applicable in practice only in the context of industrial object identification.

**Lack of Abstraction of Category Information** A more serious problem with alignment-like methods is their too literal treatment of object geometry. Alignment attempts to account for the observed location of every feature of the object; in comparison, categorization of novel objects requires abstraction of geometrical detail. This seems to call for a conceptual framework that is inherently statistical (cf. Kendall, 1984; Bookstein, 1996). Mere tolerance to certain variation in model parameters does not seem to suffice, as indicated by the relatively disappointing performance of a version of alignment that adopted this approach (Shapira and Ullman, 1991).

**Lack of an Explicit Representation of Object Statistics** From a statistical standpoint, alignment is deficient because it is geared to treating two objects at a time, instead of capturing several dimensions of variation within an ensemble. A step towards combining alignment with statistics has been made by Basri (1996), who developed an algorithm for representing object classes by their prototypes (defined as statistical averages of exemplars). However, because this method assigns the input to the closest known category (an approach known in pattern recognition as the nearest-neighbor decision), it is essentially limited to the processing of objects that resemble one of the prototypes much more closely than any of the others.

### 2.3.4 Multidimensional Feature Spaces

The structural approach downplays the representation of metric details of objects, while the geometric approach relies too heavily on such details. In comparison, the choice of a multidimensional feature space as the representation medium leads to a class of theories that steer the middle course between these two extremes. Formally, any theory of representation for recognition can be cast in terms of a feature space. For example, a structural description of an object can be recoded by specifying the location of a point that represents it in a (discrete) feature space whose dimensions are the values of the labels attached to the various parts and to their spatial relationships. Likewise, the geometric description of an object consisting, say, of $n$ points in 3D is equivalent to a vector of $3n$ continuous dimensions.[28]

The feature space approach generalizes these formulations by allowing a hybrid representation, some of whose dimensions may be discrete and defined in structural terms, others continuous and defined in terms

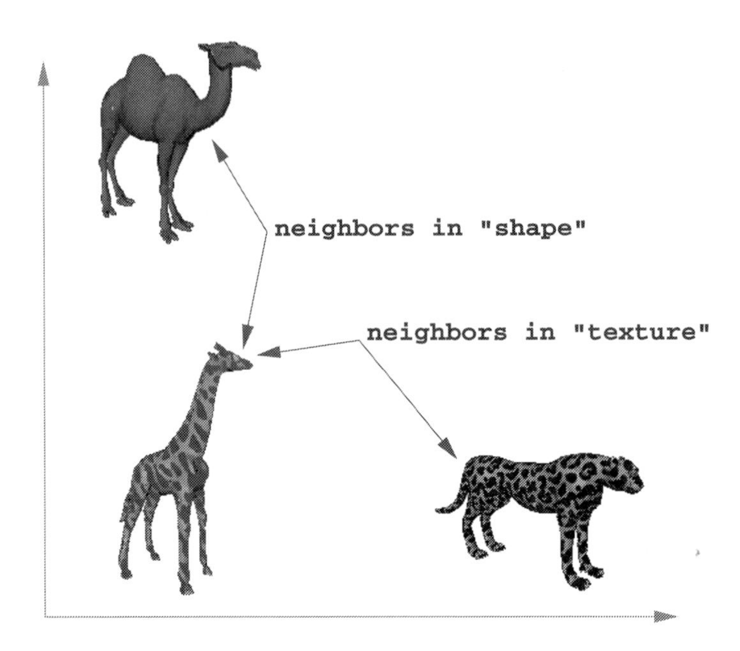


**Figure 2.6**
A novel object (*camelopardalis*), represented by two kinds of features: those having to do with shape (which make it a neighbor of camel), and those related to visual texture (according to which it is a neighbor of leopard).

of metric details, and yet others having to do with visual qualities other than shape (see figure 2.6), or, for that matter, non-visual qualities. Feature spaces also provide a natural substrate for operations that are normally performed on representations such as categorization, because the required comparison of representations in any case amounts to the estimation of similarities, which in a feature space can be made to correspond to the estimation of distances. Furthermore, the limitation imposed by the use of the nearest-neighbor decision procedure can easily be removed by reformulating the problems of recognition and categorization as clustering in a feature space (Duda and Hart, 1973). This facilitates the representation of a novel object by its membership in a number of clusters (categories) simultaneously (figure 2.6).

Of the three theories of representation discussed so far, feature space is the first one that does not necessarily fall under Shepard's rubric of $\mathcal{F}$-isomorphism. As noted above, although geometric information can be used to define dimensions of a feature space (as in the representation of a rectangle by the coordinate of its vertices), it does not have to: a rectangle can be equally well represented by its aspect ratio and perimeter (cf. Palmer, 1978). Indeed, the constraints of computational and implementational feasibility usually steer the choice of features away from the extremely convenient yet difficult to recover geometric characteristics. Consequently, a feature-space representation must be $\mathcal{S}$-isomorphic to the world of shapes in order to be able to support the visual tasks listed in sections 2.1.2 and 2.1.3.

### Multidimensional Histograms

Although pattern recognition methods based on feature spaces have been around for a long time, their applicability to object vision was widely believed to be limited. Recent developments in the choice of features and in the computational capacity of computer systems led to a considerable success of several feature-space systems. These systems represent objects by histograms (computed over the entire input image) of multidimensional vectors of measurements related to color (Swain and Ballard, 1991; Mel, 1997) and to local distributions of intensity (Mel, 1997; Schiele and Crowley, 1996). Although the spatial origin of individual feature measurements is lost in the process of histogramming, global coherence of viewed objects is validated through the effective interaction of many local features. Encouragingly, histogram-based systems exhibit a certain tolerance to variation in object details, resulting in an ability to group similar objects together (Mel, 1997).

### Computational Problems with Feature Spaces

**Combining Diagnosticity with Invariance** The main problem of feature-space methods is finding features that afford reliable discrimination among similar objects, along with invariance across object transformations [this corresponds to the issue of stability vs. sensitivity of features, mentioned by Marr (1982)]. Simple geometrical arguments (Green and Swets, 1966; Duda and Hart, 1973) can be used to show that these are conflicting requirements, which can be met jointly only as a result of a compromise (see appendix H), or following a special training (Intrator and Edelman, 1997b).[29] In practice, the histogram-based systems described in (Schiele and Crowley, 1996; Mel, 1997) do not seem to tolerate rotation in depth to the same extent that they cope with shape-preserving transformations of objects, such as translation in the image plane.

**Difficulty of Learning from Examples in Multidimensional Spaces** Because statistical representations such as those involving feature histograms must be learned, the issue of dimensionality assumes a central role in determining the viability of any given scheme. Learning from examples in a high-dimensional space is computationally problematic. The problem, known as the "curse of dimensionality" (Bellman, 1961), lies in the exponential dependence of the required number of examples on the number of dimensions of the representation space.[30] Dimensionality reduction thus becomes of primary importance (Edelman and Intrator, 1997). The challenge, then, is to reduce dimensionality while preserving the ability of the representational system to deal with novel objects, without having to come up with novel features.

**Inexplicit Representation of Structure** Another reason for dimensionality reduction in the feature-space approaches is the need to make explicit the dimensions of similarity (which may be much fewer than the total number of "raw" features). Returning to the example of figure 2.6, it seems reasonable to require of a representational system not only that it note the resemblance of a giraffe to a camel and to a leopard, but also that it realize that the former has to do with certain dimensions of the giraffe's shape and the latter with its color and visual texture. Likewise, it is also desirable to represent explicitly the manner in which shape structure is similar or different (Hummel, 1998). Consider, for instance, two objects: a sphere attached to the top of a cube, and a cube on top of a sphere. It is very easy to devise a feature space in which these objects would be represented as "different"; in fact, in a computer vision system they would differ in most of the raw image (pixel) dimensions. Such a representation of difference is, however, unstable and unwieldy. A much better representation would make explicit the commonalities of the two shapes, that is, the (local) resemblances between them, rather than their (holistic or global) difference. This, in turn, would facilitate the representation of their differences (namely, the different locations of the common features).

The challenge here is, of course, to achieve these two goals without reverting to the structural approach, which, as we saw earlier, has its own serious disadvantages.

In summary, the feature space approach would lead to a more attractive theory, if the diagnosticity of features would not have to be traded for invariance, if the dimensionality of the representation space would be low enough to allow efficient and generalizable learning, and if structure would be made explicit, at least for objects that do yield themselves to a straightforward decomposition. In the next chapter, I present a theory that pursues these goals within the general framework of a feature space; the subsequent chapters describe its implementation and testing.

## Notes

1. The entity matched to the present stimulus can also be the outcome of some processing involving memory traces rather than "raw" memories.

2. There are reasons to believe that in many situations in human vision the nature of the representations themselves is determined by the context imposed by the task at hand (Barsalou, 1987; Barsalou, 1991; Schyns, 1998).

3. For an example of such behavior, see Mel (1997).

4. Color and texture cues, when available, are intrinsically less variable under changes of viewpoint than shape cues—another reason for a designer of a recognition system to try to make the best of shape alone, before any recourse to this information.

5. The multiple-view algorithms require also correspondence (Ullman, 1979), that is, a one to one association of matching features in each pair of views. Together with the correspondence information, a set of views allows the recovery of the 3D structure of the object; multiple-view recognition algorithms bypass this recovery step. Approaches that use multiple views but not detailed (i.e., pixel-by-pixel) correspondence are properly termed "appearance-based." The implementation of the multiple-view method in chapter 5 will take the more difficult path of not using detailed correspondence, which is why I can here afford to gloss over the distinction between view and appearance, tacitly assuming that the latter is meant when the former is mentioned.

6. In practice, in deriving models of specific systems, concerns such as biological plausibility and computational complexity must be addressed in addition to theoretical considerations; see section 6.1.

7. Other examples that come to mind seem to be all connected with the aftermath of air travel: the identification of one's luggage on the conveyor belt, and of one's car in a large parking lot (both frequently done on the basis of cues that have

nothing to do with 3D shape *per se*. I am indebted to A. J. O'Toole for these examples of situations that require identity-level processing of visual objects). A similar observation has been used by some psychologists (notably, I. Biederman) as a basis for arguing that the observed viewpoint dependence of identification is a "special" phenomenon (as is face recognition). Findings that effectively refute this view are discussed at length in chapter 6.

8. The distinction between the basic level and the entry point is motivated by the exceptions to this rule: objects that are atypical in that they are usually named at a non-basic level. For example, an image of a penguin normally evokes the label "penguin" and not "bird" (the basic category to which penguins belong).

9. Biological perceptual systems routinely attribute identical category labels to stimuli that are easily distinguishable in a discrimination task (cf. Shepard, 1987).

10. For a glimpse at a debate concerning the possibility of achieving productivity and compositionality with distributed (as opposed to symbolic part-based) representations, see (Fodor and Pylyshyn, 1988; van Gelder, 1990).

11. Analogy is defined in the *Webster Revised Unabridged Dictionary* as "similarity of relations."

12. For prominent arguments against internal representations as such, see (Gibson, 1979; Brooks, 1991).

13. Representing an object during recall is more complicated than representing it while it is being viewed, in which case the world can serve, in a sense, as an external memory (cf. O'Regan, 1992).

14. Such symbols would be automatically grounded in the external world (Harnad, 1990) by virtue of the correspondence between the representations and their targets.

15. A set $X$ is said to be partitioned into equivalence classes if all members of the same class, but not members of distinct classes, are related by a two-argument relation $R : X \times X \rightarrow \{\mathtt{true}, \mathtt{false}\}$ that is reflexive and transitive: $\forall x_i \in X, R(x_i, x_i) \rightarrow \mathtt{true}$ and $\forall x, y, z \in X, R(x, y) \wedge R(y, z) \Rightarrow R(x, z)$.

16. That is, to the representations of individual objects.

17. Cf. Shepard's (1984) notion of "internalized kinematic constraints"—empirical "laws" which describe the behavior of objects and which can be put to use in situations that require prediction of motion behavior or interpretation of complex phenomena involving visual motion.

18. This is much like Shepard's (1975) distinction between "concrete" isomorphism, under which the representation of a square is another square, and its "abstract" version, under which the representation of a square can be, for example, four pairs of coordinates encoding the locations of the square's corners.

19. There it is called "The Picture Theory of Representation"—a label that is unfortunate, because in vision research pictorial representations (cf. Ullman, 1989) are traditionally associated with the "concrete" Aristotelian $\mathcal{F}$-isomorphism.

20. See Marr (1981, 133) for a list of various problems that must be overcome to make his 3-D representation feasible; some of those, such as figure-ground separation, were suspected not to have a clean (what Marr termed "Type I") theory, which would necessitate a "bag of tricks" approach.

21. Some theories, such as Biederman's (1987) Recognition By Components, discussed later, liken objects to words and components or parts to phonemes.

22. In labeled graph matching, a mapping is established between the vertices and the edges of two graphs in such a manner that the labels carried by the elements of one graph match those of the other one.

23. For a full-fledged Bayesian treatment of issues that arise in this inference task, see Richards et al. (1996).

24. The seven layers in the JIM model of Hummel and Biederman were labeled as follows: image edges, blobs, geons, enumerated relations, invariant relations, geon feature assemblies, and objects. The crucial assumption of the model was the existence of "fast enabling links" between various elements, which enabled grouping and which operated on the principle of binding by synchronization posited by some researchers (von der Malsburg, 1981). Although the temporal correlation or synchronization hypothesis has a wide following (Singer and Gray, 1995), the experimental evidence for it is inconclusive (Young et al., 1992), and alternative interpretations for the neurophysiological data have been offered (Kirschfeld, 1995).

25. Regularization is a common mathematical technique applied to problems that are formally ill-posed. By extending the definition borrowed from the theory of differential equations, a problem is considered ill-posed if its solution does not depend continuously on the data, or if more than one solution exists, as in the case of structural interpretation. Regularization attempts to reduce the solution space, by imposing additional constraints, over and above those contained in the data. References to the mathematical literature on regularization and a discussion of its relevance to low-level visual tasks can be found in Poggio et al. (1985).

26. That is, a hypothetical match that identifies certain image features as manifestations of particular object features. This hypothesis is usually verified (or rejected) by a later stage in the recognition process.

27. Fiducial geometric features are associated with fixed locations on the object's surface and can therefore be trusted to convey information about its geometry and orientation. A surface marking or a corner formed by two surfaces meeting at an angle are good geometric features; a smooth bend in a surface is not.

28. However, views (projections) of such an object do not span the entire $3n$-dimensional space, but rather reside in a linear six-dimensional subspace, as proved in Ullman and Basri (1991).

29. That is, unless the features are both absolutely diagnostic and inherently invariant to the transformation in question, as in the case, say, of the bar codes used to label goods in stores.

30. The "curse of dimensionality" refers to the exponential dependence of the number of examples required for learning a task on the number of dimensions of the representation space (Bellman, 1961). Suppose that filling a region in a 1-dimensional feature space with representative examples requires ten data points; a comparable coverage of a three-dimensional feature space would then require 1000 examples (Stone, 1982).

# 3

# 𝒮-isomorphism: The Theory

1. Objection: "Knowledge placed in our ideas may be all unreal or chimerical." . . . If our knowledge of our ideas terminate in them, and reach no further, where there is something further intended, our most serious thoughts will be of little more use than the reveries of a crazy brain. 2. Answer: "Not so, where ideas agree with things."

—John Locke
*An Essay Concerning Human Understanding*—1690

In the preceding chapter, I argued that recognition-related tasks can be well supported by representations related to their target objects via a second-order, or 𝒮-isomorphism. In other words, rather than capturing first-order qualities pertaining to shapes (e.g., their geometry), representations should encode second-order or relational qualities, such as similarity (as in Shepard's original formulation of second-order isomorphism; see Shepard and Chipman, 1970), temporal succession (Freyd, 1993), and transformation under changes in the viewing conditions (Edelman and Duvdevani-Bar, 1997b). In this chapter, I concentrate on similarity, with the aim of developing an approach to its measurement and representation which would be both intuitively satisfying and computationally tractable. As we shall see later, the resulting framework encompasses the representation of other relational qualities as well.

The definition of similarity via a metric or distance function proposed in section 3.1 is traditionally criticized on several theoretical and practical accounts. In anticipation of such criticism, I qualify that definition, and argue that when its scope is limited to *shapes* of common objects, the notion of a metric similarity space constitutes a useful basis for formal treatment of representation, and for the development of more sophisticated similarity functions.

The simplest way to embed a set of shapes in a metric space where proximities correspond to similarities is to define each shape by the coordinates of a list of fiducial points (chosen in such a manner that corresponding points can be identified in all the shapes). The resulting shape space has a number of interesting properties, which are discussed in section 3.2.

Another way to encode shape is by computing the statistics of an ensemble of object geometries and to represent each member of the ensemble in terms of a small number of parameters common to all members, as suggested in section 3.3. If principal component analysis is used for that purpose, the parameters computed from the ensemble (which may be called eigenshapes) can be used to synthesize the objects by linear superposition. Eigenshapes or any other parameterization can in turn be used to morph, or smoothly deform, one shape into another. Several independent deformations of that kind can provide a low-dimensional framework for the description of shapes; the low dimensionality of the resulting shape space is crucial in that it facilitates its subsequent representation by an S-isomorphic shape space of the observer.

Section 3.4 raises the issue of ensuring that the desired relationship—S-isomorphism—holds between distal and proximal shape spaces. Because visual systems do not have direct access to whatever shape space one may devise for the description of shapes "out there" in the world, they must necessarily rely on indirect means of obtaining information about shapes and, in particular, about similarities between shapes. This indirect route always involves measurement of features, some combination of which, it is hoped, is related in a principled manner to the desired distal quantities. The next concept to be introduced into the discussion is, therefore the *measurement space*, spanned by the chosen set of features. The principle of S-isomorphism dictates certain constraints that are to be observed in the choice of features, as discussed in this section.

One of these constraints encourages the use of extremely high-dimensional measurement spaces, as explained in section 3.4.3. Because of the high dimensionality, systems striving for a faithful representation of the visual world face the problem of dimensionality reduction—

computing a successor to the original measurement space, which would be sufficiently low-dimensional to allow useful operations (such as learning from examples) to be carried out on the ensuing representations. The search for such a low-dimensional *proximal* representation space (culminating in the following chapter) is motivated by the prior knowledge of the existence of a low-dimensional parameterization for a given set of *distal* shapes, as stressed above.

## 3.1 Similarity as Proximity in a Metric Space

The need to represent similarities between shapes calls for a formalization of the notion of similarity. The most straightforward way of doing this is to treat similarity as a function that assigns to each pair of shapes a real number. This, in turn, is easily done if one adopts the notion of a *shape space*—a metric space in which each point corresponds to a particular shape (more on this in section 3.2). In that case, similarity can be thought of as a quantity inversely related to the shape-space distance between the objects, defined through a metric function on that space.

### 3.1.1 Some Common Objections

Treating similarity as proximity in a metric space confers considerable methodological advantages because the extensive mathematical apparatus available for the treatment of metric spaces can be brought to bear on the various computational issues that arise when the theoretical framework is put to work. The metric-space approach, however, invites several objections, which at first appear devastating:

1. *The problem of arbitrariness: similarity is a useless notion, because a pair of objects can be seen as arbitrarily similar (or dissimilar).* This point has been made repeatedly in philosophy (Quine, 1969; Goodman, 1972), pattern recognition (Watanabe, 1985), and cognitive science (Murphy and Medin, 1985).
2. *The problem of context: even if various possible features of objects are weighted to pin similarity down, it cannot yet be treated as a function (that is, a certain kind of mapping) defined on pairs of objects if it is to capture the dependence of perceived similarity on the context in which it is assessed.* The role of context has been mentioned in neurobiology (Gilbert, 1994; Rolls, 1996), perceptual psychology (Biederman

et al., 1974; Marks, 1992), and cognitive science (Tversky, 1977; Medin and Schaffer, 1978).

3. *The problem of asymmetry: even if similarity can be treated as a function, it cannot be based on the notion of a metric space, because similarity relations violate the metric axioms (especially symmetry).* This observation, too, can be encountered in various disciplines, such as psychology (Tversky, 1977) and computer vision (Mumford, 1991).

In view of these concerns, the use of similarity as an explanatory tool in cognitive science has been traditionally predicated on a system of biases (Watanabe, 1985) intended to account for its observed quirks, or, more recently, on "respects" (e.g., "in what respect are those two things similar?") delineating the process of similarity estimation (Medin et al., 1993). In this section I take a diametrically opposite approach. Rather than conceding from the outset that similarity is ultimately subjective, I want to see first whether in some sense, however limited, similarity (more precisely, geometric similarity) is objective. Subjectivity can be always reintroduced later to accommodate the relevant psychological data.

## The Problem of Arbitrariness

A striking manifestation of the problem of arbitrariness in unconstrained similarity can be found in the following theorem of Watanabe (1985): "Any two objects are as similar to each other as any other two objects, insofar as the degree of similarity is measured by the number of shared predicates."[1] This theorem holds if the set of predicates (features) used to assess similarity is finite and equally applicable to all objects, and if no two objects are identical with respect to this set. Watanabe's conclusion (in which he echoes C. S. Peirce; see also Quine, 1969, and Tversky, 1977) is that different weights must be assigned to different predicates if the concept of similarity is to make any sense.

The introduction of weights into the calculation of similarities amounts to abandoning altogether the quest for objectivity. Whereas this may be unavoidable in some perceptual domains, in the calculation of *geometric* similarity this extreme can be avoided. For that, geometric objects must be construed not as arbitrary "predicates," but as collections of elementary geometric features, such as the locations of fiducial points (as is only proper). As we shall see in section 3.2, given a set of such points for each of the shapes under consideration, shape similarity can be defined formally, in a unique manner (roughly speaking, in terms of geodesic or shortest-path distance in the space of all shapes). Now, imagine a fixed number of fiducial points spread all over the surface of a geometrical object. Their exact locations are immaterial as long as the points are dense enough. The points, moreover, need not be labeled: the "shape-space" similarity alluded to earlier can be computed for each of the possible pairings of fiducial points of two objects, and the minimum over all the pairings can then be defined as their geometric similarity.

This definition of similarity involves neither attaching permanent labels to fiducial points, nor assigning differential weights to the contributions of different points to the overall similarity. Because none of the points is singled out in any manner, geometric similarity *can* be made at least as objective as Newtonian mechanics or such sub-disciplines of physics as crystallography or the theory of gases. An intuitively satisfying outcome of this definition is that it allows one to say that the Earth is more like a sphere than a cube, without having to add "to us" or expecting to be contradicted on epistemological grounds.

**The Problem of Context**

Observer bias arises out of an interaction between the subject (the system that performs the comparison) and the targets (the objects that are compared). Likewise, context effects are the product of an interaction, among the targets and other objects which the subject brings to bear on the comparison. A classical illustration of the dependence of similarity on context can be found in Tversky (1977): a majority of subjects who were asked whether Austria was most similar to Sweden, Norway, or Hungary, chose Hungary. When the choice was among Sweden, Poland, or Hungary (the latter two being members of the now defunct Eastern Bloc), the preference switched to Sweden. In tasks such as this, defined over abstract feature domains, the context effect is unstable, not the least because of the idiosyncratic nature of the background knowledge which the subjects bring to bear on similarity judgment. In Tversky's example, this is the knowledge of geopolitics. That experiment would probably yield a different result if repeated two decades later with young subjects who may be unaware of the now-extinct political subdivisions of Europe.

In the judgment of similarity of objects on the basis of their geometry, the influence of context (i.e., the set of shapes that serve as a tacit background for the comparison) weakens as its scope widens. At limit, when the entire universe of familiar shapes is taken as the background, similarity among objects becomes, trivially, a function of those objects only (simply because the omnipresent all-inclusive context is the same for all objects). This similarity function, which is effectively context-free, can serve as a basis for deriving various context-sensitive measures of similarity, just as objective geometric similarity can be transformed into various subjective similarities by imposing this or that observer-specific bias.

**The Problem of Asymmetry**

According to the axiom of symmetry, in a metric space the distance between points A and B must be the same as the distance between B and A. Violations of symmetry in psychophysically measured subject data prompted Mumford, who surveyed a list of possible metrics defined over shapes, to reject them all as irrelevant because "similarity isn't even a metric" (Mumford, 1991). In response, I note that modeling asymmetry is easy if the symmetrical cases can be accounted for (just as a context-sensitive similarity measure can be easily derived from a context-free one). More specifically, the perceptual system of the observer can warp the metric similarity space, according to his or her or its idiosyncrasies, and to the dictates of the task (Harnad, 1987; Goldstone, 1994). Furthermore, similarity need not remain restricted by the symmetry inherited from the underlying distance function; the metric-space model can be considered a starting point for a more elaborate one. For instance, metrics can be made to depend on the local density of exemplars in various regions of the representation space, resulting in asymmetric similarity judgments (Krumhansl, 1978). More generally, asymmetry can be achieved by modeling explicitly the differential salience of various dimensions of the representation space (Edelman et al., 1996b). Thus, a metrics-based definition of similarity need not prevent the replication of a considerable variety of similarity-related phenomena in human perception.

### 3.1.2 A Metric Similarity Space as a Working Hypothesis

To summarize this preliminary discussion, while similarity frequently depends on the choice of features and on context, and while it may be asymmetric, confining its scope to shape-based comparisons among a large number of objects downplays those dependencies. The resulting view of perceptual shape-based similarity as proximity in a metric shape space retains sufficient scope to meet the needs of shape recognition tasks. Eventually, however, this notion of similarity, adopted for the time being as a working hypothesis, must be tested against three criteria. First, it must be useful for the development of a theory of $\mathcal{S}$-isomorphism. Second, it must be amenable to extension in a manner that would take narrow task-dependent contexts into account and would allow asymmetric similarities. Third, it must prove to be a faithful model of human performance in object recognition tasks that comply with the narrow-scope constraints stated earlier. The theoretical usefulness of the shape space hypothesis is the main concern of this chapter; I shall return to the discussion of the other two issues later on.

## 3.2 Shape Spaces

The notion of a shape space has been introduced in the past in a number of applied fields, such as biological morphometrics (Bookstein, 1991) and computational molecular biology (Farmer et al., 1986), as well as in various mathematical disciplines such as statistics (Kendall, 1989), and complex analysis and algebraic geometry (Sundararaman, 1980). Shape spaces are useful insofar as they put the otherwise vague concept of similarity on a rigorous basis, providing tools for its principled treatment. In a given field, an intuitively satisfactory definition of a shape space leads immediately to the formalization of the associated concepts of shape classes, shape transformation, etc. (table 3.1).

### 3.2.1 Kendall's Shape Space

Probably the most straightforward formal definition of a shape space, called by Kendall (1984) $\Sigma_n^k$, construes shapes as "clouds" of $k$ labeled points embedded in an underlying $n$-dimensional Euclidean coordinate space $R^n$. The first thing to notice about the shape space $\Sigma_n^k$ is that

**Table 3.1**
Some nomenclature related to the notion of a shape space

| | | |
|---|---|---|
| all shapes | ↔ | a metric space $\mathcal{A}$ |
| all "objects" | ↔ | subspace $\mathcal{S}_p$ of $\mathcal{A}$ |
| normalized* objects | ↔ | subspace $\mathcal{S}$ of $\mathcal{S}_p$ |
| **a shape** | ↔ | **a point** |
| dissimilarity | ↔ | distance |
| similarity | ↔ | proximity |
| a class of shapes | ↔ | a cluster of points |
| transformation | ↔ | movement perpendicular to $\mathcal{S}$ |
| deformation | ↔ | movement within $\mathcal{S}$ |

*Note:* An object is *normalized* if its orientation, size and location relative to the coordinate system are set to some predetermined arbitrary standard. (See Kendall, 1984, for the explanation of this and other concepts related to shape spaces.)

its dimensionality is not $n$, but rather $kn$. Consider, for instance, the space of all triangles that can be drawn on a flat sheet of paper, i.e., all shapes defined by the locations of three points in two dimensions (Kendall, 1989). This space, $\Sigma_2^3$, is six-dimensional, because two numbers are needed to fix the location of each of the three vertices of the triangle.

The example of the space of all triangles in a plane suggests an immediate extension to solid shapes, which in vision are usually called "three-dimensional" (because three numbers are needed to specify the location of each of their points). The surface of such a shape can be approximated to any desirable precision by a mesh of triangular elements (see figure 3.1; this representation of object shape is common in computer graphics). Assuming that the resulting mesh has $k$ vertices, the solid shape is thereby embedded into the shape space $\Sigma_3^k$.

### 3.2.2 Transformations and Deformations

We may recall that the major motivation for introducing the notion of a shape space was the possibility it offers to formalize similarity (or rather, dissimilarity) by the means of a distance function. The space $\Sigma_n^k$ inherits from its underlying Euclidean space precisely the kind of natural definition of distance that we need. For two members of $\Sigma_n^k$ (i.e., two

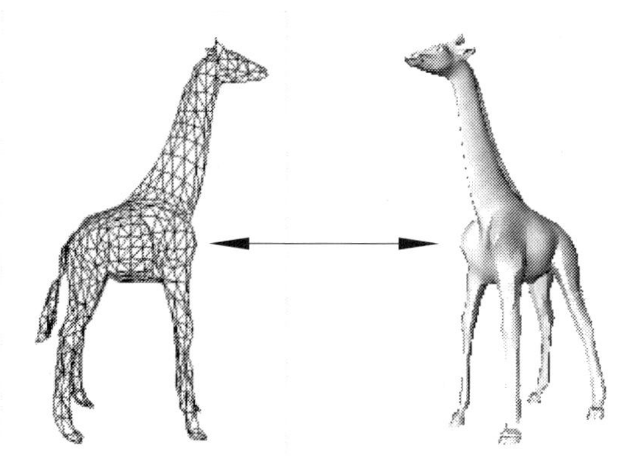

**Figure 3.1**
A shape and its triangle-mesh approximation.

clouds of $k$ points each, embedded into $R^n$) this distance is the sum of squared differences of all $kn$ coordinates of the two shapes. Note that within Kendall's framework the points are assumed to be labeled, so that correspondence is known. This assumption will be phased out in section 3.2.3.

According to this definition of distance, two objects related by translation or rotation would count as different—a situation that needs to be avoided. Thus, the notion of *shape* must include a specification of the transformations which, by definition, leave the shape invariant (Kendall, 1989). If objects are conceived as rigid configurations of points, shape is defined up to the action of the orthogonal group of transformations (that is, rigid motions and reflection).[2] From this, it follows that dissimilarity between two sets of points is to be measured by the *Procrustes distance*, defined as the sum of squares of residual distances between corresponding points, remaining after an optimal orthogonal mapping that matches one set to the other has been applied (Borg and Lingoes, 1987).

An interesting consequence of allowing for a Procrustes transformation before computing distance in $\Sigma_n^k$ is that it makes the topology of this space non-trivial. Consider again the simple example of the space of all triangles in a plane, and a particular member of that space: the equilateral triangle. Now, imagine deforming this triangle by moving one of the vertices inwards, along the perpendicular to the opposite side; this deformation corresponds to a movement of the corresponding point in $\Sigma_2^3$. At some stage, the chosen vertex will cross over the opposite side (with the triangle momentarily degenerating into a line), and will continue moving outwards. Finally, an equilateral triangle will be re-formed. This triangle is a rotated version of the original one, and therefore equivalent to it under the Procrustes metric. This exercise illustrates that a continuous movement along a straight line in the underlying space can correspond to a movement along a closed orbit in the $\Sigma_2^3$ space.[3]

### 3.2.3 Best-Correspondence Distance

The Procrustes distance provides the requisite unique, unbiased, and effectively computable measure of similarity between two "point cloud" shapes—but only if the points in each cloud are assigned unique labels which establish the necessary correspondence. As suggested in section 3.1, this last obstacle can be removed by placing *all* possible correspondences on an equal footing. To that end, let us define the *best-correspondence distance* $d_{bc} : \Sigma_3^k \times \Sigma_3^k \rightarrow R$. Let $s_1, s_2 \in \Sigma_3^k$ be two mesh objects. The best-correspondence distance is then $d_{bc} = \min_{c \in C} d_P(s_1, s_2)$, where $d_P$ is the Procrustes distance, and $C$ is the set of all pointwise correspondence pairings between the two meshes. It is easy to verify that $d_{bc}$ is a metric. Moreover, because it is based on the Procrustes distance, $d_{bc}$ inherits its properties of uniqueness and lack of bias.

Because the number of possible pairings depends exponentially on the number of points in each of the two meshes, brute-force computation of $d_{bc}$ is intractable for large values of $k$. In principle, prior constraints can be brought to bear on this problem to make its solution computationally feasible.[4] It is important to realize, however, that the status of $d_{bc}$ in the present theory is somewhat like that of an inertial coordinate system in Newtonian mechanics. The inertial system is an abstraction, whose mere *existence* suffices for grounding the theory in physical reality. That a coordinate system affixed to the earth's surface happens to be approximately inertial[5] is a convenient accident of nature, but not a prerequisite for the laws of mechanics to hold. Likewise, the existence of a unique $d_{bc}$ for any two shapes suffices for our present purpose, albeit this distance may be only approximately represented by the observer's visual system.

### 3.2.4 An Objective Shape Space

The existence of a unique best-correspondence distance $d_{bc}$ obviates the need to label the points that comprise the objects in Kendall's shape space $\Sigma_3^k$ (figure 3.2). Furthermore, the exact number of points, $k$, is immaterial, as long as $k \geq k_{res}$, where $k_{res}$ is large enough to ensure that the largest gap between the points does not exceed the resolution at which the shape is to be considered (all shapes are assumed here to be normalized to the same size; the discounting of size variation in this manner is, in fact, a part of the computation of the Procrustes distance $d_P$, which underlies $d_{bc}$).[6] We may, therefore, define a metric space $\Sigma_{bc}$ as the space of objects composed of $k_{res}$ unlabeled points, embedded in $R^3$ and endowed with the $d_{bc}$ distance.

## 3.3 Parameterization of Distal Shape Space

In the preceding section, we saw that the concept of shape space (with the concomitant measure of similarity between shapes) can be defined in a manner that makes mathematical and intuitive sense, and is independent of any observer, just as the Newtonian space is routinely assumed to be. Having achieved that, we may now re-introduce the observer, and address the question of the conditions under which the observer's internal representations could be considered formally veridical, when compared against the external (distal) world of shapes. In the remainder of this chapter, the main consideration will be the representation of similarity, which will necessarily focus the discussion on the comparison of several shapes at a time, rather than on the mere parameterization of each shape by itself.

The focus on similarity among shapes raises the issue of the *scope* of the comparison. In many cases, a visual system would be better off if it limits the range of shapes for which representation in a common space is sought (i.e., a common parameterization is assumed). Such a limitation can be imposed by the logic of the task confronting the system. For example, embedding disparate objects in distinct representational subspaces could automatically exclude the possibility of the embarrassing proverbial comparison between apples and oranges. The categorical structure imputed to the world of shapes in this manner can be made to reflect the

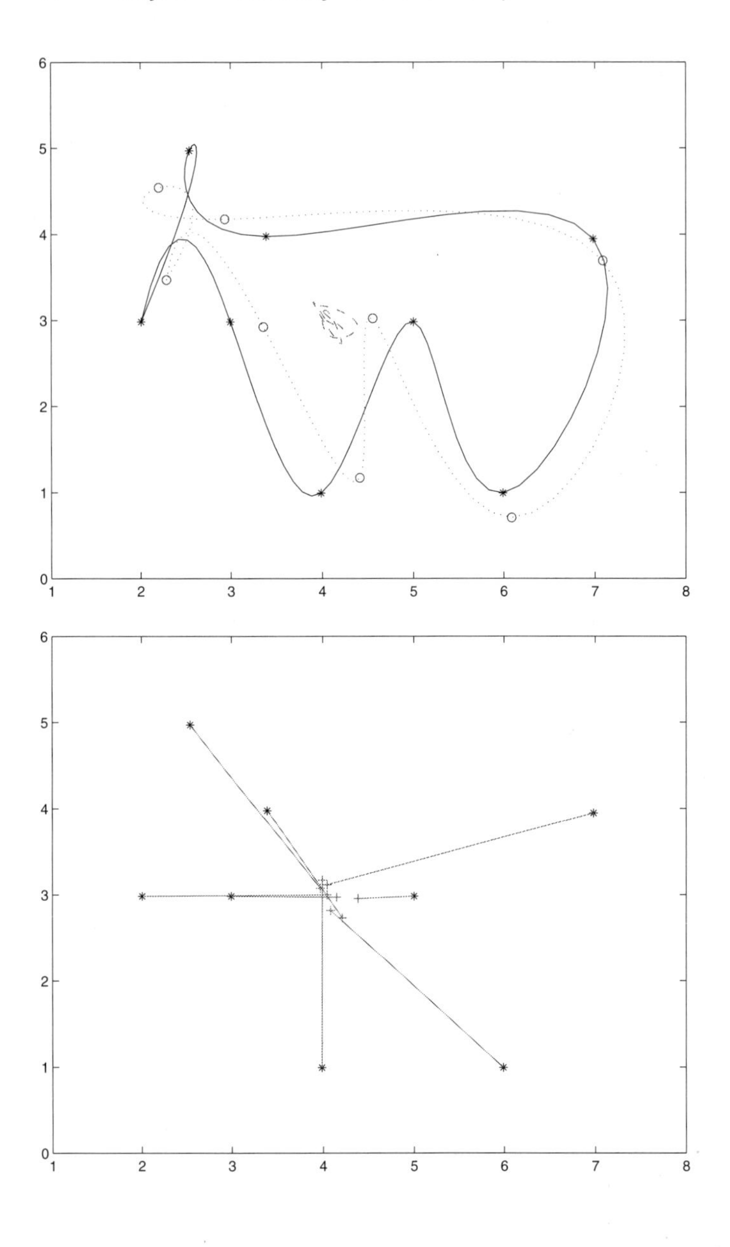
0
1
2
3
4
5
6
1
2
3
4
5
6
7
8
0
1
2
3
4
5
6
1
2
3
4
5
6
7
8

behavioral needs of the system; different observers may carve the shape space into domains of different scope.

The issue of scope is linked naturally to that of *dimensionality*. Shapes that are all like each other can be represented in a reduced-dimensionality space. Note that just as any limited-scope parameterization is necessarily biased, so is any reduced-dimensionality parameterization. Because of the many possible ways to project a high-dimensional space into a low-dimensional one, it does not make sense to talk about an objective low-dimensional shape space encompassing diverse high-resolution objects. Consequently, the question of embedding a set of shapes in a common low-dimensional space can only be properly addressed at the subjective level, where it becomes an empirical issue, specific to the given visual system. Likewise, the congruence between the low-dimensional spaces of several observers is an empirical issue. If it holds, this indicates that the perceptual systems of the observers are alike in an important sense.

### 3.3.1 Scope of Parameterization

The need to compare shapes in the parameter space dictates that the same set of parameters be used to define all the shapes relevant to a given task. The shape space $\Sigma_{bc}$ offers precisely this level of generality: when

**Figure 3.2**
*(Top)* The solid curve is a contour whose shape is determined by the coordinates of 8 fiducial points (marked by $*$'s), and which, therefore, belongs to the shape space $\Sigma_2^8$ (the points are connected by a cubic spline, to facilitate visualization). The dotted curve is a perturbed version of the solid one, obtained by displacing each fiducial point by a two-dimensional Gaussian random variable, with zero mean and a standard deviation of 0.35. The order of the points was permuted randomly, then recovered by computing the best correspondence between the original and the perturbed points (that is, the correspondence that resulted in the smallest Procrustes distance $d_P$). The recovery here is correct. As pointed out in section 3.2.4, even for disparate shapes for which the notion of intrinsically correct correspondence is meaningless, the best correspondence is still well-defined and is unique (up to a possible symmetry of the shape). Note that the difference between the best correspondence and a random one is, for similar shapes, very pronounced: the small dashed curve in this plot was obtained by Procrustes transforming the shape in which the order of points had been randomized, so as to fit the original curve. This fit is very poor, because of the incorrect correspondence. *(Bottom)* The original and the randomly permuted fiducial points (with line segments indicating the true correspondence).

considered at a given resolution, all shapes are uniquely described by $k$ fiducial points (that is, $3k$ parameters), with dissimilarities between pairs of shapes given by the best-correspondence distance $d_{bc}$.

In many cases, the best correspondence between shapes, imposed by seeking the smallest Procrustes distance $d_P$, makes no sense perceptually. For example, a grand piano can be matched to a giraffe so as to minimize $d_P$, but the result, albeit unique and objective, would not strike one as natural. In comparison, if a camel and a giraffe are matched on the basis of minimum $d_P$, the pairing of the fiducial points should appear quite acceptable.

Intuitively, the latter situation occurs when the shapes to be put into correspondence are *intrinsically similar* to each other to begin with. The notion of intrinsic similarity can be derived from the definition of the best correspondence distance $d_{bc}$ as follows. Consider, first, the extreme case in which there are two identical objects, for which the point labels are lost. Clearly, a recovery of the original correspondence in this case will result in $d_{bc} = 0$ (if the object possesses symmetries, several correspondences may lead to the same outcome; this means merely that the object is congruent to itself under some symmetry transformation). Now, consider two objects that differ by a small shift in each of the constituent points, so that the true distance $d_{tc}$ ($tc$ standing for "true correspondence") between them is nonzero. If that shift is much smaller than the mean distance between points, the probability that a wrong correspondence will give rise to $d_{bc} < d_{tc}$ should be very small. Although I did not attempt to derive an analytical bound on this probability, numerical simulations confirm that for sufficiently similar objects (those for which $d_{tc}$ is smaller than about 15% of the maximum diameter of the objects) the lowest $d_{bc}$ distance indeed results in the correct correspondence (figure 3.3).[7] When this is the case, intrinsic similarity is well-defined, and can be set to any monotonic function of $1/d_{bc}$.

These considerations are important in the context of the possible strategies for representing the distal shape space internally. Basically, the limited scope of intrinsic similarity implies that it is not reasonable for a visual system to treat all shapes within the same parametric framework, even if a common observer-independent parameterization (such as the one given by the shape space $\Sigma_{bc}$) does exist. Another considera-

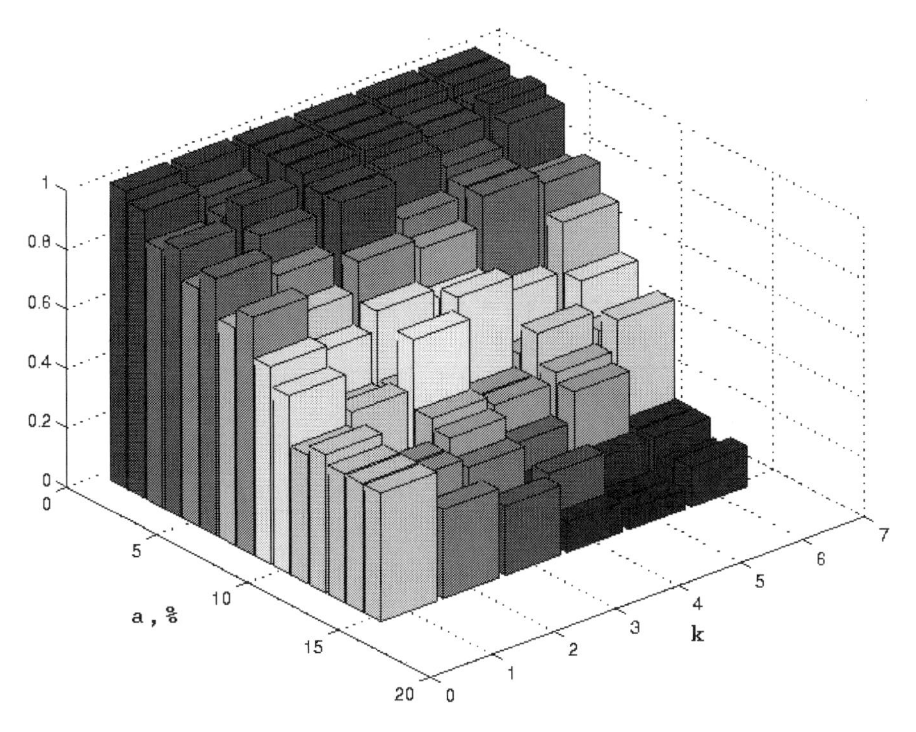


**Figure 3.3**
The proportion of randomly generated pairs of objects in $\Sigma_3^k$ for which minimizing the $d_{bc}$ distance leads to the recovery of the correct correspondence. The independent variables here are the number of constituent points, $k$, and a parameter $a$ that controls the distance between the two objects under the true correspondence, $d_{tc}$. The first member of a pair was generated by drawing each of its $k$ points independently from a uniform distribution $\mathcal{P}$ defined over the unit cube in $R^3$. The second object was derived from the first one by perturbing each point by noise $\mathbf{n} = a\mathbf{p}$, with each $\mathbf{p}$ drawn independently from $\mathcal{P}$, and the parameter $a$ varying from 0 to 0.7 in increments of 0.05.

tion is that of the goal which the representation must serve. Specifically, the stress in visual recognition tasks differs, depending on the set of objects that are involved: whereas similar shapes need to be *compared* in a detailed manner, extremely disparate shapes need to be merely *distinguished* from one another. As a consequence, in the context of a particular visual system and a given task, dispensation should be given for different classes of shapes to be encoded internally by different sets of parameters.

### 3.3.2 Dimensionality of Parameterization

What is the natural dimensionality for a shape space containing objects a human observer is likely to encounter in the visual world? Geometric common sense suggests that faithful description of complicated shapes—those, for instance, that consist of a great many points or surface elements, which may move independently of each other—may require thousands of dimensions. Indeed, the intermediate-resolution giraffe-like mesh shape in figure 3.1 took about 3000 dimensions to define. In comparison, psychophysical literature that describes experimental manipulation of shape in studies of shape perception often contains phrases such as "the shape dimension,"[8] which imply that shapes can be treated as low-dimensional entities. It turns out that both high-dimensional and low-dimensional characterizations of shape spaces are computationally relevant, depending on the circumstances of the task.

Indeed, whereas the nominal dimensionality of the shape space $\Sigma_3^k$ is equal to $3k$, a comparison between several shapes (selected by an observer in the context of a given task) opens up the possibility for considering the same shapes in a much lower-dimensional setting. This possibility is based on a method known in computer graphics as *morphing*: smooth metamorphosis of one shape into another, illustrated in figure 3.4. Consider two shapes, $s_1$ and $s_2$, each represented as a point in $\Sigma_n^k$. If we arrange the $kn$ numbers, encoding the two shapes in two vectors, $\mathbf{x}$ and $\mathbf{y}$, all the shapes that are, in a sense, "in between" $s_1$ and $s_2$ will be encoded by $\alpha\mathbf{x} + (1 - \alpha)\mathbf{y}$, $0 \leq \alpha \leq 1$.[9] Note that the difference between $\mathbf{x}$ and $\mathbf{y}$ is a one-dimensional quantity in the framework provided by this simple linear-interpolation morphing.

Thus, shape representation has both high-dimensional and low-dimensional aspects. On the one hand, to specify each of the two endpoints of a morphing sequence, $\mathbf{x}$ and $\mathbf{y}$, in isolation, one has to fix the values of $kn$ parameters. On the other hand, once those shapes are specified, a variety of other shapes can be described using a single parameter: the value of the blending coefficient $\alpha$. Importantly, it is the low-dimensional aspect of shape representation—encoding differences between shapes—that is central to the notion of S-isomorphism. This insight can be summarized by re-stating that S-isomorphism calls for the

**Figure 3.4**
Two four-legged animal shapes, cow and pig, and a shape that is halfway between them in a common parameter space. Note the distinctly porcine expression of the intermediate object. Each of the two original objects was first discretized by dividing its bounding box into $30 \times 30 \times 30 = 27000$ volume elements (voxels). Each voxel was assigned three parameters, which were set to the average values of the $x, y, z$ coordinates of the object points falling within the voxel. This procedure effectively embeds the shape into a 81000-dimensional space. Morphing was then carried out by averaging the coordinates in the corresponding voxels, and rendering the resulting shape.

representation of the morphing of shapes, rather than the representation of shape geometry *per se*.

One may wonder whether a common low-dimensional parameterization exists even for diverse sets of shapes (such as giraffes and grand pianos, an example mentioned above), which are not related by intuitively obvious morphing sequences. It is interesting to compare the situation here with other perceptual modalities where low dimensionality of the distal space is indeed a useful assumption. Consider, for example, color vision, where a typical problem is how to compute the reflectance of a surface patch from measurements performed on its retinal image. The solution to this problem is the reflectance function of the surface, which can be visualized as a plot of the ratio of reflected vs. incident light energy, specified for a range of wavelengths of the latter. The central feature of this problem is that the expected solution resides, in principle, in an infinite-dimensional space, because a potentially different (in the worst case, random) value of reflectance may have to be specified for each of the infinite number of wavelengths of the incident light (D'Zmura and Iverson, 1997). Furthermore, the spectral content of the illumination (which is confounded with the reflectance function multiplicatively, and which must be discounted to allow the computation of the reflectance) is also potentially infinite-dimensional, for the same reason.

Although the space of surface reflectances and the space of illumination profiles *could* be infinite-dimensional, they are not. In fact, quite the opposite is true. Cohen (1964) and Judd et al. (1964) demonstrated that both reflectance and illumination spaces are low-dimensional by subjecting color measurement data to principal component analysis (PCA).[10] The results showed that both reflectance and illumination data can be approximated well if represented by three dimensions each (i.e., projected onto the three leading principal components). Biological visual systems make good use of this fact. Primates exhibit color constancy under a wide range of conditions (Beck, 1972), despite maintaining only a low-dimensional neural color coding space (De Valois and De Valois, 1978). The dimensionality of their psychological (perceived) color space is the same as that of the distal color spaces revealed by principal component analysis (Boynton, 1978).

The internal representation space for color can be low-dimensional, because the distal color spaces (that of surface reflectance and that of illumination) happen to be low-dimensional. If an analogous situation prevails in the distal shape space, visual systems could take advantage of it by representing shapes locally in low-dimensional spaces, with all the ensuing computational advantages. The outcome of a simple computational exercise, illustrated in figure 3.5, indicates that representation of shapes in a common low-dimensional space is possible, as long as the shapes are sufficiently similar to each other—a condition that we regarded as plausible in the discussion of the scope of common parameterization in the preceding section.

If more than two shapes are considered at a time, one can employ PCA to compute an optimal low-dimensional linear basis for the set of shapes, in which case each constituent shape can be represented as a linear combination of the "eigenshapes" (members of the basis). If only a few leading eigenshapes are used in this representation, a dimensionality reduction (relative to the $3k$ dimensions for $k$-point shapes, or to the number of shapes, whichever is less) will ensue. This operation is illustrated in figure 3.5, where two animal shapes are rendered along with their projection onto the twelve-dimensional linear space spanned by the leading twelve eigenshapes of an ensemble of twenty-one similar objects. The high mutual similarity of these twenty-one shapes (all of them

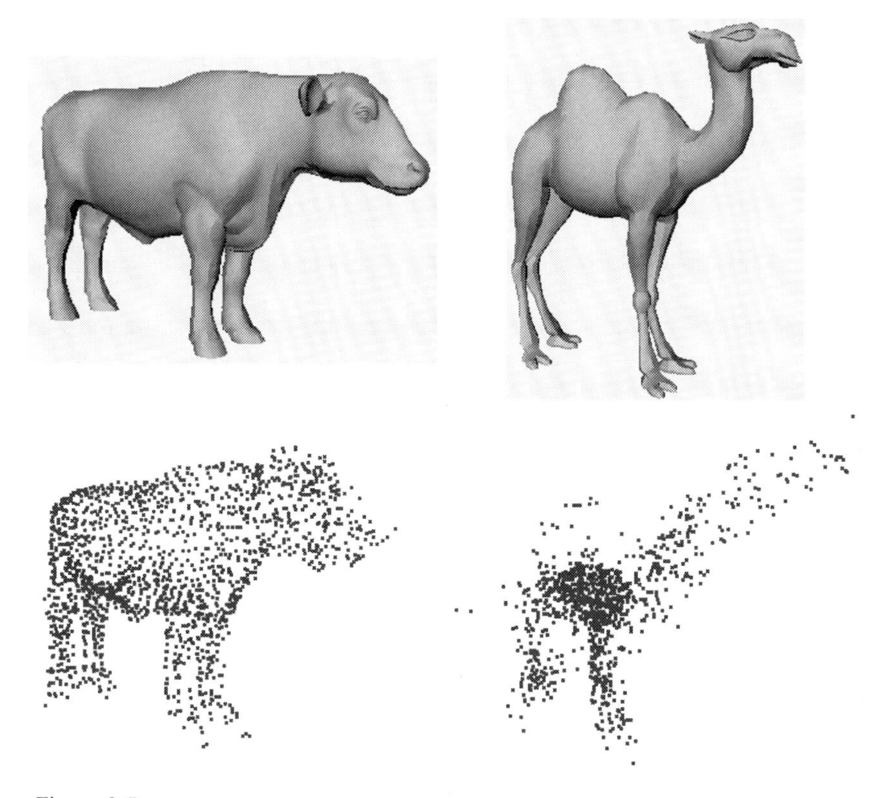

**Figure 3.5**
*(Top)* Two animal shapes. *(Bottom)* The same shapes, after discretization and embedding in a twelve-dimensional shape space by principal component analysis (PCA). The significance of this embedding is discussed in section 3.3.2. Altogether, twenty-one shapes of four-legged animals were digitized in the manner described in the legend of figure 3.4. The resulting $21 \times 81000$ data matrix $D$ was subjected to PCA, using the standard method of analyzing the $21 \times 21$ covariance matrix $DD^T$, instead of the intractable $81000 \times 81000$ matrix $D^T D$. It turned out that 75% of the variance in this data set could be explained by the leading twelve principal components. The two objects in the bottom row are the two shapes reconstructed in this twelve-dimensional space. These objects are rendered as dot clouds because the proper surface triangulation required for shading is lost as a byproduct of the discretization procedure.

four-legged animals) resulted in the twelve leading dimensions accounting for 75% of the variance of the entire set. This signifies a relatively low dimensionality (although not as low as in the color space example).

The subspace spanned by several similar shapes in $\Sigma_{bc}$ is very likely to be nonlinear (curved), in which case PCA overestimates its dimensionality. The general problem of recovering a low-dimensional curved subspace embedded in high-dimensional data is computationally nontrivial (Leen and Kambhatla, 1994; Edelman and Intrator, 1997). I shall address it in chapter 4 in the context of designing a method for reducing the dimensionality of perceptual data. For the time being, however, all we need is to realize that sets of similar shapes are amenable to relatively low-dimensional encoding.

The preceding discussion of possible parameterizations of the world of shapes can be summarized as follows:

1. The intuitive notion of the space of all possible shapes can be given a formulation that is independent of any observer, just as the notion of the regular space of classical physics can.
2. It may be advantageous for a visual system to consider separately various limited-scope shape spaces, each containing shapes intrinsically similar to each other.
3. Such limited-scope shape spaces can be considered (relatively) low-dimensional, although their reduced-dimensionality versions are no longer observer-independent.

As far as representation is concerned, the main theoretical question, is, therefore, how to get an S-isomorphic version of the low-dimensional parametric distal shape space across the gap separating the observer from the world.

## 3.4 The Distal to Proximal Mapping

The observer-independent formalization of shape space, offered in the preceding section, provides an answer to the basic ontological question of shape representation: "what is it out there that can be represented?" Given the shape space $\Sigma_{bc}$ and its locally low-dimensional versions, one may ask the next question: "How to represent it?" Consequently, I now turn to the *process* of representation, construed as a mapping from the distal to the proximal, or internal, shape space.

### 3.4.1 Levels of Representation of Similarity

My main concern being veridicality, I would like to identify the conditions under which the image of the distal shape space, under the distal to proximal mapping which I shall call $F$, would qualify as a faithful representation. Because veridicality is a matter of degree, a wide range of possible characterizations of $F$ can be considered. To impose structure on these possibilities, one may classify the various mappings by the degree of preservation of similarity that they afford. The advantage of this classification scheme is its direct relevance to the notion of $\mathcal{S}$-isomorphism, which, by definition, is a mapping that preserves second-order qualities such as similarities.

#### Preservation of Distinctness

The minimal requirement appears to be that the mapping be one to one, so that distinct points in the distal space are mapped to distinct points in the representation space (figure 3.6A).[11] To realize the implications of limiting the representational requirements to mere distinctness, note that a major reason for maintaining internal representations is *generalization*: any system, at any point in time, will have encountered only a finite number of (labeled or rewarded) stimuli. For any other stimulus, the response will have to be generalized, based on memory traces of past experiences with related stimuli (Shepard, 1987). A representation whose fidelity is limited to distinctness provides no basis for generalization, because it does not contain information concerning relationships between stimuli, beyond the identity of each of them.

#### Full Similarity Spectrum Preservation

A modicum of generalization capability is afforded by a mapping that preserves to some extent the neighborhood structure that prevails in the original space. For example, two points that are nearest neighbors of each other before the mapping may remain so after the mapping. This kind of representation may provide a limited basis for generalization (specifically, all objects more similar to some object $O_1$ than to $O_2$ could be represented as such, rather than merely as distinct both from $O_1$ and from $O_2$).

If the identity of the $k$'th nearest neighbor of each point is preserved for some $k > 1$, the resulting representation will be in closer correspondence

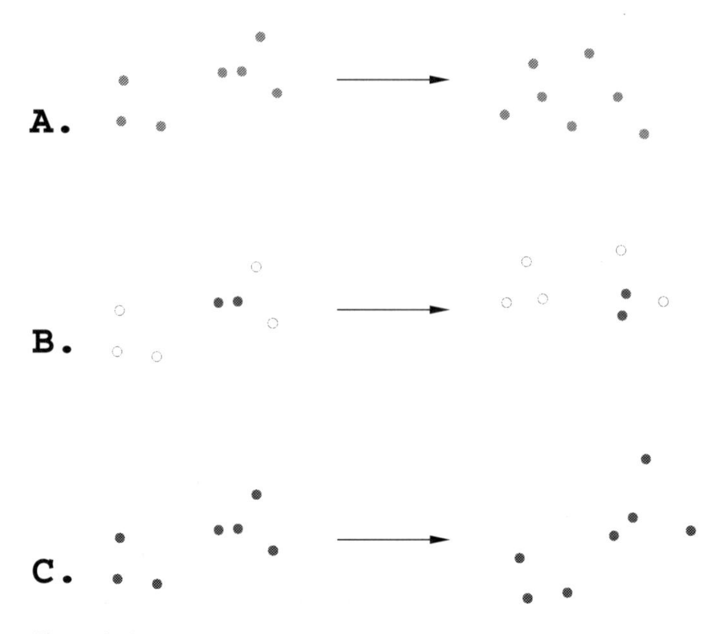


**Figure 3.6**
Degrees of veridicality of the distal-to-proximal mapping. *(A)* Preservation of distinctness. *(B)* Preservation of nearest-neighbor relations. *(C)* Full distance spectrum preservation.

with the original space. At limit, when the rank order of all interpoint distances for any finite set of points is fully preserved, the representation mapping becomes, for all practical purposes, a similitude (figure 3.6C). The original shape-space configuration of the points can then be recovered from the distance rank information, up to rigid motion (Shepard, 1962; Kruskal, 1964; Shepard, 1980; Borg and Lingoes, 1987). A representation that possesses this degree of fidelity can support categorization at a number of levels, including the determination of the identity of the stimulus, and not only of its class.[12]

### 3.4.2 The Components of the Mapping $F$

In general, $F$ can be described as a composition of three mappings: $F = f_3 \circ f_2 \circ f_1$, where the first component, $f_1$, is dictated by the properties of the world, and the other two constitute part of the system (figure 3.7).

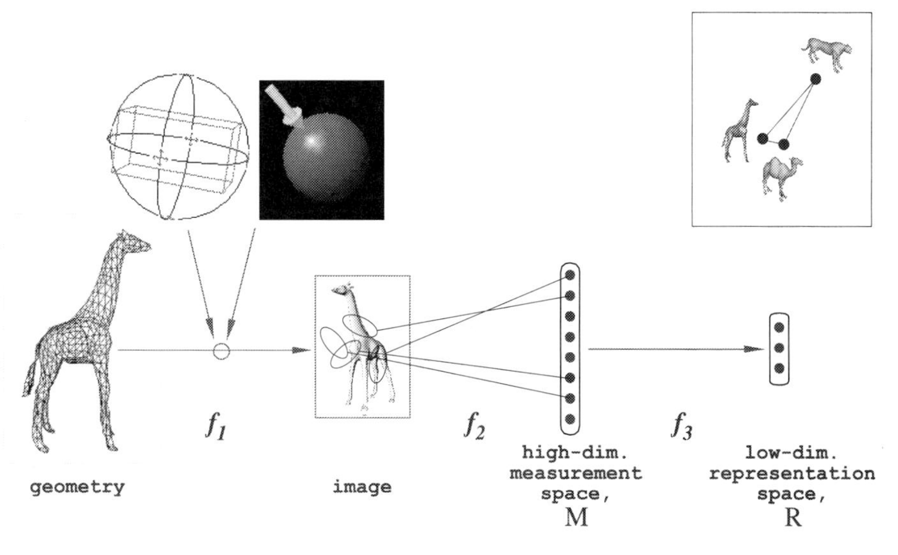


**Figure 3.7**
The components of the distal to proximal mapping $F$ (see section 3.4.2). In this schematic illustration, the appearance of the object is governed by its shape and by extrinsic factors such as pose and illumination direction. To assure proper representation of the original parameter space, a typical perceptual system must carry out many measurements, then reduce the dimensionality of the resulting space, while getting rid of the extrinsic variables. *(Inset)* Preservation of similarity relationships (e.g., mapping a giraffe and a camel closer to each other than to a cheetah) is an important constraint on the mapping $F$, discussed in section 3.4.3.

**Imaging** The first component of $F$, $f_1$, maps the geometry of an object to an image, given the viewing conditions: $f_1 : \Sigma_{bc} \times \mathcal{T} \times \mathcal{L} \rightarrow \mathcal{I}$, where $\Sigma_{bc}$ is the shape space defined in section 3.2.4, $\mathcal{T}$ is the set of possible transformations of objects (translations and rotations), $\mathcal{L}$ is the set of illuminations, and $\mathcal{I}$ is the set of images. This formulation leaves out certain factors (e.g., degrees of freedom associated with the surface material), which are not directly relevant to the issue of shape representation. I also assume that the scene consists of a single object.

**Measurement** The second component of $F$, $f_2$, corresponds to the battery of measurements carried out by the visual system on the stimulus image: $f_2 : \mathcal{I} \rightarrow \mathcal{M}$, where $\mathcal{M}$ is the visual *measurement space*. In the primate visual system (which I shall discuss at some length in chapter 6), each dimension of the measurement space can be thought of as corresponding to the activity of a retinal ganglion cell. The axons of the ganglion neurons constitute the optic nerve, which projects from the eye to the brain. The nominal dimensionality of the space $\mathcal{M}$ is, therefore, the same as the number of axons in the optic nerve: about one million.

**Representation** The third component of $F$, $f_3$, refers to the processing that occurs within the visual pathway, starting at the optic nerve, and ending at the locus where the representations of visual objects are thought to reside, in the inferotemporal cortex: $f_3 : \mathcal{M} \rightarrow \mathcal{R}$, where $\mathcal{R}$ is the *shape representation space* for objects.

The mapping $F$ establishes a correspondence between distal shapes (members of $\Sigma_{bc}$) and their internal representations (members of the proximal shape space $\mathcal{R}$). As such, the space $\mathcal{R}$ is more likely than not to be specific for a particular observer and task. Nevertheless, if the mapping $F$ fulfills certain conditions, the representation can be veridical, $\mathcal{R}$ being $\mathcal{S}$-isomorphic to the distal shape space.

### 3.4.3 Constraints on $F$

The defining feature of $\mathcal{S}$-isomorphism is that a representation should preserve similarity ranks everywhere in the shape space. It turns out that the requirement of such *global* rank preservation is quite restrictive in the class of representation mappings it allows. Specifically, a one to one mapping with this property must be a composition of scaling with rotation or reflection (Reshetnyak, 1989).[13] If the constraint of globality is relaxed, the class of admissible mappings becomes much larger. Let us assume for the moment that both $\mathcal{R}$ and the subspace of $\Sigma_{bc}$ that it must represent, are two dimensional. In this case, veridicality is a generic property of well-behaved representation functions: the requirement of *local* rank preservation is satisfied by any smooth and regular (invertible) mapping (Cohn, 1967). Such mappings are *conformal*, that is, they preserve angles, and therefore, also the similitude of small triangles (figure 3.8). In particular, a scalene triangle formed by a triplet of points in a distal shape space will be mapped into a triangle with the same ranking of side lengths in the proximal representation space. In terms of similarity preservation, this means that the representations of two objects that are more similar to each other than to a third object will be closer to

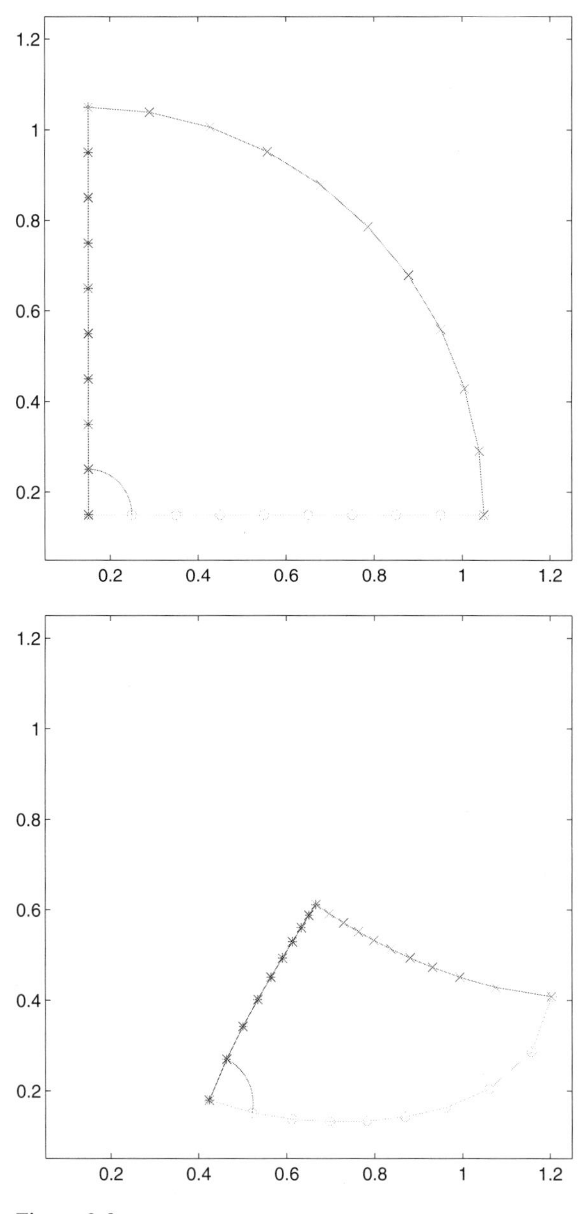


**Figure 3.8**
An illustration of the concept of conformal mapping, discussed in section 3.4.3. *(Top)* Two similar "triangles" formed by two straight line segments and two circular arcs, all meeting at right angles. *(Bottom)* The same two "triangles" under the action of the conformal mapping $\mathbf{z} = \sqrt{\text{atanh}\,(\mathbf{x})}$ (the choice of the function here is arbitrary, and is intended merely to illustrate the concept of conformality). For the small triangle, both the isosceles shape and all the angles are preserved. At a larger scale, the triangle is distorted, although the angles remain right.

each other than to the representation of the latter, as per the definition of S-isomorphism.

What happens if the dimensionality of the shape space that needs to be represented is higher than two? It may seem that we are in trouble, because conformality in high-dimensional spaces is as restrictive as global distance rank preservation. As proved by Liouville in 1850, already for $n = 3$ there are no everywhere conformal mappings from $R^n$ to itself besides those which are composed of finitely many inversions with respect to spheres, or Möbius transformations. These constitute a finite-dimensional continuous (Lie) group which includes the group of rigid motions in $R^n$ and is only slightly broader than that group (Reshetnyak, 1989).

In practice, however, the situation is much more benign than it seems: a generic smooth and regular mapping $F$ will still support veridical representation, if the aim is *approximate* and local preservation of similarity ranks. This relaxation of the main constraint corresponds to replacing the requirement of conformality with that of *quasiconformality*. Intuitively, a conformal mapping is locally an isometry; a quasiconformal mapping is locally affine.[14] Under such a mapping, the ranks of distances between points are preserved approximately, and on a small scale (Väisälä 1992, 124). Because any diffeomorphism restricted to a compact subset of its domain is quasiconformal (Zorich, 1992, 133), *any* smooth and regular mapping $F$ will result in a representation that is locally approximately veridical. In other words, similarities among shapes that are close to each other in the distal shape space will be represented faithfully (cf. appendix A).

### 3.4.4 Implications

The requirement that the mapping $F$ be *regular* means that it should preserve the original dimensions of shape variation (note that if it does not, the resulting representation will not satisfy even the distinctness requirement, stated in section 3.4.1). An interesting conjecture that can be made at this point is that the high dimensionality of the measurement space $\mathcal{M}$ in a typical biological visual system is motivated by the requirement of regularity. Specifically, diverse nature and large number of independent measurements increase the likelihood that any change in the geometry of the distal objects ends up represented at least in some of the dimensions of the measurement space. Indeed, in primate vision, the dimensionality of the space presented by the eye to the brain is roughly one million—the same as the number of fibers in each optic nerve.[15] The reduction of the dimensionality of this space to manageable proportions will be a major concern in chapter 4.

The requirement that the mapping $F$ be *smooth* means that small changes in the shape of the distal object should be mapped into small displacements of the corresponding point in the internal representation space. Mumford (1994, 143) noted that distances in the measurement space induce a "natural geometry" over shapes. One of the manifestations of this geometrical structure is that smoothly changing the shape of the imaged object causes the corresponding point to ascribe a manifold (intuitively, a smooth "surface") in the measurement space. The dimensionality of this manifold depends on the number of degrees of freedom of the shape changes. For example, simple morphing of one shape into another produces a one-dimensional manifold (a curve). Likewise, rotating the object in depth (a transformation with two degrees of freedom) gives rise to a two-dimensional manifold which may be called the *view space* of the object. Thus, despite being mostly empty (a randomly chosen combination of pixel values in an image is extremely unlikely to form a picture of a coherent object), the high-dimensional measurement space does contain a structured low-dimensional subspace that represents images of coherent objects. The structure of this proximal shape space depends on all the factors that participate in image formation, both intrinsic (the shapes of objects) and extrinsic (e.g., their pose).

The influence of the extrinsic factors that affect object appearance must be counteracted by the perceptual system through the action of the mapping $F$, to reduce the likelihood of two nearby points in the distal shape space $\Sigma_{bc}$ (i.e., two similar shapes) being mapped into widely disparate points in the representation space $\mathcal{R}$. Because some tasks may require information about extrinsic factors such as pose or illumination of the object, it would be prudent to retain this information and keep it separate from that of intrinsic shape, rather than collapse the dimensions corresponding to the extrinsic factors entirely. This idea is illustrated in figure 3.9, which depicts schematically a close-up of the measurement

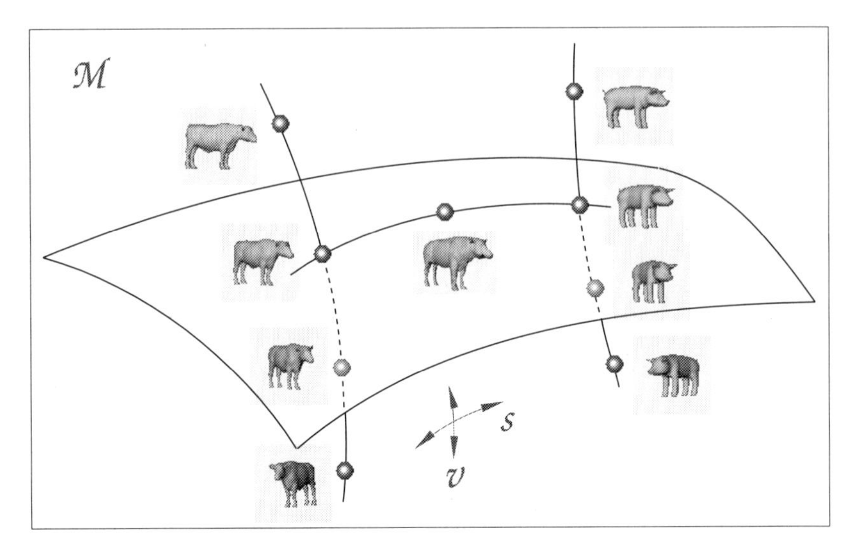


**Figure 3.9**
View spaces of two objects, and their common shape space, embedded in the measurement space $\mathcal{M}$. See text for explanations.

space $\mathcal{M}$ in the vicinity of the representations of two similar objects, cow and pig. The viewpoint information here is kept separate from the shape information in that the view spaces of the two objects are orthogonal to the trajectory through $\mathcal{M}$ that corresponds to the morphing of one into the other.

For a set of similar objects, the view spaces and the morphing trajectories arranged as shown in figure 3.9 constitute a low-dimensional local structure—the proximal shape space $\mathcal{R}$—embedded in the multidimensional measurement space $\mathcal{M}$. Provided that the distal to proximal mapping $F$ is indeed regular and smooth, this local structure will faithfully reflect the local low-dimensional structure of the distal shape space. This means that the representation is veridical for a particular observer, because distal structure is observer- and task-specific. Thus, the space $\mathcal{R}_{O_1}$ for an observer $O_1$ is $\mathcal{S}$-isomorphic to some task-specific subspace of $\Sigma_{bc}$.

One may note at this point that the conditions for the internal shape spaces of two observers, $\mathcal{R}_{O_1}$ and $\mathcal{R}_{O_2}$, to be $\mathcal{S}$-isomorphic to each other are related to the basic conditions for veridicality discussed above. In this case, the properties required of the mapping $F$ apply to the composition of the inverse of $F$ for one of the observers, with the direct mapping $F$ for the other: $F' = F_{O_1} \circ (F_{O_2})^{-1}$. In particular, two systems for which $F'$ omits some of the relevant dimensions will be separated by an unbridgeable perceptual gap (in color vision, this is exemplified by the fundamental incompatibility between the color spaces perceived by an achromat and a person with normal color vision). A less drastic discrepancy between representation spaces in different systems arises when the transformation relating two representations is invertible but highly distorting.[16] In that case, two systems may have widely different, albeit not unbridgeable, grasps on the world. Two stimuli which normally appear similar to one of the systems would seem dissimilar to the other. An example of this kind of incompatibility between object similarities as perceived by different subjects is the "other race" effect in face recognition (Brigham, 1986): people are better at distinguishing between faces of their own race, which they perceive to be less similar to each other, compared to the perception of the same faces by observers of another race.

In summary, this chapter brought together various conceptual tools needed for developing a formal theory of representation. The first of these was similarity, a concept which, as we saw, can be made precise by confining its scope to object geometry and by defining it via proximity in a shape space: a mathematical structure in which shapes correspond to points and (dis)similarities to interpoint distances. Within this framework, representations will be veridical—$\mathcal{S}$-isomorphic to their objects—exactly when the distal shape-space similarities (along with other second-order relationships between objects) are preserved by the distal to proximal "perceptual" mapping. To that end, the perceptual mapping, which I called $F$, must satisfy the following requirements:

1. *Regularity.* $F$ should be non-singular over the set of shapes that need to be represented. Specifically, it should collapse none of the behaviorally important dimensions of shape variation (i.e., dimensions of $\Sigma_{bc}$).
2. *Smoothness.* $F$ should map small changes in $\Sigma_{bc}$ into small changes in $\mathcal{R}$; this property may be local.

3. *Separation of shape from viewing conditions.* The representation space $\mathcal{R}$ obtained under $F$ should be decomposable (locally, for each class of intrinsically similar shapes), into $\mathcal{R}_v$ and $\mathcal{R}_s$, or the view space and shape space components. Note that invariance (i.e., collapsing of $\mathcal{R}_v$) is not desirable.

4. *Low dimensionality.* The representation space for each class of intrinsically similar shapes should be low-dimensional.

A computational mechanism that satisfies these requirements is described in the next chapter.

## Notes

1. This theorem was called by Watanabe the Theorem of the Ugly Duckling, because it shows that similarity in appearance, as indeed any other unconstrained similarity, is misleading.

2. Other options can also be considered here; consider the definition of geometries in terms of transformations and invariances stated in F. Klein's Erlangen program. An alternative framework, suitable for deformable shapes, is outlined in appendix C.

3. It can be shown that this space is also not flat, and contains singularities (one of which is the triangle whose three vertices coincide). Most importantly, the local Riemannian metric that takes these properties of the shape space into account leads to a global metric which is identical to the Procrustes distance (Carne, 1990; Le and Kendall, 1993).

4. The relevant constraints here are similar to those that apply in the computation of correspondence in stereopsis (Marr and Poggio, 1979), e.g., continuity (which requires that nearby points in one object map to nearby points in the other object).

5. The imprecision of this approximation is revealed by phenomena such as the precession of the plane of oscillation of Foucault's pendulum.

6. If no such limit is placed on $k$, we may end up trying to represent shape at a level of detail corresponding to subatomic distances.

7. For real objects, texture and color provide additional cues that make correspondence easier.

8. Turning to the Web in search of an example of this usage, I found an online article (Smith et al., 1995) containing the following passage: "The visual search phenomenon known as 'pop-out' (where a single unique element, say the only red one, is immediately detected by an observer) is thought to be influenced by top-down factors by some theorists who argue that performance is facilitated by knowing in advance on which stimulus dimension (e.g., color or

shape) the unique element will differ from its surroundings." Note that the word "dimension" appears in singular, as if both color and shape are one-dimensional quantities.

9. This expression is the convex linear combination of **x** and **y**. It should be noted that moving along the straight line in the $kn$-dimensional Euclidean space does not necessarily correspond to moving along a geodesic (the shortest path) in $\Sigma_n^k$; see (Le, 1991).

10. Principal Component Analysis (PCA or the Karhunen-Loève Transform) is a method for reducing the dimensionality of a data set by projecting each vector onto several "principal directions" and retaining these projections as the new representation of the data. The principal directions correspond to the eigenvectors of the variance-covariance matrix of the data. The relative importance of the projections is determined by sorting the eigenvectors in the descending order of their associated eigenvalues. For each target dimensionality $n$, retaining the leading $n$ principal components results in an approximation of the data which is optimal in the least-squares sense. (See Joliffe, 1986.)

11. It is difficult to impose this requirement over all possible objects, unless the dimensions along which objects can vary are known in advance. Thus, any perceptual system is prone to the error of omission caused by the necessarily finite set of measurements that span its internal representational space.

12. The above hierarchy is clearly not the only possible way to define the fidelity of the representation mapping. If the representation is to be used mainly for classification, one may require that points that are separable under some parametric decision surface in the original space remain so following the mapping (this is in contrast with the distance-based requirements, which are nonparametric). For example, if points in the original shape space tend to form linearly separable clusters, one may require that the clusters remain linearly separable under the mapping. Moreover, one may also require that clusters that are not originally linearly separable become so under the mapping (Cortes and Vapnik, 1995). These considerations are beyond the main concern of the present section, which is to specify a *minimal* computational basis for the processes that operate on the representation space. Still, if the original-space configuration of stimuli allows an efficient remapping, making explicit an underlying structure of linearly separable clusters, this possibility must remain open following the mapping into the representation space. Obviously, whereas the lowest-fidelity (distinction-preserving) representation does not necessarily preserve such properties, the highest-fidelity (similarity-preserving) representation does.

13. One should keep in mind that scaling and other transformations mentioned in the present context pertain to configurations formed by objects in the shape space, and not to the objects themselves.

14. A regular mapping is quasiconformal if there exists a constant $q$, $1 \leq q < \infty$, such that almost any infinitesimally small sphere is transformed into an ellipsoid

for which the ratio of the largest semiaxis to the smallest one does not exceed $q$ (Reshetnyak, 1989).

15. This observation has been made repeatedly in the past (Peirce, 1868; Poincaré, 1963), yet has escaped the attention of most vision scientists, who continue to see vision as the reconstruction of the 3D world from the 2D (!) sensorium.

16. Note that whereas two conformal maps acting back to back yield a conformal map, a composition of two $q$-quasiconformal maps will, in general, result in a map with $q' > q$.

# 4

# $\mathcal{S}$-isomorphism: An Implementation

It seems evident that, if all the scenes of nature were continually shifted in such a manner that no two events bore any resemblance to each other, but every object was entirely new, without any similitude to whatever had been seen before, we should never, in that case, have attained the least idea of necessity, or of a connexion among these objects.

—David Hume
*An Enquiry Concerning Human Understanding*—1748

To design a system for $\mathcal{S}$-isomorphism, one needs (1) to decide upon the set of features that would comprise the initial measurement space $\mathcal{M}$, and (2) to choose an algorithm that would map $\mathcal{M}$ into the ultimate internal representation space $\mathcal{R}$, in which second-order relationships such as similarities would mirror the relationships that hold among distal shapes. The main computational constraints on the composite mapping that links the distal shape space to the internal one are regularity, smoothness, and low dimensionality of the target space $\mathcal{R}$. These constraints delineate a broad class of mappings. To narrow down the range of possibilities, one must consider pragmatic issues, such as the tasks for which representations are required and the architecture of the system that is to harbor them, as well as meta-theoretical issues such as the nature of the problem of generalization in recognition.

Hume's observation concerning the importance of "similitude to whatever had been seen before" in making sense of objects provides, to my mind, a crucial insight into the latter issue. Consider, for example, a situation in which an observer is confronted with a sequence of views of an object. If these views arrive in their natural order and in close succession (as it happens when the object rotates in front of the observer), it is easy to form a useful representation of the object. As we shall see in section 4.1.1, such a representation can be made into more than the "sum" (i.e., mere association) of the individual views, because Hume's "connexion" through resemblance supports *interpolation* of successive views of an object (Edelman and Weinshall, 1991; Seibert and Waxman, 1992; Stone, 1996b; Wallis and Rolls, 1997). This, in turn, allows the system to generalize recognition to novel views of the same object (Poggio and Edelman, 1990).

A more challenging situation is the one that requires the observer to act on a single view of a potentially novel shape (in chapter 2, I called this the "analogy" problem). In principle, a visual system capable of recovering 3D shape information from cues available in a single view of an object (texture, shading, occlusion) or from two closely related views (as in binocular stereopsis) should be able to carry out such tasks. For example, it should be possible to predict what the object would look like from another viewpoint (if it lies within the same general aspect[1] as the reference view), on the basis of the 3D shape information. In practice, however, even the human visual system, which is quite good in perceiving 3D shape from the combined stereo, shading, and texture cues (Bülthoff and Mallot, 1990), does not seem to be able to use shape information to extrapolate the appearance of the object to novel views (Rock et al., 1989). Moreover, the strategy of 3D reconstruction followed by reprojection from a novel viewpoint is completely useless for estimating the appearance of the initially occluded sides of regular, non-transparent objects. These considerations reinforce Hume's basic claim: *to predict what an observed object would look like from another viewpoint, one must rely on the resemblance between its image and views of familiar shapes.*[2]

Things acquire a surprising twist if Hume's dictum is interpreted constructively, as a blueprint for a representational strategy, rather than as a statement of an inherent limitation of vision. Here is how it can be made to work: suppose that $\{\mathbf{p}_i\}$ are some reference shapes familiar to the system; then any object $\mathbf{x}$, familiar or novel, can be represented by its similarities to these shapes, $\{s(\mathbf{x}, \mathbf{p}_i)\}$. This choice of representational strategy has several interesting implications. First, because reliance on similarities to familiar shapes is the very basis of this scheme, it complies naturally with Hume's meta-theoretical constraint (namely, better performance for more familiar objects). Second, because a system can only estimate proximal, not distal, similarities, the importance of the basic design goal of $\mathcal{S}$-isomorphism—to preserve similarities between objects—is reiterated. Third, because the number of the reference shapes can be much smaller than the dimensionality of the measurement space $\mathcal{M}$, representation by similarities to these shapes offers a significant dimensionality reduction. Fourth, because various recognition problems are equivalent to pinpointing the representation of the stimulus within $\mathcal{M}$, and because the location of a point can be defined by specifying its distance to several reference points, or *landmarks*, the strategy of estimating similarities to reference shapes leads to a uniform treatment of various recognition tasks.

The tricky part, of course, is to measure the right distances in the measurement space $\mathcal{M}$. In the context of a shape space, distance means dissimilarity in shape (i.e., the amount of deformation). Consequently, its estimation must exclude components of measurement-space distance that are orthogonal to the shape space embedded in it, as well as components due to shape transformation such as rotation. A convenient computational mechanism for distance estimation that satisfies these requirements is a module tuned to a particular shape, that is, designed to respond selectively to that shape, irrespective of its transformation. A few such modules, tuned to different reference shapes, effectively reduce the dimensionality of the representation from that of the measurement space to a small number equal to the number of modules.

The resulting approach to representation is powerful and flexible in two respects. First, the choice of shapes that are to serve as landmarks is by default contingent on the system's experience, and can be tailored to its needs and resources. The main constraint on the choice of landmark shapes is operational, and can be phrased in terms of *coverage* of the shape space (the portion of the measurement space in which images generated by coherent objects, as opposed to noise-like pixel patterns, reside).[3] Second, the system's action following the estimation of proximities between the stimulus (an image of an unknown object) and the landmark is largely determined by the task at hand. In a simple situation where the system is required to decide whether or not the stimulus is exactly like one of the stored objects (as in object identification), an equally simple memory-based strategy will suffice. In comparison, if the task calls for the categorization of the stimulus (which need not be identical to any of the stored objects), the computation of similarities to a number of stored representations becomes necessary.

## 4.1 Task-Dependent Treatment of the Measurement Space

The results of chapter 3 indicate that faithful representation is theoretically possible, provided that a low-dimensional subspace isomorphic (in Shepard's sense) to a distal shape space is contained in the high-dimensional space of measurements performed by the system. The practical import of this realization depends on finding a way to identify the relevant low-dimensional structure within the measurement space (see figure 4.1 and appendix A). The possibilities here depend, in turn, on the perceptual task at hand. The rest of this section parallels the discussion of the various tasks in chapter 2, offering for each task a computational mechanism capable of forming the representation it requires.

### 4.1.1 Identification ("Is this an image of object X?")

At the most specific level, the task is to determine whether or not the image belongs to a particular well-defined object. The answer to this question cannot be determined by matching the image to a template (e.g., a snapshot) of the object because of the variability in the appearance of objects, precipitated by possible changes in the viewing conditions (Ullman, 1996). Due to the influence of viewing conditions, the measurement-space structure formed by different images of the same object is an extended entity, and not a single point (figure 4.1). Nevertheless, this structure admits a compact computational description, which can be taken advantage of when attempting to recognize the object.

Figure 4.1 shows schematically the space $\mathcal{V}$ of all possible views of an object, $\text{Cyl}_0$, under the assumption that the object is only allowed a single degree of transformational freedom (here, rotation around the line of sight). To be identified as belonging to $\text{Cyl}_0$, an image—a point in the measurement space—must be shown to lie within the *one-dimensional*

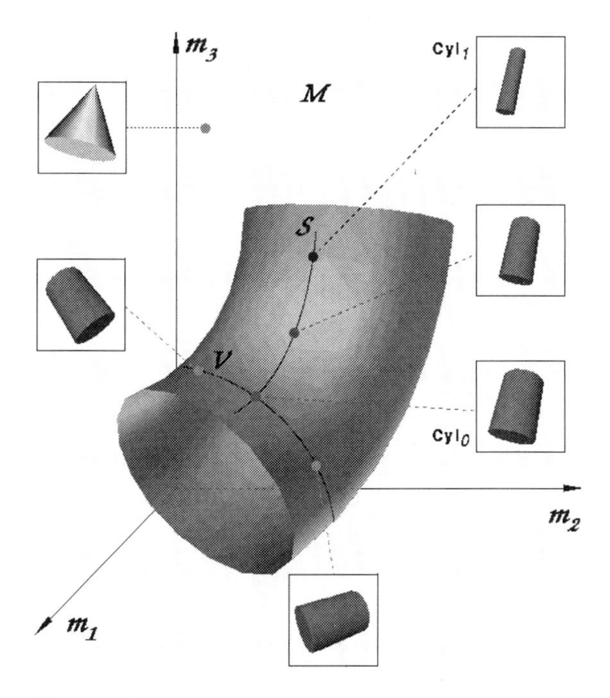


Figure 4.1
The measurement space, $\mathcal{M}$, and the (proximal) shape space $\mathcal{R}$ embedded in it. The scene here is assumed to consist of a single rigid object (a cylinder) that may either rotate around a fixed axis, or deform, by turning smoothly and gradually into another, distinct object (a thinner cylinder). The measurement space is depicted as three-dimensional, to facilitate visualization; normally, its dimensionality would run in the tens of thousands. In comparison, the spaces $\mathcal{V}$ and $\mathcal{S}$ that comprise $\mathcal{R}$ are indeed low-dimensional (see chapter 3). No matter how many dimensions the measurement space possesses, the only possible images generated by this scene are those contained in a certain two-dimensional manifold embedded in that space. Of the two dimensions of this manifold, one corresponds to the rotational degree of freedom of the object, and the other to the choice of its shape (i.e., its location within the shape space). The view space of $\mathrm{Cyl}_0$ is one-dimensional (because of the single degree of transformational freedom assumed in this example) and closed (because rotating an object around a fixed axis eventually returns it to the original orientation).

*manifold* $\mathcal{V}$ that is the view space of that object (a proof that $\mathcal{V}$ is indeed a low-dimensional manifold can be found in Jacobs, 1996). The problem of identification is thus reduced to the determination of the proximity of a point to a smooth "surface." As pointed out by Poggio and his co-workers (Poggio, 1990; Poggio and Edelman, 1990; Poggio and Girosi, 1990), a theoretical framework suitable for approaching this problem can be found in the literature on function interpolation and approximation.[4]

**Object Identification as a Problem in Function Interpolation**

We may formalize the solution of the identification problem as the construction of a *characteristic function* that maps images of the target object to some constant value (say, one), and all other images to another value (say, zero). Redundant as this statement may seem, it is important to realize that identification only makes sense if the object is familiar. At least some of the views of such an object must therefore be known to the system; any long-term representation it may have formed of the object must incorporate the information inherent in these views. Using the terminology of figure 4.1, this means that at least some of the points assured to belong to the view space $\mathcal{V}$ of the target object $\text{Cyl}_0$ are known to the system. Thus, the problem of object identification becomes equivalent to the *interpolation* of a characteristic function of the object from a number of examples or measurement-space points known to belong to the object.

Because it is possible to draw an infinite number of different functions that all pass through the specified data points, this interpolation problem is formally ill-posed.[5] In this respect, object identification is like many other problems in vision, whose straightforward solution is not unique, or is deficient—does not depend continuously on the data (Poggio et al., 1985). A possible remedy in these cases consists of bringing additional knowledge to bear on the problem when attempting to narrow down the range of possible solutions in the search for uniqueness.[6] In the present case there is a crucial piece of prior knowledge that we have not used so far: the smoothness of the manifold, spanned in a properly constructed measurement space by the different views of the same shape that undergoes a smooth transformation. In interpolation, if the target function is assumed to be smooth (e.g., if certain bounds on its derivatives are known to hold), the space of possible solutions is narrowed down, frequently to a unique solution. This approach to ill-posed problems is an instance of a technique known as regularization[7] (Tikhonov and Arsenin, 1977; Poggio et al., 1985; Bertero et al., 1988).

### Interpolation with Basis Functions

The connection between problems in vision and regularization proved especially fruitful due to the considerable variety of regularization procedures developed in the past several decades. Recently, it has been realized that one such procedure, when applied to the problem of interpolation, leads to a solution that is particularly easy both to visualize and to implement in a distributed network whose structure can be learned from examples (Poggio and Girosi, 1990; Girosi et al., 1995). This solution is *basis function* interpolation (Broomhead and Lowe, 1988). According to this method, the interpolating function is a linear superposition of basis functions. In its simplest version, one of these is placed at each data point in the input space for which the output value is known. Alternatively, a few basis functions are strategically placed to optimize the coverage of the relevant space.

The shape of the basis function reflects the prior knowledge concerning the change in the output as one moves away from the data point. In the absence of evidence to the contrary, all directions of movement are considered equivalent, making it reasonable to assume that the basis function is radial (that is, it depends only on the distance between the actual input and the original data point, which serves as its center). The resulting scheme is known as radial basis function (RBF) interpolation. Once the basis functions have been placed, the output of the interpolation module for any test point is computed by taking a weighted sum of the values of all the basis functions at that point (figure 4.2; details concerning the computations involved in basis function interpolation can be found in appendix D.1).

### RBF Interpolation Applied to Object Identification

Radial basis function interpolation has been applied to the object identification problem by Poggio and Edelman (1990), who showed that an

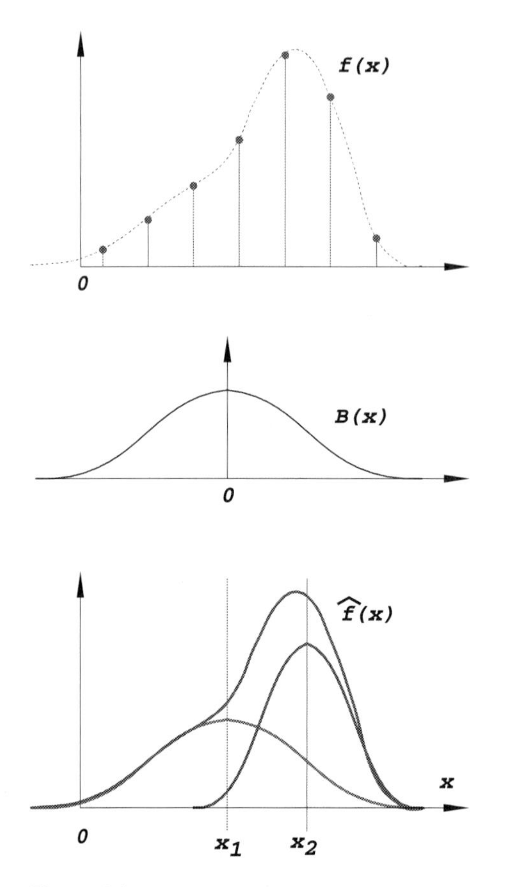


**Figure 4.2**
Interpolation by a linear combination of basis functions. *(Top)* The data points through which the target function must pass. *(Middle)* The basis function. *(Bottom)* The interpolated function, $\hat{f}(x)$, constructed by summing two weighted replicas of $B(x)$, one centered at $x_1$, and another at $x_2$: $\hat{f}(x) = B(x - x_1) + 2B(x - x_2)$.

RBF network can learn to produce a standard view of a wire-frame object when presented with an arbitrary view of the same object. The RBF model was subsequently used to replicate a number of central characteristics of the process of object identification in human vision (more on this in chapter 6).

When RBF interpolation is applied to the identification of different views of an object, one basis function is used for each familiar view (figure 4.3). The appropriate weight for each basis function is then computed by an algorithm that involves matrix inversion (a closed-form solution exists for this case; see appendix D.1). This completes the process of training the RBF network. To determine whether a test view belongs to the object on which the network has been trained, this view (that is, its measurement-space representation) is compared to each of the training views. This step yields a set of distances between the test view and the training views that serve as the *centers* of the basis functions. Because the functions are "radial," the value of each of them depends only on the distance between its center and the test point. In the next step, the values of the basis functions are combined linearly to determine the output of the network.

The output of the RBF network can be made to take a variety of forms, depending on the task assigned to it. In the case of identification, the network is trained to output a single value (a scalar), which signifies the degree of membership of the test view in the space spanned by the training views (figure 4.4). Alternatively, the output can be a vector. For instance, the network can be trained to produce a standard view of the trained object, when given any of its views, or it can be made to output the attitude of the object with respect to the imaging system. The only limitations of the RBF interpolation approach in this respect are the feasibility of interpolation as a solution to the problem at hand, and the availability of a sufficient amount of data to train the network, two issues to which I shall return later.

Just as the RBF network can be trained to produce a variety of outputs (provided that the input-output mapping it must realize is smooth, and that there are enough data points to constrain the solution), it can be made to accept a variety of input formats. This means that there is considerable freedom in the choice of the measurements that are to be

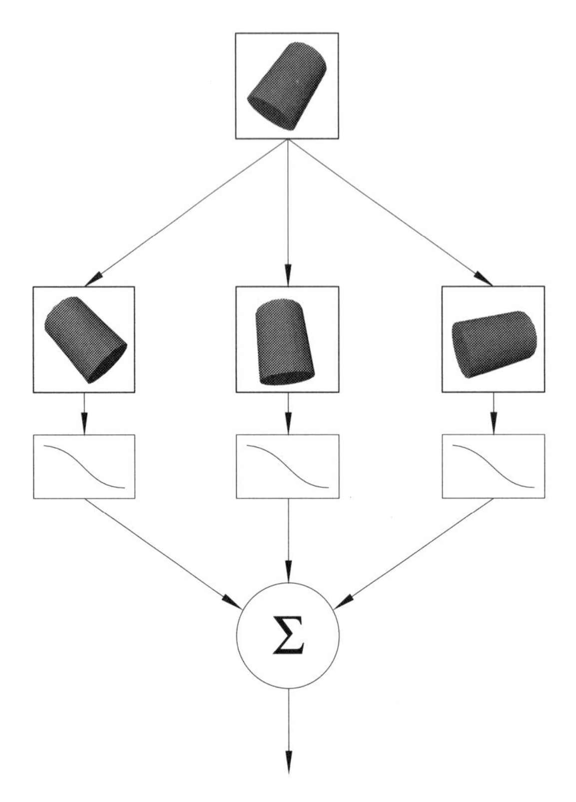


**Figure 4.3**
A schematic depiction of an RBF network trained to recognize images of a cylinder that may rotate around the line of sight. Units tuned to different views of this object serve as the basis functions, whose values are combined linearly to interpolate its view space.

performed on a visual object prior to the attempt to identify it. Consequently, the choice of the underlying measurement space can be guided by considerations specific to the particular problem with which the network is supposed to deal. If, for instance, the objects to be identified are wire-frame shapes produced by connecting a number of sticks in a series, "automatic" invariance of identification with respect to rotation around the line of sight can be achieved when the network is fed the angles between adjacent sticks, instead of, say, the coordinates of the joints at which the sticks connect to each other (Poggio and Edelman, 1990).

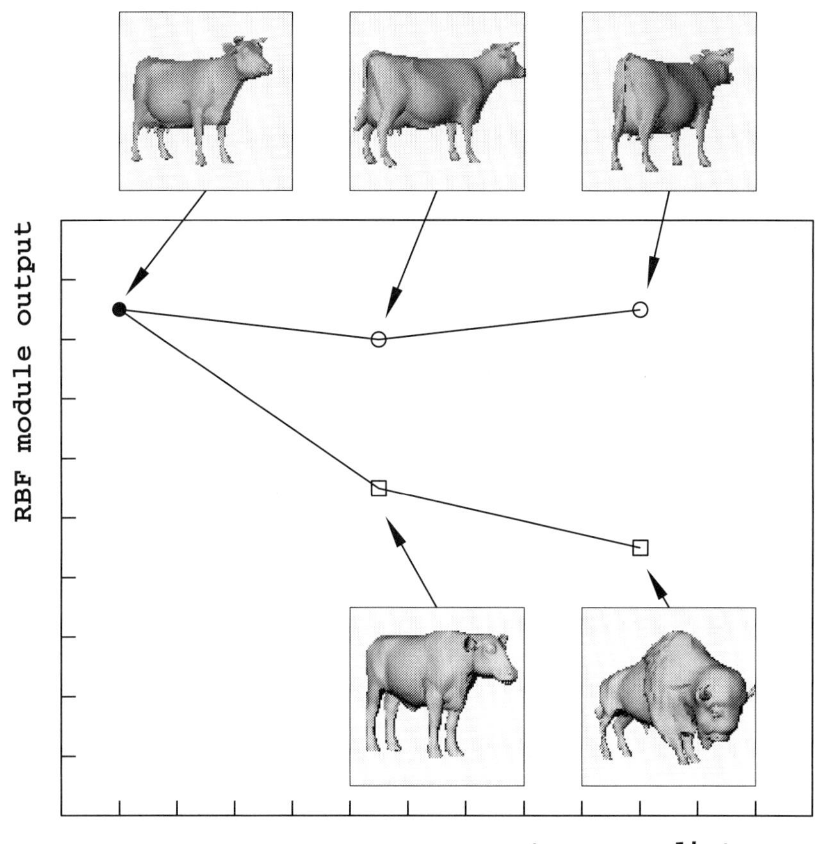


**Figure 4.4**
Effects of view and shape change on the response of an RBF module. The plot illustrates schematically a typical response pattern of a radial basis function network, trained on views of an object (here, a cow), to stimuli differing from a reference view of that object (marked by the filled circle), in two ways: (1) by progressive view change, marked by circles; (2) by progressive shape change, marked by squares (cf. Edelman and Duvdevani-Bar, 1997, figure 6). The abscissa corresponds to the measurement-space distance between the test and the reference stimuli. The insensitivity of the module's output to view-space changes relative to shape-space changes is a property of RBF networks that can be derived analytically under certain conditions (appendix D.2).

### The Sufficiency of Memory for Identification

In a series of discussions on the capabilities of RBF networks in the context of modeling brain function, Poggio and his colleagues (Poggio, 1990; Poggio and Hurlbert, 1994) noted that in their operation, RBFs effectively trade off computation for memory. Indeed, when the basis functions used in the interpolation process are infinitely narrow,[8] the RBF network becomes a lookup table: it returns the value associated with one of the training points when given that point as input, or zero if given any input that does not belong to the training set. In this case, the function of the RBF network is pure memory lookup. As the "width" of the basis functions is increased, the network becomes capable of interpolation. As a result, it can be made to cover an extended region of the input space while relying on a finite number of memorized examples.[9]

A satisfying conclusion one may draw from the foregoing discussion is that for object identification—the most specific level of object processing—a visual system needs merely the capability to store object views and interpolate among them. An immediate corollary is the computational feasibility of *generalization* to novel views: a system with those capabilities can identify novel images of a known object by interpolating the view space in which they reside between points corresponding to familiar views.

### 4.1.2 Recognition ("Is this an image of something I know?")

A straightforward extension of this memory-based strategy is likely to be effective also at the other extreme of the spectrum of possible tasks involving visual shapes. Here, at the most general task level, one may wish to find out whether the stimulus is at all close to the union of shape spaces of known objects, or, simply put, whether or not the stimulus "looks like something."[10]

Just as the identification of an object presupposes a prior exposure to it, an object can be recognized as familiar (*re*-cognized), by definition, only if it belongs to the set of previously encountered objects (the consequences of relaxing this rather strict definition will be considered at length in the following section, which deals with categorization). This truism suggests that a quantitative measure of familiarity of a stimulus may be formed by taking the strongest response among those of the object-specific modules available to the system. Other operations—pooling the similarities of the stimulus to all explicitly represented objects (Nosofsky, 1988; Nosofsky, 1991b), or computing the variance of these similarity values—are also possible.

In terms of the example illustrated in figure 4.1, the responses of the individual modules convey information concerning the proximity of the stimulus to the view spaces of their respective objects. Thus, the strongest response is merely a measure of the proximity of the stimulus to the view space of the object that happens to be the closest, while the summed responses measure the proximity to all the known view spaces taken together. In many cases, these proximity values carry much less information than demanded by the task. For instance, if only a few objects are known to the system well enough to have justified the allocation of a dedicated RBF module, most stimuli will fall in between the explicitly encoded view spaces. Such stimuli will be correctly deemed unfamiliar. Unfortunately, that will be all the system can find out about these stimuli, unless care is taken to ensure that novel objects receive a special treatment, as suggested below.

### 4.1.3 Categorization ("What is this thing?")

Categorization is what one does when faced with the most basic of all possible questions about an object: what is it? Although the nomenclature introduced in chapter 2 distinguished among several categorization-related problems, they all share a common trait: the potential novelty of the stimulus. Unlike identification or recognition, categorization is more than remembrance of things past, making one wonder whether the memory-based approach to which I adhered so far in this chapter would not have to be abandoned. Entities, however, should not be multiplied without necessity, so let us not give up just yet.

#### The Problem of Radically Novel Objects

A fully trained system relying on memory alone would have to form tens of thousands of object-specific modules if it were to approximate the human ability to categorize objects (Biederman, 1987). It is easy to see, however, that the real challenge for such a system is not the high demand for memory as much as the inability to deal with *radically* novel objects (by "radically" novel I mean an object that is substantially similar to several familiar ones; novel objects of the less interesting kind are those which are not similar to any familiar object).

Indeed, let us assume for the moment that there is no limitation on the amount of memory dedicated to the representation. Assume also that the system has taken advantage of the unlimited memory supply, and has somehow come into possession of a record (i.e., a special RBF module) for each member of a very extensive library of objects. Each of these familiar objects can then be recognized by the kind of template matching we discussed before (with the RBF mechanism supporting the recognition of potentially unfamiliar views). Furthermore, moderately deviant versions of the familiar objects can be recognized as well, using the nearest neighbor strategy (Duda and Hart, 1973), according to which the stimulus is assigned the label of its closest neighbor in the underlying feature space (in our case, the measurement space). However, such a system would still fail on the first radically novel object it encounters.

It is important to realize that this failure stems from a conceptual and not a technical flaw of the approach. This flaw has to do with the inherent unsuitability of rote memory, even when augmented by the nearest-neighbor option, to deal with (that is, to make sense of) radically novel objects. To see that, let us consider the following example: a traveler from the Levant, having crossed the Sahara for the first time, sees a living thing that stands as high as the treetops, has small horns, is yellow with brown spots, and eats leaves. A recollection of the Mediterranean fauna will not avail here, no matter how good the traveler's memory: the thing is sufficiently unlike any of the familiar beasts to make recognition (*re-*cognition) amount to self-deception. For that same reason, a conscious invocation of the nearest-neighbor principle will not do: deciding that this thing is really just a strange-looking camel is not any better justified than deciding that it is merely a malformed leopard.

## The Sense of "Sense"

Our thought experiment, intended to find out whether a visual system equipped with unlimited memory and full knowledge of thousands of objects can make sense of one additional object, has resulted in a strange impasse. The imaginary traveler has at his disposal all the relevant visual information about a giraffe, but is totally unable to make heads or tails of it. The absurdity of this situation suggests that memory alone cannot impart to a visual system the ability to make sense of visual objects, if "making sense" is taken to mean template matching of the winner-take-all variety.

To me, this suggests not a failure of the memory-based approach to recognition, but rather a need for a better notion of "making sense" of visual objects. On the one hand, identifying the object in front of one's eyes (or, rather, its measurement-space representation) with the memory item that resembles it the most does not count as understanding (and neither does having the proper label to go with the picture; see figure 4.5). On the other hand, the sum total of the memories of visual objects stored in the system, coupled with some, as yet unidentified computational mechanism, must result in the ability to understand novel objects.

The upshot of the above two observations is that the computational mechanism we are after should endow the memory system with the ability to make explicit the relationships among stored objects, and not merely to store each object along with some unique label. One step in the right direction would be to organize the memory hierarchically, so that a given item would be assigned a number of labels, chosen from different levels of categorization. Because diverse objects (e.g., cats and dogs) would be labeled by common inclusive labels (e.g., quadrupeds) in addition to their names, a variety of similarity relationships would thus be automatically made explicit. Note that this trick would only work for novel objects if the procedure enabling the system to determine category membership is universally applicable. The only two distinct procedures of the required kind that I am aware of are discussed next.

### The Structural/Analytic Approach

In contemporary theories of vision, the traditional attempt to impart open-endedness to a categorization scheme—that is, to let it deal with novel objects—has been to postulate the use of generic parts which can be joined together in various combinations by specifying their spatial relationships (Binford, 1971; Marr and Nishihara, 1978; Marr, 1982; Biederman, 1985; Biederman, 1987). On the structural account (cf. section 2.3.2), making sense of the image of a newly encountered giraffe would proceed as follows. First, the unknown object would be decomposed into parts, using some method guaranteed to work in a bottom-up

Figure 4.5
A picture is worth a thousand words . . . or is it? In this variation on figure 1.1, a perplexed observer tries to make sense of an object seen for the first time. Note that the problem is in the *kind* of representation used, and that having the object accompanied by its proper category label does not help: a mere label carries with it no "added value" in terms of information content. For a way out of this predicament, see section 4.1.3.

fashion, that is, without prior knowledge of the structure of the object (see Hoffman and Richards, 1984). In the safari example, the parts would be some generalized cylinders corresponding to the giraffe's limbs, body, neck, head, etc. Second, the relative disposition of the parts would be determined. According to the structural theories, making explicit (in Marr's sense) the description of the parts and of their spatial relationships is all there is to making sense of the object.

It is interesting to note, however, that even the staunchest proponents of the structural theory of visual representation do not stop at that, as illustrated by the analysis of a novel "do it yourself" object described in (Biederman, 1987). Having stated that this object (figure 4.6) is best represented as a composition of boxes, cylinders, etc., Biederman goes one crucial step further, by pointing out its similarity to a "New York City street corner hot dog cart." This culmination of the representational process in an estimate of similarity suggests that similarities to other, familiar objects, over and above the structure of the novel object, must be made explicit to understand an object well.

One may suspect that the estimation of similarity of a shape to objects embedded in a scene would suffer from the same computational problems as the recovery of a structural description of the scene (in fact, in figure 2.5, I used a snapshot of a real hot-dog cart to illustrate some of these problems). This apprehension is, however, unfounded. Whereas the *interpretation* of a scene (i.e., describing the real hot-dog cart structurally) is problematic, the *verification* of a presence of a certain object there (i.e., finding the do-it-yourself shape in the picture) is computationally straightforward; viz. the alignment algorithms (Ullman, 1989). Thus, the estimation of similarity of an object to some member of a scene is computationally feasible, even if structural decomposition of the scene is not.

### Towards Memory-Based Categorization

If the structural decomposition of the object is not an end in itself, but rather a means towards computing its similarities to some familiar objects, it becomes tempting to find out whether representation can be based directly on the computation of such similarities. The foremost advantage of such an approach to representation would be the possibility of basing categorization on memory. In other words, the same mechanism capable of identifying familiar objects would help make sense of novel ones.

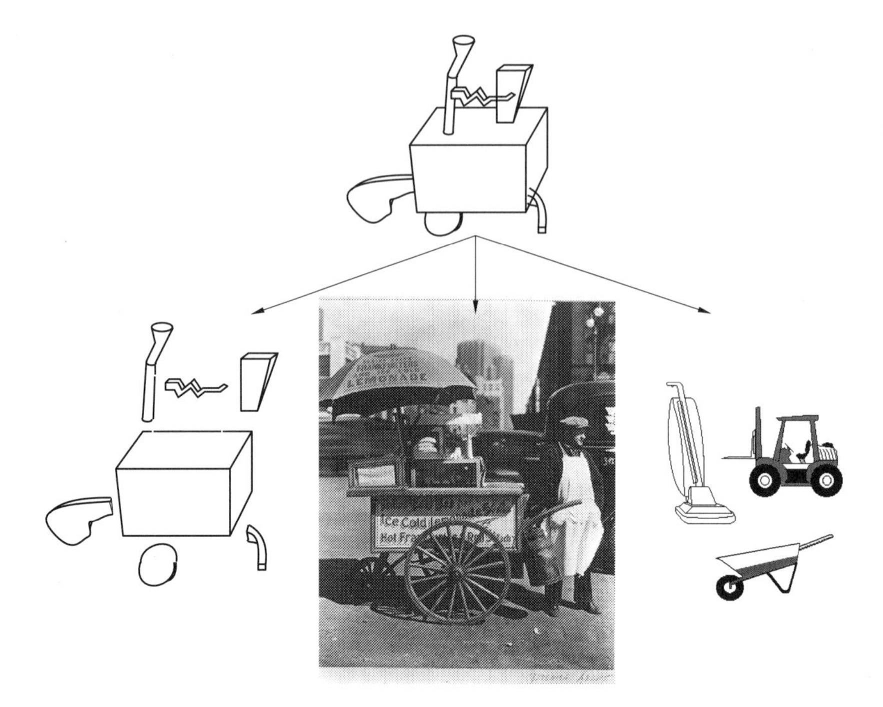


**Figure 4.6**
*(Top)* A novel object, after Biederman (1987, figure 1). *(Bottom)* According to Biederman, the way to make sense of this object is to decompose it into primitive parts and to determine their spatial relationships, as illustrated on the left. It may be, however, that we can make sense of this shape simply because it resembles a fragment from a familiar scene, as illustrated in the middle pane. Moreover, even if we never saw a hot dog cart before, this shape can be understood (and, if necessary, committed to memory) in terms of its similarities to some common familiar objects, such as those shown on the right.

To make this approach work, it is crucial that similarities to *several* familiar objects be involved in the representation of a novel one. A nearest-neighbor strategy does not work for radically novel objects, as we saw in the example of the traveler and the giraffe. In comparison, representation by similarities to *multiple* "reference objects" is quite feasible: describing a giraffe to a friend who never saw one as a camelopard is, indeed, useful—provided that the friend is familiar with camels and leopards (figure 4.7).

We are now ready to translate the newly acquired intuitions concerning the nature of categorization and the role of memory in object representa-

**Figure 4.7**
Giraffe as a camelopard. *(Left)* On the structural account, the giraffe is represented as a labeled graph, listing its parts and their spatial relationships, and the texture of the entire thing. The similarity of a giraffe to a camel and a leopard (whose computation is a prerequisite for "making sense" of the giraffe as a visual object; see figure 4.5) is then assessed by comparing the appropriate graphs and texture data. *(Right)* Here, in comparison, similarities between the giraffe and a camel and a leopard *are* its representation. This approach bypasses the complicated computation of a structural description, by basing representation on similarities, as explained in section 4.1.3. Note that the old name for the giraffe, derived from the Roman *camelopardalis* (spotted camel), is a much more useful label than either camel or leopard alone, for reasons discussed in section 4.2.

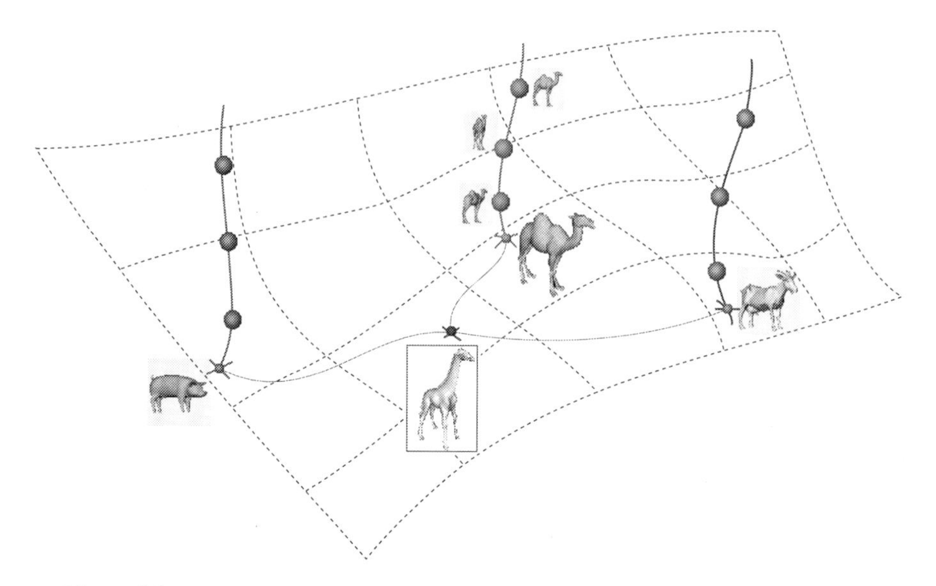

**Figure 4.8**
Describing a new shape (giraffe) in terms of its proximities to three shape-space landmarks: camel, goat, pig (cf. figure 3.9). For an intuitive explanation of this approach, see section 4.2.2.

tion into practical terms. Recall that a radically novel object corresponds to an arbitrary point within the proximal shape space $\mathcal{R}$ (itself a subspace of the measurement space $\mathcal{M}$; see figure 4.1). Within this framework, similarities between objects translate into proximities between shape-space points. In particular, representing a new object by its similarities to several familiar ones corresponds to representing a point in the shape space by its proximities to several reference points, or landmarks (figure 4.8). The computational implications of this analogy are explored further in the next section.

## 4.2 Categorization as Navigation in Shape Space

The problem of locating the stimulus (an image of a novel object) within the proximal shape space is analogous to the problem of determining the location of a point on a terrain, which arises in navigation and in orienteering,[11] as well as in the preparation of topographic maps. Because "location" makes sense only when defined relative to some frame of reference, the first issue to be settled before venturing into the open is what could serve as such a frame in shape representation.

### 4.2.1 Defining the Frame of Reference

In cartography (and, more generally, in the geometry of two-dimensional manifolds), the frame of reference is normally provided by two orthogonal families of curves, which together constitute a coordinate system. While specifying a pair of coordinates is perfectly suitable for defining a location on a map, it is rather useless on a terrain, unless a correspondence is established between the terrain and the map. In practice, the only way to achieve such a correspondence is to choose a set of *landmarks* on the terrain (see figure 4.8), and to identify their counterparts on the map. Once this is accomplished, localization is reduced to finding one's position with respect to the landmarks; the isomorphism between the map and the terrain assures that a corresponding location relative to the reference points on the map can then be computed in a straightforward manner.

Whereas the general importance of landmarks for navigating a terrain is undisputed, the particular choice of features that are to serve as landmarks depends on the problem at hand. For instance, the location of a buried treasure on an island in the South Seas can be specified as being fifty paces to the north of the lone palm tree. The landmarks here are the palm and, implicitly, the North Pole; the latter defines a (directed) line along the surface of the island, while the former picks a point on that line. In a more prosaic setting, the location of a well in a valley can be defined by the bearings of two prominent hilltops, as seen from the well. If these are visible from anywhere in the valley, a traveler should be able to locate the well by following a simple procedure that requires only a compass equipped with an azimuth scale.

We can now use the analogy of orienteering to develop a practical approach to shape representation. Under this analogy, a parallel is drawn between the terrain and the (proximal) shape space. To describe or represent a shape then means to find its proper location in the shape space (the "terrain"). Furthermore, just as a location on a terrain can be specified by its geographical relationships with respect to some landmarks, so the location of an object's shape in the shape space is encoded in terms of some reference shapes.

Should such an encoding rely on angular bearings or on distances in the shape space? In the terrain example, the choice of method depends on the circumstances. For instance, measuring out a preset distance of a few dozen paces is easy enough on the beach of a treasure island, but is impractical when the distances are large, or when the landmarks and the test point are separated by water. In some cases (notably, in map-making) the distances must eventually be made explicit; this is done by measuring some distances directly, and computing the others by trigonometric means.

In the implementation of the idea of a shape space, distances and not bearings seem to be a natural choice: computing distances between a test object and some reference shapes amounts to the assessment of some similarity relationships, whereas the bearings from one shape to another do not have an equally intuitive counterpart. Consequently, the shape of an object is to be represented by the vector of its proximities[12] to a chosen set of landmarks (reference shapes).

An interesting feature of the analogy between the shape space embodied in a representational system and a stretch of terrain is the difference in the ontological status of the various points in the two spaces. The terrain exists independently of this or that set of landmarks chosen by a cartographer or employed by a navigator. In comparison, the shape space embedded in a given representational system is, in a sense, a virtual one, and is merely outlined by the collection of reference shapes (unless the system represents explicitly, continuously, and simultaneously all the points in that space, i.e., all possible shapes).

### 4.2.2 Active Landmarks

Clearly, in the latter case the reference shapes or the landmarks do more than provide a frame of reference—they are the bootstraps whereby the shape space lifts itself into existence. In this space, the landmarks have a special status: the $i$th landmark can be readily recognized as the vector whose $i$'th component (corresponding, as suggested above, to the point's proximity to the $i$'th landmark) is at ceiling. Furthermore, any object for which at least some of the proximities do not vanish can be *potentially* represented—but is not until it is shown to the system (objects that are sufficiently unlike any of the reference shapes are all effectively mapped to the null vector). Thus, the fabric of the shape space woven by the landmarks is invisible everywhere except where you look; given a test point (an object), its location (shape) can be determined simply by measuring off its proximities to the landmarks.

Any system that embodies this approach must provide mechanisms for an efficient storage of the landmarks, and for their use in the process of locating the test point. In the terrain example, a landmark can be simply a cairn on a hilltop; this simplicity is paid for by the need for nontrivial computation in the process of localization, which then involves the evaluation of trigonometric functions. The default assumption is that this computation is carried out by an intelligent agent faced with the task of determining its location from the observation of the landmarks (think of a hiker navigating the terrain). In this situation, the computation, in a sense, focuses on the test point, and not on the landmarks: it seems natural that the navigator—the consumer of the information made explicit in the process of localization—should bear the main burden of computation and representation.

This anthropomorphic division of navigational labor does not become a system that relies on the spatial representation paradigm for encoding shapes of objects. In such a system, the "continuity" (in the cinematographic sense) of representation is provided not by an agent moving from one test point to another in the shape space, but by the collection of landmarks, which, together, define that space. This suggests that a *distributed* approach to representation, in which the landmarks are assigned a more important role, may be a more natural choice. In particular, in a distributed system both functions required for landmark-based navigation—storage and use—may be combined in a single computational mechanism.

Consider an active landmark, realized by a computational unit that responds to the shapes of objects presented to it, and, specifically, responds more strongly to objects that are more similar to some prototypical shape peculiar to that landmark (its optimal stimulus). Such a *tuned unit* is merely a functional abstraction of the RBF module discussed earlier in this chapter.[13] Let us now identify the computational properties required of a tuned unit over and above the basic need for selectivity in the measurement space.

## 4.3 Tuned Units as Active Landmarks

In addition to selective response along the dimensions relevant to the representational task at hand, a tuned unit must fulfill certain other conditions if it is to serve as a universal and basic building block for the construction of a representation space.

### 4.3.1 Relevance

First, if a tuned unit is to be useful as a landmark designator in a certain region of the represented space, its preferred stimulus must reside there. This requirement seems so obvious as to be not worth mentioning. Nevertheless, neglecting to see that it is fulfilled can lead to a representation that is numerically unstable or downright useless.

To see what happens when the requirement of relevance is violated, let us return to the example of locating a well in a valley. If the bearings with respect to two stars, rather than two hilltops, are used to define the location of the well, the navigator is likely to become lost. Stars, unlike hilltops, are too far from the valley floor for their azimuth to change from one location to another. As a result, all the places in the valley will turn out to have the same "coordinates" within this frame of reference.

### 4.3.2 Coverage

A subtler problem arises when the reference points are clustered in a certain region of the space, so that their bearings are pretty much the same, even when measured from nearby locations. In this case, triangulation may become numerically unstable because of the need to base the computation on differences between nearly equal quantities. Thus, the landmarks to be used in charting a region of space must not only be close to that region (that is, close to any of its points), but also be sufficiently evenly distributed throughout the region.

### 4.3.3 Smoothness

If the response of each tuned unit depends continuously on the dissimilarity between the test stimulus and the preferred shape, an ensemble of units realizes a smooth distal to proximal mapping. Now, a mapping that is smooth and nonsingular is conformal,[14] which means that it can serve as a substrate for veridical representation of the original parameter space, as argued in chapter 3. A smooth response curve of the tuned units is, therefore, a key ingredient in faithful representation.

### 4.3.4 Invariance to Irrelevant Dimensions

The third requirement—invariance to irrelevant dimensions—is peculiar to systems of tuned units that use measurements of distances rather than directional bearings for localization. According to this requirement, the distance signaled by an individual unit must exclude any component that is perpendicular to the "terrain." To see why this is important, consider attempting to establish a correspondence between a map and a real terrain on the basis of measurement of distances between some test point (such as the well in the valley, mentioned in the earlier examples) and a few landmarks (such as several hilltops in its vicinity). Distances measured on a map will normally ignore the vertical component (unless the navigator painstakingly integrates the elevation data and takes these into account when computing distances). In comparison, distances measured along the terrain (e.g., by counting the number of paces between the endpoints of the path that is traversed) certainly include the vertical component.

A simple example of an irrelevant dimension, in a system of tuned units geared to representing visual objects, is illumination. When the illumination level is very low, the tuned units, naturally, respond very weakly. It is important that the system be able to distinguish between the situation in which a unit responds weakly because there is not enough light, and one in which the unit simply does not like what it sees. Obviously, comparing the responses of many units acting in parallel may help to make this distinction (indeed, this is one of the mechanisms of adaptation to illumination found in the initial stages of even the simplest biological visual systems).

It is every bit as important to ensure that *orientation* of the objects does not affect distance (similarity) measurements if the goal is to represent shape. It has been pointed out (Ullman, 1996) that if distances are measured in the raw pixel space, images of the same shape taken from different viewpoints may be deemed as less similar to each other than images of somewhat different shapes taken from the same vantage (figure 4.9). The above considerations suggest that a unit tuned to shape must be made to compensate for this effect.

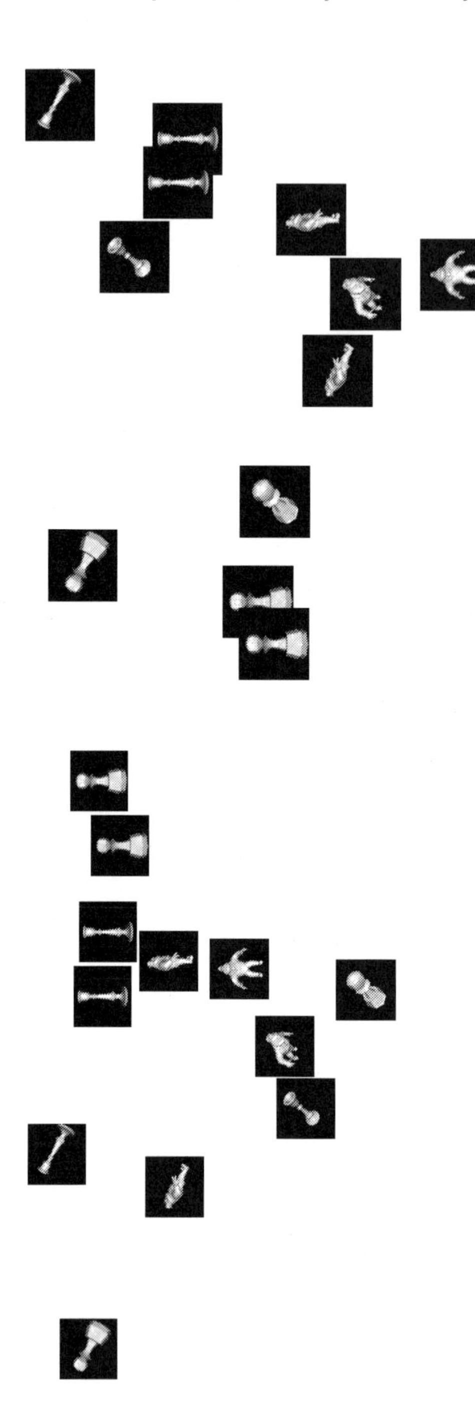

**Figure 4.9**
On the importance of discounting distance along measurement-space dimensions that are irrelevant to shape. *(Left)* The visualization in 2D of mutual similarities of different images of three objects, derived by multidimensional scaling (MDS) from their pairwise distances computed in the "raw" measurement space of the outputs of 200 filters covering the images. Note that the MDS procedure places similar images near each other (see appendix F). In this case, view-space distance (i.e., measurement-space distance due to orientation changes) dominated shape-space distance, causing the images to be clustered by the orientation of the object. *(Right)* The arrangement of the same images according to their similarities in the space spanned by the outputs of three RBF modules, each trained on one of the objects. Here, the view-space distance is downplayed, resulting in clustering by object shape.

Although this sounds like a call for an absolute invariance of the relevant features (i.e., the responses of the ensemble of the tuned units), the real requirement is, in fact, much less taxing, and therefore easier to implement. To realize that, note that radically different shapes are not likely to be confused, even if considerable freedom is allowed in the viewing conditions; a comparison between such shapes does not require prior cancellation of the effect of viewpoint. Thus, surprisingly, a tuned unit is just the mechanism that is needed here. Such a unit can combine invariance to the extraneous variables with selectivity to a particular class of shapes; if the stimulus is too different from that class, the viewing conditions no longer matter, because the unit can be excluded from consideration on the basis of its weak response (presumably, some other unit in the system will then take over the representational chore for that stimulus).

### 4.3.5 Monotonicity

The unique value of a tuned unit as an active representational tool stems from its ability to signal shape-space proximity between its preferred stimulus, and the current input. Although this ability has been taken for granted so far, there is no a priori reason to expect that responses of tuned units would signal distance along the manifold corresponding to the proximal shape space—the "right" distances needed for pinpointing a location in that manifold. Instead, it is more likely that the responses would depend on distances along straight lines through the measurement space. The sub-units tuned to individual views, out of which the RBF modules are built, certainly measure the measurement-space and not the manifold distance. When joined together, a number of such units form a module that is relatively insensitive to distance parallel to the view space of the object on which it is trained. In the directions to which the module remains sensitive, it still measures distance straight through the measurement space.

Fortunately, this shortcoming of estimating proximities to landmarks using an ensemble of tuned units need not interfere with their representational capabilities. Suppose that each unit's response, while determined by the measurement-space proximity between the current and the preferred stimuli, happens to be monotonically related to the corresponding shape-space proximity. Then the shape-space location of the current stimulus relative to the landmarks can be recovered from the measurements of the unit responses (Edelman, 1995c), just as in nonmetric multidimensional scaling (Shepard, 1962; Shepard, 1966; Shepard, 1980) the coordinates of a set of points can be recovered from mere ranks of interpoint distances (of course, a monotonic transformation of proximities preserves their ranks; see appendix F). Note that for direct measurement-space distance to be monotonically related to the manifold (shape-space) distance, the manifold must not be too undulating. This property, in turn, is related to the smoothness of the mapping from the visual world to the measurement space.

The monotonicity of the measurement-space distances (to which the tuned units respond), as a function of the shape-space distances, ensures that the outputs of the tuned units contain a faithful representation of the proximal shape space. To ensure, further, that the distal shape space is well represented, the same kind of monotonicity must be imposed also on the mapping from the world to the measurement space. We may observe, however, that this is already implied by two of the constraints stated above: if the mapping from the distal shape space to the measurement space is smooth, and if the irrelevant dimensions of variations in the distal stimuli are projected out (by virtue of the tuned units being trained to ignore these dimensions), then the response of a tuned unit will depend monotonically on the distal shape change. This, in turn, will result in a veridical representation of the distal shape space by the ensemble of tuned units.

Because of the importance of the monotonicity constraint, I digress now to mention some empirical results concerning human perceptual performance, which indicate that monotonicity of the requisite kind is a rule, rather than an exception there. One group of such results (to be discussed in full in chapter 6) emerges in a class of experimental paradigms that require the subject to judge perceived similarities among various stimuli.[15] Similarity ranks are then used to embed the stimuli in a low-dimensional space in such a manner that the distance between any two stimuli is monotonically related to their perceived similarity.

The procedure used for this purpose is nonmetric multidimensional scaling, already mentioned above. Along with estimating the coordinates for the stimuli in the embedding space, this procedure also yields the form of the monotonic function relating distance in that space to perceived similarity. As noted and discussed by Shepard (1987), this *generalization gradient* function (so called because it expresses the likelihood of obtaining the same response for progressively less similar stimuli) is monotonically decreasing in a wide variety of similarity judgment tasks. Shepard's paper, which appeared on the tercentenary of the publication of Newton's *Philosophiae Naturalis Principia Mathematica*, was explicitly motivated by a quest for psychological laws that would match those of mechanics. This expectation has been met in at least one respect: the empirical result concerning the form of the generalization gradient is extremely robust. Shepard's (1987) survey of dozens of studies that yielded generalization gradients showed that they can be described by a decaying exponential, $P(x; x_0) = e^{-d(x,x_0)/\sigma}$, where $P(x; x_0)$ is the probability of generalizing to stimulus $x$ the response previously made to $x_0$, and $d(x, x_0)$ is the normalized distance in the representation space. In a later work, Shepard and Kannappan (1992) incorporated this finding into a computational model of generalization.[16]

### 4.3.6 Learnability

The sketch appearing in figure 4.1, which was used to support the analogy between categorization and landmark-based navigation, depicted the measurement space as three-dimensional. Now, a manifold corresponding to the shape space can hardly be missed if embedded in a three-dimensional volume. Choosing landmarks on this manifold under such circumstances is, likewise, quite easy. Thus, it should be possible, at least in this simple case, to *learn* veridical representation by training a few tuned units to develop the appropriate response selectivity, while adhering to the other constraints listed above. A visual system that follows this approach has a good chance of scoring a victory over nature, by bridging the gap between its internal representation space and the objective space of shapes it represents.

#### The Curse of Dimensionality

In a more realistic situation, when the use of a high-dimensional measurement space is mandatory, the victory may well turn to be Pyrrhic: the proliferation of dimensions would increase the likelihood of capturing as many dimensions of variation of distal shape as possible, but, at the same time, would make the handling of measurement data difficult. It has been known for some time that high-dimensional spaces present computational challenges that may make the problems that give rise to such spaces intractable. In particular, the computational complexity of controlling a process (Bellman, 1961), approximating a function (Stone, 1982), or, more generally, learning from examples (as in learning to interpolate a function from a small number of data points; see section 4.1.1), grows exponentially with the number of dimensions. This phenomenon has been termed "the curse of dimensionality" (Bellman, 1961).

The potential susceptibility of learning algorithms to the curse of dimensionality is easily illustrated on an example we discussed before in which the issue of *coverage* of a representation space by data points was encountered. Consider the construction of a mechanism whose function is to represent the view space of a given object, given several of its views as examples (section 4.1.1). What would happen if this problem were approached using brute-force memory-based strategy, such as nearest-neighbor classification? The most important indicator of the success of a learning mechanism—its generalization capacity—is manifest in its performance on novel test points. For a nearest-neighbor classifier, this is determined by the spacing of the training data: the farther apart the data points, the higher the likelihood of a test point falling too far from any of the examples. Thus, the performance of the nearest-neighbor method clearly depends on the degree to which the memorized examples cover the measurement space. Assuming that $n$ examples are required to assure a close enough spacing of memorized examples along each of the $d$ dimensions of the measurement space, the total number of examples necessary for a uniform coverage of that space is $n^d$. The exponential dependence of the number of examples on dimensionality makes learning from examples infeasible even for moderate values of $d$.

### The Lifting of the Curse

A system whose goal is to represent the shape space hiding in the heaps of measurements may be able to circumvent the computational problems associated with high-dimensional spaces if it takes advantage of the low-dimensional and smooth nature of the manifold containing the relevant data. In the view-space example discussed above, this can be done by abandoning the nearest-neighbor approach in favor of an interpolating scheme such as the RBF mechanism. The number of examples required for valid generalization can be reduced by orders of magnitude, depending on the order of differentiability that may be assumed for the target function (for some numerical examples, see Stone, 1982).

Unlike object identification, which can be formulated in terms of interpolation in a space of views of the same object, categorization inherently involves dealing with multiple objects. Although interpolation among views of different objects does not make sense (Edelman and Duvdevani-Bar, 1997c), here too the smoothness of the space in which they are embedded (i.e., the shape space) mollifies the computational complexity of learning. As we saw above, smoothness and low dimensionality of the shape-space manifold ensures that measured distances to landmarks are monotonic in the true (manifold) distances, making the required coverage of the example space less dense.

To summarize this discussion, we may conclude that a representational scheme based on active landmarks is effectively learnable in two respects. First, a learning algorithm is readily available: one can use any of the published algorithms for RBF or nearest-neighbor learning, such as the $k$-means (Duda and Hart, 1973) for placing the basis function centers (Moody and Darken, 1989), followed by matrix inversion for computing the basis function weights (Poggio and Girosi, 1990). Second, the success of the learning process is assured, as indicated by prior work on the complexity of learning function interpolation in well-behaved spaces (Haussler, 1992).

## 4.4 The Chorus of Prototypes

We are now ready to spell out the details of the representational scheme which consists of a collection of active landmarks. This scheme, which I call the *Chorus of Prototypes* (Edelman, 1995c), employs vectors of proximities to a small number of reference objects to span the shape representation space.[17] The Chorus scheme implements the idea of $\mathcal{S}$-isomorphism, subject to a combination of theoretical and practical constraints. The main objective of this implementation is to zero in on the shape space $\mathcal{R}$ embedded in the multidimensional measurement space $\mathcal{M}$, while preserving veridicality, that is, $\mathcal{S}$-isomorphism between $\mathcal{R}$ and the distal shape space, defined by the task at hand and by the selection of objects. As we found out early on, making sense of the measurement space in this manner is rather easy if the goal of the system is merely the recognition of previously seen objects. In that case, a memory-based mechanism operating on the principle of interpolation among stored views was shown to be capable of fulfilling the requirements posed by the task. The real challenge arose when the task demanded the categorization of shapes not encountered before; nothing short of an open-ended approach, able to deal with radically novel objects, would count as a satisfactory solution to this problem.

In a natural extension of the treatment of the identification task, the approach to categorization proposed in this chapter chose to describe the structure of a novel object in terms of memory records of similar structures, rather than as a combination of generic primitive shapes. This approach was inspired by an analogy between categorization of novel objects and navigation, with the role of the terrain played by the (proximal) shape representation space $\mathcal{R}$ embedded in the high-dimensional measurement space $\mathcal{M}$, and the role of landmarks by the memorized objects.

This solution to the problem of novel objects takes advantage of the properties of $\mathcal{R}$ to limit the memory demands on the system. Due to the low-dimensional and smooth nature of the space $\mathcal{R}$, it proved possible to retain in memory only a small number of object representations, which, nevertheless, provide the basis for the representation of novel shapes, just as the knowledge of the locations of some chosen landmarks can be used to pinpoint the location of any point on the terrain from which several landmarks are visible simultaneously.

### 4.4.1 Persistent and Ephemeral Representations

In Chorus, the representation space for objects is built over a high-dimensional measurement space of primitive features. Recurring stable patterns of primitive features, which correspond, by definition, to statistically *persistent* objects are represented explicitly; these constitute the prototypes that span the shape space. Each persistent prototype may be represented by an interpolating mechanism similar to an RBF network tuned to a number of the object's views (Poggio and Edelman, 1990), and may be learned from examples.

In distinction to the persistent entities, rare or *ephemeral* patterns of primitive features are represented implicitly, by the distributed activity they induce in the prototype detectors. Some of the mathematical aspects of the idea of representing points in a space by their distances to some fixed reference points or landmarks are discussed in appendix B.

### 4.4.2 The Underlying Principles

The Chorus scheme derives its ability to represent and categorize a large variety of objects, most of which are ephemeral (in a statistical sense) and are represented implicitly, from explicit storage of information concerning objects that are deemed persistent and are each assigned a dedicated recognition mechanism (a tuned unit). The power of this approach stems from the same principle that makes multidimensional scaling work: in a metric space, fixing the relative distances of a set of points effectively determines their coordinates up to a translation and rotation of axes (Shepard, 1980). If several basic requirements, listed in section 4.3, are satisfied, and if the manifold spanned by the input stimuli in the measurement space is well-behaved, this method is assured to recover a faithful replica of the pattern of inputs in the measurement space, solely from qualitative (rank order) similarity data, contained in the responses of the tuned units trained on persistent objects.

Another principle, which I have discussed at length in chapter 3, makes the resulting representations reflect properties of the distal stimuli, and not merely of their proximal (measurement-space) traces. The principle is that of preservation of distance ranks by well-behaved mappings (on an appropriate spatial scale, and subject to some other, not too restrictive conditions). As we saw, if the measurements carried out by the system depend smoothly on distal shape characteristics (as they do generically, for a wide class of functions), and if irrelevant dimensions are downplayed (as they are by tuned units discussed in this chapter), the proximal shape space constitutes an approximately veridical replica of the distal one. The proximal shape space can then be charted with the aid of landmarks, implemented by the tuned units.

### 4.4.3 The Applications

The representation of a distal shape space created by Chorus can be put to work in a variety of categorization tasks. Possible ways of doing this are outlined below.

#### Categorization at Different Levels

Consider first the action of Chorus on images of familiar objects (that is, objects for which the system possesses persistent representational modules). The identification of such an object involves singling out the strongest-responding module, and verifying that its response exceeds some preset threshold. The basic-level category of the object is signaled by the identities of several of the stronger-responding modules. A secondary stage of processing may be conceived, which could associate labels with such patterns of module responses. Alternatively, a self-organizing categorization method, such as adaptive resonance (Carpenter and Grossberg, 1990), can be used in conjunction with Chorus. Finally, general familiarity with the object can be estimated by computing the variance of the responses of the more active modules. High variance would mean that some of the modules really like what they see, and others do not, signifying familiarity.

#### Treatment of Novel Objects

If the sum of the responses of the active modules is low, then low variance in the computation of familiarity signifies a stimulus that does not look at all like any of the object classes known to the system. Alternatively, if the sum of the responses is non-negligible, the object is radically novel, but still deserves consideration. This event may trigger a learning routine (in which case a dedicated module can be trained using the approach mentioned earlier in this chapter), or the system may choose to leave the object in its ephemeral status, and let it be represented by the vector of activities of those modules which respond above some threshold. These ideas are put to test in the next chapter, which describes an implementation of Chorus and reports its performance on a database of dozens of objects.

## Notes

1. The formal notion of an aspect (Koenderink and van Doorn, 1979) refers to a set of views of a object in which its *qualitative* appearance, as determined, e.g., by the number of corners (as opposed to the image-plane location of each corner), remains the same.

2. This predicament is related to the induction problem, discussed by Hume: we must rely on an analogy between the presently viewed object and other, familiar ones, to predict the effect of its rotation, just as we must rely on an analogy between today and tomorrow to predict that the sun will rise tomorrow as it did today (cf. section 2.1.3).

3. Likewise, in computational learning theory, the expected performance of a system can be related to the degree to which the examples on which it has been trained are representative of the domain of the function the system tries to learn (Haussler, 1992).

4. Formally, interpolation seeks a function that passes through the data points, while approximation settles for mere proximity of the target function to the data. In the present context, these two terms are used interchangeably.

5. In his work on the theory of differential equations, Hadamard (1923) terms a problem ill-posed if it has no solution, or if the solution is not unique, or if it does not depend continuously on the initial conditions.

6. This approach has also been advocated by Marr (1982), who pointed out that the recovery of the geometric structure of the world would be impossible in the absence of prior assumptions about physical properties of objects and of the imaging process.

7. Regularization is a common mathematical technique applied to problems that are formally ill-posed. By extending the definition borrowed from the theory of differential equations, a problem is considered ill-posed if its solution does not depend continuously on the data, or if more than one solution exists, as in the case of structural interpretation. Regularization attempts to reduce the solution space by imposing additional constraints over and above those contained in the data. A discussion of regularization in the context of low-level visual tasks can be found in (Poggio et al., 1985).

8. An example of such a function is Dirac's $\delta$, which is defined as the function that satisfies $\int f(x - x_0)\delta(x_0)dx = f(x)$ for any $f(x)$.

9. This fact runs contrary to the intuition that tells us that an infinite number of examples is needed to cover the domain of the target function, if the latter is defined over real numbers. Russell's (1921) notion that a representation of an object should be equated with the set of its views has been rejected by Marr (1982),

presumably on the basis of that intuition. If the connection between object identification and memory-based approaches such as interpolation between examples were discovered earlier, Marr's monumental work on a theory of memory (Marr, 1971) could have provided an interesting alternative starting point for theorizing about visual recognition.

10. The alternative being that it looks like nothing familiar. Note that there are very many ways in which this can be true. Because of the high dimensionality of the measurement space, a point picked at random is overwhelmingly likely to correspond to a snapshot of noise, such as the "snow" one sees on a TV set tuned to a dead channel.

11. Orienteering is the competitive sport of finding one's way on foot across rough country with the aid of a map and compass.

12. The proximity of two points $\mathbf{x}_1, \mathbf{x}_2$ in a metric space can be defined as $e^{-d(\mathbf{x}_1, \mathbf{x}_2)}$, where $d$ is the appropriate distance function. Thus defined, proximities are conveniently bounded between 1 (for coinciding points) and 0 (for infinitely distant points).

13. It may be also considered a functional model of a sensory cortical neuron, whose main characteristic is selective response to those inputs that are confined to a subspace of the space of all effective stimuli (those that evoke a response at least in some members of the neuronal population in a given cortical area). I shall discuss the parallels between the landmark-based approach and biological representational systems at much greater length in chapter 6.

14. Strictly speaking, it is quasiconformal, as is any diffeomorphism restricted to a compact subset of its domain (Zorich 1992, 133), which means that it can be considered conformal on a small scale (see appendix C).

15. The judgment can be explicit, in which case the subject is asked to give an estimate of the perceived similarity of a pair of stimuli, or rank two pairs by similarity. Alternatively, the reliance on similarity can be implicit, as in delayed match to sample experiments, where the response latency and the error rate in a same/different task depend on the perceived similarity.

16. Shepard (1987) also showed that the exponential generalization law can be derived from first principles, and is relatively insensitive to the form of the distance function entering the computation. I will return to the discussion of its ramifications in chapter 7.

17. Webster's Dictionary entry for chorus is: \'ko-r-*s, 'ko.r-\ n [L, ring dance, chorus, fr. Gk choros] 1a: a company of singers and dancers in Athenian drama participating in or commenting on the action. In a chorus, unlike in Selfridge's (1959) Pandemonium, the contributions of the individual actors are in harmony with each other. Lee Brooks (1987, 165) uses the expression "chorus of instances" in his discussion of Medin and Schaffer's (1978) theory of representation.

# 5

# 𝒮-isomorphism: Experiments

I must appeal to experience and observation whether I am in the right: the best way to come to truth being to examine things as really they are, and not to conclude they are, as we fancy of ourselves, or have been taught by others to imagine.

—John Locke
*An Essay Concerning Human Understanding*—1690

In theory, the most exciting feature of the principle of second-order or 𝒮-isomorphism is that it makes veridical representation of the world of shapes a generic property: any system that realizes a well-behaved distal to proximal mapping will have formed a veridical representation of some chunks of the distal shape space. This promise, however, carries with it a qualification: because only local and approximate veridicality is generic, the resulting representation may be of limited use in practice. The need to settle for an approximate solution arises also in the implementation I proposed for 𝒮-isomorphism, the Chorus of Prototypes (figure 5.1). There, the partial rather than the absolute suppression of noninformative dimensions of the measurement space by the action of the tuned modules is the price one seems to have to pay for computational simplicity and (as we shall see in chapter 6) biological relevance of the scheme.

To demonstrate that the rather prolonged theoretical prelude has not been aired in vain, and that the various approximations made along the way leave room for the actual performance, I shall now describe an implementation of Chorus and its testing on a database of real objects. Geometrical descriptions of these objects (ten of which were used as

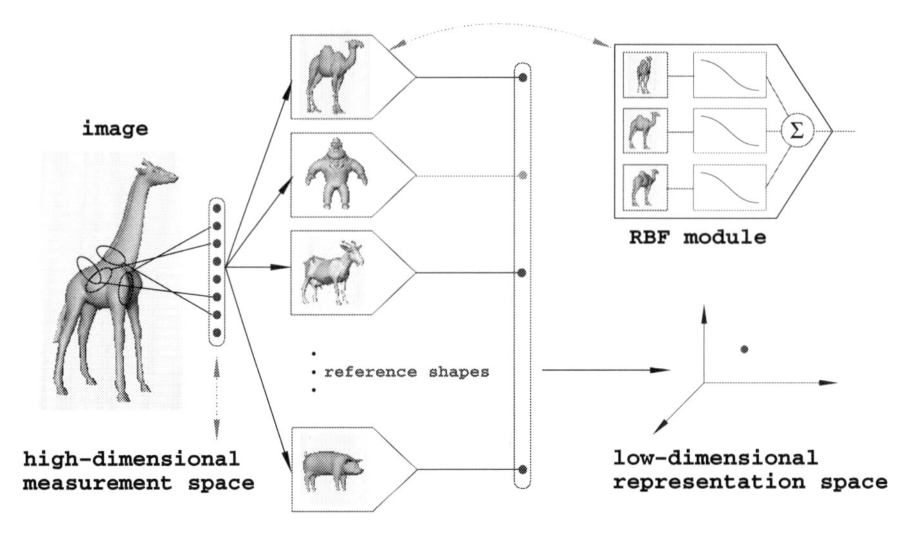


Figure 5.1
The Chorus scheme. The stimulus is first projected into a high-dimensional measurement space, spanned by a bank of receptive fields (appendix A). Second, it is represented by its similarities to reference shapes. In this illustration, three of the modules (camel, goat and pig) respond significantly, spanning a shape space that is nominally three-dimensional (in the vicinity of the measurement-space locus of giraffe images). The inset shows the structure of each module. Each of a small number of training views, $\mathbf{v}_t$, serves as the center of a Gaussian basis function $\mathcal{G}\left(\mathbf{a}, \mathbf{b}; \sigma\right) = exp\left(-\|\mathbf{a} - \mathbf{b}\|^2/\sigma^2\right)$; the response of the module to an input vector $\mathbf{x}$ is computed as $y = \sum_t w_t \mathcal{G}\left(\mathbf{x}; \mathbf{v}_t\right)$. The weights $w_t$ and the spread parameter $\sigma$ are learned as described in appendix D.

reference shapes by the Chorus system, and about sixty as test shapes) are available commercially. They can be manipulated (e.g., deformed or rotated) and rendered by computer graphics software, producing realistic looking images such as those shown in figure 5.2.

Because the focus of this book is on shape-based recognition, nonshape cues to object identity were minimized during rendering. Objects were rendered under the Lambertian shading assumption, using a simulated point light source situated at the camera, a uniform gray surface color, and no texture. Each object was presented to the system separately, on a white background, at the center of a $256 \times 256$ window; the maximal

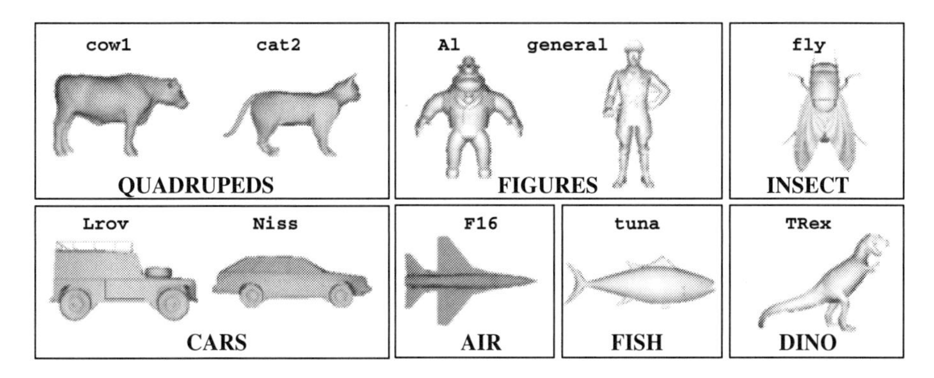


Figure 5.2
The ten training objects used as reference shapes in the computational experiments described in the text, organized by object categories. The objects were chosen at random from a collection available from Viewpoint Datalabs, Inc. (http:/www.viewpoint.com/).

dimensions of the 3D bounding boxes of the objects were normalized to a standard size (about one half of the size of the window). Thus, the problems of figure-ground segmentation and of translation and scale invariance were effectively excluded from consideration. Images obtained in this manner were mapped into a 200-dimensional measurement space, as described in appendix A.

## 5.1 A Chorus of Ten Reference-Object Modules

The aim of the Chorus of modules tuned to various shapes is to approximate the dimensions of the shape representation space $\mathcal{R}$ (itself embedded in the multidimensional measurement space $\mathcal{M}$). In section 4.3, this goal was translated into a series of constraints on the functional properties of the individual modules. Most importantly, a module tuned to a particular shape has to be insensitive to its transformations (which can be achieved by training the module to respond equally to different views of the target shape), and to respond differentially to different shapes (for which it suffices to train the module to be selective to the target shape).

### 5.1.1 The RBF Module

In practice, only a few target views are usually available for training. The problem, therefore, is to interpolate the view space of the target object, given some examples of its members, while rejecting views of other objects. I chose to approach this problem using radial basis function (RBF) interpolation (Broomhead and Lowe, 1988; Poggio and Girosi, 1990). Although other computational solutions are possible,[1] it is worth noting that the RBF model has been used to replicate a number of central characteristics of object recognition in primate vision (Bülthoff and Edelman, 1992; Logothetis and Pauls, 1995; Logothetis et al., 1995). I shall return to discuss this choice in chapter 6.

An application of RBF interpolation to object recognition has been described in Poggio and Edelman (1990). In its simple version, one basis function is used for (the measurement-space representation of) each familiar view. The appropriate weight for each basis is then computed by an algorithm that involves matrix inversion (a closed-form solution exists for this case). This completes the process of training the RBF network. To determine whether a test view belongs to the object on which the network has been trained, this view (that is, its measurement-space representation) is compared to each of the training views. This step yields a set of distances between the test view and the training views that serve as the centers of the basis functions. In the next step, the values of the basis functions are combined linearly to determine the output of the network (see figure 5.1, inset, and appendix D).

### 5.1.2 A Multiple-Module Network

Multiple landmarks are needed to pinpoint an object within the shape space $\mathcal{R}$ (and, indeed, to sequester $\mathcal{R}$ from the measurement space $\mathcal{M}$). A multiple-module network is constructed by combining several single-shape modules, each tuned to a different shape. The training of the individual modules must be coordinated, e.g., to increase the likelihood that more than one module responds significantly to any shape. This can be done by training the modules together, aiming simultaneously for good performance of the individual modules, and for an optimal cover of the set of reference objects, as described in appendix E.

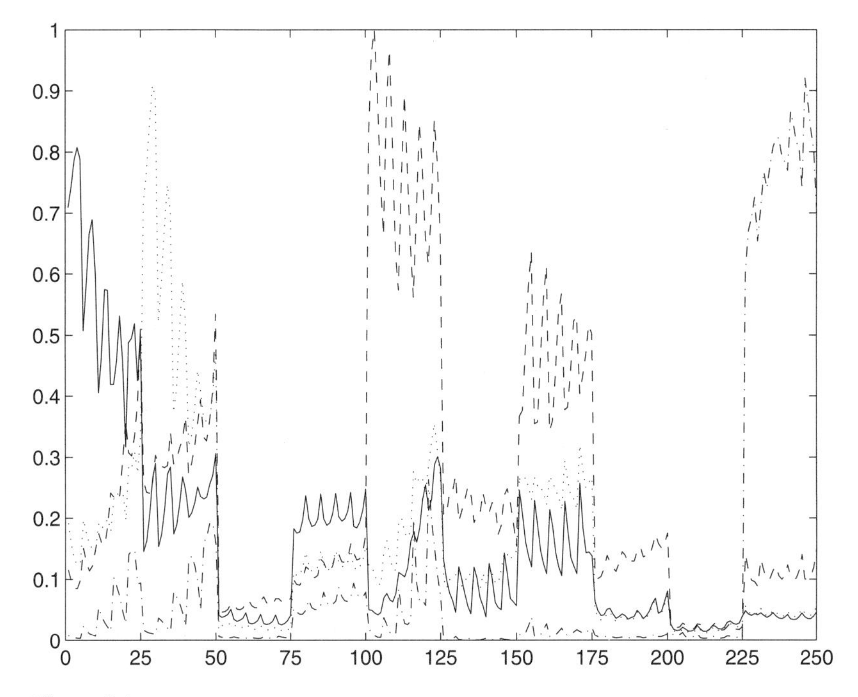


**Figure 5.3**
Normalized activity of several RBF modules obtained for 100 test views (twenty-five views for each of four objects). The views, which vary along the abscissa, are grouped, so that the first twenty-five views belong to the first object (cow, solid line), with the subsequent views, in groups of twenty-five, belonging, respectively, to cat (dotted line), tuna (dashed line), and TRex (dash-dotted line). Note that each module responds strongly to views of its target object, and significantly less to views of other objects. At the same time, more than one module generally responds to any given view.

The response properties of a network trained using this algorithm are illustrated in figure 5.3, which shows the activity of several RBF modules for a number of views of each of the objects on which they had been trained. As expected, each module's response is the strongest for views of its target shape, and is weaker for views of the other shapes. Significantly, the response is rarely very weak. This feature contributes to the distributed nature of the representation formed by an ensemble of modules, by making several modules active for most stimuli. Much more information concerning the shape of the stimulus is contained in the entire pattern of activities that it induces over the ensemble of the reference-object modules, compared to the information in the identity of the strongest-responding module (Edelman et al., 1992).[2] Let us now see how this information can be put to use in solving various recognition-related problems.

## 5.2 Experimental Results: Recognition-Related Tasks

Ten objects were chosen at random from the database, to serve as the reference shapes or prototypes for the multiple-module Chorus (see figure 5.2). The performance of the resulting ten-module system, implemented in cooperation with S. Duvdevani-Bar (Edelman and Duvdevani-Bar, 1997a; Edelman and Duvdevani-Bar, 1997d) was first assessed in three recognition-related tasks: (1) *identification* of novel views of the ten objects on which the system had been trained, (2) *categorization* of forty-three novel objects belonging to categories of which at least one exemplar was available in the training set, and (3) *discrimination* among twenty additional novel objects, chosen at random from the database.

### 5.2.1 Identification of Novel Views of Familiar Objects

The ability of the system to generalize identification to novel views was tested on the ten reference objects, for each of which a dedicated RBF module had been trained. The performance of three different identification algorithms was evaluated on a set of 169 views, taken around the canonical orientation specific for each object (Palmer et al., 1981). The test views ranged over $\pm 60^\circ$ in azimuth and elevation, at $10^\circ$ increments.

The performance of each of the ten RBF modules in isolation was first tested using individually determined thresholds. For each module, the threshold was set to the mean activity on trained views[3] less one standard deviation. The performance of each of the ten modules on its training object is summarized in table 5.1. The generalization error rate (defined as the mean of the miss and the false alarm rates, averaged over the ten reference objects) for the individual-threshold algorithm was 7%.

**Table 5.1**
Performance of individual shape-specific modules

| | cow1 | cat | Al | gene | tuna | Lrov | Niss | F16 | fly | TRex |
|---|---|---|---|---|---|---|---|---|---|---|
| miss rate | 0.11 | 0.14 | 0.02 | 0.01 | 0.13 | 0.04 | 0.03 | 0.10 | 0.16 | 0.05 |
| false alarm rate | 0.08 | 0.11 | 0.07 | 0.02 | 0.11 | 0.05 | 0.04 | 0.12 | 0.12 | 0.03 |

*Note:* The table shows the miss and the false alarm rates of modules trained on the objects shown in figure 5.2. The generalization error rate (defined as the mean of the miss and the false alarm rates) was 7%.

Model-based recognition systems in computer vision typically decide the identity of the stimulus by performing a Winner-Take-All (WTA) operation on the outcome of a series of comparisons involving the stimulus and each of the familiar objects. In a Chorus of modules, this corresponds to determining the label of the module that gives the strongest response to the stimulus (cf. table G.1 in appendix G). The error rate of the WTA method was 10%.

As I already noted, the WTA decision effectively discards valuable information present in the entire pattern of module responses (as opposed to the mere identity of the strongest-responding module). For example, two distinct stimuli can cause the same module to become the "winner," yet have distinct modules in the "runner-up" position. To take into consideration the entire distributed pattern of module activities when deciding upon the identity of the stimulus, one can process that pattern further, instead of merely finding its most prominent component. To that effect, we trained a second-echelon RBF module to map the ten-element vector of the outputs of the reference-object modules into another ten-dimensional vector only one of whose elements (corresponding to the actual identity of the input) was set to a nonzero value of one; the other elements were set to zero. This approach takes advantage of the distributed representation of the stimulus by postponing the Winner-Take-All decision until after the second-echelon module has taken into account the similarities of the stimulus to *all* reference objects (Edelman et al., 1992). The WTA algorithm applied to the second-echelon RBF output resulted in an error rate of 6%.

The conclusion of this first round of experiments is that individual reference-object modules can be trained to identify novel views of those objects. The satisfactory performance of the RBF modules, which did generalize to novel views of the training objects, justified testing the entire system in a number of representation scenarios involving novel shapes, as described next. Because one cannot expect the performance on novel objects to be better than on the familiar ones, the figure obtained in the present section—about 10% error rate—sets a bound on the performance in the generalization tasks.[4]

### 5.2.2 Categorization of Novel Object Views

The second experiment examined the ability of Chorus to support categorization of "moderately" novel stimuli, each of which belonged to one of the categories present in the original training set of ten objects. To that end, we used the forty-three test objects shown in figure 5.4. To visualize the utility of representation by similarity to the training objects, we used multidimensional scaling (Shepard, 1980; see appendix F) to embed the ten-dimensional layout of points, each corresponding to some view of a test object, into a two-dimensional space (see figures 5.5 and 5.6). An examination of the resulting plots reveals two satisfying properties: first, views of various objects clustered by object identity (and not, for instance, by pose, as in patterns derived by multidimensional scaling from distances in the original measurement space; cf. figure 4.9); second, views of the same category (e.g., QUADRUPEDS) formed distinct "super-clusters."

The ten-dimensional distributed representation inherent in the activities of the ten reference-object modules can support object categorization. To demonstrate that, we (1) assigned a category label to each of the ten training objects (for instance, cow and cat were both labeled as QUADRUPEDS), (2) represented each test view as a ten-element vector of RBF-module responses, and (3) employed a categorization procedure to determine the category label of the test view. The category labels were the same as the ones given to the various groups of objects in figure 5.2. It is worth noting that a certain leeway exists in the assignment of the labels; human observers, in particular, base categorization on a number

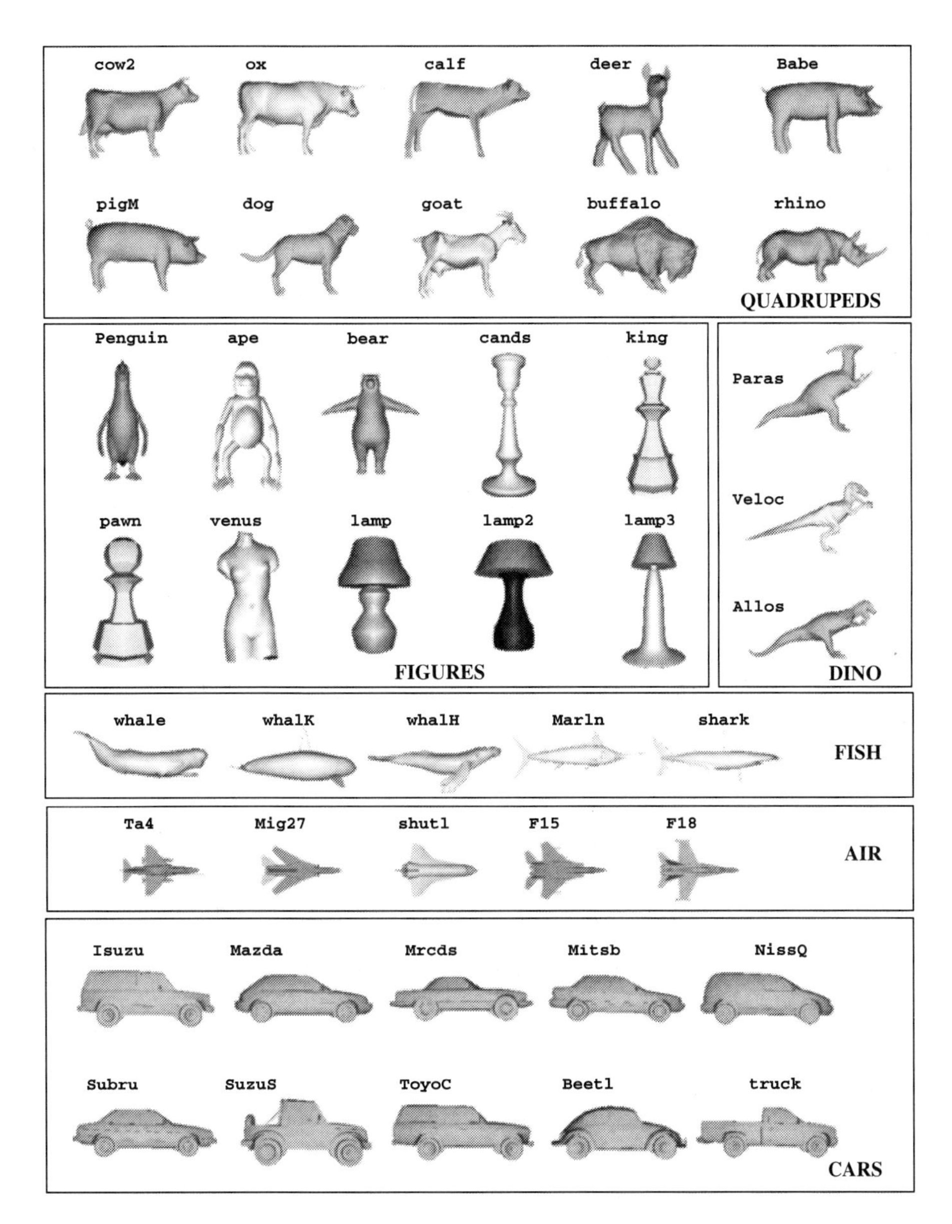


Figure 5.4
The forty-three novel objects used to test the categorization ability of the model (see section 5.2.2); objects are grouped by shape category.

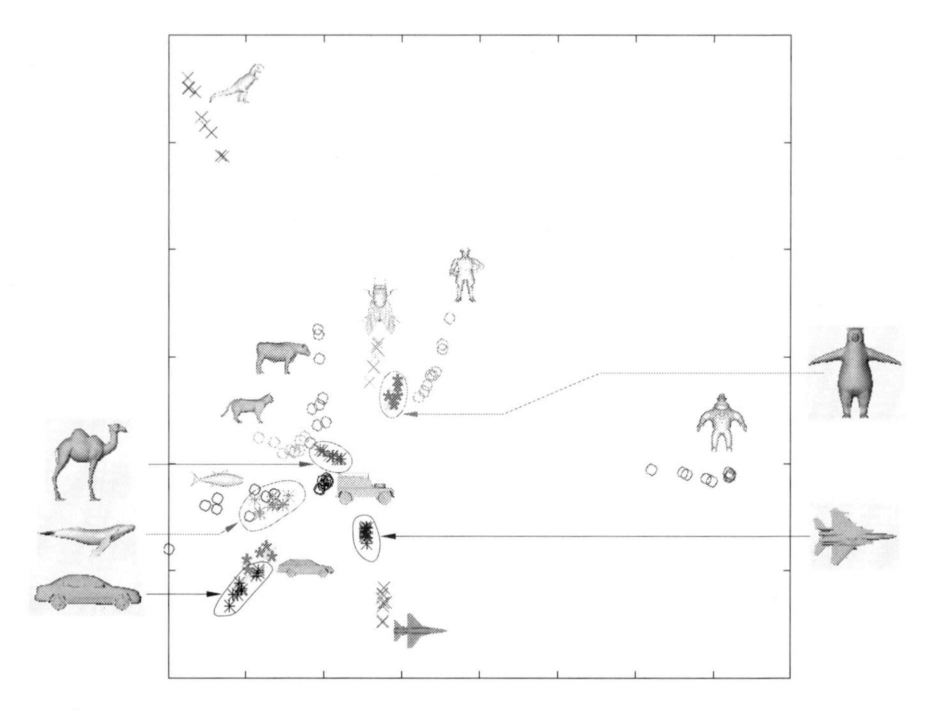

**Figure 5.5**
An illustration of the ten-dimensional shape space spanned by the outputs of the ten reference-shape RBF modules. Locations of the reference shapes and of five novel objects unfamiliar to the system (camel, whale, car, bear, F15) are shown. Multidimensional scaling (MDS) was used to render the 10D space in 2D, while preserving as much as possible distances in the original space (Shepard, 1980). Each point corresponds to a test view of one of the objects. Altogether, nine views are shown for each of the ten reference shapes and the five novel objects. Note that views belonging to the same object tend to cluster (part of the residual spread of each cluster can be attributed to the constraint, imposed by MDS, of fitting the two dimensions of the viewpoint variation *and* the dimensions of the shape variation into the same 2D space of the plot). Also, clusters corresponding to similar objects (e.g., the QUADRUPEDS) are near each other. The icons of the objects appear near the corresponding view clusters; those of five novel objects are drawn in the margins. See figure 5.6 for another plot of this kind.

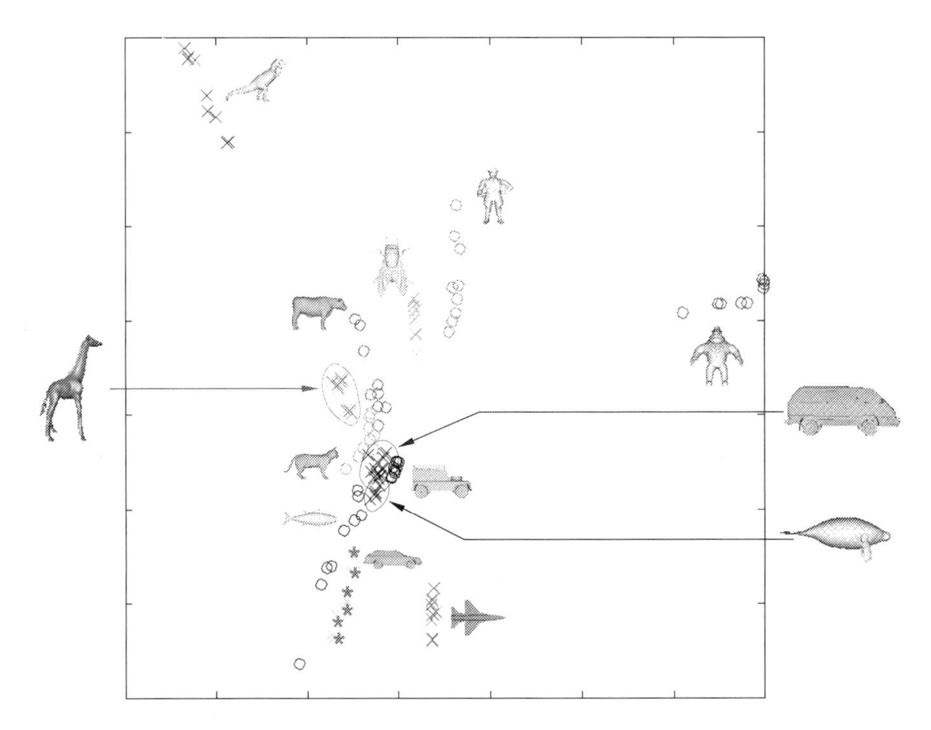

**Figure 5.6**
Another illustration of the ten-dimensional shape space spanned by the outputs of the reference-shape RBF modules, this time with a different selection of three novel objects (giraffe, manatee, van; cf. appendix G). As in the previous figure, each point corresponds to a test view of one of the objects.

of factors, of which shape similarity is but one. For example, a fish and a jet aircraft are likely to be judged as different categories; nevertheless, if shape alone is to serve as the basis for the estimation of their similarity, these categories may coalesce.[5]

An examination of the confusion tables produced by the categorization algorithm we describe below revealed the expected miscategorization errors. First, the fly classifier turned out to be highly sensitive to the members of the FIGURES category. Second, the tuna module was in general more responsive to AIRcraft than the F16 module (the sole representative of AIRcraft among the reference objects). To quantify the effects of this ambiguity in the definition of category labels on performance, we compared three different sets of labels for the reference objects. The first set of category labels is the one shown in figure 5.2. The second set differs from the first one in that it labels the fly as a FIGURE; in the third set, the tuna and the F16 have the same category label.

### Winner Take All (WTA)

Only two of the several categorization procedures described in Edelman and Duvdevani-Bar (1997d) are mentioned here. The first of these is the WTA algorithm, according to which the label of the module that produces the strongest response to the novel stimulus determines its category membership. Note again that the WTA method is incompatible with the central tenet of the Chorus approach—that of distributed representation. To be informative, a representation based on similarities to reference objects requires that more than one module respond to any given stimulus. A system trained with this requirement in mind is expected to thwart the WTA method by having different modules compete for a given stimulus, especially when the latter does not quite fit into any of the familiar object categories. Indeed, in this experiment the WTA algorithm yielded a high misclassification rate: 45% for the first set of category labels. Adding a second-echelon RBF module (cf. section 5.2.1) reduced this figure to 30%. When the second and the third set of category labels were used, misclassification rate decreased to 32% and 25% respectively. Carrying out the WTA algorithm in the second-echelon RBF space reduced both those figures to 23%.

### *k*-NN Using the Training Views

The other categorization method was based on the *k* Nearest Neighbor (*k*-NN) principle (Duda and Hart, 1973). According to this principle, the category of a test view is determined by polling the *k* reference views that turn out to be the closest to the test view in the representation space: the label of the majority of those *k* views is assigned to the test view. In our case, each of the RBF modules is made to store *N* views of its reference object as a part of its training procedure; each such view can be represented as a point in the ten-dimensional space

Table 5.2
The individual errors for each category of test objects

| Category Labeling | QUAD | FIGS | FISH | AIR | CARS | DINO |
|---|---|---|---|---|---|---|
| Set I | 0.08 | 0.34 | 0.14 | 0.50 | 0.11 | 0.33 |
| Set II | 0.08 | 0.10 | 0.14 | 0.50 | 0.11 | 0.33 |
| Set III | 0.08 | 0.10 | 0.14 | 0.28 | 0.11 | 0.33 |

*Note:* (See section 5.2.2 and table G.2 for details.) Note how the error rates decrease for the test objects of the FIGURES category in the second set, and for the test objects of the AIR category in the third set of labels.

Table 5.3
A summary of misclassification error rates exhibited by the two methods of section 5.2.2, for the three sets of category labels, using both the 200-dimensional measurement space $\mathcal{M}$ and the ten-dimensional shape space $\mathcal{R}$.

| | | Method | | |
|---|---|---|---|---|
| | | WTA | | |
| Representation Space | Category Labeling | 1st echelon | 2nd echelon | k-NN C |
| | Set I | 45 | 30 | 23 |
| $\mathcal{R}$ | Set II | 32 | 25 | 16 |
| | Set III | 23 | 23 | 14 |
| | Set I | | | 23 |
| $\mathcal{M}$ | Set II | | | 22 |
| | Set III | | | 20 |

of module outputs, and used as a labeled reference view in the $k$-NN algorithm.

This method yielded mean misclassification rates of 23%, 16%, and 14% for the three sets of category labels (averaged over values of $k$ ranging from one to nine). Table 5.2 summarizes the errors obtained for the third set of category labels, for $k = 3$ (for details, see table G.2 in appendix G). Note how the definition of category labels of the reference objects affects the resulting misclassification rate.

All in all, the pattern of the performance of the Chorus scheme in the categorization task conformed to the expectations (table 5.3).

Specifically, the performance based on the distributed representation of novel shapes in the ten-dimensional shape space $\mathcal{R}$ (14% error rate, nearly as good as the identification of the reference objects by the same system), was better than in the "raw" 200-dimensional measurement space $\mathcal{M}$ (20% error rate). The full distributed use of $\mathcal{R}$ also led to a better result than a Winner-Take-All decision involving each of its dimensions separately (23% error rate).

### 5.2.3 Discrimination Among Views of Novel Objects

Whereas the novel test shapes in the second experiment were chosen from one of the categories represented in the reference-object set, the third experiment involved twenty novel objects picked at random from the same database (figure 5.7). The experiment examined the ability of Chorus to represent these objects and to support their discrimination from one another.

The representation of these test objects in the ten-dimensional shape space $\mathcal{R}$ is described in table G.3 in appendix G, which shows the activation of the ten reference-shape RBF modules produced by each of the objects. It is instructive to consider the patterns of similarities revealed in this distributed representation. For instance, the giraffe turns out to be similar to the two quadrupeds present in the training set (cow and cat), as well as to the dinosaur (TRex), for obvious reasons. It is also similar to the tuna and to the fly, for reasons which are less obvious, but immaterial: both these reference shapes are similar to most test objects, which makes their contribution to the representation uninformative. Thus, in the spirit of figure 4.8, the giraffe can be represented by the vector [1.87 1.93 1.72] of similarities to the three reference objects which turn out to be informative in this discrimination context (cow, cat, TRex).

As in figure 5.5, the model clustered views by object identity, and grouped view clusters by similarity between the corresponding objects. To obtain a quantitative estimate of the separation of clusters corresponding to different test objects in the ten-dimensional space $\mathcal{R}$ in this case, we conducted a discrimination experiment. All 169 test views of the twenty test objects were first mapped into the $\mathcal{R}$-space. Each test view was then classified by the $k$-nearest neighbors algorithm, using all the

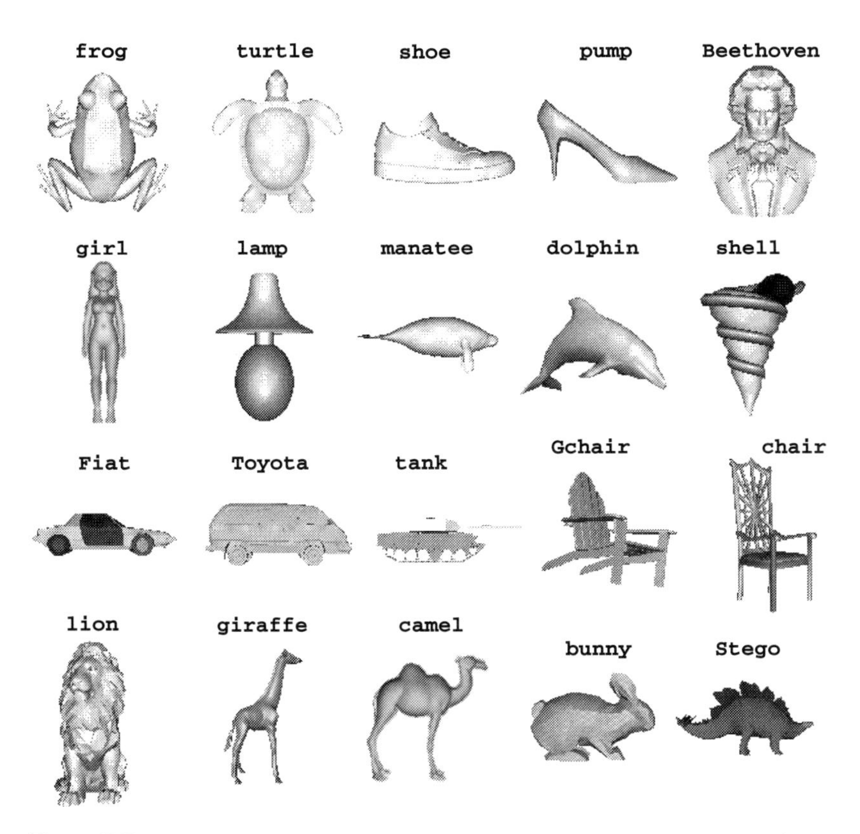


Figure 5.7
The twenty novel objects, picked at random from the object database, which we used to test the representational abilities of the model (see section 5.2.3).

other views as reference, and with labels corresponding to object identity (rather than to object category, as in the preceding section). The error rate (averaged over the 169 views of each of the twenty test objects, and over values of $k$ ranging from one to nine) was 5%. In the measurement space $\mathcal{M}$, the same experiment yielded an error rate of 1%.[6] It is worth noting that even though the $\mathcal{M}$-space representation yields a lower discrimination error rate, its dimensionality is higher than that of the $\mathcal{R}$-space by a factor of twenty, making it less suitable for generalization (Edelman and Intrator, 1997), as well as more memory-intensive (in advanced biological systems, the dimensionality of $\mathcal{M}$ runs in the tens of thousands if not millions).

Some light on the dimensionality issue is shed by another experiment, in which the performance of the Chorus system was estimated with a varying number of reference objects, holding the size of the test set fixed. A related experiment quantified the extent of dimensionality reduction that could be achieved under the constraint of a specific preset discrimination error. Figure 5.8, top, shows the discrimination error rate obtained with the 3-NN method (using twenty-five views per test object, 10° apart), plotted against the number of reference and test objects (see also table G.4 in appendix G). Figure 5.8, bottom, shows the number of reference objects required to perform the discrimination task (using the 3-NN method on twenty-five views per test object) with an error rate of less than 10%, for a varying number of test objects. The results indicate that the model's performance scales well with the number of test objects, although the relatively small size of the database limits the scope of this conclusion.

## 5.3 Experimental Results: Analogy-Related Tasks

Simulation results surveyed so far in this chapter show that the Chorus scheme can process relatively novel shapes that resemble some familiar objects, but are not necessarily identical to any of them. Chorus also provides a low-dimensional representation for completely novel objects, which do not necessarily resemble any of the familiar categories. These features of Chorus stem from its reliance on representation by similarities to *several* reference shapes. This categorization-oriented approach may be contrasted with the standard formulation of recognition, whose goal is to determine the *single* model shape that is the most similar to the stimulus.

The computational substrate for the estimation of similarities of the stimulus to the multiple reference shapes is provided in Chorus by a number of modules whose function is to signal difference in shape, while downplaying difference in extrinsic factors such as orientation. In the terminology of chapter 4 (see figure 4.8), this amounts to collapsing the view spaces of shapes, so as to preserve the shape space component of the total distance, as measured in the space $\mathcal{M}$. One may observe, however, that it is precisely the view space of a shape that contains

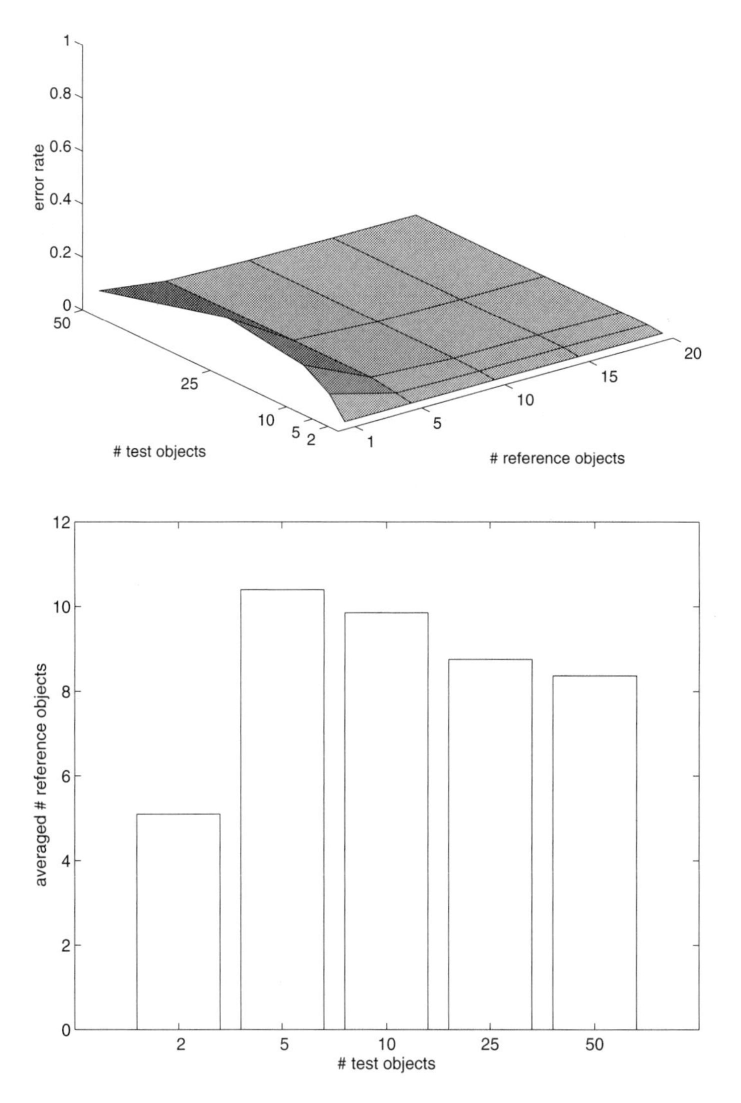


**Figure 5.8**
*(Top)* The mean discrimination error rate plotted against the representation dimensionality (the number of reference objects) and the size of the test set (the number of test objects). The means were computed over ten random choices of reference and test objects. See table G.4 for performance figures. *(Bottom)* The dimensionality of the representation (the number of reference objects) required to perform discrimination with an error rate of 10% or less, for a varying number of test objects. The data for this plot was obtained by repeating the task of discriminating among the views of $N_t$ test objects represented by the activities of $N_p$ reference objects 2500 times; this corresponded to ten independent choices of $N_t$ test objects out of a set of fifty test objects (five values of $N_t$ were tested: 2, 5, 10, 25, 50), and to ten random selections of $N_p = 1, 5, 10, 15, 20$ out of the twenty available reference objects.

information concerning the way its appearance changes with rotation. Because the knowledge of the view space of an object would allow the prediction of its appearance from novel viewpoints, transformation-related tasks (what I termed analogy) call for a somewhat different treatment of view spaces than that of invariance-related tasks such as recognition and categorization, discussed earlier. In this section, I describe a Chorus-based approach to a number of analogy tasks.

Let us consider again the structure of the multidimensional space of measurements $\mathcal{M}$. A view of an object corresponds to a single point in $\mathcal{M}$, and a smoothly changing scene such as a sequence of views of an object rotating in front of the observer—to a smooth manifold that is the view space of the object. The dimensionality of the view space depends on the number of degrees of freedom of the object. A rigid object rotating around a fixed axis gives rise to a one-dimensional view space (see the curve labeled $\mathcal{V}_1$ in figure 5.9).

Given a transformation of an object, the structure of its view space is determined by the object's geometry.[7] The view spaces of two nearly identical shapes will be very close to each other; a smooth deformation of the object will result in a concomitant smooth evolution of its view space. This observation can serve as the foundation for a principled treatment of novel objects in analogy tasks. Specifically, a system that has internalized the view spaces of a number of object classes can treat a view of a novel object intelligently, to the extent that it resembles the familiar objects.

### 5.3.1 Mechanism for Supporting Analogy

The computational mechanism whereby this can be done is interpolation. The particular interpolation problem that arises here involves irregularly spaced data. Among the many methods developed for this case (Alfeld, 1989), the simplest one is inverse-distance weighting, due to D. Shepard, in which the contribution of a known data point to the interpolated value at the test point is inversely proportional to the distance between the two (Shepard, 1968a; Gordon and Wixom, 1978).

In our case, the data "points" are actually entire manifolds: the view spaces of the reference objects. Accordingly, the viability of interpola-

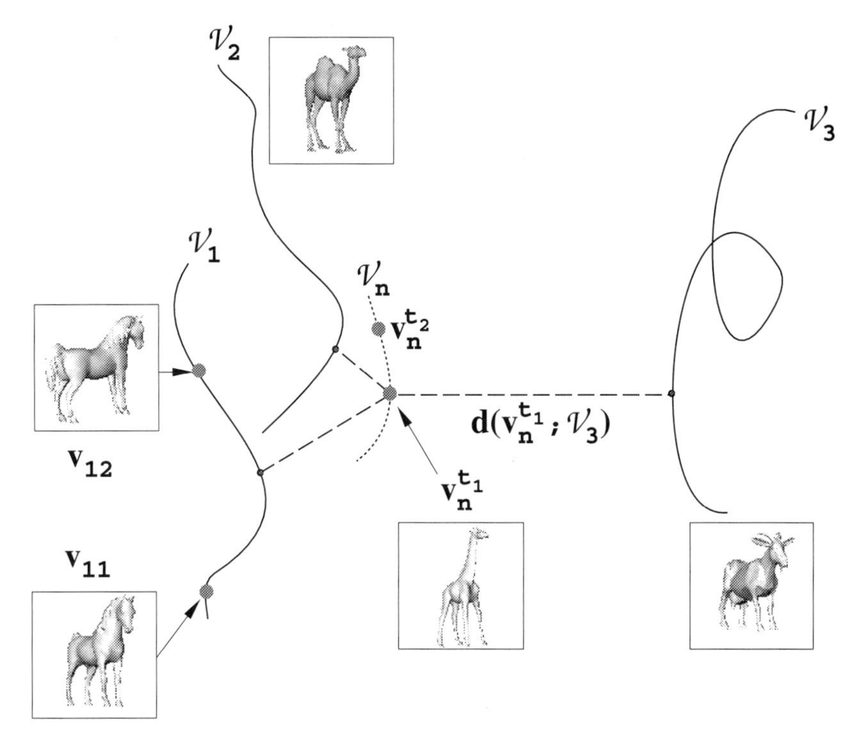


**Figure 5.9**
Interpolation of prototypical view spaces. The change in the view (appearance) of an object unfamiliar to the system (in this example, giraffe) can be estimated by interpolating corresponding changes in the appearance of reference (prototype) objects (here, horse, camel and goat).

tion among view spaces depends on the prior availability of a mechanism for dealing with view spaces of individual objects. Because such a mechanism can be implemented in different ways (one possibility is the RBF module discussed at length elsewhere in this book), I shall treat it here as a "black box" (cf. figure 5.10) that can be trained to output a constant for different views of some target object (and a zero for views of other objects), or to estimate the pose of the target, or to transform one of the target views to another (e.g., to a "standard" or canonical view). All these possibilities are put to use in the rest of this section.

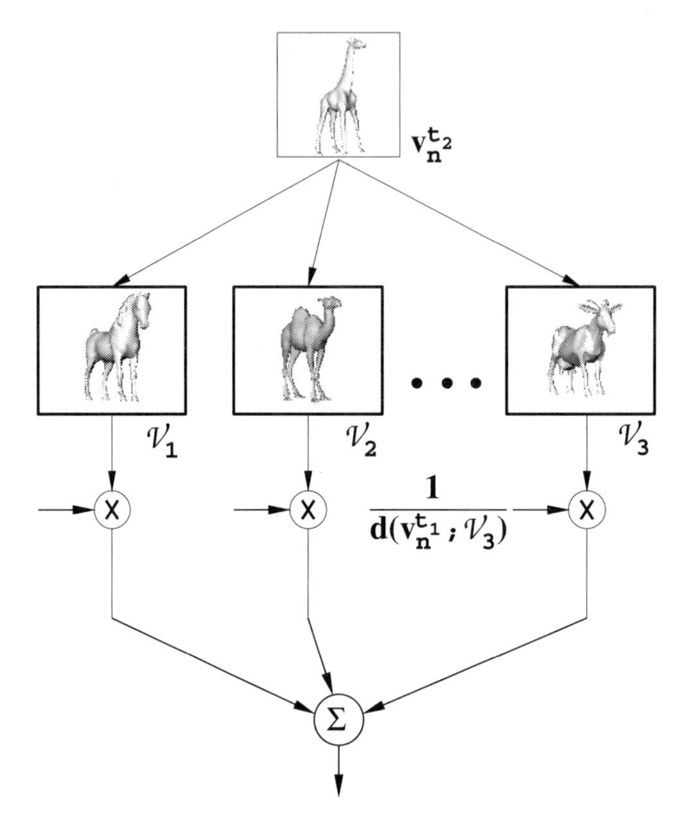


**Figure 5.10**
A mechanism for the interpolation of prototypical view spaces. The inverse-distance weighting method of Shepard (1968) is used to combine the outputs of a few "black boxes"—classifiers tuned to various prototypical or reference objects (Edelman and Duvdevani-Bar, 1997c). This scheme can estimate the view space of a novel object by interpolation of the familiar ones. As a result, it can support a range of tasks related to categorization, as described in the text.

### 5.3.2 Local Viewpoint Invariance for Novel Objects

Consider a system composed of $k$ modules, each of which outputs a value that is close to one for various views of its reference object and generally smaller values for views of other objects. The output of such a module can be interpreted as the similarity (i.e., proximity, or inverse distance) between the stimulus image and the view space of the module's target object. Formally, the output of the $i$'th module for a given test view $\mathbf{v}_n^t$ of a novel object, $x_i(\mathbf{v}_n^t)$, can serve as an indicator of the relevance of the $i$'th prototypical view space $\mathcal{V}_i$ to estimating the structure of the view space of the novel object $\mathcal{V}_n$. Consequently, the weight of $\mathcal{V}_i$ in determining the shape of $\mathcal{V}_n$ should be set to $x_i(\mathbf{v}_n^t)$.

We can apply this principle to the computation of a quantity $Y$ that is intended to remain constant over changes in the test view $\mathbf{v}_n^t$ of a novel object. First, compute the vector of responses of the $k$ modules to a test view $t_1$; denote it by $\mathbf{w} = \mathbf{x}(\mathbf{v}_n^{t_1})$. The estimate of $Y$ for another test view $t_2$ is then $Y(\mathbf{v}_n^{t_2}) = \mathbf{w}^T \mathbf{x}(\mathbf{v}_n^{t_2})$, where $T$ denotes the transpose. Note that this is an instance of Shepard's interpolation method; the weights are pre-computed for a certain input, then used for other inputs (i.e., in other parts of the input space). Clearly, $Y(\mathbf{v}_n^{t_2})$ will remain approximately constant, as long as the test view $\mathbf{v}_n^{t_2}$ is not too far from the view $\mathbf{v}_n^{t_1}$ used to estimate the weights $\mathbf{w}$, and as long as the novel object is not too different from at least some of the reference ones.[8] The results of an evaluation of this approach to object constancy (which, it should be stressed, works for novel objects) are shown in figure 5.11.

### 5.3.3 Recovery of a Standard View for Novel Objects

One may introduce a variation on the theme of the preceding section, by training each object-specific module to output a *standard view* $\mathbf{v}_k^s$ of its respective object (Poggio and Edelman, 1990). The standard view of a novel object $\mathbf{v}_n^s$ can be estimated from a given test view $\mathbf{v}_n^t$ by applying Shepard's interpolation method: $\mathbf{v}_n^s = \sum_k \mathbf{w}^T \mathbf{v}_k^s$, where the weights $\mathbf{w}$ are the same as before. This method requires a set of modules trained, as previously, to output a constant, in addition to the modules trained to output a standard view.

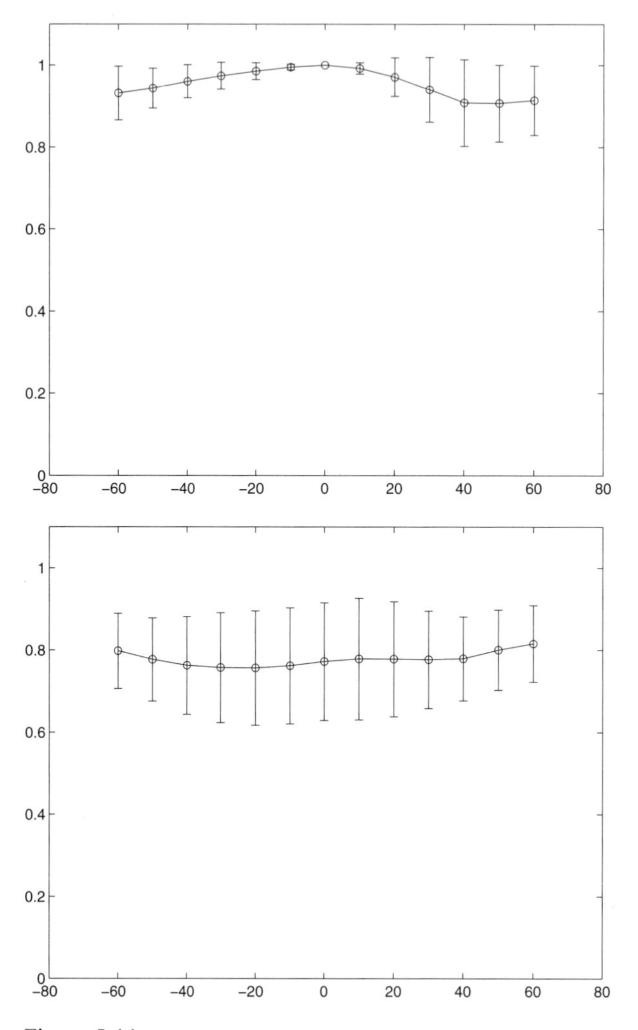


**Figure 5.11**
Local viewpoint invariance. The plots show the weighted sum of activities of ten modules tuned to reference objects (figure 5.2), evoked by different views of a test object; the data are the means and the standard errors computed over fifty test objects (figure 5.4). The computation follows the interpolation method illustrated in figure 5.10. *(Top)* The output with the weights pre-computed for a standard (canonical) view of each test object. *(Bottom)* The output with the weights computed for one of the test objects (camel), then used for the other forty-nine objects. Note that the output on the bottom is consistently less than on the top.

The performance of a system trained to recover standard views of reference objects is illustrated in figure 5.12. This system was tested on fifty novel objects, in addition to the ten reference ones. As one may expect, the performance of this method improves if the novel object belongs to the same category as the reference objects (figure 5.12, bottom left).

### 5.3.4 Recovery of Pose for Novel Objects

Information concerning the pose (i.e., orientation) of an object is contained in its image, provided that the object's shape is familiar, or that it can be related to some familiar shapes in a principled manner. This observation can be combined with the method of figure 5.10 to estimate the pose of novel objects, using a system trained to recover the pose of reference objects. The performance of the resulting method is illustrated in figure 5.13. As in the estimation of a standard view, the performance improves if the novel objects belong to the same category as the reference ones (figure 5.13, bottom right).

### 5.3.5 Prediction of View for Novel Objects

The last experiment in this series examined the ability of the view space interpolation method to support the prediction of a novel view of a novel object, given its "standard" view. Intuitively, this corresponds to an attempt to guess what a novel object would look like from an unfamiliar viewpoint, a task that people are not very good at, if the objects are totally unfamiliar (Rock et al., 1989). The performance of our method in this experiment is illustrated in figure 5.14.

### 5.3.6 Comparison with Related Methods

View space interpolation on the basis of similarity, or inverse-distance weighting, can support a variety of visual recognition, categorization and analogy ("imagery") tasks (figures 5.11 to 5.15). This method is related to a number of previously examined approaches. For example, (Poggio and Edelman, 1990) demonstrated both pose and standard-view recovery for wireframe objects (their system was not tested on novel objects, though). More recently, Lando and Edelman (1995) averaged the viewpoint transformations of a number of objects to recover the standard

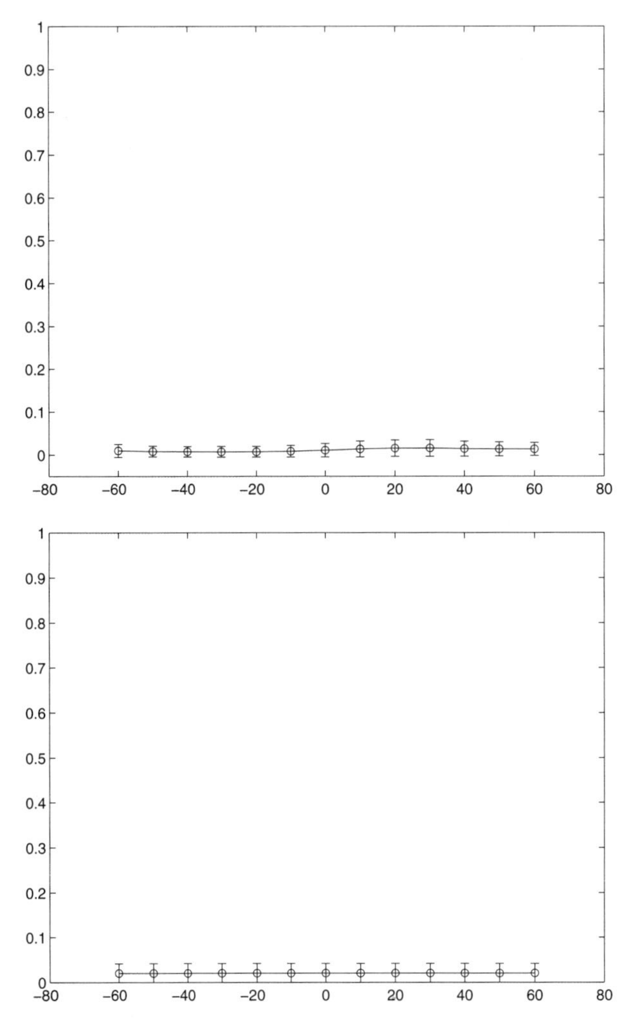


**Figure 5.12**
Recovery of a standard view. Each of the ten modules was trained to output the standard view of one of the reference shapes. Then, for thirteen test views (spaced at 10° around the canonical view) of each of the test objects, the *distance* between the estimated standard view of that object and its true standard view, $d = \cos(\hat{\mathbf{v}}^s, \mathbf{v}^s)$, was calculated and plotted against the angular distance between the test and the standard view. *(Top left)* Performance on views of the ten training objects. *(Top right)* Performance on the fifty test objects. *(Bottom left)* Performance on views of the twenty objects of the CARS category. Here, the results are significantly better, because the novel objects belong to the same category as

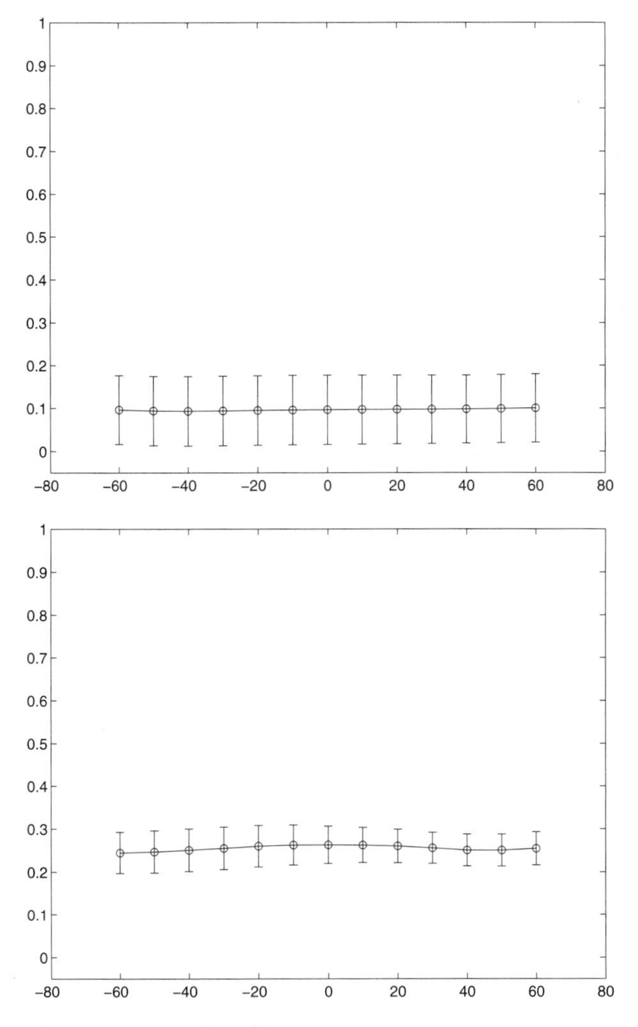


**Figure 5.12** ***(continued)***
the reference objects. *(Bottom right)* Distance between the recovered view and the standard view of a "wrong" object (randomly chosen out of the fifty test objects); the distances in this control plot are consistently larger than in the other plots in this figure.

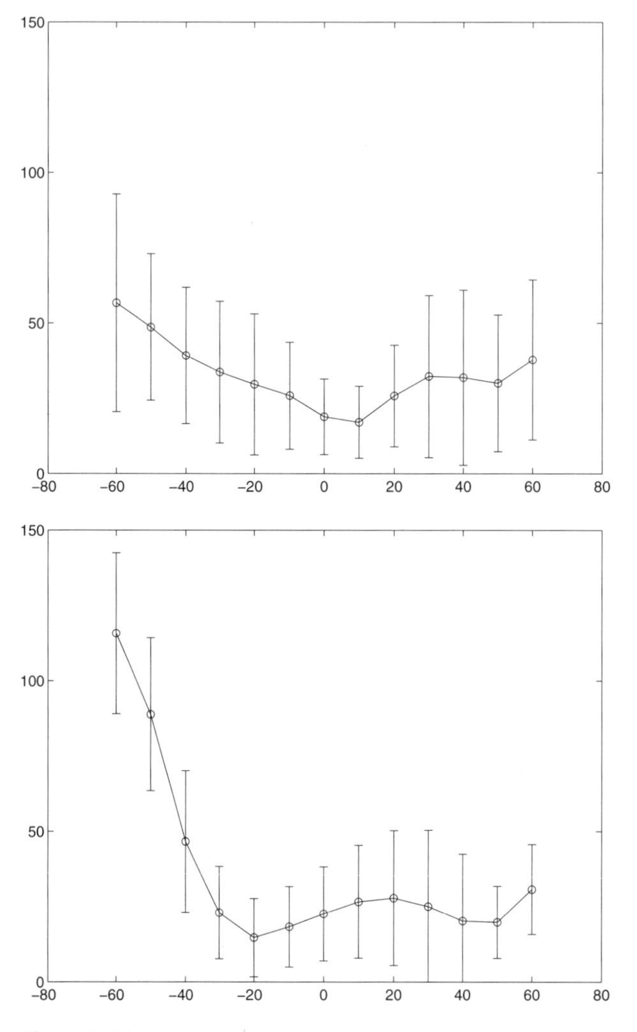


**Figure 5.13**
Recovery of pose. The system was trained to estimate the orientation of an object from its view. The plot shows the difference between the estimated pose and the true one, for several values of pose (ranging between $-60°$ and $60°$, $10°$ apart). *(Top left)* Results for the ten training objects. *(Top right)* Results for the fifty test objects. *(Bottom left)* Results for the twenty objects of the CARS category. *(Bottom right)* Recovery of the pose of the twenty CARS, based on the outputs of the two CAR modules. As in figure 5.12, performance is better for novel objects that belong to the same category as the reference ones.

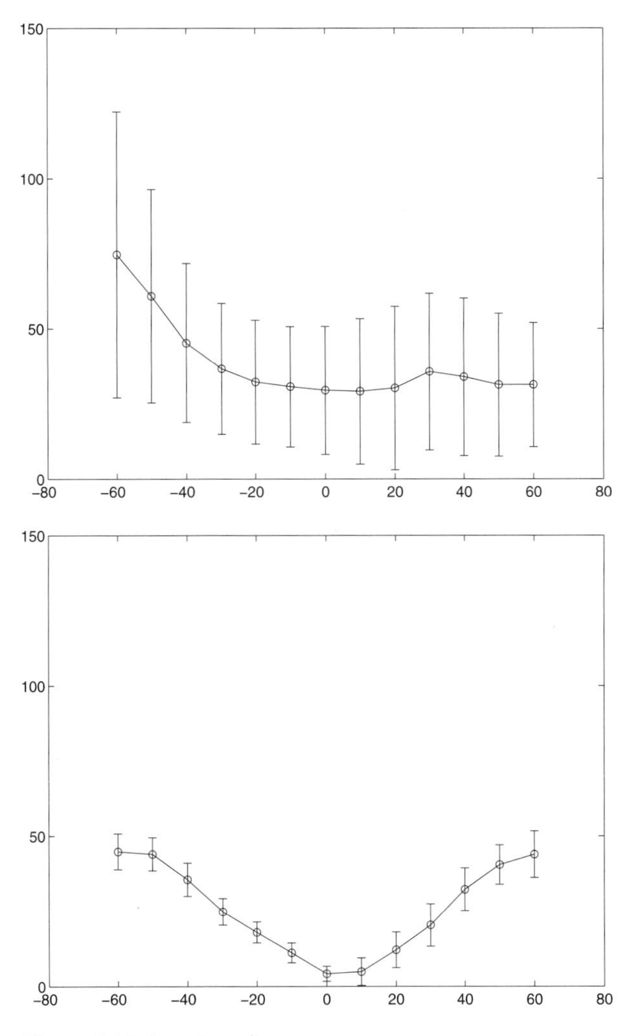


Figure 5.13 *(continued)*

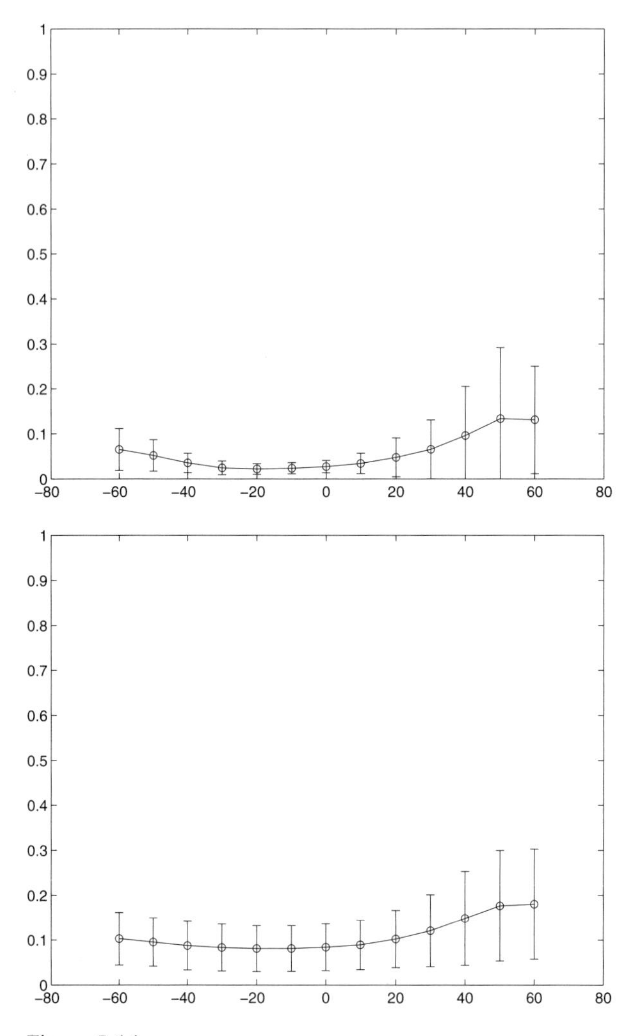


**Figure 5.14**
Prediction of transformed views. The plot shows the cosine distance between predicted and true views of an object, for several pose values, ranging between $-60°$ and $60°$ at $10°$ intervals. *(Top)* The distance averaged over the ten reference objects. *(Bottom)* The distance averaged over the fifty test objects.

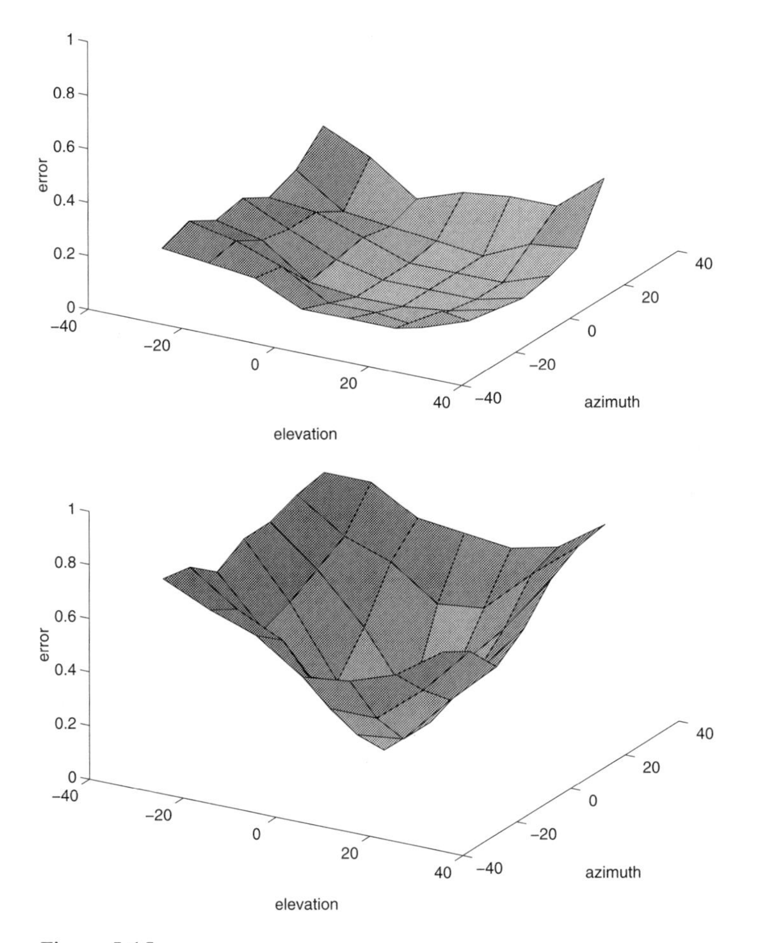


**Figure 5.15**
*(Top)* Categorization error for forty-nine test views, covering a 30° × 30° portion of the view sphere centered on the single training view (mean error over fifty test objects: 10%). *(Bottom)* Discrimination error under the same conditions (mean error: 49%).

view of a novel member of the same category (human faces). Likewise, Beymer and Poggio (1996) used the view space of one face to predict the appearance of unfamiliar views of another face. This approach is related to Basri's (1996) two-stage recognition algorithm, in which an input view is first associated with the most similar prototype (object class), then mapped into a standard view using a transformation specific for that class.[9] The present method, based on the Chorus framework, extends these earlier approaches, as follows: (1) it uses interpolation among several view spaces, rather than averaging or selection of the one nearest to the test view of the novel object; (2) it is shown to work for a relatively wide range of shaded 3D shapes.

## 5.4 Interim Summary: Second-Order Isomorphism and Chorus (SiC)

The treatment of the topics of representation and recognition in this book have, up to this point, adhered to the standard practice in computer vision. I started with a computational analysis of the problem, compared several theoretical approaches, and chose one of them, a particular version of S-isomorphism. This was followed by its implementation by a bank of object-specific modules (a Chorus of Prototypes), and by testing the resulting scheme—which may be called SiC ("sic" for S-Isomorphism/Chorus)—in a series of computational experiments involving shaded images of 3D objects. Before proceeding to examine the biological aspects of SiC, to which the next chapter is devoted, let us pause to compare it with other computational approaches to object representation and recognition, such as pictorial alignment, structural matching, and feature spaces.

According to the pictorial approach, objects are represented by the same kind of geometric information one finds in a picture: *coordinates* of primitive elements, which, in turn, may be as simple as intensity values of pixels in an image. Because of the effects of factors extrinsic to shape, pictorial representation can be used for recognition only if it is accompanied by a method for normalizing the appearance of objects (Ullman, 1989), or, more generally, for separating the effects of pose from the effects of shape (Ullman and Basri, 1991; Tomasi and Kanade, 1992). Given the many ways in which this can be done (Lowe, 1987a; Ullman,

1989; Poggio and Edelman, 1990; Ullman and Basri, 1991; Breuel, 1992; Tomasi and Kanade, 1992; Vetter et al., 1997), the main challenge facing the pictorial approach seems to be categorization rather than recognition (that is, making sense of unfamiliar shapes rather than identifying familiar ones). One reason for that is the excessive amount of detail in pictures: much of the information in a snapshot of an object is unnecessary for categorization.[10] Although a metric over images that would downplay within-category differences may be defined in some domains, such as classification of stylized "clip art" drawings (Ullman, 1996, 173), attempts to classify pictorially represented 3D objects (vehicles) met with only limited success (Shapira and Ullman, 1991).

The extension of pictorial alignment-like approaches from recognition to categorization is problematic for another, deeper reason than mere excess of information in images of objects. To realize that, note that both stages in the process of recognition by alignment (namely, normalization and comparison; see Ullman, 1989) are geared towards pairing the stimulus with a *single* stored representation (which may be the average of several actual objects, as in Basri's 1996 algorithm). As I have pointed out repeatedly, this strategy, designed to culminate in a Winner Take All decision, is inherently incompatible with the need to represent radically novel objects.

So far, the ability to deal with novel objects has been considered the prerogative of structural approaches to representation (Marr and Nishihara, 1978; Biederman, 1987). The structural approach employs a small number of generic primitives (such as the thirty-odd geons postulated by Biederman), along with spatial relationships defined over sets of primitives, to represent a very large variety of shapes. The classification problem here is addressed by assigning objects that have the same structural description to the same category.

In principle, even completely novel shapes can be given a structural description, because the extraction of primitives from images and the determination of spatial relationships is supposed to proceed in a purely bottom-up, or image-driven fashion. In practice, however, both these steps have proved impossible to automate. Perhaps as a result of this situation, mainstream approaches to recognition in computer vision tend to ignore the challenge posed by the problems of categorization and of representation of novel objects (Murase and Nayar, 1995), or else treat categorization as a kind of imprecise recognition (Basri, 1996).

In contrast to all these approaches, SiC is designed to treat both familiar and novel objects equivalently, as points in a shape space spanned by similarities to a handful of reference objects. According to Ullman's (1989) taxonomy, this makes it an instance of the feature-based approach, the features being similarities to entire objects. The minimalistic implementation of this idea described here achieved recognition and generalization performance approaching that of state of the art computer vision systems (Murase and Nayar, 1995; Mel, 1997; Schiele and Crowley, 1996), despite relying on very impoverished, low-level information (the outputs of 200 Gaussian filters). Furthermore, this performance was achieved with a low-dimensional representation (ten nominal dimensions), whereas the other systems typically employ about one hundred dimensions (for a discussion of the importance of low dimensionality in this context, see Edelman and Intrator, 1997). Finally, SiC also exhibited significant capabilities for shape-based categorization and for useful representation of novel objects—a goal which I consider to be of greater importance than mere recognition of previously seen objects, and which, up till now, has eluded the designers of computer vision systems.

The most severe shortcomings of the present implementation of S-isomorphism are (1) the lack of tolerance to image-plane translation and scaling of the stimulus, (2) the lack of a principled way of dealing with occlusion and interference among neighboring objects in a scene, and (3) the lack of explicit representation of object structure (a shortcoming it shares with many other feature-based schemes). I shall return to a discussion of these issues in chapter 7.

## Notes

1. For example, multilayer perceptrons seem to perform better than RBFs when the measurement space is "crowded," as in face discrimination (Edelman and Intrator, 1997).

2. In comparison, a typical object recognition system in computer vision opts for the latter, impoverished, representation of the stimulus, by carrying out a Winner Take All decision. The limitations of this choice vis à vis novel objects were discussed in section 4.1.3.

3. Only about one tenth of the 169 views determined by canonical vector quantization (see appendix D.3.1) had been used in training the modules.

4. To improve that figure, one should probably start with a more informative measurement space: the low basic resolution afforded by the 200 Gaussian filters used as the front end to the present system makes it legally blind according to the US federal definition.

5. This assumption was tested in an independent psychophysical experiment (Duvdevani-Bar, 1997), in which human subjects were required to judge similarity among the same shapes used in the present study, on the basis of shape cues only. Similarity scores gathered using the tree construction method (Fillenbaum and Rapoport, 1979) were submitted to multidimensional scaling analysis (SAS procedure MDS, 1989) to establish a spatial representation of the different shapes. The result revealed a clustering of object shapes in which the fly belonged to the FIGURES category, and AIRcraft were interspersed within the FISH category.

6. When the same procedure was carried out for the forty-three test objects of figure 5.4, the error rate was higher, because these objects resemble each other more closely. The mean error rate was 15% in the $\mathcal{R}$ space and 7% in the $\mathcal{M}$ space.

7. Certain features are common to view spaces of all objects: the view space always closes upon itself as the object undergoes a complete rotation. Other features are peculiar to certain classes of objects: the view space of a rotationally symmetric object is a point; the view space of an object that possesses a mirror symmetry with respect to the axis of rotation crosses itself once.

8. This observation is related to an old method for achieving invariance with respect to a group of transformations by summing over the elements of the group (Pitts and McCulloch, 1965); more recently, similar ideas were advanced by Nosofsky (1988).

9. All these methods (except Lando and Edelman, 1995), rely on detailed correspondence information. In such methods, features in the input image and in the stored representations must be matched before any further processing can be done. The correspondence problem for objects such as those in figure 5.2 remains, at present, largely unsolved.

10. It is interesting to note in this context that human observers classify line drawings of common shapes as reliably as full-color professional slides (Biederman and Ju, 1988; Price and Humphreys, 1989).

# 6

# Biological Evidence

There are many positive advantages, which result from an accurate scrutiny into the powers and faculties of human nature. . . . And if we can go no farther than this mental geography, or delineation of the distinct parts and powers of the mind, it is at least a satisfaction to go so far; and the more obvious this science may appear (and it is by no means obvious) the more contemptible still must the ignorance of it be esteemed, in all pretenders to learning and philosophy.

—David Hume
*An Enquiry Concerning Human Understanding*—1748

My aim in the present chapter is to examine the ability of SiC to serve as a model of representation and recognition in primate vision. In theories of biological vision, models of representation are frequently coached in terms that are too broad or ill-defined to be given a computational interpretation (see Palmer, 1978, for a discussion). Even when the theory behind a model is rigorous, the issue of the model's ability to carry out its purported function is more often than not glossed over as merely implementational (Marr, 1982). In contrast, adopting SiC as a working model amounts to taking a concrete stance both on theoretical and on implementational issues. In adherence to this commitment, I now proceed to compare the requirements posed by SiC with the repertoire of recognition-related mechanisms found in neurobiological studies, and to examine its predictions in the light of the recognition performance data available from psychophysical studies.

## 6.1 Neurobiology: Computing with Receptive Fields

Can SiC be constructed out of building blocks that are likely to be found in a biological visual system? We saw that the main requirement imposed by the $\mathcal{S}$-isomorphism theory on sensory transduction, and on the later processing stages that map the stimulus into the measurement space $\mathcal{M}$, is that of smoothness of the transfer function. The subsequent dimensionality reduction by Chorus required, in turn, a mechanism that could be tuned to particular stimuli, and whose tuning curve would be wide and shallow. It is difficult not to note the similarity between these computational requirements and the properties of the most ubiquitous of the various functional abstractions of cortical information processing mechanisms—the receptive field (RF).

In sensory neurophysiology, the RF of a cell is defined traditionally as the part of the visual field in which a stimulus must appear to elicit a response from the cell (Kuffler and Nicholls, 1976). More generally, one may put the space of qualities to which the cell in question responds selectively on an equal footing with the "real" or retinal space. For example, the space in which the RFs of the orientation-selective cells in the primary visual cortex[1] reside may be thought of as having five dimensions: two for the retinal location, one for orientation, one for the direction of motion, and one for the length of the stimulus.[2] The notion of RF generalized in this manner, by specifying the preferred stimulus of the cell, constitutes a useful characterization of its input-related function.

According to a commonly encountered simplified notion of sensory cortical information processing, each cell integrates information linearly over its (spatial) receptive field, then funnels the outcome through a non-linearity, and sends the resulting signal to the next stage of processing. Arguments to the effect that every detail of this oversimplified view is wrong in some situation or other are now becoming equally common. Even the very basic aspects of RFs, such as spatial contiguity and selectivity in the stimulus space, are contested (in regard to the non-classical RFs and context-dependent selectivity). A recent review of these issues can be found in Gilbert (1994).

The proposed extensions to the classical concept of RF invariably add to the computational power of RF-based mechanisms. Consequently, the strongest constraints on the kind of information processing that can be supported by the cortex are those imposed by the run-of-the-mill, classical RFs. It is interesting to find out, therefore, whether or not the more common observations and generalizations concerning cortical RFs are in line with the needs of SiC. Several interrelated generalizations of this kind are proposed and defended below.

## 6.2 Neurobiology: Properties of RFs at the Lower Levels of Processing

### 6.2.1 Broad Tuning

At all stages of visual processing, cells respond preferentially to some patterns as compared to others. Returning to the example of the primary visual cortex, cells that exhibit tuning to the orientation of intensity gradients have rather broad selectivity profiles; the orientation of the optimal stimulus may change by tens of degrees before the response is reduced to the baseline (Bishop et al., 1973). Another manifestation of this general phenomenon is the high degree of spatial overlap (in retinotopic terms) between the RFs of neighboring cells. This corresponds to a broad tuning in retinal space.

As far as SiC is concerned, broad tuning at the lower level (that of the measurement space) is beneficial: together with the high dimensionality, it serves to increase the likelihood that an arbitrary change in the stimulus will precipitate a change in the representation.

### 6.2.2 Graded Response

At the lower end of the object processing stream, the response evoked by a stimulus decreases, as a rule, gradually rather than abruptly as the stimulus undergoes a continuous change away from the optimum for the given cell (Shapley and Victor, 1986).

Functionally, a graded, broadly tuned RF can be considered a transducer, which smoothly maps changes in some feature space into changes along the dimensions represented in the output of the cell (a single dimension, if the response is taken to be the firing rate of the cell; possibly several dimensions, if the temporal properties of the firing are taken into account). This is precisely the kind of measurement mechanism that SiC needs.

## 6.3 Neurobiology: Properties of RFs at the Higher Levels of Processing

According to SiC, smooth transduction, which is the unifying functional characteristic of the lower-level RFs, is augmented at the higher levels of

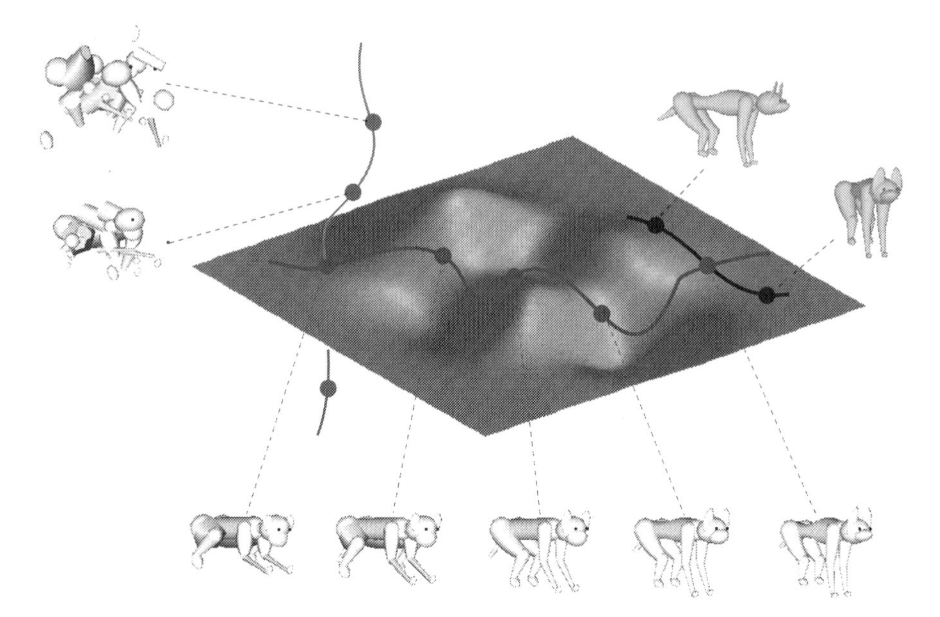

**Figure 6.1**
An illustration of the concept of admissible deformation for a real-world object. The appearance of a flexible/articulated object such as an animal can change in many ways while remaining coherent. Two examples of such changes are those induced by a rotation of the object (*right*) and those due to a deformation (*middle*). The number of these admissible degrees of freedom is tiny, however, compared to the total number of possible ways in which a high-resolution image (or a measurement-space snapshot) of an animal can be changed. Response profiles of RFs at the higher end of the visual processing stream are expected to be smooth and graded along the admissible directions in the measurement space, and to drop abruptly to baseline when the stimulus is changed inadmissibly (*left*).

processing by increasingly specific response to complex features, up to and including entire objects. The high complexity of such features entails a very high-dimensional space of potential deformations and transformations. Of these, only a small subset is admissible (figure 6.1). Accordingly, the RF profiles at the higher levels are expected to drop abruptly if the manipulation of the stimulus takes it outside the admissible subspace, while retaining the graded response property carried over from the lower levels along the admissible dimensions. As we shall see next, these characteristics are indeed found in the RFs of cells near the end of the object-processing stream, in the inferotemporal (IT) cortex.[3]

### 6.3.1 Selectivity to Objects

Spatially, the RFs of cells in the IT cortex extend over several tens of degrees (less in the posterior portion and more in the anterior portion of IT), and always include the fovea (Tanaka, 1992). Their selectivity characteristics along dimensions other than retinal displacement space became clear only gradually, over the course of two decades.

The functional equivalent of the top-level apparatus used by Chorus—modules tuned to particular classes of objects—was first identified by electrophysiological means in early 1970s, when reports of IT cells responding selectively to faces started to appear in the literature (Gross et al., 1972). For a long time, such reports were routinely misinterpreted and rebuffed as attempts to give credibility to the grandmother cell doctrine, first stated and rejected by Sherrington in 1941, and resurrected around 1972: the same year that Barlow published what proved to be a controversial paper on the convergence of information in higher cortical areas (Barlow, 1972). A widespread confusion concerning Barlow's position contributed to the status of the grandmother cell doctrine as a favorite straw man of theoretical neurophysiology. Whereas Barlow mentioned the "grandmother cell" once (on the penultimate page of his paper) and then only to dismiss it in favor of a sparse distributed code, Blakemore, writing in 1973 in the *New Scientist*, referred to a "great debate . . . known as the question of the grandmother cell" (Rose, 1996).[4]

The central theoretical argument raised against the very idea of cells tuned to specific objects is combinatorial: presumably, too many such cells would be required to encode all the objects which a visual system may have to represent. The main fallacy in this argument is in a hidden assumption it makes concerning the selectivity of the tuned cells. If the (feature-space) RF of each such cell is so narrow that it only responds to a particular individual object (in the extreme, one's grandmother, or a yellow Volkswagen), then indeed it is difficult to see how a proliferation of cells can be avoided. If, on the contrary, each RF is wide and shallow and overlaps (in the shape space or in other feature spaces) the RFs of other cells in the system, then a large variety of objects can be represented by the activities of a limited number of cells, making the combinatorial argument void.

Independently of the above considerations, and well before any computer vision system actually applied distributed coding to object representation, steadily accumulating evidence in support of cells tuned to object classes precipitated a major change in the mainstream view of the function of IT cortex. Although neither the guiding principles nor the mechanisms behind the emergence of the object-specific responses in IT were as yet given an account as detailed as that of the primary visual cortex, the idea itself has gained a wide acceptance (Rolls, 1996; Logothetis and Scheinberg, 1996; Tanaka, 1996).

Some of the more recent experimental evidence from the IT cortex is especially important for judging the biological relevance of Chorus and of earlier models that dealt with the recognition of objects across changes of viewpoint. That evidence bears on the central prediction of the view interpolation theories of recognition (Poggio and Edelman, 1990; Edelman and Weinshall, 1991). Along with Barlow's (1972) doctrine, these theories predict the existence at some stage of the object processing stream of cells tuned to specific views of objects.

First intimations of evidence in support of this idea were provided by a series of works by Perrett and his collaborators, who found that most of the cells responding preferentially to heads are actually selective for specific views of heads, that is, for full face, profile, etc. (Perrett et al., 1985; Desimone et al., 1984). A typical width of the tuning profile of these cells with respect to rotation in depth was about 60° (at the height of $\frac{1}{2}$ of the peak response). A minority of cells responded to multiple views, and very few responded to head images irrespective of the view.

A direct quantitative demonstration of view-tuned cells was produced subsequently in a study that utilized controlled computer-generated objects (Logothetis et al., 1995). The monkeys in this study had been trained to recognize wire-like stimuli such as the one illustrated in figure 6.6. Following extensive training (hundreds of thousands of trials), responses of cells tuned to some of the wire-like objects could be routinely isolated and recorded (Logothetis et al., 1995). Of the ninety-three cells found to respond preferentially to wires, sixty-one responded to one or two views and three responded to all views; these numbers are comparable to those reported in (Perrett et al., 1991) for face stimuli. To quantify the selectivity of the RFs, Logothetis et al. (1995) fitted Gaussians to the view selectivity profiles; their width—60° at $\frac{1}{2}$ the height—was found to be about the same as in Perrett's studies.

The findings of face-selective cells in IT were frequently accompanied by reports of cells that responded to monkey and human hands, and others that responded to various household objects that happened to be tested. The first systematic studies of responses to common objects were undertaken when the existence of "face cells" became relatively well-established. Such studies revealed that selectivity of response is by no means an exception. Moreover, selectivity to common objects could be observed following relatively brief exposure. For example, Rolls (1996, 341) describes cells that could be activated by images of ten real plastic objects, which had been placed in the monkey's cage a few weeks prior to the experiment. As in the studies mentioned above, most of the cells responded in a view-specific manner, although some did exhibit viewpoint independence.

Over the past decade, K. Tanaka and his collaborators used a variety of colorful 3D plastic objects to probe the characteristics of IT cells. To determine which of the many visual features of these objects were critical for the activation of the cell in a particular recording session, these researchers employed a manual "stimulus reduction" method. According to this method, the 3D stimulus object was replaced by a 2D paper cutout, which was then progressively simplified, until the cell stopped responding (Tanaka et al., 1991). Because a given stimulus can be reduced in many ways, the painstaking search for the simplest effective stimulus did not always succeed. Nevertheless, for ninety out of the 208 cells in anterior IT that responded to the original objects but not to simple stimuli such as gratings, the critical feature could be reconstructed by a 2D paper cutout. For eighty-seven cells the reduction process failed, although these cells did respond to some of the 3D stimuli. The remaining thirty-one cells responded preferentially to faces. Not surprisingly, the size of the RFs increased from visual area V4 through posterior IT to anterior IT; likewise, the proportion of cells that required complex features increased from V4 to posterior IT (from 2% to 12% in Tanaka et al., 1991; from 38% to 49% in Kobatake and Tanaka, 1994). Cells in anterior IT did not respond at all to simple features (bars and spots).

The "reduction" study provided the first clear data concerning the nature of object features represented in IT, which in the monkey was hitherto thought to be devoted mainly to faces and only incidentally to some other objects.[5] Besides the existence of RFs for complex object features, this method revealed several characteristics of such features and of the spatial arrangement of the corresponding IT cells in the cortex:

1. *Critical features.* The critical features were, as a rule, simpler than actual images of the stimuli objects. In a typical example (see figure 4 in Kobatake and Tanaka, 1994), the response of a cell to a picture of a monkey's face was 0.87 of the response to a stylized face that could be obtained, e.g., by removing the texture and the nose and by averaging over many real faces. The selectivity profile in "feature space" was usually rather sharp, but not absolute.
2. *Shape over texture/color.* For a large majority of cells (sixty-seven of the ninety cells in Tanaka et al., 1991), the critical feature had to do with the shape of the stimulus contour and its contrast sign; a minority of the cells required some combination of texture and color in addition to the shape information. The reversal of contrast produced a reduction of the response compared to the optimal stimulus by more than 50% in 60% of the tested cells; outlining (leaving only the lines, without the mass) resulted in a similar reduction of response in 70% of the cells (Ito et al., 1994).
3. *Columnar structure.* Having found that face cells selective to frontal and profile views clustered in distinct clumps in IT, Perrett et al. (1987) suggested that a columnar arrangement similar to that found in the primary visual area V1 (Hubel and Wiesel, 1968) may also be present in IT. Indeed, Tanaka and his colleagues found that cells from the same vertical penetration tended to exhibit similar selectivity properties, effectively forming columns for visual features. Fine differences in preferred shape and various differences in orientation were found within columns, while larger differences in preferred shape existed across columns (Fujita et al., 1992; Tanaka, 1992; Kobatake and Tanaka, 1994; Wang et al., 1996). The size of the column was estimated at $0.5 \times 0.5$ *mm*, which translates into 1300 columns in anterior IT (Tanaka, 1993b).

### 6.3.2 Ensemble Encoding

Having scanned the latest findings on response patterns of cells in IT cortex, I find it particularly instructive to return for a moment to Barlow's views of the cortical hierarchy, expressed in his 1972 paper. As anticipated by Barlow and others, fewer cells respond to a given stimulus in progressively higher visual areas; at the same time, because of the broad tuning and the graded response profile of individual RFs, the shape of the stimulus is nevertheless adequately described by the *population response*.

Population coding (Hinton, 1984) is a well-known concept in theories of neural information processing. In biological systems, in view of the properties of broad tuning and graded overlapping RFs, the population response confers the additional advantage of hyperacuity. Specifically, the resolution (in retinal or feature space) supported by the ensemble response can be far better than what can be derived from the responses of the individual RFs (Snippe and Koenderink, 1992; Weiss et al., 1993). Both the graded profile of the RFs and their broad spread are crucial for this phenomenon. The former property is necessary to make sure that even small changes in the stimulus configuration are reflected in the RF output, while the latter is required for information gathered from a wide area to be pooled in forming the ensemble response.

Barlow's theory of cortical representation goes beyond mere population coding, by postulating that the code should be also *sparse* (Barlow, 1994). In a sparse distributed representation, the total number of dimensions may be quite large, but the number of dimensions along which the response is significant for any given stimulus is small. The sets of active dimensions differ over various categories of stimuli, and may have little overlap for radically dissimilar or incomparable objects. As pointed out by Barlow (Barlow, 1959; Barlow, 1990), this characteristic of a representation makes it especially suitable for supporting probabilistic learning: if two features do not normally overlap in the representation space (i.e., are statistically independent), the likelihood of the appearance of their conjunction in a particular stimulus can be estimated by a simple computation (taking the product of their individual likelihoods). If the actual rate of appearance of the conjunction is higher than predicted in this manner, it will be easily noticed by the system, which should be on the lookout for such "suspicious coincidences."

The observations made so far concerning the nature of the object code in IT consistently support the idea of a distributed code, although the sparseness of the code was quantified only relatively recently. A tuned cell will respond to a number of stimuli—and, conversely, a number of cells will respond to a given stimulus—if its RF in the space of the relevant features (that is, features that are effective for a particular population of cells) is wide. The wide selectivity profiles of RFs in IT were noted in Desimone et al. (1984): "Many IT cells responded nearly equally to nearly every stimulus tested, and most of the stimulus-selective cells gave at least a small response to virtually every stimulus tested, especially visually complex stimuli" (2061). This observation has been corroborated repeatedly, in studies that used faces, toys, images scanned from magazines, and many other kinds of visual stimuli:

• (Sakai and Miyashita, 1991). This work, in which the monkeys were trained to remember pairwise associations among twenty-four two-dimensional patterns obtained by Fourier synthesis, reports data from ninety-one cells; of these, thirty-two responded to one picture, and fifty-nine to more than two.

• (Young and Yamane, 1992). The population response of cells in IT to faces was analyzed by subjecting the data to multidimensional scaling (see appendix F). An interpretation of the resulting configuration of the stimuli yielded meaningful dimensions of physical variation among the faces.

• (Miyashita et al., 1993). The stimuli in this study were ninety-seven fractal 2D patterns, used in a delayed matching to sample task. In eighty-eight of the 121 picture-selective cells from which recordings were made, the similarity between responses to the best, second best and third best stimuli could be computed. In these cells, the response pattern was rather wide: a histogram of the number of stimuli vs. firing rate was approximately linear.[6]

• (Miller et al., 1993). This study used as stimuli 500 complex multicolored pictures scanned from magazines; the task was delayed matching to sample with a variable number of intervening stimuli. Out of a total of 146 visually responsive neurons, 124 were selective for the sample stimuli. Discriminant analysis showed that the responses of an individual neuron could be used to classify a stimulus as matching or nonmatching in about 60% of the trials. To achieve the same performance as that of the monkey (about 90%) would require averaging the responses of twenty-five neurons (assuming uncorrelated responses).

• (Logothetis and Pauls, 1995). In this exploration of responses to wire-like computer-generated objects, most cells responded to some extent to all the test objects (sixty or 120, depending on the experiment), although responses to a small subset of those (five to ten objects) were much more pronounced. Cells responsive to wires also responded in an apparently nonselective manner to several kinds of distractor objects (figure 10 in the paper).

• (Rolls and Tovee, 1995b). Twenty-three faces and forty-five non-face natural images were used as stimuli in this experiment. The sparseness of the population response was estimated at 0.65 on the average over the sixty-eight stimuli.[7] The response data were subjected to multidimensional scaling, which produced a layout of the stimulus space represented by this population of neurons. In this representation space, different faces were well separated, whereas different non-face stimuli were grouped together.

• (Abbott et al., 1996). These researchers used information theory and neural decoding techniques to determine how the capacity to represent faces depends on the number of coding neurons. Monte Carlo simulations based on experimental data showed that the information grows linearly with the number of neurons. Firing rates of the fourteen recorded neurons could be used to distinguish between twenty face stimuli with approximately 80% accuracy. The representational capacity of N neurons of this type was estimated at about $3(2^{0.4N})$ different faces, at 50% discrimination accuracy.

• (Rolls, 1996). In a study involving ten plastic objects (shown to the monkey for a few weeks prior to the recording), each object-sensitive neuron was found to respond to a subset of the stimuli, rather to single stimuli.

Very recently, it became possible to apply functional magnetic resonance imaging (fMRI) techniques to the quantification of ensemble response properties of object-selective cells in the human brain. The impetus for this development was provided by an independent characterization of the lateral occipital (LO) object-selective complex (Malach et al., 1995). The results of this and related studies indicated that a cortical area responding to complex images and objects, but not to textures and simple stimuli, could be isolated and its functional properties could be defined. The discovery of the columnar organization of the IT cortex in the monkey and the evidence in favor of distributed rather than localized response patterns in that area together suggested that in addition to trying to associate stimulus categories with localized sub-regions within LO (Kanwisher et al., 1996; Kanwisher et al., 1997), it may be worth attempting to derive the structure of the object representation space from the entire response pattern across LO.

A series of fMRI experiments reported in (Edelman et al., 1998) provides an initial corroboration of this idea. In one experiment, subjects placed in a magnet were shown images of natural objects; some of the images were subdivided and scrambled. The results of this experiment showed that the activation of most voxels in object-related areas remains unaffected by a coarse scrambling of the images, suggesting that features optimally activating cells in LO are less complex than entire objects. In another experiment, subjects viewed images of objects from several shape categories. A map of the representation space derived by multidimensional scaling from the distributed pattern of voxel activation in LO showed a significant separation between the categories, indicating that distributed population response is a useful model of representation in LO (see figures 6.2 through 6.4).

### 6.3.3 Selective Invariance

Maximal invariance to viewing conditions is a desirable trait of any visual system. The Chorus model, which relies on relatively few object-specific modules to represent any stimulus, cannot be expected to exhibit uniformly high invariance for all objects. Specifically, the performance of Chorus is the nearest to full invariance for objects that are the most similar to the reference shapes on which the modules are trained.

Encouragingly, the invariance to viewing conditions found in the behavior of cells in monkey IT cortex is limited precisely in this manner: however invariant with respect to rotation, translation, scaling, etc., the response of an IT cell is necessarily specific to some class of objects. For those objects to which the cell responds optimally, the response is typically generalized over about $\pm 30^\circ$ rotation in depth, or a scale factor of two, or translation of about $10^\circ$ in the visual field.[8] The earlier studies did not report quantitative estimates of the extent of invariance regions along various dimensions of stimulus change. For example, the head-specific cells described in (Perrett et al., 1987) responded preferentially to certain orientation of the head in depth, and were said to generalize over other transformations, such as image position, size, image-plane orientation and illumination changes; no details were provided. In the "critical

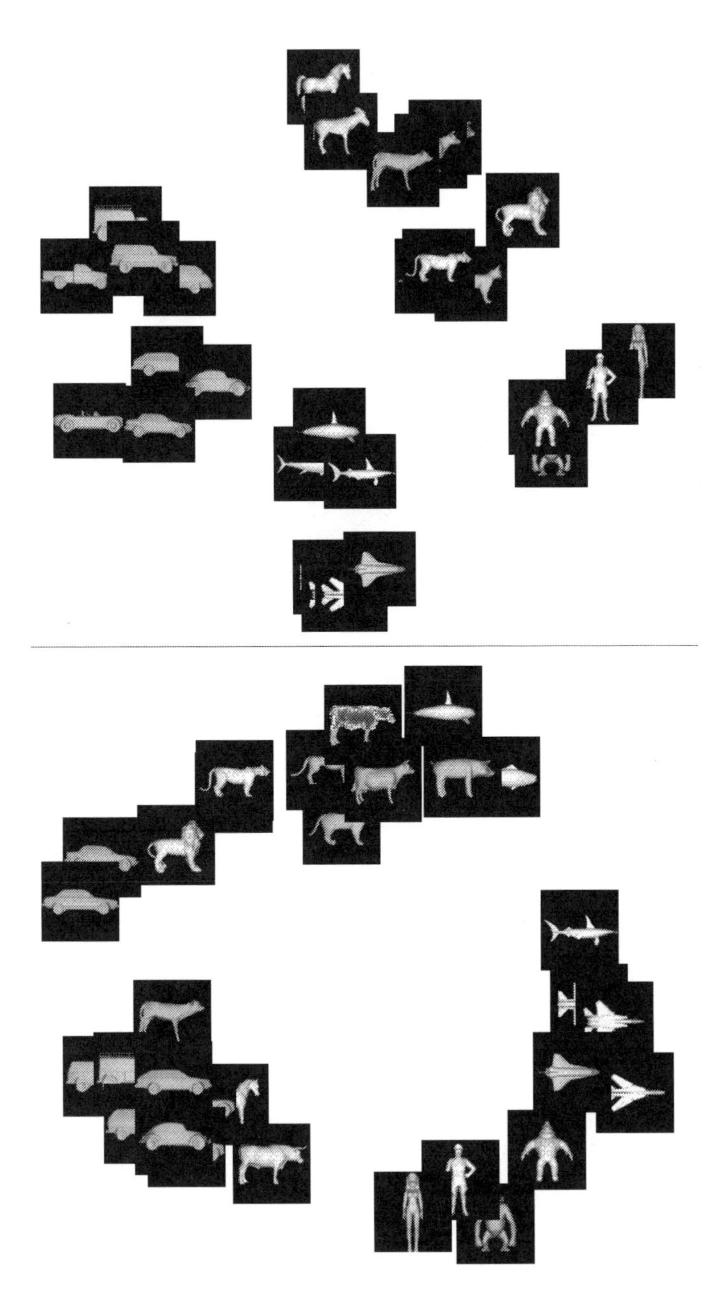

**Figure 6.2**
*(Top)* A two-dimensional MDS configuration of the thirty-two objects, recovered from the *psychophysically determined* dissimilarity matrix combined from all subjects. *(Bottom)* A two-dimensional MDS configuration of the thirty-two objects, recovered from the combined *voxel-space representation* derived from the most significant object-related voxels in all subjects. (See Edelman et al., 1998, for details.)

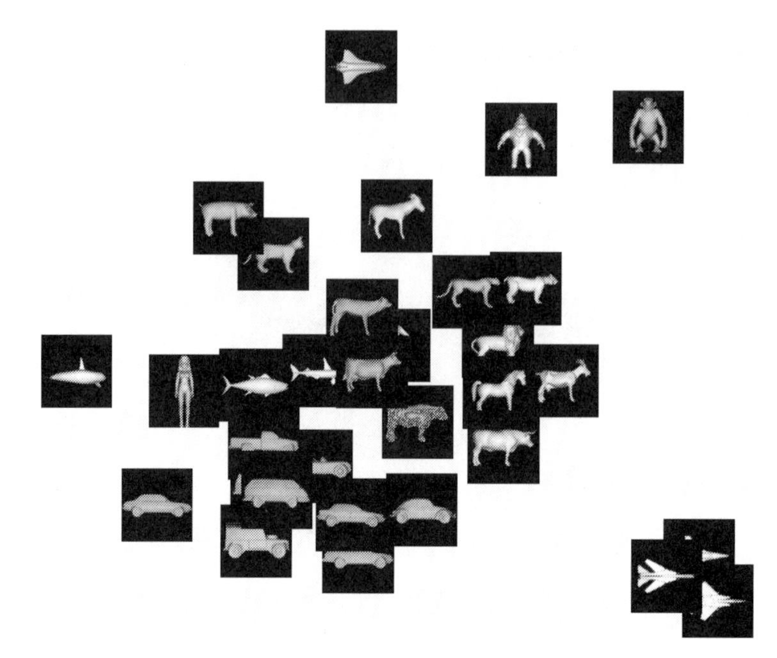

**Figure 6.3**
This two-dimensional MDS configuration of the thirty-two objects was recovered from the activation of 136 most significant object-sensitive voxels in five fMRI slices of a *single subject* (Edelman et al., 1998). Note how airplanes, cars and four-legged animals are clustered separately. In principle, this result allows an experimenter to make an educated guess as to the shape of a stimulus observed by a subject solely from the fMRI data of the observer (provided that the stimulus falls more or less within the region of the subject's shape space defined by the shapes that appear in this map).

feature" study (Tanaka et al., 1991), the cells were reported to exhibit some tolerance for size and location (about 13° × 13° in anterior IT).

Logothetis et al. (1995) found cells tuned to views of wire-like objects in the IT cortex, and reported a range of sensitivities to translation. Most cells only responded to stimuli within the parafovea; no response was elicited by stimuli at 7–10° eccentricity. For some cells, a translation of 2° reduced the response to baseline. The range of object sizes to which cells responded was 1–6°.

Tovee et al. (1994) measured the responses of IT cells in a fixation task, in which the stimuli could be placed in various locations of the visual field. The neurons were found to respond (at a level greater than $\frac{1}{2}$ of the

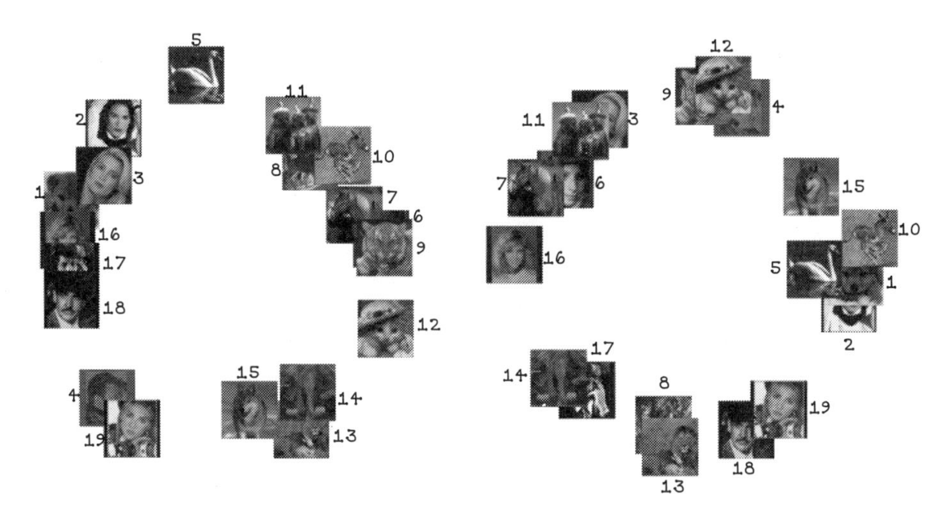


**Figure 6.4**
Post hoc shape space analysis of data from an experiment in which images of common objects were progressively scrambled to determine the "grain" of the representation in successive visual areas (Grill-Spector et al., 1998). *(Left)* MDS was applied to the most significant voxels in area LO which responded preferentially to entire objects but not to scrambled versions of these objects. Data were taken from seven subjects. Each image is labeled by its serial number in the epoch. Note that animals and faces form separate (in fact, nearly linearly separable) clusters. *(Right)* The significance of the results depicted on the left was assessed by a bootstrap procedure, in which the MDS analysis was applied to randomly permuted time-courses. Note that this plot reveals no clustering, indicating that the clusters on the left are statistically unlikely to be due to chance or to a data artifact.

maximum) even when the fixation spot was 2–5° beyond the edge of the face stimulus (which itself subtended 8–17°). Although the amplitude of cell responses varied with eccentricity, they maintained their selectivity across different faces.

Working with "critical features" of plastic toy objects, Ito et al. (1995) found that responses of seventeen out of thirty-three cells (responsive to critical features) were limited to a two-octave range of sizes; others responded over a wider range. The mean extent of a RF was 24°. Selectivity for shape was largely preserved over the size changes. Interestingly, the distribution of the optimal stimulus sizes was prominently bimodal, with peaks around 3.4° and 27°.

Rolls (1996) argued that translation invariance in cortical cells should be tested in situations where more than one stimulus is present in the visual field. Indeed, the amplitude of the responses of cells in one study was found to be modulated by the presence of other objects in the receptive fields of the cells (Rolls and Tovee, 1995a). This finding is reminiscent of the interactions among simultaneously presented stimuli reported in (Moran and Desimone, 1985). In that work, single cells were recorded in extrastriate area V4 of monkeys trained to attend to stimuli in one location in the visual field and to ignore stimuli at another location. When both locations were within the RF of a V4 cell, the response to the unattended stimulus was "dramatically" reduced (this was not true for cells in the primary visual area V1). In other words, a stimulus that was demonstrably effective when attended to, was rendered completely ineffective when ignored by the animal. A similar ability of IT cells to "switch" from one object to another was described more recently by (Chelazzi et al., 1993).

### 6.3.4 Plasticity and Learning

The stimulus-specific quasi-invariance of tuning properties of cortical cells is complemented by an ever-present capacity for modification of these properties in response to changing patterns of stimulation (Gilbert, 1994). Although novel stimuli are not likely to be treated in an optimal fashion, learning processes operating on a time scale of weeks or months ensure the emergence of mechanisms tuned to such stimuli (Kobatake et al., 1992).[9] In the latter study, twenty-eight two-dimensional shapes (black polygons on white background) were presented to the monkey on a daily basis, in an animal-initiated delayed matching to sample task, for a year. Following this training period, 39% of cells in IT gave a maximum response to one of the twenty-eight trained stimuli in trained monkeys; only 9% did so in untrained monkeys. This malleability of the representations in IT led Tanaka to hypothesize that "new columns are created in the IT cortex as a result of training" (Tanaka, 1993a).

Short practice with stimuli can also cause re-tuning of the system (Li et al., 1993; Rolls et al., 1989). In some cases, even one-shot learning leads to a markedly improved performance. For example, Rolls, Tovee and Ramachandran (1993) reported learning on a five-second time scale. The monkeys in their experiments were shown high-contrast black and white faces blended with the background. Human subjects cannot recognize such pictures easily, unless the object depicted in the image is familiar to them. A few seconds later, the monkeys were shown easily recognizable gray-scale images of the same faces. Amazingly, cells that responded to the latter stimuli but not to the original high-contrast images, did respond to the originals when these were returned after a few more seconds.

Another kind of plasticity, which combines the ability to represent novel objects with the ability to form associations between pairs of such objects, was found by Miyashita and his colleagues (Sakai and Miyashita, 1991; Sakai et al., 1994). The monkeys in these experiments learned to associate images whose only relationship was that of successive presentation; following training, neurons encoding the newly learned associations were found in the IT cortex.[10]

### 6.3.5 Speed of Processing

The last characteristic of the cells in IT cortex to be mentioned in the present brief survey is that of response time. Because Chorus is an essentially feedforward model, it predicts that the outcome of recognition should be discernible in IT a very short time after the onset of the stimulus. Indeed, backward masking experiments, in which the processing time available for a given stimulus is limited artificially by following it up with a disruptive mask, indicated that as little as twenty to thirty milliseconds suffice for the development of a full response in IT. Specifically, the activity of neurons that respond to non-scrambled faces (but not to scrambled faces) was found to become significant as the SOA (stimulus onset asynchrony, or the delay between the stimulus and the mask) is increased over twenty *msec* (Rolls et al., 1994).

It is interesting to note that in the same displays, human subjects could identify one out of six faces (Rolls and Tovee, 1994). Although the response time of individual neurons cannot be measured directly in humans, indirect methods such as the analysis of event-related scalp potentials (ERPs) can be brought to bear on the issue. In one study using ERPs (Thorpe et al., 1996), the subjects had to detect the presence of an animal in previously unseen photographs flashed for twenty *msec* (without subsequent masking of the stimulus). The fifteen subjects tested in this experiment (each for at least 700 trials) exhibited a 94% mean correct rate. Importantly, a negative ERP associated with the successful detection of an animal in the image was found at a delay of just 150 *msec* after stimulus onset.

### 6.3.6 A Summary of Neurobiological Support for SiC

The neurobiological findings just surveyed suggest that all the mechanisms necessary for supporting a biological implementation of SiC are actually present in primate vision. One may recall at this stage that the basic building block of SiC is a module tuned (i.e., responding selectively) to a particular object. Evidence for the existence of such modules has been available for a long time, ever since the first reports of face cells found in the inferotemporal (IT) cortex in the monkey were made around 1972. Theories of object representation based on storing specific views, developed in the last decade, offer a concrete and credible computational interpretation to the findings of the face cells.

Furthermore, what seems to have been the main objection to those findings—the implausibility of the very notion of a grandmother cell—is neutralized by the idea of distributed coding as it is applied to shape. According to the opposition, the existence of grandmother cells was implausible because too many cells would have been required to represent the many combinations of the primitive features likely to be found in the real world. This objection, however, does not take into account the possibility of new objects being represented by graded patterns of activities of modules (cells) tuned to familiar ones—a possibility that has been proved workable by the results described in chapter 5.

In summary, the mechanisms needed to support SiC seem to be present in the primate visual system. It is possible, however, that their actual function is different, or that they are altogether irrelevant to the process of object recognition. For example, it may be that the principle on which the IT cortex operates is that of reconstruction and subsequent structural representation. In that case, the finding of object-tuned cells would be a by-product of the process of representation, rather than its implementational substrate. At the same time, another mechanism would assume the central role. For example, if a theory of the kind espoused by Hummel and Biederman (1992) were a good model of the object recognition in primate vision, then the crucial finding would be that of the binding mechanisms postulated by that theory. Indeed, phenomena possibly indicating the existence of such mechanisms have been reported recently. It seems clear, therefore, that neurophysiology alone cannot decide the issue, mainly because of the difficulty of determining unequivocally whether the cells' function in representation and recognition is actually that which they seem to perform in an experimental setting.

## 6.4 Psychophysics: Effects of Viewpoint

The ambiguities in the interpretation of neurobiological data can be reduced to some extent by bringing behavioral evidence to bear on the distinction between the competing models. If the predictions of such a model are found to be incompatible with the outcomes of psychophysical experiments designed to test them, it is likely that the explanation of the workings of that model at the level of neurobiology is misguided. In the remainder of this chapter, the various theories mentioned in this book will be put just to such a test.

Psychophysical studies of recognition typically report two kinds of variables that measure the subject's performance: those that have to do with response time, and those that pertain to the accuracy of the response. Most frequently, the former is simply the response time (RT) itself, and the latter the error rate (ER), computed over a number of trials (e.g., over the repetitions of some combination of experimental conditions). There is a good reason for treating RT and ER effects separately: algorithmic solutions to an information processing problem may differ in their computational complexity, yet obey the same underlying constraint dictated, for example, by the choice of architecture.[11] Thus, while the examination of response time data may reveal something about the processes involved in recognition, insights into the limitations of those processes and the nature of the underlying representations require an analysis of the error rate patterns.

### 6.4.1 Canonical Views

The most glaring dependence of recognition performance on orientation is found, not surprisingly, in objects that can be *expected* to possess a preferred orientation, either because it is part of the definition of their shapes, or because they only appear at a limited range of orientations. Two families of such objects are alphanumeric characters and faces (Rock, 1973; Rock et al., 1994; see figure 6.5). For characters, both

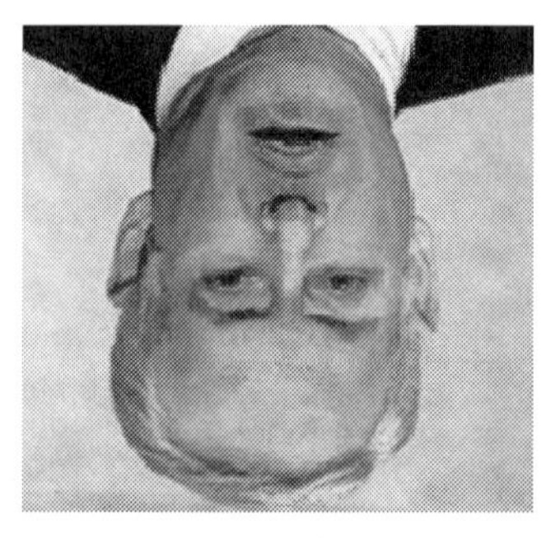

**Figure 6.5**
Words and faces possess a preferred orientation, which may be the main reason they appear strange when rotated. *(Left)* A modified inverted text. *(Right)* A modified (Thatcherized) inverted face, after Rock (1974) and Thompson (1980). Turn the book upside down to see the extent of the illusions.

factors just mentioned contribute to the effect of orientation: an inverted p is identical to a d. Perhaps because character orientation is important, people rarely pay attention to inverted or even mildly rotated text, even when they are exposed to it. In fact, the predominance of characters oriented "the right side up" in the visual experience of a reader is so overwhelming that one wonders not why inverted words appear difficult to read, but rather why they can be read at all without having to be physically reoriented.

For faces, statistics of exposure is the main determinant of the orientation preference. People, unlike, say, monkeys, rarely see faces upside down.[12] Presumably as a result of this bias, one is surprised to see that a processed face image in which the mouth and the eyes have been cut out and pasted back after being flipped appears only mildly strange when viewed upside down, but does look bizarre when viewed the right side up (Thompson, 1980).

Statistics of exposure may affect recognition of objects rotated in depth, and not only around the line of sight. Thus, objects that are normally seen from a limited range of angles are *expected* to be easier to recognize when seen from a familiar orientation. The first indication that not only characters or faces possess a preferred orientation came from a seminal study involving recognition of rotated common objects—horse, house, car, etc. (Palmer, Rosch and Chase, 1981).[13] It turned out that some views of such objects are easier to process, as indicated by the shorter response times elicited by those views (Palmer et al., 1981). In a series of experiments, Palmer et al. found that those views, termed *canonical*, were also judged as subjectively "better" than randomly picked views, and were consistently chosen by independent observers as the preferred views from which representative photographs of the objects should be taken, or the views from which these objects were most typically imagined. The canonicalness of a view could be predicted from the visibility of its surfaces and from its subjective importance for determining the identity of the object.

The possibility that the existence of canonical views and other effects of orientation stem from mere statistics of the subjects' prior exposure to the stimuli and not from factors intrinsic to the processes of representation and recognition was the main reason for the introduction of novel objects into the transformation experiments. Novel objects offer the experimenter a better control over the orientation (and hence the appearance) of the stimuli at the time of the formation of their representation in the subject's long-term memory. Recognition experiments involving novel objects can exert such control in several ways. First, the novel stimuli can be shown to the subjects during a familiarization stage from a wide range of attitudes covering the entire viewing sphere, so as not to create a bias towards any particular view (Edelman and Bülthoff, 1992b; Cutzu and Edelman, 1994). Second, the subjects can be given control over the views they are to be shown, and their choices can be kept track of (Perrett and Harries, 1988; Blanz et al., 1996). Third, the range of views with which the subjects are familiarized prior to testing can be artificially restricted, allowing the degree and the manner of generalization to novel views to be assessed (Tarr and Pinker, 1989; Bülthoff and Edelman, 1992). I shall return to describe experiments belonging to each of these categories later in this chapter.

### 6.4.2 Mental Rotation

In certain matching tasks, such as deciding whether or not two simultaneously viewed objects can be brought into congruence by rotation, the solution can be achieved, in principle, by constructing and transforming representations that are geometrically isomorphic to the stimuli. Under certain assumptions, the matching time will then grow monotonically with some measure of the extent of the transformation, such as the difference in orientation between two objects.[14] In particular, if the rotation is presumed to be carried out at a constant angular speed, the decision time will depend linearly on the extent of necessary transformation.

Following this logic, Shepard and Metzler (1971) presented subjects with a task that required them to decide whether two shapes shown side by side were congruent (related by a rigid motion—in that case, rotation in the image plane or in depth) or enantiomorphic (related by a mirror transformation in addition to rotation). They found that if the objects were congruent, the subjects indeed took longer to respond when the orientation difference between the objects was larger. Moreover, the dependence of RT on misorientation between the two stimuli was found to be nearly linear. This remarkable finding led to a flurry of experimental studies of mental rotation; some of these are summarized in Shepard and Cooper (1982).

The classical setup in which mental rotation was first found did not involve referral to long-term memory representations. Some of the subsequent studies exploring issues related to mental rotation did require the subject to match the viewed stimulus against a stored representation. These studies concentrated on the response times of subjects required to name misoriented stimuli. Initially, these were line drawings of common objects rotated around the line of sight (Jolicoeur, 1985; Jolicoeur and Landau, 1984). Later experiments examined both image-plane and in-depth rotation, using a variety of objects which could be rendered at progressively greater degrees of photorealism (Rock and DiVita, 1987; Tarr and Pinker, 1989; Bülthoff and Edelman, 1992; Edelman and Bülthoff, 1992b; Humphrey and Khan, 1992; Tarr, 1995).[15]

Mental rotation experiments in which the two stimuli to be compared are shown side by side leave no doubt as to the orientations that are to be matched. In comparison, in memory or recognition experiments only one of the orientations is known—that of the stimulus. The "orientation" of the object encoded in the memory trace that is compared to the stimulus, and, indeed, the very possibility to treat representations of objects as orientable in some sense, should be considered in this case open to theoretical debate. The theory that seems to be the most closely related to the notion of mental rotation—normalization by alignment (Ullman, 1989)—does not, in fact, provide an unequivocal prediction concerning either the time course of recognition or the orientedness of memory representations of objects. For one thing, several distinct versions of alignment algorithms were proposed. According to one of them, the memory representation of an object is a 3D geometrical construct, which can be rotated at need, until its projection matches the appearance of the stimulus to be recognized. In this version, the notion of a "home" orientation is ill defined, and experimental findings of such orientations (to be discussed in a moment) can be accommodated post hoc.

In another version of alignment, a number of 2D views of each object are stored and transformed as necessary. An experimental assessment of this kind of alignment, also known as multiple views plus transformation,[16] was reported in Tarr and Pinker (1989). Subjects in that study were trained on some views, then tested on new views of the same objects. Letter-like asymmetrical patterns were used in conjunction with image-plane rotation; the results were later extended to 3D stimuli composed of small cubes. Tarr and Pinker found that RT grows with misorientation between the test view and the stored one. Following practice, this effect disappears, but is restored once another new view is introduced.

In mental rotation, the effects of rotating objects in depth are more interesting and potentially more revealing about the underlying computational substrate than those of image-plane rotation, because the former changes the apparent shape of objects, and may cause self-occlusion. Rotation in depth was the focus of the study of Tarr (1995), which involved seven asymmetric objects composed of cubic parts, similar to those used in the original mental rotation study (Shepard and Metzler, 1971). The stimuli were assigned nonsense labels; the subjects had to learn these, and had to learn to construct the objects from Lego-like cubes, to familiarize themselves with the stimuli prior to the experiment. In each experimental trial, the subject had to decide whether the stimulus image belonged to a target object or to an enantiomorph; auditory feedback was given for wrong responses. The data in this experiment revealed RT effects consistent with the idea of rotation to the nearest familiar view. Another experiment reported in Tarr (1995) used a naming instead of a handedness decision task; it revealed the same effects as the first one.

Other researchers corroborated the findings of Tarr and Pinker (1989) and Tarr (1995) in a variety of experimental conditions. The telltale dependence of RT on viewpoint was found in a series of one-interval forced-choice experiments involving novel wireframe objects (Edelman and Weinshall, 1991; Edelman and Bülthoff, 1992b). Importantly, the ER was always affected in the same way as RT (that is, views that took longer to recognize were also causing more mistakes). These findings were taken to support the idea that objects are represented by collections of views, with familiar views being recognized faster and more accurately than novel ones (more on that in section 6.4.4).

The debate between proponents of object-centered representation theories and viewpoint-centered models (of which Chorus happens to be an example) pervades much of the discussion that surrounds mental rotation and related phenomena. According to some researchers (Perrett et al., 1987), viewpoint-centered representations are merely an intermediate stage in the formation of an object-centered, *nec plus ultra* representation envisaged by Marr. On this account, findings of viewpoint-dependent performance result from experiments that tap the early stage of object representation. At any rate, it seems to be very difficult to coax the visual system to bypass this early viewpoint-dependent stage altogether, even if the proper (i.e., "object-centered") information is included in the stimulus. For example, the subjects of Gibson and Peterson (1994), confronted with a figure-ground discrimination task, were given orientation cues (outlines of figure parts) which preceded the appearance of rotated stimuli. These advance cues did not, however, speed up the response times, leading Gibson and Peterson to conclude that their subjects could not access object-centered representations of the stimulus before its actual presentation and presumed normalization by an alignment-like process.

Although the visual system seems to be reluctant to take advantage of artificially introduced orientation cues, it is sensitive enough to object-centered information that is naturally present in the stimulus. This was demonstrated by ingenious experiments that estimated the amount of various kinds of shape information present in wireframe stimuli and compared these to the actual information taken into account by the subjects (Liu et al., 1995). These experiments showed that subject efficiency with respect to the information present in the stimulus can be as high as 20%.

Moreover, human efficiency with respect to an 2D ideal observer (that is, a process that takes into account *all* the 2D shape information present in a stimulus) exceeded 100%, indicating that shape cues in addition to the 2D information must have been processed by the human subjects.

The obvious candidates for such additional cues are depth and other kinds of 3D information.[17] The situation here is, however, more complicated than it seems at first glance. A study that specifically explored the role of depth in the recognition of wireframe objects revealed that binocular stereo (available both during familiarization with the objects and during subsequent testing) had the unexpected effect of lowering the mean error rate without reducing the dependence of ER on misorientation of the object with respect to a familiar view (Edelman and Bülthoff, 1992b). At the very least, this means that 3D cues are not encoded in the human visual system in an object-centered manner (which would have resulted in better viewpoint invariance across the board).

### 6.4.3 Nonlinearities and the Effects of Practice

Although the initial reports of mental rotation by Shepard and his colleagues described the dependence of RT on orientation as linear, significant nonlinear components were found in subsequent studies (Koriat and Norman, 1985; Edelman and Bülthoff, 1992b; Tarr, 1995). It is difficult to decide whether or not this nonlinearity is an embarrassment for the mental rotation hypothesis. On the one hand, if something is being rotated inside the subject's head, it should have momentum (Freyd, 1983) in addition to velocity, leading to nonlinearities in the plot of rotation angle vs. time. On the other hand, in mechanics an object must have mass to possess momentum, and the notion of mass is hardly relevant to the psychobiology of representation.

Cutzu and Edelman (1994) attempted to characterize in computational terms the nature of canonical views of a class of wireframe objects (figure 6.6) and to decide whether fixed-rate rotation is a good functional model of the process whereby novel views of such objects are recognized. The observers were first familiarized with the stimuli, which were shown rotating on the computer screen for several revolutions, with the axis of rotation slowly precessing. Thus, all views that were subsequently tested were shown to the subject for the same duration. The subjects were then

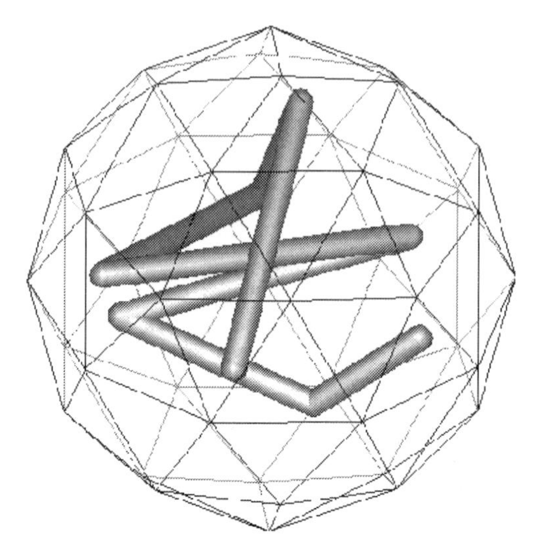

**Figure 6.6**
Stimuli such as this seven-segment wire-like object were used in a controlled quantitative study of the canonical views phenomenon (Cutzu and Edelman, 1994). The amount of visible surface of the objects as seen from different viewpoints was kept nearly constant by equalizing the three principal moments of inertia to within 5%. The vertices of the enclosing polyhedron in this illustration indicate the viewpoints for which recognition was tested.

required to perform a yes/no recognition tasks on views of target objects, interspersed with views of distractors that belonged to the same general class.

Perhaps the most surprising finding in this experiment was the very existence of preferred or canonical views (these were defined as views for which the combined RT and ER score was the lowest). Such views were far from universal: the best view according to one subject's data was often hardly recognized by the other subjects. A subject by subject analysis showed that the RT/ER scores were not linearly dependent on the shortest angular distance in 3D to the best view, as predicted by the mental rotation theories of recognition. Rather, the performance was significantly correlated with an image-plane feature by feature deformation distance between the presented view and the best (shortest-RT and lowest-ER) view (figure 6.7). These results undermine the mental rotation hypothesis, and suggest that measurement of image-plane similarity

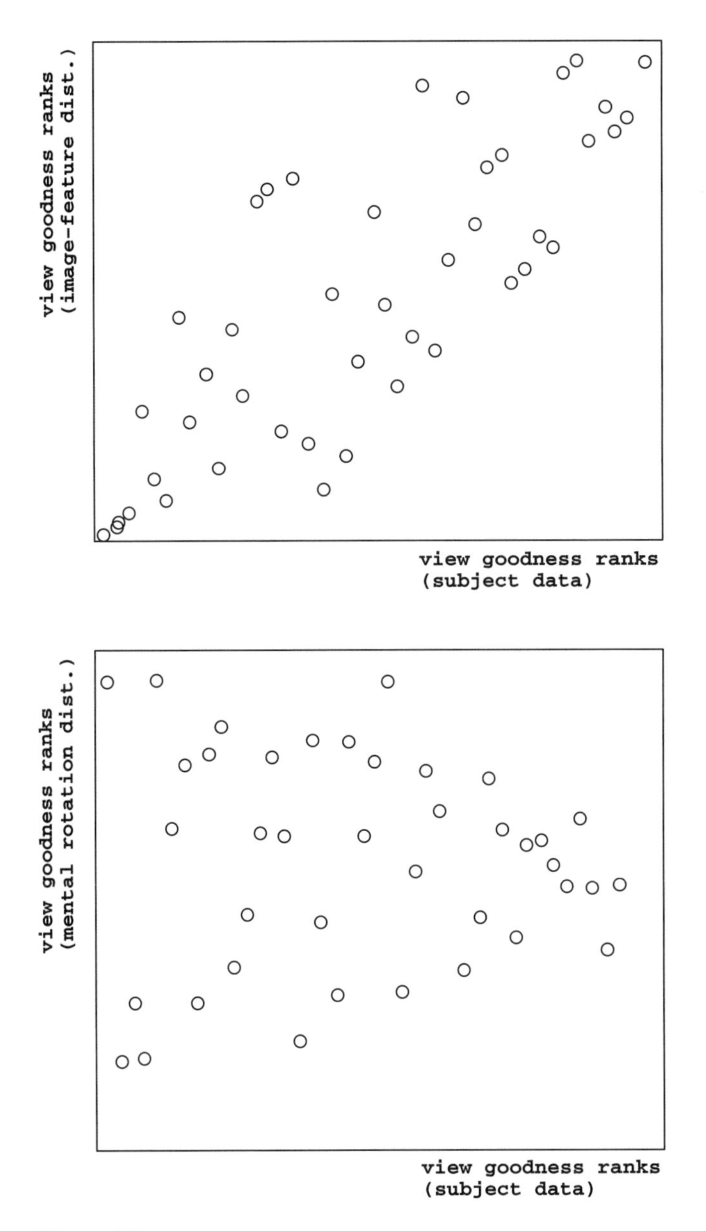


Figure 6.7
View goodness data for one of the subjects and one of the stimuli, replotted from Cutzu and Edelman (1994). *(Top)* A scatter diagram plotting view goodness ranks predicted by an image-based feature distance formula against ranks derived from subject data. Spearman (rank) correlation is 0.7 ($p < 0.0001$). *(Bottom)* View goodness ranks predicted by the mental rotation distance to the canonical view, plotted against subject data. Spearman correlation is 0.03, n.s.

to a few (subject-specific) feature patterns is a better model of the process whereby the human visual system recognizes objects across changes in their 3D orientation.

A central component of these results is the possibility not only to account for the dependence of RT on orientation, but also to bring into consideration the observed ERs, which were included in the definition of view goodness. For reasons I already mentioned, ER patterns offer a better insight into the workings of a recognition system than RT patterns. Most importantly, unlike the "regular" mental rotation effects having to do with RT, the ER effects do not disappear with practice.

Consider, for example, the study of Tarr (1995), where the dependence of RT on the angle of rotation was found to become gradually weaker with practice. Although this result was described as an increase in the rate of putative rotation, it is better seen as a gradual disappearance of the mental rotation effect with practice. The fading of the RT effect, the nonlinearity of rotation in the sessions where it was present, and the similar effect involving the ER, none of which can be accounted for by the classical mental rotation hypothesis, all suggest that the explanatory value of this hypothesis is more limited than is usually thought.

This conclusion is borne out by the outcome of a series of experiments described in (Edelman and Bülthoff, 1992b). The novel wireframe objects in these experiments were shown in motion or binocular stereo, so as to give the subjects the opportunity to form a viewpoint-independent (i.e., object-centered) representation, if they could. The first experiment tested the recognition of objects seen repeatedly from the same set of viewpoints. Although the RTs in this experiment became uniform with practice, the differences in ER for the different views remained stable. In the second experiment, this result was replicated in the presence of a variety of depth cues in the test views, including binocular stereo. In the third experiment, recognition under monocular and stereoscopic conditions was compared over four testing sessions. In those two experiments, it was found that the addition of stereo depth reduced the mean ER, but affected neither the general pattern of performance over different views, nor its development with practice. The fourth experiment probed the ability of subjects to generalize recognition to unfamiliar views of objects previously seen at a limited range of attitudes, both under monocular and stereoscopic viewing. As I already mentioned briefly in the preceding section, the same increase in the error rate with misorientation relative to the training attitude was obtained in the two conditions. Taken together, these results support the notion that 3D objects are represented by multiple specific views, possibly augmented by partial viewer-centered three-dimensional information, if it is available through stereopsis.

### 6.4.4 A Model of Canonical Views and Mental Rotation

Although effects that are usually interpreted as mental rotation require practice to fully manifest themselves and disappear with further practice, they are clearly present in a wide range of situations. The ability to transform mentally the image of an object presupposes a particular kind of representation, namely, mental images. How are these representations related to computational models such as Chorus and to neurobiologically defined mechanisms such as units tuned to particular objects?

As pointed out by Palmer (1978), a great deal of confusing terminology and improperly posed questions must be overcome before one can get down to investigating these questions. For example, it was once widely believed that the interpretation of the results of mental rotation studies touched on a deep controversy: the distinction between "analog" (image-like) and "symbolic" (proposition-like) representations (Pylyshyn, 1973; Kosslyn et al., 1979). This particular theory-laden dilemma became irrelevant following the emergence of alternative theories, which avoided both of its horns (a tuned unit is neither an analog nor a symbolic representation in the usual sense).

Attempts to make headway while skirting empty dogmas have been made by asking what is rotated in mental rotation. Two distinct possibilities here are the stimulus image and the reference frame (Koriat and Norman, 1984). However, even when experimental evidence is obtained in support of one or the other of the possibilities, the mechanisms behind the phenomena—the very meaning of "rotation"—remain unclear. As before, an unexpected third alternative offers the most promising answer to the question "what is rotated, the image or the reference frame?" The answer, implicit in Cooper (1976), is "neither." According to Cooper, a gradual analog process whose successive stages can be put into a one-to-one correspondence with successive orientations of the stimulus gives rise to a semblance of rotation.[18] This process need not operate on "analog" representations such as images: activation spread in a network of "laterally" connected tuned units, each responding preferentially to some view of the stimulus, can do the job.

A network of units tuned to different views of an object (Seibert and Waxman, 1990; Edelman and Weinshall, 1991; Wallis and Rolls, 1997) is the backbone of an RBF module of the kind used in the preceding chapters to implement Chorus. To make such a network simulate mental rotation, view-specific units must be connected in a particular order, reflecting the order of views encountered during the object's rotation or its circumnavigation by the observer (this requirement may explain the initial improvement of rotation with practice). This creates within the network a pattern of connected units that is isomorphic to the view space of the target object—a *footprint* of the view space. The spread of activation in the network can then simulate mental rotation, as envisaged by Cooper.[19]

Here is what happens in this model when activation is injected at a specific point of a footprint as a result of the system's exposure to a test view (Edelman and Weinshall, 1991). First, activation spreads to the footprint-neighbors of the tuned unit corresponding to the test view. Second, a higher-stage unit computes a (weighted) sum of the activities of the footprint constituents and compares the result to a threshold. The degree of similarity between the pattern of activity and the pattern of weights is interpreted as the model's analog of response time. The dependence of this measure on viewpoint (that is, on the initial locus of activation) is the counterpart of the canonical views phenomenon (see figure 6.8, top).

The simulated response time not only varies with viewpoint: because of the sequential structure of the footprint, it depends on the viewpoint in an orderly fashion, resembling the typical pattern of mental rotation. When the same views on which the model had been trained appear in a different order, the original sequential structure of the footprint is weakened, because of the emergence of new "lateral" links between different tuned units that are not necessarily adjacent to each other in the footprint (see figure 6.8, bottom). Eventually, the interconnection pattern of the

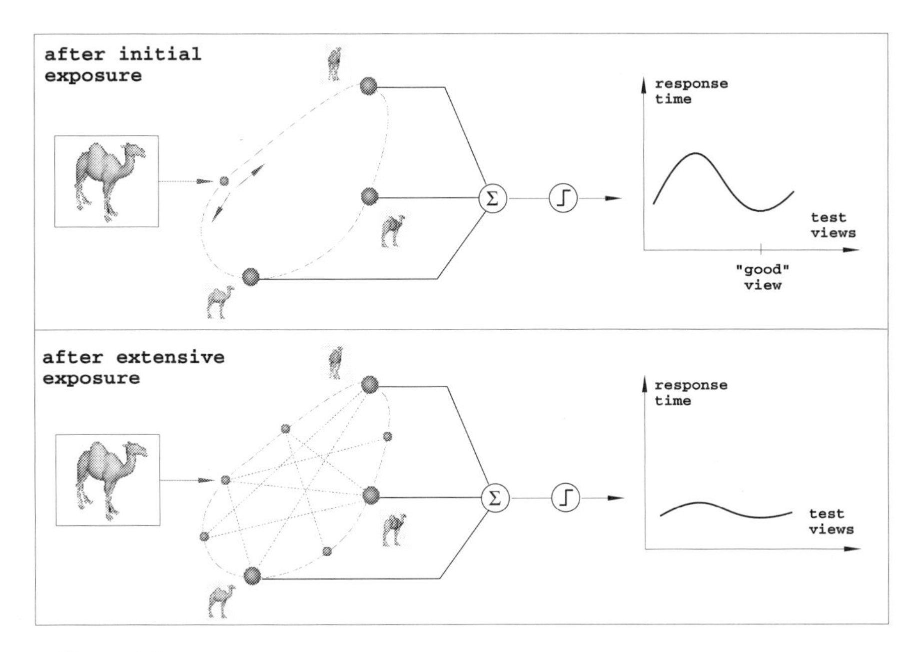


Figure 6.8
A model of "mental rotation" in recognition (after Edelman and Weinshall, 1991; Edelman, 1991). *(Top)* A schematic illustration of the *footprint* of an object—a distributed representation of its view space (see text). Immediately after training with an orderly sequence of views that arises, e.g., when the object is rotating, its footprint (dashed line) possesses a sequential structure. The spread of activation through the footprint (illustrated by the arrows) following exposure to a test view (shown surrounded by a frame) creates a semblance of mental rotation: (1) a higher stage charged with comparing the distribution of activities of view-specific units to a pattern stored during training reaches its firing threshold in a shorter time for some test views (termed canonical), but not for others; (2) the time to firing depends monotonically on the misorientation of the test view relative to the canonical one. *(Bottom)* Practice-induced association between non-neighbor views creates shortcuts across the footprint. Because of this, the initial dependency of "response time" on viewpoint is lost, due to the weakening of the original footprint structure.

participating units becomes amorphous, causing the manifestation of mental rotation, which is epiphenomenal to the structure of the footprint, to disappear.

This model, which was shown to replicate both the basic mental rotation phenomenon and its disappearance with practice (Edelman and Weinshall, 1991), embodies an isomorphism between the temporal succession of views of a rotating object and the spatial adjacency of the representations of these views in a selectively interconnected network (Seibert and Waxman, 1990; Stone, 1996b; Sinha and Poggio, 1996; Wallis and Rolls, 1997). It is interesting to consider the theoretical underpinnings of this idea in view of the distinction between first-order ($\mathcal{F}$) and second-order ($\mathcal{S}$) isomorphic representations, proposed by Shepard at about the same time that the first mental rotation studies were carried out in his laboratory. It may seem that the representations that are transformed must be $\mathcal{F}$-isomorphic to their objects, to enable a meaningful comparison following transformation.[20] The conceptually problematic $\mathcal{F}$-isomorphism is, however, unnecessary. If the representational system is $\mathcal{S}$-isomorphic to the world—that is, if relationships among objects rather than (or in addition to) the objects themselves are being mirrored in the system—the transformation of representations can be substituted for the transformation of the objects.[21] Thus, the model described above fits within the SiC framework both architecturally (because it relies on an RBF-like network of units tuned to specific views) and conceptually (because it conforms to the basic idea of $\mathcal{S}$-isomorphism).

### 6.4.5 Viewpoint Invariance as a Tool for Testing Theories of Representation

The model outlined in the preceding section aims to explain both the existence of mental rotation effects and the eventual shift towards viewpoint-invariant performance. The elementary building block of this model, and, more generally, of the Chorus scheme, is a unit tuned to a particular view of a particular object, and the basic operation is interpolation between such views. Accordingly, when considered as a psychological model of recognition, Chorus leads one to expect inherently viewpoint-dependent performance, although this can become effectively invariant following extensive practice with a given object.

A competing school of thought in the psychology of recognition claims that objects are represented as qualitatively defined structures composed of generic parts (Biederman, 1985; Biederman, 1987). In contrast to Chorus, models derived from this theory predict an inherently viewpoint-invariant performance, because both the generic parts and their structural relationships are presumably discernible no matter what the orientation of the object is. Because the universal quantifier implied by this claim is clearly unwarranted by the experimental data (for example, by the canonical views and mental rotation phenomena), its scope is usually narrowed down to the effect that recognition is, as a rule, invariant for most objects, or in most tasks that count as recognition (in other words, generically), and that viewpoint-dependent performance is a rare exception to the rule.

Predictions concerning viewpoint invariance can be derived also from the other theories mentioned in chapter 2. Theories that rely on geometric constraints generally predict a uniformly low error rate across different views (the dependence of response time on viewpoint in this case remains unspecified, because geometric constraints can be brought to bear on recognition in a variety of ways, according to a particular algorithm). A uniform low error rate is predicted also by the feature-space theories. Unlike view interpolation and structural description theories, geometric constraints and feature spaces have not been championed as models of human vision. The following discussion will, therefore, concentrate on the two former theories.

### Evidence Concerning Viewpoint Invariance

The current central role of viewpoint invariance in deciding between competing theories of representation is rather curious, given that for most of the history of visual psychophysics it was assumed to be a non-issue. As late as 1980, Marr could (and did) take invariance of human recognition performance safely for granted; the only exceptions to the rule of invariance seemed to be the cases where objects were presented in severely foreshortened views. The year 1981 saw the beginning of a revolt against this dogma, in the form of the seminal paper on canonical views (Palmer et al., 1981) and Rock's pioneering work on the effect of rotation in depth on recognition performance.[22]

The next decade brought about an intense debate rather than a settlement of the viewpoint invariance issue (Biederman and Gerhardstein, 1995; Tarr and Bülthoff, 1995; Bülthoff et al., 1995). On the one hand, viewpoint-invariant recognition performance was reported for both common and novel objects in a variety of tasks (Eley, 1982; Biederman, 1985; Cooper et al., 1992; Biederman and Gerhardstein, 1993; Biederman and Gerhardstein, 1995; Bar and Biederman, 1995). On the other hand, performance was found to fall short of invariance in at least as many cases. Specifically, lack of invariance was reported for the following kinds of stimuli: line drawings of common objects (Bartram, 1976; Jolicoeur and Kosslyn, 1983; Lawson et al., 1994), photographs of common objects (Ellis et al., 1989), and a spate of novel 3D objects such as paperclip shapes (Rock and DiVita, 1987; Bülthoff and Edelman, 1992; Edelman and Bülthoff, 1992b), cube structures (Tarr, 1995), widgets composed of "geons" (Humphrey and Khan, 1992; Kurbat, 1994; Hayward, 1998), amoeboid blobs (Bülthoff and Edelman, 1992), as well as whole potatoes (Perrett and Harries, 1988) and objects shaped like potato chips (Farah et al., 1994). Furthermore, departures from invariance were found in tasks such as imagination and long-exposure recognition (Rock et al., 1989), naming (Tarr and Pinker, 1989; Tarr, 1995), handedness discrimination (Tarr and Pinker, 1989), one-interval forced-choice target recognition (Bülthoff and Edelman, 1992; Edelman and Bülthoff, 1992b), priming (Srinivas, 1993; Lawson et al., 1994), delayed matching to sample (Edelman, 1995a), and picture matching (Lawson and Humphreys, 1996). Finally, the viewpoint-dependent performance found in human subjects has been also replicated in monkeys (Logothetis et al., 1994). A review of the extensive literature that reports various violations of viewpoint invariance can be found in (Jolicoeur and Humphrey, 1998).

These days, when a reasonable reply to the question "is recognition viewpoint invariant?" seems to be, "yes and no" (Farah et al., 1994; Tarr, 1995), one wonders how the conflicting psychological data can be brought to bear on theoretical issues such as the choice of a proper computational model of human performance. As always, experiments specifically designed to test particular theories are the most promising option. Such a study, which used novel objects to achieve a better control over the experimental conditions, provided the first direct support for the view-interpolation theory that constitutes the basis of the Chorus scheme (Bülthoff and Edelman, 1992). This experiment explored the ability of the human visual system to generalize recognition from familiar to novel views of paperclip-like objects, such as the one shown in figure 6.6. The relative arrangement of familiar and novel views in the view space, illustrated in figure 6.9, was chosen carefully, so as to test three theories of object recognition: viewpoint normalization or alignment of 3D models (Ullman, 1989) and linear combination of 2D views (Ullman and Basri, 1991) (both of the geometric constraint variety), and view interpolation (Poggio and Edelman, 1990).

The three theories predicted different patterns of generalization to novel views, ranging from uniformly good performance on all three kinds of test views (INTER, EXTRA and ORTHO; see figure 6.9) for 3D alignment, through uniformly good performance for test views that can be expressed as a linear combination of the familiar views (that is, INTER and EXTRA) for the linear combination theory, to better performance for INTER compared to EXTRA or ORTHO views for view interpolation. The outcome of this experiment was compatible with the latter prediction. It was replicated by a computational model that consisted of an RBF network whose basis functions in the view space were centered on the familiar views that had been presented to the subjects during training. Taken together, these results suggested that the human visual system is better described as carrying out nonlinear view interpolation (of the kind required by Chorus) than geometrically precise operations such as alignment.

**Recognition by Components (RBC) as a Theory of Viewpoint Invariance**

A serious shortcoming of the experiment described above, which it shares with a number of other studies that found recognition performance to be viewpoint-dependent (Rock and DiVita, 1987; Tarr and Pinker, 1989), is its reliance on unnaturally looking stimuli. In the paperclip shapes, for example, the absence of extended surfaces is an advantage insofar as it stretches the range of orientations that can be tested without self-occlusion. However, this very feature makes those shapes unlike most objects encountered in real life, and may contribute to the poorer viewpoint invariance for paperclips, compared to the same shapes filled in

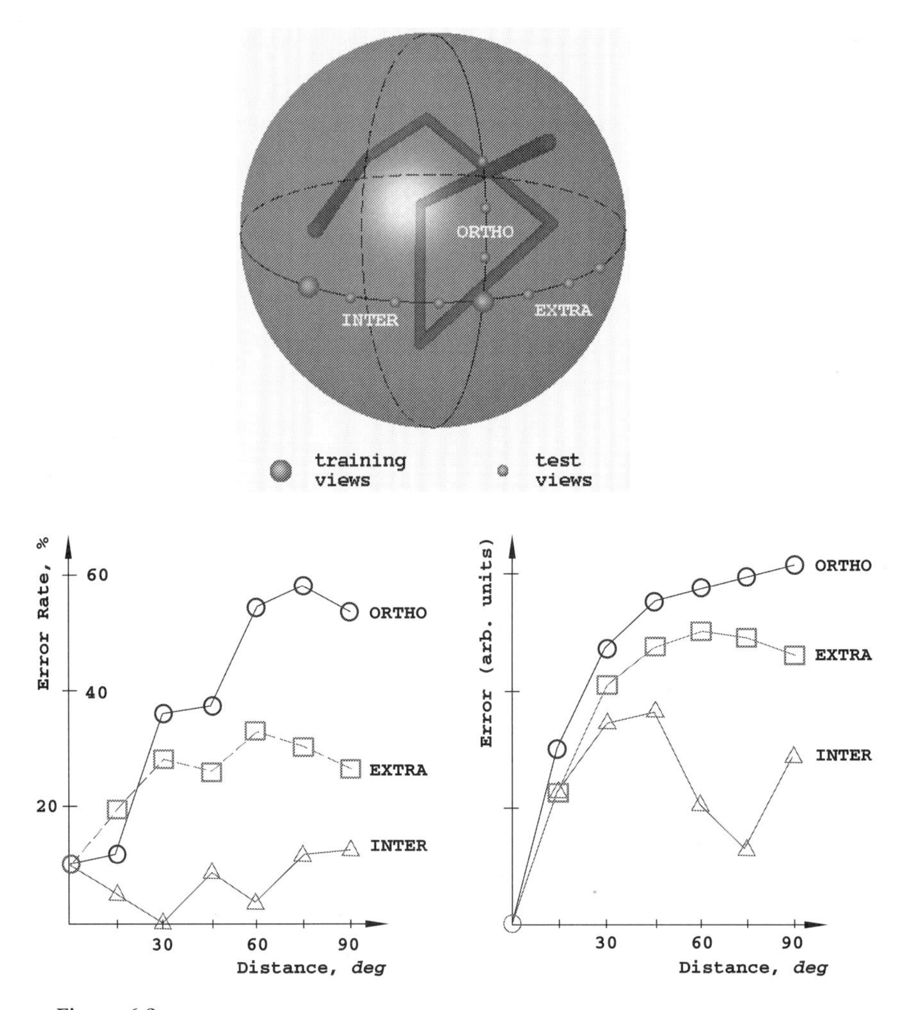


Figure 6.9
*(Top)* An illustration of the INTER, EXTRA and ORTHO conditions in the experiments of Bülthoff and Edelman (1992). The imaginary viewing sphere is centered around the recognition target. Different training and testing views are distinguished by various symbols. During training, subjects were shown the target from two viewpoints on a great circle of the viewing sphere, 75° apart, oscillating (±15°) around a fixed axis. Recognition was then tested in a two-alternative, forced-choice task that involved static views of either target or distractor objects. Target test views were situated on the shorter part of the same great circle (INTER condition), on its longer portion (EXTRA condition), or on a great circle orthogonal to the training one (ORTHO condition). *(Bottom left)* The performance of four subjects in the first experiment (error rate vs. great-circle distance from the reference view, after Bülthoff and Edelman, 1992). The mean error rates in the INTER, EXTRA and ORTHO conditions were 9.4%, 17.8% and 26.9%. *(Bottom right)* The performance of a view-interpolation model in the same experiment (see Bülthoff and Edelman, 1992, for details).

so as to resemble potato chips (Farah et al., 1994). Attempts to circumvent this criticism by demonstrating that similar results can be obtained with other stimuli, e.g., 3D amoeba-like shapes (Bülthoff and Edelman, 1992) or cubist constructs (Tarr, 1995), miss the point, because those stimuli look just as unnatural. Worse, mere replication of the results with a few more object classes offers no principled way to predict in advance what degree of viewpoint invariance should be expected for a given set of shapes.

A comprehensive theoretical framework intended both to account for the entire spectrum of invariance results and to predict the outcome of new experiments was advanced in mid-1980s by Biederman. The research program undertaken by Biederman and his collaborators, who aimed at proving that recognition is basically viewpoint invariant, is best understood in terms of his theory of representation, known as Recognition by Components, or RBC (Biederman, 1987). We may recall that this theory, which follows the structural approach (see section 2.3.2), postulates a small number of volumetric primitives, or geons (see figure 6.10), which, together with some spatial relationships, are used to describe qualitative shape features of objects (or rather, of basic categories of objects, such as a mug or a briefcase). A typical example of a qualitative feature would be the distinction between convex and concave parts; in comparison, the length of a part is called, by Biederman, a metric feature. The main purpose of the experiments summarized in Biederman (1987) was to demonstrate the sufficiency and the necessity of RBC as a theory of object recognition in human vision.

**Arguments for the Sufficiency of RBC** Biederman's argument for sufficiency proceeded from two findings. The first of these was the recognition of partial objects in which only a few of the original geons were included (Biederman, 1987). The stimuli were line drawings of common objects, selected so as to require two, three, six, or nine components to look complete. Seventeen geon types were found to be sufficient for representing these objects in terms of their parts. The results of this experiment (figures 14 and 15 in Biederman, 1987) indicate that, for a given complexity level, increasing the number of components leads to more accurate naming responses. This outcome is compatible with RBC, as well as with any reasonable alternative, such as the idea that information in local contour

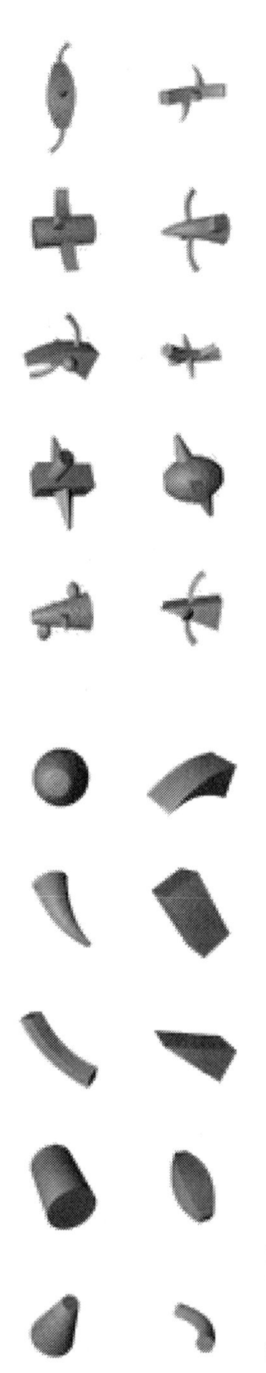

**Figure 6.10**
*(Left)* "Geometric ions" or geons—volumetric primitives postulated as the generic parts used to represent objects in the structural description theory of Biederman (1987). *(Right)* Novel objects composed of geons used by Hayward and Tarr (1997) to probe the degree of viewpoint dependence in recognition.

features is accumulated under partial exposure, until recognition is certain (Bar and Ullman, 1996). Biederman's second argument for the sufficiency of RBC is based on the equally rapid and accurate recognition of color photographs and of line drawings of common objects. In this experiment (Biederman and Ju, 1988), the subjects were required to name or perform name verification of objects that were presented in two versions: professional full-color photographs and simplified line drawings showing only the object's major components. The equivalent performance in these two conditions constitutes an important indication of the kind of information necessary for recognition (namely, contours or "edges"),[23] although it does not, of course, say anything about the grouping of these contours into parts.

**Arguments for the Necessity of RBC** The experiments mentioned above show that RBC is sufficient as a theoretical account of recognition, but does it offer a better explanation than the alternatives, such as Chorus? Because the main technical distinction between RBC and Chorus lies along the componential/holistic axis, the proponents of RBC must show that human recognition performance cannot be accounted for without invoking an intermediate representational stage in which the part structure is made explicit. Indeed, the argument advanced in Biederman (1987) in favor of the necessity of RBC was based on the effect of part-based image degradation on recognition performance. One experiment that addressed this issue explored priming of contour-deleted line drawings of common objects (Biederman and Cooper, 1991b). Half of the contour in each image was removed either by deleting every other image feature (i.e., line or curve) from each geon, or half the geons. It was found that deletion of entire geons had a much more disruptive effect on recognition than deletion of every other contour. Similarly, partial deletion of contours comprising line junctions was more disruptive than the deletion of an equal amount of mid-segment contour (Blickle, 1989).

The interpretation of these results is less straightforward than it may seem. The claim that geons mediated the priming in these experiments can be countered by observing that their results are equally compatible with the idea that a contour completion mechanism (Grossberg and Mingolla, 1985; Shashua and Ullman, 1988) is interposed between the stimulus image and the recognition stage. This idea is supported by a model described in (Kalocsai and Biederman, 1997). That work examined a simulation of the primary visual cortex composed of simple-cell receptive fields augmented by "extension fields," which introduced long-range lateral interactions among simple RFs. The action of this simulation on contour-deleted images boosted the recognition of images shown to be recoverable by human subjects, and increased the similarity of feature-deleted but not part-deleted images, essentially replicating the effects reported in Biederman and Cooper (1991b).[24] It is interesting to note that the possible relevance of contour completion in this context was hypothesized (but not tested computationally) earlier by Blickle (1989). Most of his psychophysical findings, such as the continuous nature of performance degradation following contour deletion (Blickle, 1989), also favor the idea of a contour completion mechanism over a part-based explanation.

**Metric vs. Qualitative (Geon) Differences** An important prediction of RBC is that qualitative changes (e.g., a convex contour turning into concave) should be more salient than metric ones (e.g., a moderate lengthening of a part). Cooper and Biederman tested this prediction by comparing the effects of metric and qualitative changes on subject performance in classification and discrimination tasks (Cooper and Biederman, 1993). Their experiments used thirty-two pairs of common objects (depicted as line drawings); the members of each pair had the same name, but differed in one major geon. Prior to the main experiments, four subjects created metrically perturbed versions of one member of each pair, by adjusting the length of the distinctive geon until the subjective (perceived) difference between the resulting object and the original matched the qualitative difference between the members of the pair. In the first experiment, the subjects had to judge whether sequentially presented stimuli had the same name. The accuracy of the "same name" decisions was higher when the objects differed metrically, even if the metric difference had been found subjectively larger than the qualitative difference. In the second experiment, the subjects had to decide whether sequentially presented stimuli were exactly the same or differed in any way. Here, the objects were better discriminated when they differed qualitatively. Cooper and Biederman concluded that qualitative changes are more important for recognition than subjectively equal metric changes in object shape.

Bar and Biederman (1995) extended the method of equal subjective differences to probe the interaction of metric and qualitative changes with viewpoint invariance. They started by manipulating a metric difference between derived and reference objects until its *detectability* at a preset attitude (at 0°) matched that of a geon difference (note that Cooper and Biederman, 1993, used subjective equality as the criterion for a match). Bar and Biederman then showed that rotation in depth by about 60° away from the 0° orientation reduced the detection of metric differences to chance, without affecting the detection of geon differences.

If these results were to be taken at the face value, they could support the idea that recognition operates on a representation in which geon changes carry more weight than random image changes and remain salient across different viewpoints. (Note that this effect would not be expected in what I called the measurement space $\mathcal{M}$.) However, the results of Cooper and Biederman (1993) can be given an alternative explanation in terms of the variability of a parameter they assume to be constant: the names of the stimuli. Specifically, the "standard" versions of the objects used in that study all appear to possess more informative names than the geon-changed objects (e.g., "Martini glass" vs. "glass," "milk bottle" vs. "bottle," and "top hat" vs. "hat"). Thus, the basic manipulation in that experiment—transforming standard versions of the stimuli by changing single geons—involved a change in the name of the object, and not only in its shape, confounding the conclusions of Cooper and Biederman.

The result of Bar and Biederman (1995) could, likewise, be offset by an imperfect control. Whereas the similarity of the stimuli in the 0° condition was controlled by design, that for the 60° condition (i.e., following rotation in depth) was not, making the "original" and the "geon-difference" objects unequally salient. In particular, the difference between the substituted and the original geons, as illustrated in Bar and Biederman (1995), seems to be much less prominent in the 0° condition than in the 60° condition.

**Testing the Predictions of RBC on Viewpoint Invariance** As I already noted, the main challenge in connection with viewpoint invariance is not to demonstrate that it does or does not exist, but rather to give an account of the conditions in which invariance is expected to hold better. Contrary to a common misconception, RBC does not dictate that recognition is to be absolutely invariant, even in principle, although a description of an object in terms of geons and their relationships is likely to be stable across a wide range of viewpoints. As mentioned in Biederman (1987), one factor that limits the scope of the expected invariance is self-occlusion: not all geons comprising an object will be visible from a particular viewpoint. Another factor is the nature of the spatial relations themselves: two geons on top of each other will appear side by side when the object is rotated around the line of sight.

These and other qualifications assumed a central role in Biederman's later work (Biederman and Gerhardstein, 1993), which attempted to account for the growing body of evidence against absolute invariance in recognition. According to Biederman and Gerhardstein, recognition will not be invariant with respect to viewpoint, unless (1) the objects have readily identifiable geon-like parts, (2) the parts form qualitatively distinct configurations for different objects, and (3) the same parts are visible over the entire range of viewpoints for which invariance is expected.

The degree to which this crucial set of predictions is borne out by experimental data is subject to controversy. Gerhardstein and Biederman (1991) reported viewpoint-invariant performance in a priming experiment involving depth-rotated object images, provided that the same geons components were in view in both images. Furthermore, Biederman and Gerhardstein's (1993) replication of the experiments of Edelman and Bülthoff (1992b) showed the predicted pattern of results: performance was not invariant for the paperclip objects that violated condition (2) above, yet became invariant when one of the cylinders comprising the paperclip was replaced by a distinctive geon. This finding, however, was promptly countered by the results of a more extensive study by Tarr et al. (1997), who varied the number of distinctive geons systematically, and found generally non-invariant performance (the case of a single distinctive geon, for which a better approximation to invariance was found, being somewhat of an exception). Furthermore, even isolated geons turned out neither to be recognized in a manner independent of viewpoint (Hayward and Tarr, 1997),[25] nor to pop out preattentively in experiments using the search paradigm (Brown et al., 1992). These latter results seriously weaken the claim of geons to the role of elementary viewpoint-invariant parts, central to RBC.

**Chorus as a Theory of Viewpoint Invariance** The predictions of the Chorus scheme concerning viewpoint invariance can be spelled out on the basis of its theoretical foundations (chapter 4) and the actual performance of its implementation (chapter 5). Recall that the elementary building block of Chorus—a unit tuned to a specific view of a specific object—is inherently viewpoint-dependent. However, because the tuning curves of the individual units are wide (that is, they also respond, albeit weakly, to views that differ somewhat from their optimal stimuli), a collection of such units, each tuned to a different view, can interpolate the entire view space of a given object (this is what RBF networks do). Viewpoint invariance achieved in this manner will be approximate and specific for the given object. A system designed for the recognition of multiple objects will have to maintain a commensurate number of object-specific modules. In such a system, the degree of viewpoint invariance will decrease when the objects to be discriminated are similar to each other. This will happen because shape similarity entails similarity of view spaces. As objects are made to resemble each other more closely, their view spaces approach each other, making discrimination more difficult. Finally, a system (Chorus) of several object-specific modules of this kind is expected to exhibit a modicum of viewpoint invariance for novel objects, essentially by interpolating between the view spaces of the familiar ones.

The interaction between the degree of viewpoint invariance and object similarity in a given task was tested in a series of psychophysical experiments, in which similarity between the stimuli varied in a controlled fashion (Edelman, 1995a). Subjects were trained to discriminate between two classes of computer-generated 3D objects, one resembling monkeys, and the other dogs (figure 6.11). Both classes were defined by the same set of fifty-six parameters, which encoded sizes, shapes, and placement of the limbs, the ears, the snout, etc. Linear interpolation between parameter vectors of the class prototypes yielded shapes that changed smoothly between monkey and dog. Within-class variation was induced in each trial by randomly perturbing all the parameters.

After the subjects reached 90% correct performance on a fixed canonical view of each object, discrimination performance was tested for novel views that differed by up to 60° from the training view. In Experiment 1 (in which the distribution of parameters in each class was unimodal) and

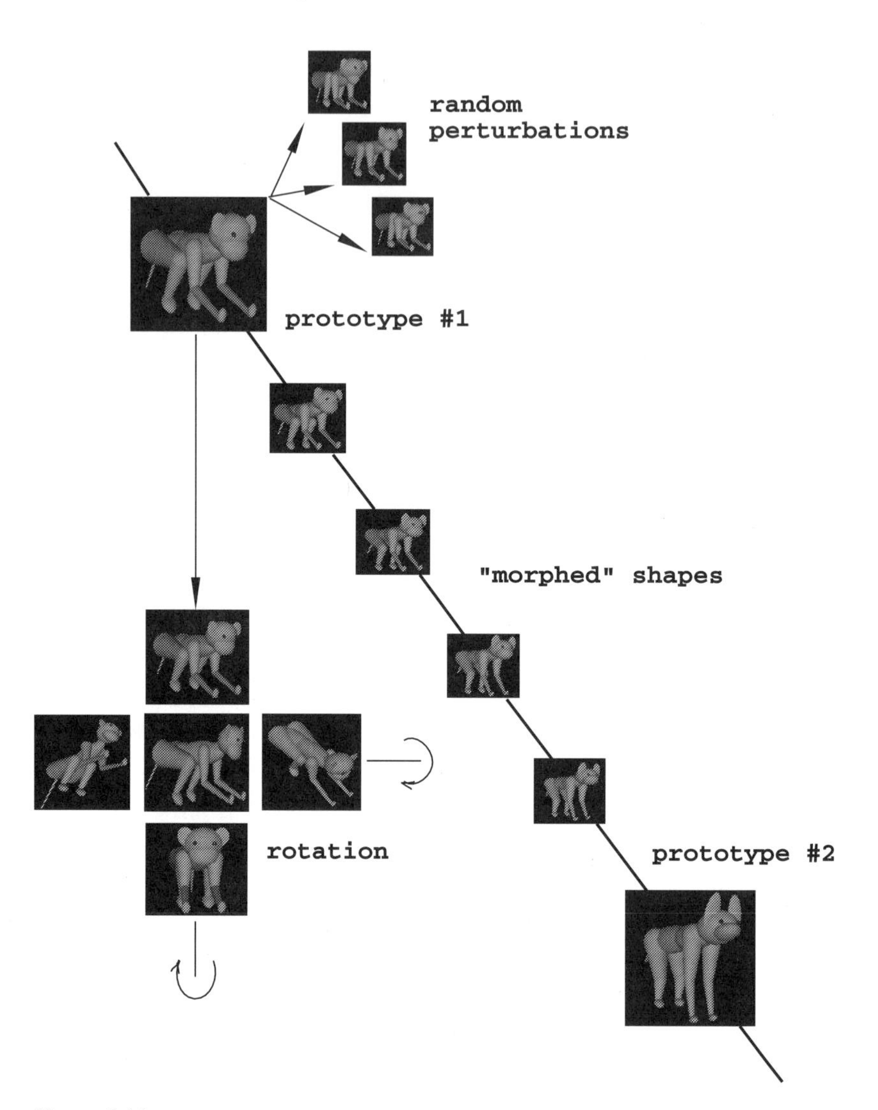


Figure 6.11
A family of images of two classes of parameterized 3D objects, obtained by morphing (Edelman, 1995a). The illustration shows the two class prototypes, four blended objects obtained by forming convex linear combinations of the prototype parameter vectors, and the effects of random perturbation of parameters (*top*) and of object rotation (*bottom left*). The class prototypes were inspired by objects #183 (raccoon) and #145 (monkey), (Snodgrass and Vanderwart, 1980).

in Experiment 2 (bimodal classes), the stimuli differed only parametrically and consisted of the same geons. Nevertheless, they were recognized virtually independently of viewpoint in the low-similarity condition, contrary to the prediction of Biederman and Gerhardstein (1993).

In the third experiment, the prototypes differed in their complement of geons (that is, they could be distinguished by local qualitative contrasts). Nevertheless, the subjects' performance depended significantly on viewpoint in the high-similarity condition, again contrary to (Biederman and Gerhardstein, 1993). In all three experiments, higher inter-stimulus similarity was associated with an increase in the mean error rate and, for misorientation of up to 45°, with an increase in the degree of viewpoint dependence.[26] These results suggest, *contra* RBC, that a geon-level difference between stimuli is neither strictly necessary nor sufficient for viewpoint-invariant performance (figure 6.12).[27]

The results of the experiments of Edelman (1995a), summarized above, are in line with one prediction of Chorus: there is an interaction between inter-stimulus similarity and the degree of viewpoint invariance in the discrimination task. The experiments of Moses et al. (1996) complemented that study by examining another, related prediction of Chorus, according to which the degree of viewpoint invariance for a novel object should depend on the similarity of that object to familiar ones. This prediction was tested by assessing the ability of subjects to generalize face recognition across changes in viewing position.[28] The subjects carried out a three-alternative forced-choice face discrimination task, with either upright or inverted face stimuli. Each of seven subjects ran four sessions on three upright and three inverted face triplets in a mixed order. Subjects first learned to discriminate among images of three faces, taken under a fixed viewing position. They were then tested on images of the same faces taken under five viewing positions (−34°, −17°, 0°, 17°, and 34° from the frontal view in the horizontal plane, controlled by a moving robot arm).

For upright faces, the subjects generalized remarkably well to novel conditions: the mean performance was 97% correct. For inverted faces, recognition performance after training was similar to the performance for upright faces ($98.6 \pm 0.7\%$ vs. $99.1 \pm 0.6\%$ correct). Notably, the generalization to novel views was significantly worse for inverted compared

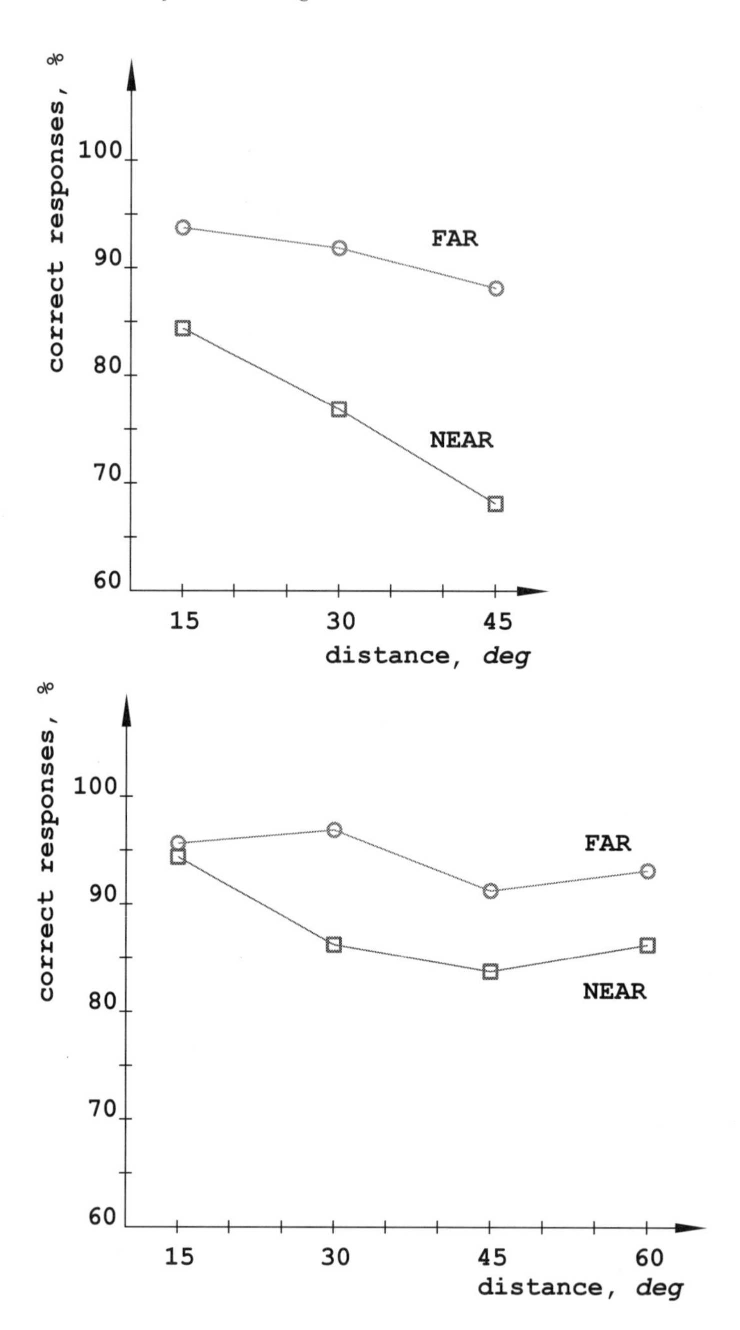
correct responses, %
100
90
80
70
60
FAR
NEAR
15
30
45
distance, deg
correct responses, %
100
90
80
70
60
FAR
NEAR
15
30
45
60
distance, deg

to upright faces (the initial performance in the discrimination of a new triplet of faces from novel viewpoints was $86.5 \pm 1.5\%$). The generalization in the inverted condition improved with practice (despite the absence of feedback). In the fourth session, the performance was $95.0 \pm 1.0\%$ for novel viewpoints. This improvement, however, was face-specific: the subjects reverted to the initial level of performance with the introduction of a new triplet of inverted faces.

These results indicate that at least some of the processes that support generalization across viewpoint are neither universal (because subjects did not generalize as easily for inverted faces as for upright ones), nor strictly object-specific (because in upright faces nearly perfect generalization was possible from a single view, by itself insufficient for building a complete object-specific model). This led Y. Moses (1993) to propose that generalization in face recognition occurs at an intermediate computational level that is applicable to a *class* of objects, and that at this level upright and inverted faces initially constitute distinct object classes.[29]

The computational notion of class-based processing (Moses, 1993; Poggio and Vetter, 1992; Beymer and Poggio, 1996) is supported by a growing list of psychophysical findings concerning the interaction of similarity and generalization. One example here is a study of generalization across image-plane rotations for novel line-drawn objects (Gauthier and Tarr, 1997). This study found significant priming for novel orientations of unfamiliar shapes, to the extent that they resembled familiar shapes of the

**Figure 6.12**
The effects of similarity on viewpoint dependence of recognition (after Edelman, 1995a). *(Top)* Percentage of correct responses (CR) in the low and high inter-class similarity conditions (FAR and NEAR modes; upper and lower curves, respectively), plotted vs. the angular distance to the training orientation. The results indicate that a geon-level difference between stimuli is not *necessary* for nearly viewpoint-invariant performance: the two stimuli differed only parametrically, and had the same complement of geons, yet were recognized relatively independently of viewpoint in the FAR condition. *(Bottom)* Percentage of correct responses (CR) for the two similarity conditions, FAR (upper curve) and NEAR (lower curve), plotted vs. the angular distance to the training orientation. The results suggest that a geon-level difference between stimuli is not *sufficient* for achieving viewpoint invariance, as indicated by the significantly viewpoint-dependent performance of subjects in the NEAR condition.

same class. It is important to note that the advantage conferred by class similarity was not traded off for confusion among members of the same class: objects were easily discriminable, yet were perceived as being "the same" insofar as their transformation was concerned. Interestingly, the pattern of orientation priming effects in the five experiments reported in Gauthier and Tarr (1997) could not be explained by postulating transformations of abstract reference frames, in agreement with earlier findings (Koriat and Norman, 1984; McMullen et al., 1995). Gauthier and Tarr concluded that "it is not unreasonable to propose that the representation of Object A at 120° is strongly connected to the representation of Object B at 120° when A and B are visually similar."

Another study, described in Tarr and Gauthier (1998), corroborated this conclusion using novel 3D objects rotated in depth. Some of the stimuli in this experiment had been shown to the subjects at many orientations, while others were shown at only a few. Tarr and Gauthier found significant generalization over viewpoint for the latter shapes, insofar as they resembled the former (more familiar) shapes; the generalization was better for novel views at which the familiar shapes had been seen before, in accordance with the predictions of the Chorus model.

In summary, recognition performance for a given view of an object depends (1) on the frequency of the appearance of that object at that viewpoint, (2) on the frequency of the appearance of visually similar objects at that viewpoint, and (3) on the variability of that object's appearance across over its different views (Tarr and Gauthier, 1998). A viable computational account of this pattern of generalization across viewpoints is offered by Chorus, which predicts, over and above the intrinsic viewpoint dependence of recognition, a better generalization over viewpoint for novel objects that are more similar to the explicitly represented prototypes.

### Beyond Viewpoint Invariance: Evidence for Multiple-Prototype Encoding

In principle, class-based processing of a novel stimulus can rely on an analogy between its expected transformation and the previously experienced transformation of its closest counterpart among the familiar objects. Alternatively, the processing of a novel shape may involve the pooled knowledge concerning a number of familiar shapes similar to it. The former option (which is, in a sense, a variety of the Winner Take All approach), is exemplified by a two-stage algorithm called recognition by prototypes (Basri, 1996). According to Basri's algorithm, the stimulus is first transformed into alignment (Ullman, 1989) with the prototype (here, the average shape) of the class of shapes which it resembles the most; a subsequent adjustment stage refines the match. The priority of categorization over identification in this method is appealing: for human observers too the categorization is easier and faster than exact identification (which, in fact, is not even defined for a novel stimulus).

Unlike this single-prototype class-based processing method, the Chorus scheme is geared to make full use of information derived from multiple related classes. In addition to its computational appeal (see chapter 4), this alternative also seems to be more in line with the general propensity for ensemble-based representations in biological vision. We came across neurobiological evidence in favor of this principle in the first part of the present chapter; the psychophysical case for it is outlined next.

The ensemble, or coarse coding (Hinton, 1984; Ballard, 1987), principle states that percepts formed by a representational system are superpositions of the activities of a number of functional units, each tuned to a somewhat different aspect of the feature space spanned by the stimuli. A compelling manifestation of this principle has been discovered by the early experiments of J. J. Gibson (1933), whose subjects perceived an objectively curved line as nearly straight, following adaptation to curves of the same sense. A straight line was subsequently perceived as curved in the opposite direction. In auditory perception, analogously, the pitch of a tone appears higher than it is, following adaptation to a somewhat lower tone; the reverse effect is obtained when the adapting tone is higher than the test one (von Békésy, 1929). Likewise, in two-way classification of parametrically-defined stimuli arranged along a line in some feature space, the performance on unseen stimuli situated progressively farther from the class boundary first gets better, then worse than the performance on trained stimuli (Mackintosh, 1995). In all these examples, the peculiarities of observed performance can be explained by positing a pool of functional units that (1) are differentially tuned to line orientation, or tone pitch, or whatever feature dimension is used in the definition of the classification task, (2) are adaptable, and (3) whose joint pattern of activation determines the subjective quality of a percept: curvature of a line, pitch of a sound, and category of a shape (Intrator and Edelman, 1997a).

An attempt to demonstrate that categorization of 3D shapes too involves comparing them with multiple class prototypes is described in Edelman et al. (1996a). Subjects in two experiments performed forced-choice classification of novel shapes composed of four geon-like parts, emanating from a common center. There were two classes of shapes, distinguished by what Biederman terms qualitative contrasts (bulging vs. waist-like limbs; figure 6.13). The subjects were trained to discriminate between the two class prototypes (shown briefly, from a number of viewpoints, in stereo) in a one-interval forced-choice task, until they reached a 90% correct-response performance level.

In the first experiment, test shapes were obtained by varying the prototypical parameters both orthogonally (ORTHO) and in parallel (PARA) to the line connecting the prototypes in the parameter space (figure 6.14). The error rate for these test shapes increased with the ORTHO parameter-space displacement between the stimulus and the corresponding prototype (the effect of the PARA displacement was marginal). Clearly, the parameter-space location of the stimuli mattered more than the qualitative contrasts (which were always present). This effect is in line with the expectations derived from Chorus, but not from RBC.

To find out whether both prototypes or just the nearest neighbor of the test shape influenced the decision, the second experiment (figure 6.15) tested new subjects on a fixed set of shapes, while the test-stage distance between the two classes assumed one of three values (FAR, INTERMEDIATE, and NEAR; test trials were blocked by condition, the order of the blocks being randomized across subjects). The error rate in this experiment, computed for physically identical stimuli presented under different conditions, was higher in the NEAR block than in the other two conditions. This result supports the notion of a metric (as opposed to a qualitative) representation space, with the subjects' performance determined by distances to more than one reference point or prototype, again as predicted by Chorus.[30]

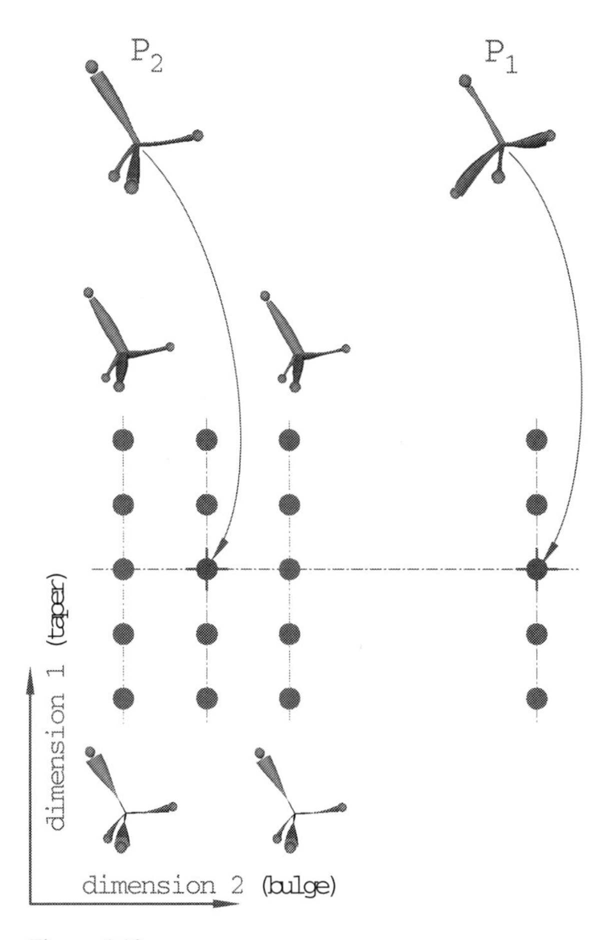


**Figure 6.13**
The parameter-space arrangement of stimuli in the experiments of Edelman et al. (1996). The parameter-space locations of the two prototypical objects are marked by $p_1$ and $p_2$. The two orthogonal directions of shape variation are bulge (increase/decrease) and taper (proximal to distal or vice versa). Specifically, the shift from $p_1$ to $p_2$ corresponds to a gradual change from a waist-like to a bulging profile of the hedgehog's limbs; the orthogonal direction corresponds to an equally gradual change of limb shape that tapers from the proximal towards the distal end to a shape that tapers in the opposite direction.

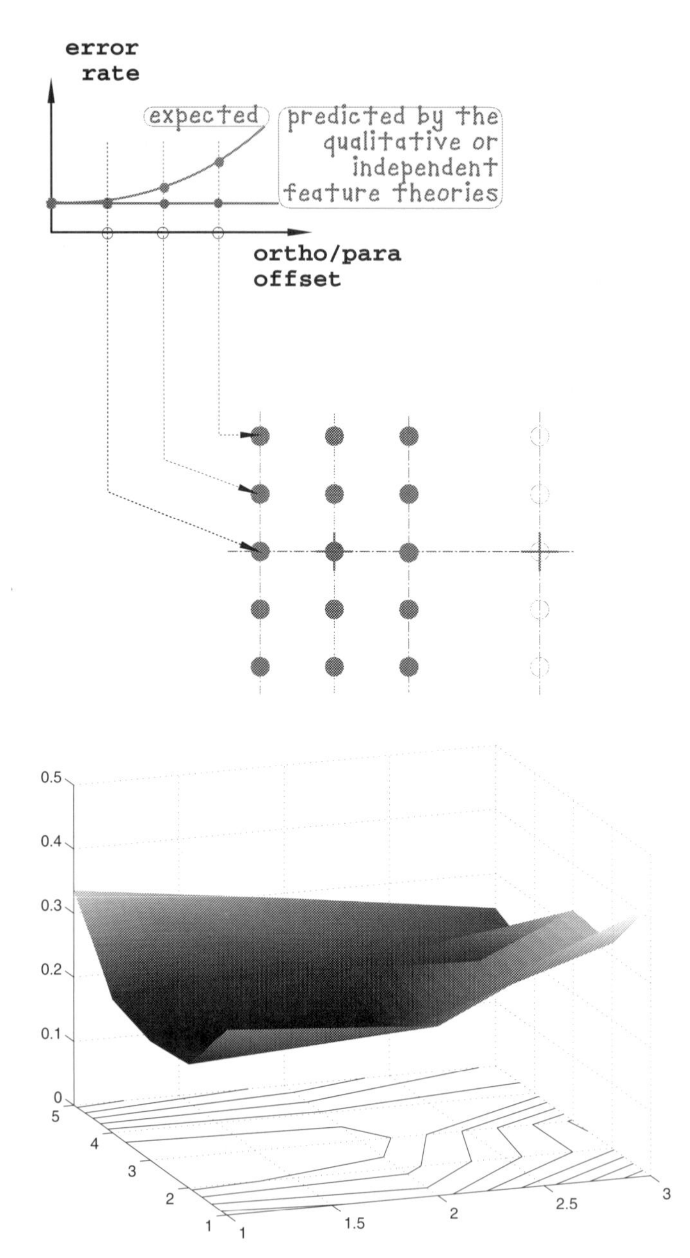
error
rate
expected
predicted by the
qualitative or
independent
feature theories
ortho/para
offset
0.5
0.4
0.3
0.2
0.1
0
5
4
3
2
1
1
1.5
2
2.5
3

## 6.5 Psychophysics: Veridicality of Shape Representation

I have introduced the Chorus model in chapter 4 as a computationally convenient means to achieve $\mathcal{S}$-isomorphism between the similarity structure of the internal shape representation space $\mathcal{R}$ and geometric similarities among distal shapes. Insofar as those predictions of Chorus that we discussed in the preceding sections are reasonably compatible with neurobiological and psychophysical data, it is interesting to see whether the hypothesis which gave rise to it—veridical representation by $\mathcal{S}$-isomorphism—has any grounding in human behavior.

As in the case of viewpoint invariance, a wide range of phenomena must be brought into consideration, if all aspects of the issue of veridicality in human perception are to be discussed. The visual system certainly behaves nonveridically, nonlinearly, or downright peculiarly in a variety of situations (Gregory, 1978). Even in shape perception tasks, such as the estimation of local surface orientation (Koenderink et al., 1996), of local curvature (Phillips and Todd, 1996), or even of object size (Gregson and Britton, 1990), human perception can be far from veridical. One may observe, however, that all those tasks involve attempts on the part of the human visual system to recover object geometry. In the terminology of chapter 2 this corresponds to the establishment of a first-order or $\mathcal{F}$-isomorphism—an undertaking where one can only expect to run into

**Figure 6.14**
*(Top)* The parameter-space arrangement of the stimuli, and the expected performance in the ORTHO experiment. The subjects were trained to discriminate between the two prototypes, $p_1$ and $p_2$. They were then tested on the discrimination of stimuli produced by a shape-space variation orthogonal to the contrast between the two prototypes. *(Bottom)* The mean error rate of the eight subjects who responded above chance in the first experiment, plotted against the ORTHO and the PARA displacement. The three PARA displacement values, denoted symbolically by the numerals 1, 2, 3, appear along the abscissa in the contour plots; the five ORTHO values correspond to the ordinate. The location of prototype $p_2$ corresponds to the point whose coordinates are (2, 3). Altogether, the fifteen data points are arranged in a $3 \times 5$ grid around prototype $p_2$ (see figure 6.13); the direction towards the other prototype in these plots is along the increasing abscissa values. The adjacent lines in the contour plot are spaced at 2.5%. Note the general increase in the error rate for test stimuli that are closer to the other prototype.

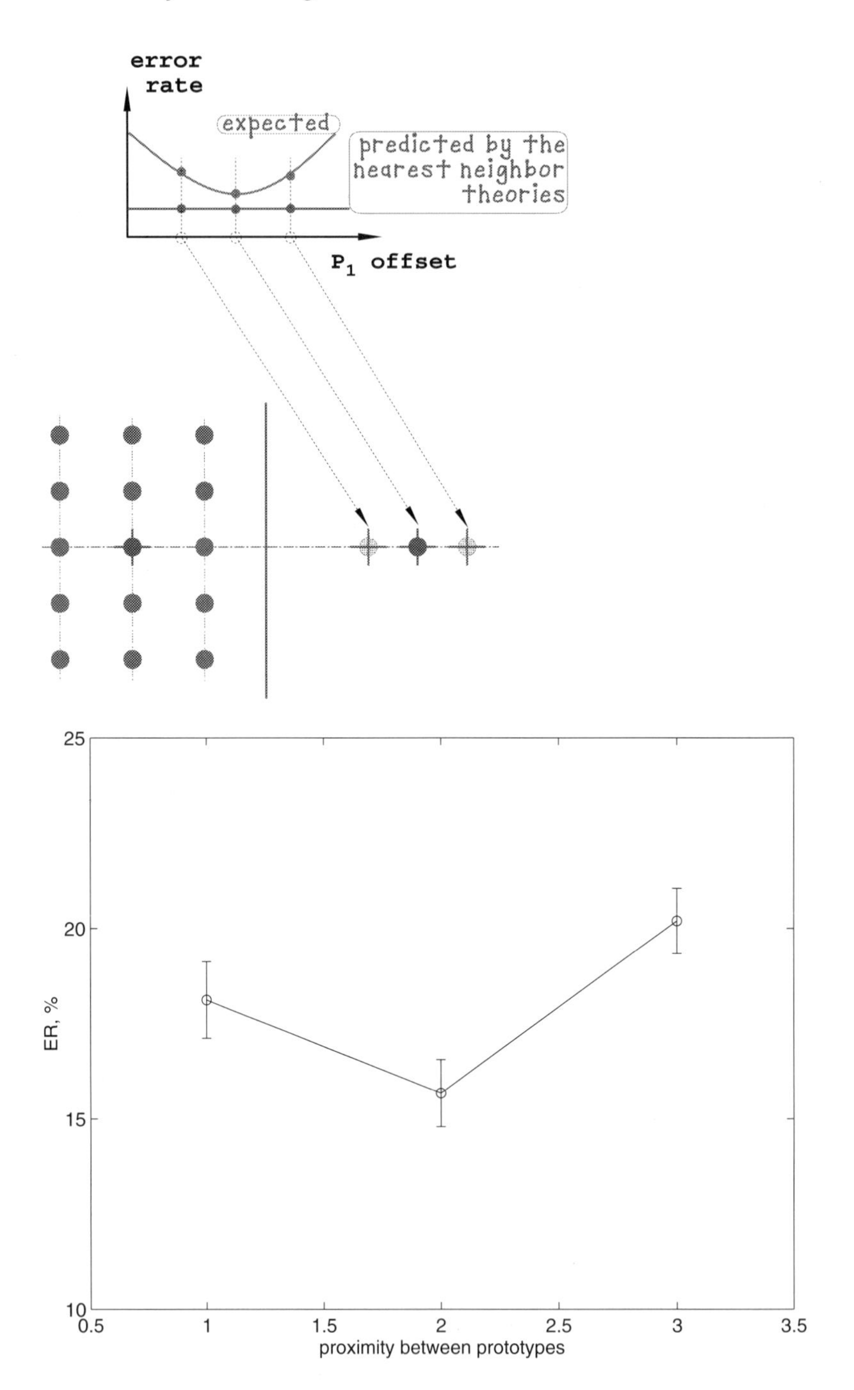
error rate
expected
predicted by the nearest neighbor theories
$P_1$ offset
25
20
15
10
ER, %
0.5
1
1.5
2
2.5
3
3.5
proximity between prototypes

difficulties. In comparison, $\mathcal{S}$-isomorphism, or veridical representation of similarities among shapes, seems to hold as a rule in recognition and categorization tasks, which involve comparisons among objects (Shepard and Chipman, 1970; Shepard and Cermak, 1973; Edelman, 1995b; Cortese and Dyre, 1996; Cutzu and Edelman, 1996).

### 6.5.1 Perceived Similarity as Proximity in an Internal Metric Space

A central characteristic of perceived similarity is the possibility to consider similarities as proximities between points corresponding to the various stimuli, when the latter are embedded into a metric space using multidimensional scaling, or MDS (Shepard, 1980; Shepard, 1987). This feature of similarity emerges from numerous studies that concentrated on different perceptual modalities and employed a variety of distinct experimental paradigms (Shepard, 1980; Nosofsky, 1992; Clark, 1993).

A degree of caution is called for when interpreting this state of affairs. First, the applicability of multidimensional scaling is ultimately determined by the relevance of the resulting solution: "Even though it is always the case that, if we are prepared to tolerate a high enough dimensionality and if we are prepared to tolerate degenerate, clustered, or lumpy configurations, we can get a spatial representation, ultimately, the criterion for accepting a representation is the sense that can be made of it, and the results that can be retrieved or predicted, by rules invariant over the space, from it" (Gregson 1975, 134).

Second, one should not assume too lightly that the internal similarity space is metric in the full sense employed in differential geometry. In that

**Figure 6.15**
*(Top)* The parameter-space arrangement of the stimuli and the expected performance in the NEAREST-NEIGHBOR experiment. The two prototypes, $p_1$ and $p_2$, are as before. In this experiment, the location of $p_1$ relative to $p_2$ varied along the line connecting the two prototypes. Performance (discrimination between the two classes) was tested for the same physical stimuli, whose location in the parameter space corresponds to the middle column in the $3 \times 5$ grid of points surrounding $p_2$. *(Bottom)* The mean performance of the thirteen subjects who responded above chance in the second experiment, plotted against the PARA displacement of prototype $p_1$. The error bars show the standard deviation of the means. The three values along the abscissa (prototype proximities 1, 2, 3) correspond, respectively, to the FAR, INTERMEDIATE, and NEAR conditions.

space, as pointed out by Clark (1993, 147), "Distances are monotonically related to similarities, but there is no presumption that sums or ratios of distances are interpretable. There may be no common unit to express distances along different axes." Fortunately, in visual shape processing these concerns seem to be largely mitigated; as we shall see next, both the metric space assumption and the applicability of MDS are justified by the human performance data.

### 6.5.2 Veridical Perception of Distal Shape Contrasts

Psychophysical experiments that use MDS to map the internal shape representation space can be classified according to the kind of stimuli they employ. Historically, a great majority of the experiments have been using sets of shapes that are not controlled parametrically, and for which the distal shape space is, therefore, unknown to the experimenter. Although a given set of images can be always post-processed in an attempt to represent it in a low-dimensional "stimulus space," the technology for such processing has not been widely available to psychologists until recently. Moreover, even when a set of images, such as human faces, is subjected to dimensionality reduction of this kind, there is no guarantee that the resulting space will be sufficiently low-dimensional to allow effective visualization, or that the stimuli will form a prominent configuration in that space (which then would have to be sought after in the subject data, using MDS).

Despite these limitations, the application of MDS to subject data in a post-hoc manner, followed by attempts to make sense of the resulting configuration, led to some interesting findings. An early study that used MDS to map a shape space was described by Shepard and Chipman (1970), whose subjects judged similarities among outline shapes of fifteen of the US states, in two conditions: memory recall and visual inspection. Shepard and Chipman found that the MDS configuration derived from the inspection trials was amazingly close to the map derived from the recall condition. They offered an explanation of this result in terms of Shepard's idea of second-order isomorphism between representations and the world. Another example, the study of Young and Yamane (1992), was mentioned earlier in this chapter; there, the application of MDS to the response patterns of inferotemporal cortex cells in monkeys presented with face stimuli yielded maps whose dimensions could be interpreted in terms of physical similarity among the faces. My third example is the work of Rhodes (1988). The subjects in that study sorted forty-one face photographs by similarity; these images were also processed by hand, to yield thirty-nine objective geometric measures of similarity. The original aim of the experiment was to compare the relative importance of the so-called first-order and second-order geometric features (e.g., lengths and angles, vs. ratios of lengths and differences of angles). The conclusion reached by Rhodes in this matter (namely, that similarity along both kinds of dimensions correlated equally well with the subjects' performance) was accompanied by what seems to me a much more striking finding: the MDS analysis of the perceived similarity data revealed that the leading dimensions were best correlated not with the geometric features at all, but with holistic (that is, whole-image) "features" such as the age and the weight of the person in the photograph.

The experiment of Shepard and Chipman did not provide *direct* support for the idea of $\mathcal{S}$-isomorphism because it had no control over geometric similarities among the stimuli. Shepard and Cermak (1973) addressed this problem by exerting parametric control over the stimuli. In this, they made the first step towards using MDS, which is essentially an exploratory tool, in a confirmatory mode (Borg and Lingoes, 1987). The general procedure for this is to start with a certain parameter-space configuration according to which the stimuli are to be generated. For example, the experimenter can take two objects and blend them parametrically to obtain a shape that is situated, in the parameter space, at the midpoint of the segment that connects (points corresponding to) the two original shapes. The three stimuli are then presented to a subject in some recognition-related task, and the subject's responses are processed by MDS to yield a map of his or her internal representation space $\mathcal{R}$; data from multiple subjects can be combined using the individually weighted version of MDS described in Carroll and Chang (1970). The veridicality of the representation of the three stimuli in $\mathcal{R}$ can then be measured (1) by testing for consistency among subjects, and (2) by comparing the parameter-space pattern formed by the stimuli (in this example, a straight line) with their arrangement in the MDS map.[31] The agreement between the configuration built into the stimuli and the one obtained from subject data can be assessed visually (Shepard and Cermak, 1973; Cortese and Dyre, 1996), or using quantitative statistical means (Edelman, 1995b; Cutzu and Edelman, 1996).

In their ground-breaking experiment, Shepard and Cermak used eighty-one "free form" stimuli: closed contours parameterized by coefficients of their Fourier series expansion. The stimuli were placed at the vertices of a $9 \times 9$ square grid in the parameter space. A standard MDS analysis revealed this grid in the subject data. Reassuringly, subsets of the stimuli that could be given consistent cognitive interpretations were found to be contiguous in the resulting map of the subjects' shape space (Shepard and Cermak, 1973). The same kind of parametric control over 2D outline stimuli was used in Cortese and Dyre (1996), with similarly veridical recovery of the parameter-space grid from similarity judgment data.

With the aid of computer graphics, parametrically controlled 3D shapes can be used to study the veridicality of representation in a more realistic setting. The first attempt to assess quantitatively the degree of fit between the parameter space underlying a set of 3D shapes and their configuration in the subjects' internal representation space was described in Edelman (1995b). The stimuli in that study were stylized animal-like shapes similar to those depicted in figure 6.11. They had been arranged in the parameter space in the form of two clusters, a configuration that was subsequently revealed in the MDS plot of the subject data. Importantly, the configurations recovered from subject data were progressively less ordered for scrambled animal shapes (in which parts have been rearranged), paperclips-like objects with distinctive geon parts, and plain paperclips. This pattern is expected if the subjects could perceive better the similarities among those objects for which they had "reference shapes" (as in the Chorus model) ready at hand. Note that this hypothesis is also compatible with the consistent findings of poor generalization across viewpoints for nonsense shapes such as the paperclip objects (Bülthoff and Edelman, 1992; Edelman and Bülthoff, 1992b; Biederman and Gerhardstein, 1993). According to Chorus, the degree of viewpoint invariance for a test shape should depend on prior exposure to many views of similar objects, which is presumably available for animal-like shapes, but not for the paperclips.

These findings were corroborated and extended in a subsequent study that used a new set of parametrically controlled animal-like shapes (Cutzu and Edelman, 1996). In addition to the delayed matching to sample task employed in Edelman (1995b), perceptual judgment and long-term memory recall experiments were conducted (see figure 6.16). The stimuli in all the experiments formed regular planar configurations (line, triangle, star, cross, square) in a common seventy-dimensional parameter space. These configurations were fully recovered by multidimensional scaling from proximity tables derived from the subject data (see figure 6.17).[32] A computational model—a simple version of Chorus, in which shapes were encoded by their similarities to a number of prototypes—replicated this result.[33] As in Edelman (1995b), the ability of the subjects in these experiments to represent the low-dimensional pattern of similarities among stimuli did not seem to extend to nonsense objects, as indicated by the results of control experiments involving "scrambled" shapes (Cutzu and Edelman, 1998). For such objects, the resemblance between the original and the MDS-recovered configurations was consistently lower than for animal-like shapes.

When the exact geometric similarity relationships built into the set of stimuli are known, the veridicality of the representation space revealed by MDS can be assessed in statistical terms. A quantitative measure of deviation from veridicality in such a case is simply the discrepancy between the stimulus configuration in the distal parameter space and the configuration produced by MDS from subject data. Neither translation, nor rotation, scaling or even reflection of one of these configurations with respect to the other affects the relative proximities of the points (which correspond to the relative similarities of the stimuli shapes). Consequently, the MDS configuration can and should be normalized before comparison, by subjecting it to a Procrustes transformation: a combination of translation, rotation, scaling, and reflection that minimizes the sum of squared discrepancies between two labeled sets of points (Borg and Lingoes, 1987).

In the experiments described above, deviation from veridicality was defined as the sum of residual squared pointwise discrepancies that remained after the Procrustes transformation step. By itself, this measure does not provide any statistical insight into the significance of the

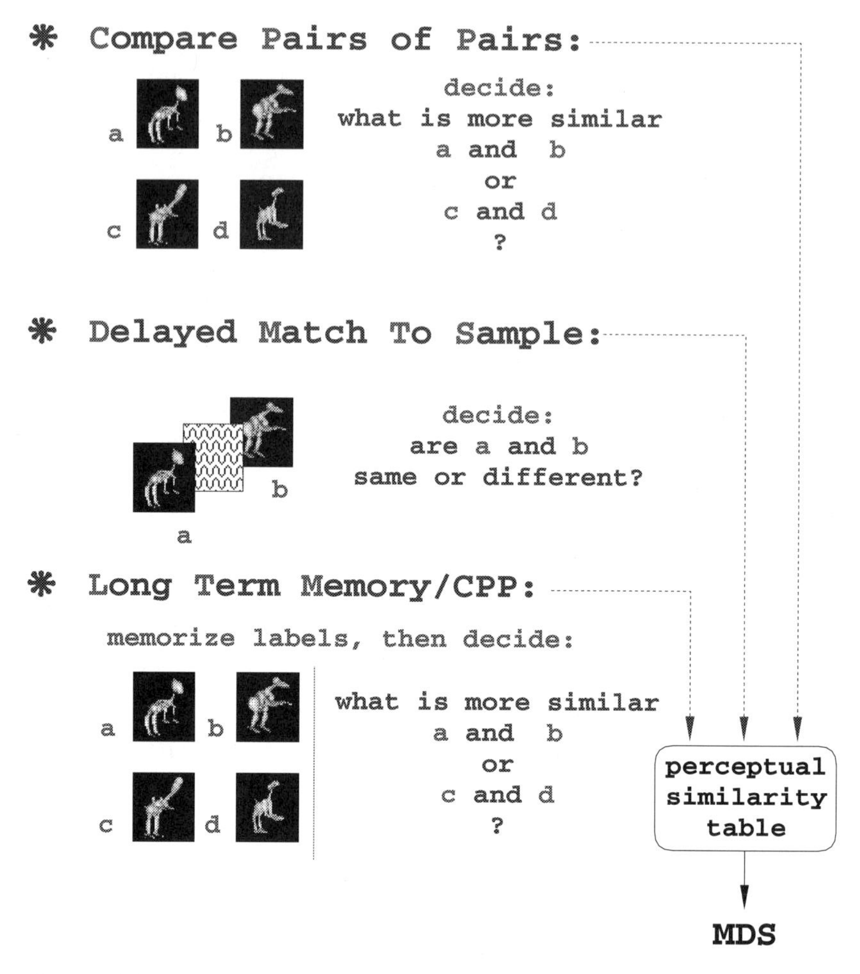


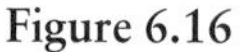

**Figure 6.16**
The three experimental methodologies used by Cutzu and Edelman (1996) to explore the structure of the internal shape representation space in human subjects.

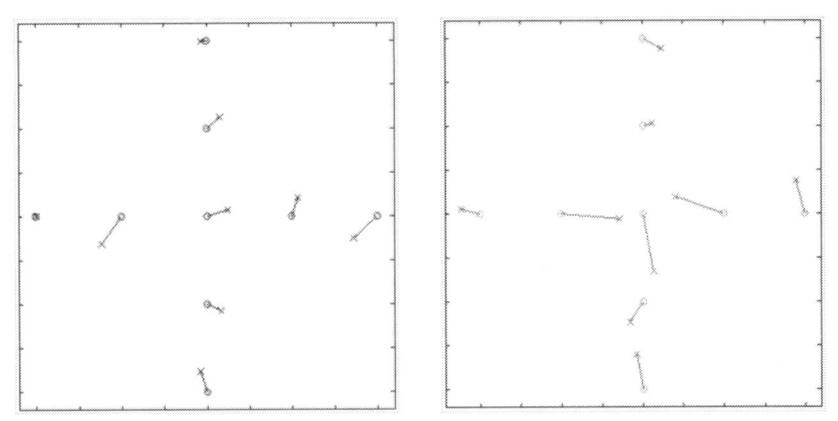


**Figure 6.17**
*(Top)* The original cross-like arrangement of nine stimuli in a common parameter space in one of the experiments described in Cutzu and Edelman (1996). *(Bottom left)* The arrangement of the same nine stimuli in the subjects' internal representation space, derived by MDS from delayed matching to sample data. Ideal and actual locations of the points denoting the stimuli are marked by o's and x's, respectively; lines connect corresponding points. *(Right)* The nine stimuli as they appear in the $\mathcal{R}$-space of a Chorus of four modules, in which the objects situated at the endpoints of the parameter-space cross served as the reference shapes.

result, because no confidence interval is obtained along with it (the same problem arises in the interpretation of MDS stress; see appendix F). Confidence bounds can, however, be computed using Monte Carlo simulations in conjunction with the bootstrap method (Efron and Tibshirani, 1993).[34] To do that, the MDS analysis and the Procrustes normalization are repeated a large number of times, using permuted data (in this manner, the basic statistics of the subject data are preserved, yet the structure that presumably gives rise to the pattern revealed by MDS is destroyed). This procedure yields a statistical estimate for the mean deviation from veridicality expected to arise by chance, and an estimate for the standard error of that mean. A comparison of those figures to the measure derived from the unperturbed subject data invariably indicated that the veridicality reported in Edelman (1995b; Cutzu and Edelman, 1998) was statistically significant.

## 6.6 Psychophysics: Effects of Translation

Computational theories of recognition based on structural descriptions, which are inherently free of ties to any particular coordinate system, foster the notion that translation is relatively easy to tolerate or to compensate. Likewise, geometric alignment espouses representations in which positions of fiducial points on an object are described relative to each other, rather that in an external coordinate system. Consequently, in computer vision, translation in the visual field is usually considered as the least problematic of the various object transformations with which a recognition system must cope. The situation in neural network models of recognition is radically different.

Some of the difficulties facing network models in achieving translation invariance have been widely publicized following the investigation of perceptrons reported in Minsky and Papert (1969). Indeed, although designs for translation-invariant neural networks have been proposed very early on (Pitts and McCulloch, 1965), it took several decades for viable models for learning translation invariance to emerge (Foldiak, 1991; O'Reilly and Johnson, 1994). The main challenge facing these models is to combine translation invariance with discrimination power. Translation invariance in itself is easily achieved by methods such as weight sharing (i.e., forcing the connection strength patterns at the input to the network to be invariant; see LeCun and Bengio, 1995) or computing histograms of feature values over the entire image and using these as secondary, translation-invariant features (Schiele and Crowley, 1996; Mel, 1997). These methods, however, typically trade off discrimination power for invariance, so that the resulting representation is prone to confuse objects that are similar in their local statistics, yet differ in their structure.[35]

Much of the translation in the visual field that an object may undergo can be compensated for by a saccade that brings it back into fixation (McCulloch, 1965). Because in principle the fixation point may fall anywhere within the object's outline, this still leaves the system with the problem of compensating for some random translation whose extent may equal the apparent size of the object. In the chapter that described the computational implementation of Chorus, I assumed tacitly that this residual compensation can be carried out by an independent mechanism. I shall now examine that assumption in view of the available psychophysical evidence.

Is object recognition in biological visual systems invariant to translation? Although one may imagine that problems encountered in neural network theory in this matter would have been taken as an omen, in psychology, translation invariance used to be commonly taken for granted. The finding that lower animals such as flies do not exhibit position-invariant processing (Dill et al., 1993; Dill and Heisenberg, 1993) cast doubt on this assumption. An increasing number of recent studies (Foster and Kahn, 1985; Nazir and O'Regan, 1990; Dill and Fahle, 1997a; Dill and Fahle, 1997b) indicate that in humans too, the recognition of novel complex stimuli is not completely invariant to translation. Typically, subjects who have to discriminate whether two sequentially flashed random-dot clouds are the same or are different, are faster and more accurate when both stimuli are presented to the same rather than to different locations in the visual field (Foster and Kahn, 1985; Dill and Fahle, 1997a). This effect seems to be gradual (i.e., larger displacements produce poorer performance), and specific for *same* trials.[36]

While *same-different* matching involves only short-term memory, Nazir and O'Regan (1990) also found positional specificity in learning experiments that lasted at least several minutes. They trained subjects to discriminate a complex target pattern from a number of distractors. Training was restricted to a single location in the parafoveal field of view. Having reached a criterion of 95% correct responses, subjects were tested at three different locations: the training position, the center of the fovea, and the symmetric location in the opposite visual hemisphere. Discrimination accuracy dropped significantly for the two transfer locations, while at the control location the learned discrimination was not different from the training criterion.

More recently, Dill and Fahle (1997b) isolated two components of learning to recognize patterns. Following the first few trials, subjects perform clearly above chance. Their performance, subsequently, improves slowly, until they reach the accuracy criterion required by the experimental task. This second learning stage can last up to several hundred trials. Dill and Fahle showed that accuracy at transfer locations (that is, generalization across translations) is at about the same level as the performance at familiar locations at the beginning of the slower learning phase. This suggests that the rapidly acquired component of recognition performance is translation-invariant, while the other, slowly learned component is more specific to the location of the stimuli in the field of view.

### 6.6.1 Translation Invariance for Line Drawings of Common Objects

The basic requirement imposed on the stimuli in psychophysical studies of translation invariance is novelty: if the stimuli are familiar, the subjects are likely to have been exposed to their transformed versions prior to the experiments. Because of this constraint, the typical stimuli both in *same-different* matching and in recognition learning studies tended to be highly unnatural and complex (e.g., random dot or checkerboard patterns). With familiar patterns, one may expect performance to be less sensitive to translation. Indeed, priming experiments with images of common objects showed complete invariance (Ellis et al., 1989; Biederman and Cooper, 1991a).

In one example, Biederman and Cooper (1991a) tested subjects with line drawings of familiar objects in a naming task. Repeated presentation reduced the naming latency, in a manner largely independent of the relative location in the visual field of the priming and the test presentations.

Some of the priming, however, may have been nonvisual: Biederman and Cooper found a reduction of the naming latency also if a different instance of the same object class was presented (e.g., a bird in flight instead of a perched one). As pointed out by Jolicoeur and Humphrey (1998), the visual part of the priming effect may be too small to detect an influence of position, size or other transformations.

### 6.6.2 Translation Invariance for Controlled Synthetic Animal-like Shapes

Dill and Edelman (1997) attempted to determine whether *same-different* discrimination of novel 3D shaded shapes would be translation-invariant, as in Biederman and Cooper's (1991) priming experiments involving line drawings of common objects, or location-specific, as in the *same-different* discrimination of 2D noise-like patterns (Nazir and O'Regan, 1990; Dill and Fahle, 1997b).

Their first two experiments tested positional specificity of *same-different* discrimination among six computer-graphics animal-like shapes (see figure 6.18). These stimuli were adapted from an earlier study (Edelman, 1995a) that had shown significant effects of rotation in depth on the discrimination of these objects. These experiments found translation-invariant performance, which did not depend on the similarity between the stimuli. In experiment 3, invariance was also obtained with "scrambled" versions of the animal-like stimuli (figure 6.19), indicating that novelty as such does not necessarily lead to a breakdown of invariance.

In experiment 3, the spatial relations among the limbs were identical for the two stimuli in each trial; the only difference between the stimuli was in the shapes of the limbs. Experiment 4 examined a complementary situation: both scrambled animals in a given trial were now composed of identically shaped limbs, and only differed in their spatial arrangement. If, for example, the first stimulus was a scrambled monkey, then the second stimulus was a differently scrambled monkey (cf. the rows in figure 6.19). In comparison, in experiment 3, the second object would have been, for example, a scrambled dog or mouse (cf. columns in figure 6.19). Consequently, experiments 3 and 4 distinguished between effects of local features (limb shapes) and feature relationships (limb configuration).

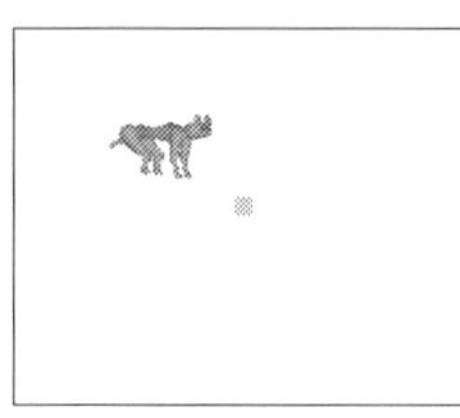



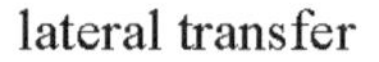


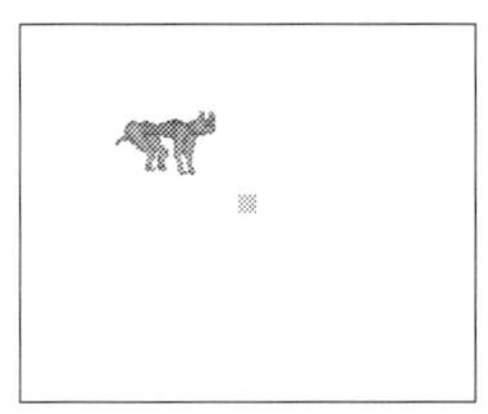

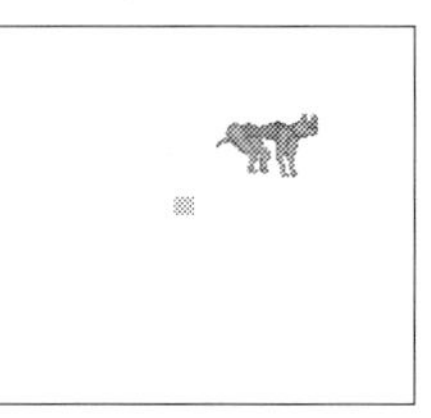



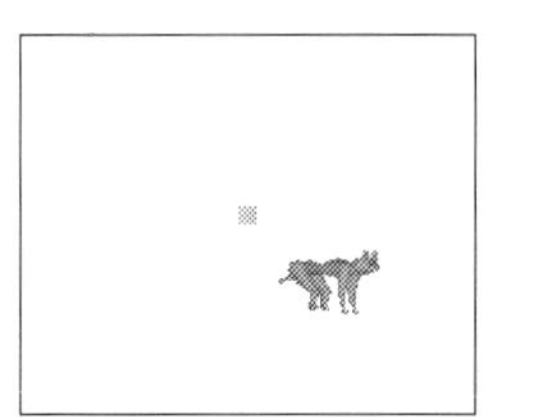

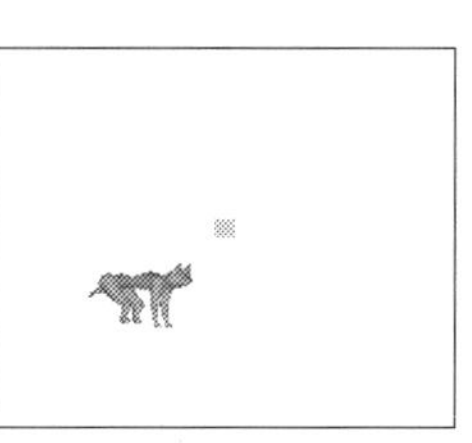

**Figure 6.18**
The four transfer conditions in the study of translation invariance described in Dill and Edelman (1997). In each trial, the first animal-like stimulus was shown at one location, followed by random masks at all four possible locations of the stimuli. The second animal appeared after 1.4 seconds, either at the same location (*control*) or at one of the other three positions corresponding to *lateral*, *vertical*, and *diagonal* transfer (figure 6.18). Lateral and vertical transfer corresponded to displacements of about 5.5°, while the diagonal displacement was 8°.

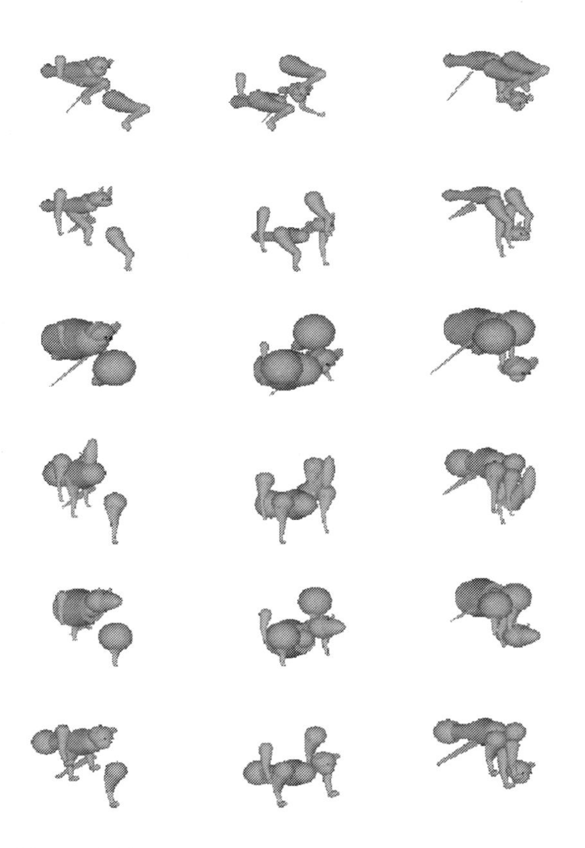

**Figure 6.19**

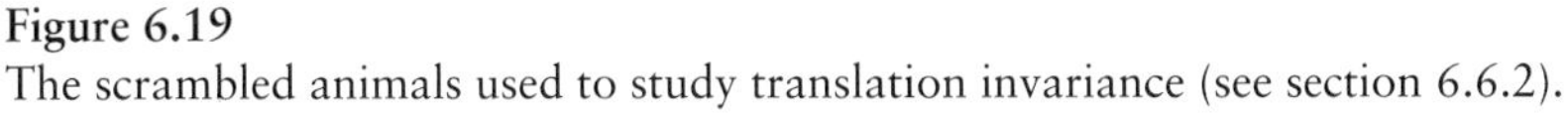

The scrambled animals used to study translation invariance (see section 6.6.2).

The seemingly slight modification of the task between experiments 3 and 4 produced a considerable difference in the results. In experiment 4, the occurrence of a particular limb was not diagnostic for discrimination (except maybe via a chance occlusion). Under these conditions, performance was not completely invariant to translation, while discrimination by local features in experiment 3 was.

The possible link between the need to consider relationships among features (i.e., structural information) and the breakdown of translation invariance was investigated further in experiment 5, which used new animal-like objects created by randomly combining limbs from different animals (cf. figure 6.20). These chimerae were difficult to categorize into

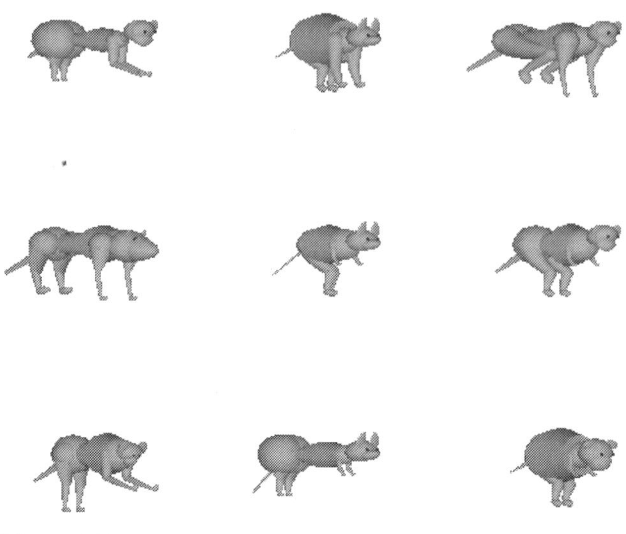

**Figure 6.20**
The "chimeric" animals used to study translation invariance (see section 6.6.2).

familiar animal classes; as new chimerae were created for each trial, the subjects were prevented from learning to categorize them. Importantly, the identification of a particular feature (e.g., the head) in two chimerae did not necessarily indicate that the two stimuli were identical, because all other features could still be different. This forced the subjects to attend to the entire configuration of each chimera. The results of this experiment were consistent with those of experiment 4: the subjects exhibited a significant effect of object translation.

Taken together, the experiments of Dill and Edelman (1997) indicate that complete translation (and scale) invariance can be obtained with a set of 3D shapes known to evoke pronounced viewpoint dependence in *same-different* judgment. At the same time, these findings qualify Biederman and Cooper's (1991) claim that visual priming is completely translation-invariant, by identifying a particular condition in which invariance breaks down: that in which the stimuli cannot be distinguished on the basis of local features. This qualification provides yet another reason to doubt the relevance of Biederman's RBC theory as a model of human object recognition. However, the observed pattern of performance cannot be accommodated by the Chorus scheme either. In chapter 4, I assumed that translation is taken care of prior to recognition, in a manner that does not depend on the nature of the recognition task. This assumption is challenged by the discovery that the degree of translation invariance for 3D shapes does, in fact, depend on an interplay between the structure of the stimuli and the nature of the task. This result also makes it more difficult to write off the previously discovered effects of translation on dot-cloud and checkerboard-pattern discrimination (Foster and Kahn, 1985; Nazir and O'Regan, 1990; Dill and Fahle, 1997a; Dill and Fahle, 1997b) as non-representative cases. Thus, the mechanisms that allow visual objects to be recognized independently of retinal location seem to be far from universally effective for all kinds of objects. In the next chapter, I propose a revision of Chorus that is motivated by this observation, and outline a research program, combining theory and experiments, which starts where Chorus leaves off.

## Notes

1. That is, the primary visual cortex of primates. This qualification will be implied throughout this chapter.

2. Additional dimensions such as the speed of motion may also be included. Alternative formulations in terms of completely different variables are also possible, but will not be discussed here.

3. The major subdivisions of IT cortex are called posterior and anterior (pIT and aIT, also known as TEO and TE). To simplify the nomenclature, these details are omitted from the literature survey in this chapter.

4. Frustratingly, Rose exonerates Barlow only to perpetrate further confusion by misconstruing reviews of contemporary work on response patterns of IT cells (Tanaka, 1996; Logothetis and Scheinberg, 1996).

5. It should be noted that the time-consuming process of manual reduction dictated that these experiments be conducted in anesthetized monkeys.

6. Interestingly, the histogram had a long tail, indicating the presence of a few vigorously responding cells. For ninety-seven new stimuli unfamiliar to the monkey, the histogram looked similar, but the tail of strong responses was absent. This may be interpreted as a sign of the involvement of very few cells in the representation of familiar stimuli; such a clique could be recruited from a larger pool of cells responding more moderately to the given stimulus.

7. Sparseness was defined as $s = \left(\sum_{i=1}^{N} r_i/N\right)^2 / \sum_{i=1}^{N}(r_i^2/N)$, where $r_i$ was the mean firing rate to stimulus $i$ in the set of $N$ stimuli. If the neurons were binary

(either firing or not), $s = 0.5$ would mean that the neuron responded to 50% of the stimuli.

8. Psychophysical correlates of such partial invariance and of the interaction between invariance and familiarity will be discussed in section 6.4 below.

9. Indeed, learning may operate even on an evolutionary time scale. It has been hypothesized that the receptive fields at the initial stages of visual processing have evolved to match the statistics of the natural images (Field, 1994), so as to optimize various properties of the representations (e.g., the informativeness) evoked by natural stimuli.

10. The ability to encode temporal succession is useful in forming representations of object viewspaces that can give rise to interesting psychophysical phenomena such as mental rotation (see section 6.4.4). Another issue raised in Miyashita's work, that of sensitivity to geometric and parametric transformations of the stimulus, is discussed further in chapter 7.

11. This point can be illustrated on a simple task—sorting a list of numbers in ascending order of magnitude—as follows. On a serial computer, a straightforward algorithm (such as "bubble sort") takes on the order of $n^2$ pairwise comparisons to sort $n$ numbers; a more sophisticated algorithm (such as Mergesort) will take $n \log n$ comparisons—the theoretical lower limit (Aho et al., 1974). On an analog computer, however, the lower limit can be transcended; for example, if each number is represented by the length of an (uncooked) piece of spaghetti, the "numbers" can be sorted in one "comparison" step, by placing the bunch of spaghetti on its end against a table.

12. Whereas cells tuned to both upright and upside-down faces have been reported in the monkey inferotemporal cortex, in sheep, which are less likely to be seen suspended upside down in a tree, only cells responsive to upright sheep faces have been found.

13. Out of the twelve objects, only one (horse) was not man-made.

14. Note that this dependence is predicted only for "positive" trials, in which the objects in fact do match. In "negative" trials, in which the objects do not match under any transformation, the mental rotation model does not generate any prediction as to the processing time (see Cutzu and Edelman, 1994).

15. These two kinds of rotation had generally similar effects. One exception was the lack of ER effect in image-plane rotation (Edelman and Bülthoff, 1992a); this is understandable, as it is a nondistorting transformation.

16. That is, transformation to the closest stored view.

17. Subjects (but not the computer models Liu et al. tested) were helped by planarity and symmetry of the stimuli.

18. Likewise, Kubovy (1983) distinguishes between two formulations: "imagine rotation of object" (acceptable) and "rotate image of object" (problematic) (see also Shepard, 1984, 421).

19. The model described in this section does not address the question of rotation of unfamiliar objects. This issue can be addressed by postulating the involvement of "transformation boxes"—hard-wired mechanisms capable of transforming an image of an object into another image, corresponding to its appearance under a fixed rotation around a fixed axis, as in the schematic model for visuomotor coordination proposed in Churchland (1987, 447). This model of mental rotation of novel objects generates psychophysical predictions that can be tested experimentally. For example, it predicts that the response time for such objects should grow by discrete steps (corresponding to the quanta of rotation hard-wired into the transformation boxes), and that rotation around mutually orthogonal axes should be amenable to manipulation that would uncover the independence of the underlying mechanisms.

20. This kind of representation is more conventionally designated as *analog* (Pylyshyn, 1973; Palmer, 1978).

21. This property of representations, which is frequently referred to as commutativity, is discussed in Holland et al. (1986, figure 2.3, 33). A related issue is treated by Amari (1978), who analyzes feature spaces that are commutative in the sense that they allow the representation of a transformed stimulus to be computed by subjecting the representation of a reference one to a certain feature-space processing, rather than by projecting the actual (distal) transformed stimulus into the representation space (cf. Shepard, 1984).

22. Earlier indications of viewpoint effects in object perception tasks were probably deemed irrelevant, either because the task did not involve matching to long-term memory, as in mental rotation (Shepard and Metzler, 1971), or because object orientation affected response latency but not accuracy, as in the recognition of 2D shapes rotated around the line of sight (Rock, 1973). A prominent pre-1980 study of the recognition of depth-rotated objects published by Bartram (1976) was not referred to by Marr (1982).

23. The idea of such convergence is supported by fMRI data on the equivalent processing of different cues to shape in the human counterpart to the monkey IT cortex (Grill-Spector et al., 1997), as well as by electrophysiological data on the effectiveness of outline stimuli in monkey V4/IT areas (Ito et al., 1994).

24. A simpler model of the primary visual cortex, which did not include the extension fields, could not reproduce this result (Fiser et al., 1997). Note that the existence of *temporal* extension fields, linking views connected by apparent motion, is consistent with Freyd's (1983) notion of representational momentum. Such a mechanism may also be responsible for the one-shot viewpoint invariance on the basis of a single given view, reported in Kourtzi and Shiffrar (1997).

25. This study explicitly tested the conditions for invariance specified by Biederman and Gerhardstein. It reported two experiments, using sequential matching and naming tasks, that satisfied all three criteria (Hayward and Tarr, 1997): the stimuli were 3D objects composed of geons (figure 6.10) and the viewpoint

changes were controlled appropriately. The first experiment showed that for qualitatively distinct objects both RT and ER are affected by viewpoint difference. The second experiment showed that this effect is due to changes in qualitative features in stimulus *images* (e.g., in the outline) and not in the geon structural descriptions.

26. The same interaction between the difficulty of the task (here, similarity between the objects that are to be discriminated) and the degree of generalization of performance across stimulus transformations (here, viewpoint changes) is found in a variety of tasks (Ahissar and Hochstein, 1997). As shown in appendix H, it is a common trait of feature-space representations, which can be derived from some simple assumptions (Green and Swets, 1966). In the present case, the feature space corresponds, presumably, to the internal shape space $\mathfrak{R}$; see chapter 4.

27. The results of Edelman (1995a) cannot be used to determine whether a single mechanism or a dual system (Jolicoeur, 1990) is responsible for the various gradations of the subjects' performance. One way to address this question is by exploring the time course of categorization. Posner (1978) pointed out that the experimenter's ability to manipulate the time courses of two phenomena would indicate that they must be supported by distinct (perhaps sequentially related) representations. This approach was adopted by Ellis et al. (1989), whose subjects had to decide whether two sequentially presented objects had the same name under a varying time constraint. The stimuli in this experiment were photographs of depth-rotated objects, named by frequency-controlled names; unlike in Bartram (1976), the rotation of these stimuli did not cause radical alteration of the object's visible features. For longer stimulus presentation times (stimulus onset asynchrony SOA = 200 *msec*), Ellis et al. found both an object benefit (that is, faster RTs if the two images were of the same object) and a view benefit (faster RTs if the images were of the same view). Interestingly, the object benefit, but not the view benefit, was reduced if the SOA was only 100 *msec*. This may be taken as an indication of the existence of two distinct (perhaps successive) stages of object representation: a view-based code that is generated faster but supports only viewpoint-dependent performance, and a slower object-based code, which can support viewpoint-invariant performance.

28. The effects of changes in the illumination were also explored in that study, but will not be discussed here.

29. Such drawing of conclusions concerning general object recognition from face recognition data has been criticized on the basis of the claim that faces are "special" in the sense of being processed by the visual system differently from other objects (Fiser et al., 1997). This claim is, however, unwarranted, in view of the demonstration that the expertise-related effects observed in face processing (e.g., the inversion effect and class-based generalization) can be replicated with other objects following exposure over a course of several thousand trials (Tanaka and Gauthier, 1997; Gauthier et al., 1998).

30. The literature on the representation of perceptual categories is too extensive to be surveyed here. The stance of Chorus on this issue is close to that of the

exemplar-based representation theories (Nosofsky, 1988; Nosofsky, 1991b); the distinction between exemplars and prototypes in this case is immaterial, as long as it is understood that more than one prototype participates in each decision. According to an alternative theory, categories are represented by the decision surfaces that separate them in the relevant feature space (Maddox and Ashby, 1993). The former approach (which can be cast formally in terms of statistical mixture modeling) is preferable on purely computational grounds, e.g., because of the greater flexibility of exemplar-based representations (Bishop, 1995).

31. Agreement between patterns derived from different perceptual modalities, e.g., between visual and haptic data, can also be tested (Garbin, 1990).

32. These results have been replicated in psychophysical experiments in the monkey, using delayed matching to sample and two separate sets of stimuli arranged in triangular configurations in the parameter space (Sugihara et al., 1998).

33. All the stimuli shared a common "qualitative" (geon) structural description, making it difficult to account for the observed results within the RBC framework.

34. I thank an anonymous reviewer of Edelman (1995b) for bringing this technique to my attention.

35. Such neglect of the global structure of the stimulus in favor of its local shape features seems to prevail in the pigeon visual system, which treats intact and scrambled (i.e., cut and rearranged) cartoon drawings as equivalent (Cerella, 1987).

36. Control experiments here ruled out explanations in terms of afterimages, eye movements, and shifts of spatial attention (Dill and Fahle, 1997a).

# 7

# Dialogues on Representation and Recognition

Their books are also different. . . . Those of a philosophical nature invariably include both the thesis and the antithesis, the rigorous pro and con of a doctrine. A book which does not contain its counterbook is considered incomplete.

—Jorge Luis Borges
*Ficciones*—1956

The reconstructionist dogma, which dominated vision intellectually for decades, generated along the way considerable theoretical *ressentiment*. In the spirit of the times, many vision researchers these days regard their subject matter as a bag of tricks—what Marr (1981) referred to as a Type II theory.[1] This stance is certainly consistent with the flood of artifices applied to this or that problem in computer vision, which, in turn, is matched and exceeded by the flood of data produced in visual neurophysiology and psychophysics. Against the backdrop of all this activity, attempts to put together a coherent picture of what, if anything, is going on behind the scenes seem especially scarce.

This book has been motivated by my belief that something *is* going on out there, and that a unified treatment of a core problem in vision, such as shape representation, is a goal both worthy and attainable, albeit contrary to the zeitgeist of theoretical fragmentation. Such a unified theory of representation would have to be viable in all respects: abstract computational, algorithmic, and experimental-observational. Any attempt to cover this much ground constructively (as opposed to being merely critical of all and sundry) runs the risk of reading like a grant proposal: single-minded and a bit overly optimistic. In many cases, a good cure for this syndrome is the one prescribed by the epigraph to this chapter.

Borges, I suspect, would have loved to submit two antithetical proposals under the same cover, were he ever in need of soliciting research support.

If this chapter is not quite the antithesis to its predecessors, it is because the situation in the current debate concerning representation and recognition in vision is not so simple as to allow a single antithesis for each thesis. The volume and the variety of questions that are raised in this debate are best envisaged by unconventional means. We can imagine, in the spirit of Stanislaw Lem and Douglas Hofstadter, a gigantic machine—a kind of oversized mechanical theorist's apprentice—with a multitude of knobs, each controlling the machine's opinion on one of the issues relevant to the field at hand. A choice of settings for all the knobs makes the machine adopt a particular set of theoretical beliefs along with a relevant body of evidence. As a result, it prints out refutations of competing theories, generates accounts for the observed data, and maybe even makes suggestions for new experiments.

Abstracting the machine away, we may think of a multidimensional landscape in which each choice of knob settings defines a point—a theory. The elevation of a point—the worth of the theory—is decided by the usual meta-theoretical means: refutability, agreement with observations, parsimony of explanation, and beauty. The trek through the six chapters of this book brought us to what I believe is a local maximum in this landscape. Having built a cairn in this place, I would like now to examine the various turns I made along the way, note the roads not taken, and perhaps discern other heights of land in the vicinity. The remainder of this chapter is, therefore, a retrospective on our journey through Theoryland, in the form of a series of dialogues between two fellow hikers.

## 7.1 Dialogue 1: On the Problem of Representation

*In the beginning of the book, you illustrated the problems you were going to address in terms of a few very concrete questions; can you now suggest some equally concrete answers? For example, what, indeed,* is *common to the brains of two people who see a cat on the mat?*

Let me try. . . . The first answer that suggests itself is simply "the cat!" This is what I meant by the claim that the world is its own best representation, which I made elsewhere (Edelman, 1998). I believe this is also what Putnam, Millikan, and Dretske had in mind when they made similar statements. Specifically, Putnam (1988, 73) wrote that "We cannot individuate concepts and beliefs without reference to the environment. Meanings aren't 'in the head.' " Likewise, Millikan (1995, 170) argued that "[It is an] error . . . to suppose that cognitive systems are located inside people's heads. Rather, cognitive systems are largely in the world. I no more carry my complete cognitive systems around with me as I walk from place to place than I carry the U.S. currency system about with me when I walk with a dime in my pocket."

Leaving the burden of the representation of a cat to the cat itself creates an explanatory dilemma. On the one hand, it is intuitively plausible: in our heads we have brains, not meaning (whatever that may be); a dollar bill is not a unit of buying power (whatever that is), but a signed promise to give the bearer some gold if they ask for it; a book is paper with some ink marks, and you won't find hobbits there (whatever they are). On the other hand, brains do generate meanings, dollars have more buying power than candy wrappers, and we can get to know a lot about hobbits from reading books. Dretske (1995, 38) clarifies the situation by making a distinction between a representation and its content: "The representations are there, but their content is not. In this sense, the mind isn't in the head any more than stories (i.e., story contents) are in books." To save the day, the insides of representational systems must be connected to their outsides properly, and neither Putnam, nor Millikan, nor Dretske tell us *how* to go about it.

Getting back to our example, if brains of different observers are to share the visual experience of a cat, each of them must tie its representation of the cat (an entity that is presumably internal to a brain) to its content (which resides on the mat). Connecting the inside of a visual system to the outside—specifying the wherewithal of the representation, so to speak—is the Himalaya of the philosophy of mind, and trekking there can be dangerous. Still, we can try to avoid the slopes and the crevasses where other hikers are known to have foundered. The base camp I propose is actually safer than it may seem: it is the old idea of a symbol.

Before you protest, assume for the moment that the representation of a cat is indeed a symbol or a place holder for the cat inside the visual system—its *locum tenens* (the cat's lieutenant, as it were). Now, let us *ground* all such symbols (Harnad, 1990) by tying each to the external event it is supposed to represent. We have at our disposal just the mechanism we need to do that: a module tuned to a specific object and trained to signal its confidence (Barlow, 1990) in the presence of that object within the field of view. If the object happens to be unfamiliar, a Chorus of modules will join in the representation. Here, then, is an answer to the question we started with: if you and I see a cat, your symbol for a cat becomes active, and so does mine.

*The symbols, then, have "strings" attached to them, which lead to the outside world . . .*

Quite right—without such grounding,[2] a system of symbols would have no natural semantic interpretation (as Stevan Harnad pointed out in 1990), and it would be impossible to claim that my symbol for a cat indeed refers to the cat and not to the mat, let alone arguing that my symbols and yours refer to the same objects.

*Wouldn't the brain need to employ a homunculus to push the symbols around?*

Certainly not. Consider this: to a first approximation, the reason for an embodied intelligence to do anything at all with the symbols that land in its "in" tray stems from the need to link perceptions to actions. To connect every possible percept to every possible action, one can use what electrical engineers call a crossbar switch (figure 7.1). As always, getting the engineers involved in a project is a good way to avoid science fiction solutions. In this case, associating raw visual inputs (say, activities in the optic nerve) with raw motor commands (activations of fiber bundles in the muscles) is infeasible, because of the high dimensionality of the input and output spaces: a crossbar with 1,000,000 lines on each side would need 1,000,000,000,000 switches. This underscores the importance of reducing the dimensionality of the problem (Edelman and Intrator, 1997). If dimensionality is kept under control, associations between inputs and outputs—the settings for the crossbar switches—can be learned from examples (Willshaw et al., 1969), and the homunculus can go into retirement.

*You argue for the importance of low dimensionality of the representation space, yet there is at least one approach to learning and classification that does not seem to suffer from the curse of dimensionality: Vapnik's support vector machine.*

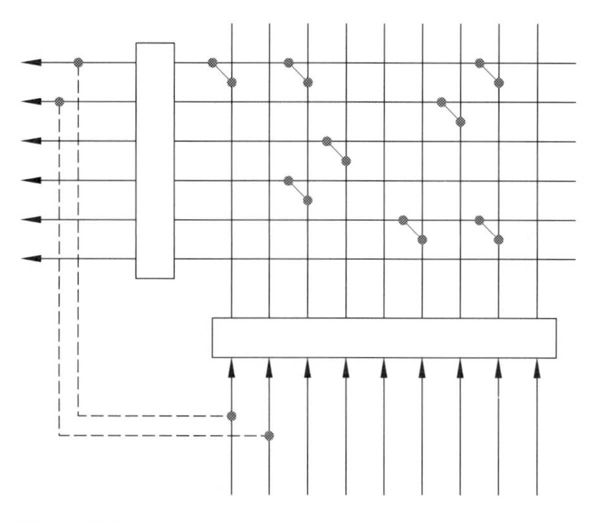

**Figure 7.1**
A crossbar switch, allowing patterns presented on the input lines to be associated with patterns generated on the output lines. Associative memories of this kind are discussed, for example, in Willshaw et al. (1969); the recurrent connections are required by certain dynamical-system models of memory. The anatomy of some brain regions, such as the hippocampus, resembles the orderly interconnection structure illustrated here. Because the number of links connecting inputs with outputs grows quadratically with the dimensionality of the representation space, the latter must be kept low to make the association feasible.

The difference between the support vector method and my approach is in the meta-theoretic (philosophical if you wish) outlook. Let me explain. Intuitively, Vapnik's work is based on the following observation: if the two clusters of data points in a two-way classification situation are well-separated, only a few of the points actually influence the location of the optimal hyperplane (linear discriminant surface) separating the classes. These special points are the support vectors; algorithms for finding and using them are outlined in Cortes and Vapnik (1995). One consequence of the support vector idea is the realization that high dimensionality can be beneficial: adding dimensions to a representation (i.e., taking additional features into account), increases the separation between the classes. Classification thus becomes easier, without falling prey to the curse of dimensionality, because the relevant dimensionality corresponds to the number of support vectors (which, in turn, depends on the data set), and not to the number of features.

From a mathematical standpoint, this happens because the difficulty of classification—the number of support vectors—is related to the VC (Vapnik-Cervonenkis) dimension, which is basically a combinatorial and not a geometric characterization of the complexity of a solution to a problem (Vapnik, 1995). The VC dimension can be low for very high-dimensional problems (which signifies their combinatorial tractability), and it can be high for geometrically low-dimensional problems (which means they would be very difficult). The claim that the geometric dimensionality of the problem is irrelevant at least in some cases is supported by the following counter-example to the curse of dimensionality, due to V. Vapnik. Consider a random mixture of points belonging to two classes in one dimension; the two classes in this example can be separated by a one-parameter decision "surface" such as a sine function of controlled period. This solution (which, because of its high separating power, has a high VC dimension) will, however, generalize very poorly to new data points, showing that low dimensionality is not a guarantee of good (generalization) performance. Together with the efficiency of support vector algorithms in the dimensionality-inflated space, this seems to indicate that the quest for low-dimensional representations is misguided.

In my view, the kind of difficulty illustrated by this example—separating two classes that are thoroughly intermixed—does not arise in typical real-world situations, where events linked by some small smooth and continuous transformation are more likely than not to call for the same label. Consider, for example, the set of images generated by viewing an object undergoing a rotation. These images are presented to an observer in a natural order; the sequence of internal representations that arises in this case, all of which must be classified as "the same" (i.e., images of the same object) will be conveniently mapped into a sequence of nearby points in a measurement space, if the measurements satisfy certain basic conditions (see chapter 3 and appendix A). An analogous situation prevails in examples that deal with smooth deformation (morphing) rather than transformation of the objects. My conclusion from this observation is that the internal representations of real-world objects and events consist of more or less contiguous clusters of points, the corollary being the importance of low dimensionality (without which learning the cluster structure from examples would be intractable).

Under this "nice world" (i.e., contiguous clustering) assumption, the low combinatorial dimension requirement becomes tautological, being reduced to the observation that a problem is easy if the clusters are well-separated. This, of course, is true also for the approaches that stress the importance of low geometrical dimensionality. The two approaches (perhaps I should say, world views) differ as to the next processing stage. According to Vapnik, dimensionality should be inflated, to facilitate linear separation between the classes. In contrast, according to the view that motivates my work, the high dimensionality of the measurement space *must* be reduced to facilitate learning from examples (Edelman and Intrator, 1997); more importantly, it *can* be reduced, because the data that are of interest to the observer reside in a low-dimensional smooth manifold in the measurement space in the first place.

*But why not just stick to the support vector idea and work directly in the high-dimensional space? According to Vapnik's results this classification problem should be tractable.*

The reason for trying to recover the low-dimensional manifold in which the data live, instead of constructing a decision surface for a given classification problem involving these data, has to do with transfer of learning or expertise across tasks. The hyperplane constructed by the support vector algorithm may be easy to learn, and it may afford good generalization to new examples of the same problem, but it is useless for generalization of expertise to different sets of labels for the same data. In comparison, a good feature extraction algorithm—one that produces a smooth low-dimensional representation that preserves the cluster structure of the data—can facilitate the learning of an entire range of tasks involving the same data points (Intrator and Edelman, 1997b). This is a special case of a more general observation, championed by G. Hinton and others, which states that a characterization of the (class-conditional) probability density of the data is much more informative and potentially useful than a characterization of the decision surface for a given task (Bishop, 1995). In theory, density estimation is a very difficult problem; in practice, the kind of estimation exemplified by methods such as Chorus is tractable, because the relevant aspects of the world are smooth and low-dimensional.

*Is there neurobiological support for the idea of low-dimensional representations of object shapes or of association between such representations?*
I believe there is. Let us start with the dimensionality issue. In this connection, it is useful to consider the parallel between the Chorus modules and the functionally defined columns found by Keiji Tanaka's group in the inferotemporal (IT) cortex in monkeys (Fujita et al., 1992; Tanaka, 1992). By the latest estimates, there are about 2,000 columns in IT (Wang et al., 1996), which means that at a coarse functional level of description the dimensionality of the output of IT is equal to 2,000. This makes the idea of input-output association plausible both anatomically and computationally: a 2,000 × 2,000 crossbar switch is not too much to ask for.

It may also be possible to identify brain mechanisms that use the low-dimensional representations provided by the IT cortex. In motor control, a structure that both resembles a crossbar switch, and is implicated in learning, is found in the cerebellum. The principal feature of the cerebellum is the Purkinje cell, which receives excitatory input from two sources: the parallel fibers (which are the axons of the granule cells), and the climbing fibers. Importantly, the dendritic trees of Purkinje cells are planar, and always meet the parallel fibers at a right angle. A given Purkinje cell receives input from numerous parallel fibers, each of which, however, makes only a few synapses with a given Purkinje cell dendrite. This structure can be compared to the illustration in figure 7.1. Many theories implicating this system in motor learning have been proposed, starting with (Marr, 1969).

For the purpose of general associative learning, low-dimensional representations originating in IT may be processed in the hippocampus, one of the areas situated upstream from the IT cortex. The particularly relevant structure in the hippocampus in this connection is the "trisynaptic" circuit (Amaral and Witter, 1989). In the first leg of this circuit, area IT projects (via the entorhinal cortex) to the granule cells of the dentate gyrus. Second, the granule cells of the dentate gyrus project to the large pyramidal cells in subfield three of cornu Ammonis or Ammon's horn, (CA3). Third, the CA3 pyramidal cells project to the pyramidal cells of the CA1 subfield, via the Schaffer collateral system. Thus, in the hippocampus one finds not only an amazing anatomical approximation of a crossbar switch, but also evidence for recurrent connections (cf. figure 7.1). As in the case of the cerebellar circuits, there are many models of learning and recall in the hippocampus (see Hasselmo et al., 1995).

## 7.2 Dialogue 2: On Theories of Representation

*You discussed various tasks that require representation before introducing any of the theories, as if the tasks are conceptually prior. I always thought that task-dependent representations are for frogs, and that primates are supposed to have a pretty good notion of what is where, even if they don't have to do anything about it.*

Try to look at it from a different perspective. Primates are good at deciding which representations may be required in a given setting and at putting these together on the fly. Cunning and flexibility act together to mask possible deficiencies in the quality of the representations, which can be brought into the open by experimental means. The poverty of the representation of everyday scenes came under scrutiny only recently, with the accumulation of results that show how little information is carried over from one visual fixation to another (Grimes, 1995; Simons and Levin, 1997).[3] At the same time, many studies (starting with the early recordings of eye movement traces by Yarbus) show that scene characteristics to which the observer pays special attention do get represented and committed to memory. The effects of task and context on the features of objects for which representations are formed are surveyed in (Schyns et al., 1998).

*I have a problem with your analysis of the analogy task. Basically, you claim that for a novel object generalization from a single view can only work by analogy with familiar objects. Doesn't this limitation only apply to systems that do not reconstruct the object's shape? If you use stereo and shading cues and carry out such a reconstruction, you can turn the resulting 3D model whichever way you choose and see what it looks like from a novel viewpoint.*

In principle, you are right. A perfect recovery of the object's 3D shape would obviate the need for analogy to other objects in guessing the transformation of its appearance under rotation. Such recovery is, however, very difficult, which is, presumably, what makes human observers rely on partial, viewpoint-dependent depth information when they are confronted with a recognition task (Edelman and Bülthoff, 1992b; Sinha and

Poggio, 1996). Efficient algorithms for computing viewpoint-dependent depth from just a few "frames" are known (Koenderink and van Doorn, 1991). I wouldn't be surprised if it is found that the human visual system uses similar algorithms alongside the kind of analogy-based computation described in section 5.3.

*Isn't the formalization of representation as a mapping between two spaces too general? This way, anything could end up being a representation of anything else.*

If the mapping were left unspecified, this would be true (see Cummins, 1989, 102ff). Specifically, mere covariation, as envisaged by Locke, between events external and internal to the system is not enough. The activity of cells in the primary visual cortex of primates covaries with the direction of motion of a grating stimulus, yet if a group of these cells is taken out, the animal ends up with a scotoma (a local blind spot), not motion blindness. So, these cells cannot be said to represent motion to the rest of the organism. However, if the intervention is done upstream by injecting very weak electrical current ($10\mu A$) in the proper site in the middle temporal area MT (known to specialize in motion processing), the animal's perception of motion is affected (Salzman et al., 1990) without creating a scotoma. In view of these considerations, a unit inside the brain (or a symbol in some other physical symbol system) can be said to represent a class of events if it fires in the presence of these events (i.e., if the symbol is properly grounded), and if its activity has a causal effect on the rest of the system.

*This criterion seems to be under-specified: if we record from a brain, how many spikes per second does a given cell have to fire before its activity merits the label of a proper representation?*

Well, in the kind of system I have in mind—a Chorus of modules—the symbols are patterns of activity across the entire population (the vectors that are fed into the crossbar switch, if you wish). The question of how much activity on each line is enough is not relevant there; one should ask instead whether the entire pattern of activity is properly grounded. The conditions for it to be so were discussed at length in chapters 3 and 4. Note, by the way, that one expects the response of a system to an external event to depend on the context in which this event is experienced. Thus, the conditionals in the definition of representation should really have a *ceteris paribus* clause added.

*Haven't you given short shrift to the structural decomposition theory? The detection of individual primitives can be improved if multiple cues are combined and if top-down guidance is used. Top-down Bayesian techniques can also tackle the combinatorial interpretation problems facing structural theories.*

I agree that this kind of structural approach is potentially a very serious contender for the title of a comprehensive theory. The natural way in which structural models handle representation and categorization of novel shapes makes them especially appealing. I guess this is what motivates the current efforts to make them work (Geman, 1996). Unfortunately, the success of these efforts is limited. Consider the widely cited example of JIM, which is an implementation of Biederman's Recognition By Components (RBC) theory (Hummel and Biederman, 1992). This seven-layer neural network dreadnought model is habitually confined to port, for fear of capsizing even in moderate seas (see Kurbat, 1994).

In computer vision, the only recognition system that adopts the structural approach and achieves an impressive performance on anything other than a toy example is the one described in (Zhu and Yuille, 1996). In a sense, this is the Marr-Nishihara (1978) method done right. Like M-N, Zhu and Yuille work in the 2D domain, dealing only with outlines of animal shapes. It remains to be seen whether full-fledged structural methods (Mumford, 1994; Geman, 1996) ever become practical.

## 7.3 Dialogue 3: On S-isomorphism

*I understand that S-isomorphism is about representing distal similarities. There seems to be a problem when that notion is used in the context of veridicality: how can one speak about* the *distal similarity when everybody knows that similarity is subjective?*

In one sentence, my reply would be that we must recognize the objectivity of *geometric* shape similarity, or else jeopardize the objectivity of Newtonian mechanics, as I argued in chapter 3. In cognitive science, a typical argument against the objectivity of similarity is voiced in Murphy and Medin (1985) with regard to the number of attributes shared by plums and lawn-mowers being infinite: both weigh less than 1000 kilograms (and less than 1001 kilograms), both cannot hear well, both have a smell, etc. In a similar vein, Watanabe (1985) proved that any two objects are as similar to each other as any other two objects, insofar as the degree of similarity is measured by the number of shared predicates (provided that the set of predicates is finite and equally applicable to all objects, and that no two objects are identical with respect to this set).

The standard resolution of this conundrum consists of bringing into the consideration an *observer*, whose system of "values" (Watanabe, 1985) or "prior spacing of qualities" (Quine, 1969) removes the ambiguity by introducing a bias (Goldstone, 1994). In a discussion of veridicality of perception, the logical next step is to consider the nature of the mapping between the representational systems of two observers, instead of the mapping between the world and the observer's similarity space. A straightforward rephrasing of the relevant passages in chapter 3 (substituting "another observer's" for "distal") leaves the computational conclusions concerning veridicality, *mutatis mutandis*, intact. In particular, if the composition of the mappings of the two observers is smooth, and if no dimensions are lost (projected out) along the way, the two representation spaces will be locally $\mathcal{S}$-isomorphic.

*This merely shifts the focus from veridical perception to veridical communication between two observers. My doubt, however, goes deeper than this distinction: your arguments for veridicality look suspiciously like a revival of the correspondence theory of truth.*

You propose to give up the notion of objective similarity altogether just to defuse the standard philosophical arguments against it. I contend that, as far as shape *geometry* is considered, this amounts to throwing out the baby with the bath water. Let's return to the lawn-mower example, this time concentrating on geometric similarity. Intuitively, the geometry of a plum is very different from that of a lawn-mower, because any shape-preserving transformation[4] applied to the former would leave a residual discrepancy that is large relative to the size of the smaller of the objects involved in the comparison—and also large relative to the residual that is left when a plum and a melon are compared. This line of reasoning can be put on a more formal basis using tools from the mathematical theory of shape spaces developed in the last decade (Kendall, 1984; Carne, 1990; Le, 1991; Le and Kendall, 1993; Bookstein, 1996). The bottom line is that the notion of shape can be formalized naturally, in such a manner that similarity is unique (defined by proximity along minimal geodesics in the shape space) in all but a few degenerate cases.

*So plums and lawn-mowers share the same distal shape space?*
In principle, yes, but we need only concern ourselves with one of its local approximations at a time. A high-resolution shape space common to very disparate objects would be very high-dimensional, with all the problems stemming from this property. A geodesic in such a space connecting two distant points is likely to be unstable, in the sense that a large set of alternative paths would be nearly as short as the shortest one. Intuitively, this means that a plum can be morphed into a lawn-mower in many ways, which differ in the intermediate shapes, yet are nearly equivalent as far as the cumulative distance along the deformation path is concerned.

In practice, the problems of high dimensionality and indeterminacy of the geodesic (similarity) are largely neutralized by the local nature of the tasks for which we need a shape space in the first place. For example, we need to know that plums are different (shape-wise) from lawn-mowers, not that they are more similar to lawn-mowers than to grand pianos (or vice versa, as it may be the case). Locally, it's a different matter: the shapes of plums and other roundish things reside in a low-dimensional subspace of the shape space, where the higher similarity of a greengage plum to an apple than to a lemon is a stable shape feature.
*I presume that all these low-dimensional distal shape spaces are then to be mapped into the internal representation system.*
Yes, as I tried to illustrate in figure I.1. The main complications along the way are (1) the adduction of spurious dimensions due to variation in viewpoint, illumination and other such factors, and (2) the general high dimensionality of the measurement space $\mathcal{M}$, dictated by the need not to lose the relevant dimensions of shape variation. So, for each shape class we have two kinds of low-dimensional subspaces embedded in $\mathcal{M}$: the shape space, spanned by morphing the members of the class into each other, and the view spaces of the individual members, which are basically orthogonal to the shape space (see figure 3.9).

The view space of an object that looks the same from all angles (a perfect sphere) degenerates into a point. It may seem that a recognition system would need to collapse the view spaces of all objects, to allow their recognition irrespective of viewpoint. In fact, it is better to represent the view spaces explicitly, because that provides a basis for intelligent processing of novel shapes in analogy-like tasks. Given the knowledge of the view spaces of several objects (i.e., of the way their appearance changes under viewpoint transformation), a new view of a new shape can be guessed by interpolation, as described in section 5.3.

## 7.4 Dialogue 4: On the Chorus of Prototypes

*Chorus relies on the possibility to construct a module responding invariantly to views of a given object. This seems to me to be asking for too much up front. Building an oracle that reports the presence of an object would amount, after all, to solving the recognition problem.*

Even if the individual modules each behaved like an oracle, they would not have solved the categorization and the analogy problems. In this sense, a Chorus of modules is more that the sum of its parts, because of its ability to deal with novel stimuli. It is important to realize also that the individual modules need not—in fact, should not—behave like oracles. Unlike an oracle, which merely signals object identity, a Chorus module produces a smoothly and monotonically decreasing response to shapes that are progressively less similar to its assigned prototype. An ensemble of such modules addresses the recognition problem in a broader manner, by effectively reducing the dimensionality of the measurement space so that the resulting representation, which is $\mathcal{S}$-isomorphic to the distal shape space, can be used for a variety of tasks.

*Is Chorus the only way of doing that?*

No, it is not. Any computational architecture that fulfills the requirements for veridical representation, listed in chapter 3, should do just as well, or even better. Consider, for example, the method for extracting low-dimensional representations described in Intrator and Edelman (1997b). There, a multilayer perceptron (MLP) trained by backpropagation formed a representation of a set of shapes that was veridical in the sense defined in this book: a low-dimensional parametric structure underlying the set of shapes was reflected faithfully in the space of activities of the hidden units of the MLP. This veridicality broke down if the training procedure did not comply with the theoretical requirements (e.g., if the network was not forced to collapse the dimensions orthogonal to the distal shape space). It is interesting to note that an RBF model trained and tested using the same procedure did not perform as well as the MLP, presumably because of the computational advantage conferred (for the particular task at hand) on the latter model by the nature of its hidden-unit response surface (Intrator and Edelman, 1997b).

*Isn't Chorus just Pandemonium resurrected?*

The Pandemonium (Selfridge, 1959; Lindsay and Norman, 1977) consisted of a three-level hierarchy: feature demons (responsible for the detection of lines, corners, etc.), cognitive demons (responsible for entire objects), and a master demon (responsible for the recognition decision). The first problem I see there is the choice of all or none primitive features, such as edges, corners, etc. This choice, which clearly violates Marr's (1976) principle of least commitment, is likely to lead to the loss of valuable information at an early processing stage. It also renders the distal to proximal mapping non-smooth, lessening the likelihood of veridical representation. This situation can be amended, if probabilistic features are used instead (Barlow, 1990; Barlow, 1994). As Barlow has been arguing since 1959 (with too few people listening most of the time), probabilistic representations can be extremely useful for learning if they include records of recurring and co-occurring events. In Barlow's Probabilistic Pandemonium, the response strength of a demon would be proportional to log $P$, where $P$ is the probability of occurrence of the feature the demon detects (cf. Intrator and Cooper, 1992).

The second problem with the Pandemonium lies at the level of decision-making (the "master demon"), where the stimulus is essentially described by the identity of the strongest-responding "cognitive demon." This Winner Take All decision (another violation of the principle of least commitment) does provide some information about the stimulus (namely, the identity of a reference stimulus to which the current one is the most similar), while discarding much more; the representation it provides qualifies only as nearest-neighbor-preserving. Chorus improves on this essentially by retaining the response levels (not only the identities) of a number of cognitive demons.

*How is Chorus different from coarse coding, then?*

It isn't; Chorus coding is coarse coding in the space of similarities to reference shapes, whose representational power stems, by design, from a particular collection of properties that are dictated by the theory of $\mathcal{S}$-isomorphism.

*I still wonder why you have not built any top-down effects into Chorus: earlier on you acknowledged that top-down resolution of interpretation ambiguities, as proposed by Mumford and by S. Geman, may be a good idea.*

In fact, I do see at least one role for a top-down control pathway in a Chorus-like model: taking task and context into account. As I already pointed out, treating the internal representation structure as a single shape space will not do: disparate shape classes are better taken care of separately. This does not, however, mean that the model disintegrates into a collection of unrelated entities, because the same object can participate in multiple local maps. In Chorus, when two different stimuli activate two partially overlapping sets of object modules, the objects in the intersection of those two sets effectively participate in two distinct shape spaces at the two moments. To enable the comparison between widely different objects, whose "influence spheres" do not normally intersect, the system can use two simultaneous thresholds, controlled by a top-down mechanism.

On the one hand, it can gradually raise the cutoff threshold, below which a module is considered as non-responding to a particular stimulus. This would bring new modules into play, making the system "realize" new aspects of the stimulus (i.e., its similarity to less and less likely reference objects). On the other hand, to keep the dimensionality of the resulting representation shape under control, the modules that respond the strongest should be quenched (perhaps by a mechanism related to that which enforces the refractory period in the firing of individual neurons). In this manner, the influence sphere of the stimulus can be made to widen and to include more and more new objects, while keeping the dimensionality at bay. Note also that new modules can be brought to bear on the stimulus by letting active modules pass activation on via associative links. In this case, similarity (even remote resemblance) ceases to be the only factor in the processing of the stimulus, making the system's response potentially much more flexible and versatile.

## 7.5 Dialogue 5: On the Performance of Chorus

*Why did you not equip Chorus with a better front end? The 200 Gaussian filters are not even close to the number or the variety of features that seem to be computed in the primate visual system by the time the signal reaches the primary visual area, V1.*

One reason for sticking to a minimal measurement space ("front end") was the desire to see what kind of performance would result from forgetting basically everything we know about the primary visual cortical area, V1. The theory of S-isomorphism predicts that the details of the measurement space should not matter for the issues that interested me most: categorization and veridicality. This prediction was confirmed: about 85% correct identification and categorization performance, along with veridical representation of distal similarities, was obtained with a system whose acuity is worse than some of the retinal prosthesis implants under development now.

*Isn't this performance level somewhat disappointing, compared to the state of the art in computer vision and the near-perfect recognition rates reported with the histogram-based approaches (Schiele and Crowley, 1996; Mel, 1997)?*

If you look at the bare figures, those systems indeed outperform Chorus by about 10%. One might argue that their performance in categorization and veridicality was not measured, but that would not be entirely fair, because those systems were not designed to address these problems. I would like to point out instead that the high recognition performance of a V1-like feature space that uses histogramming for achieving viewpoint invariance is actually good news for Chorus, because such a feature (measurement) space should complement the dimensionality reduction capability of Chorus.

*Why do you think that a combination of a good front end with Chorus will outperform each of these two methods working separately?*

Precisely because they address complementary aspects of the recognition problem: a good measurement space will go a long way towards combining the ability to discriminate between very similar objects with viewpoint invariance, while Chorus will support categorization and the representation of novel shapes, insofar as they resemble familiar ones. There are reasons to believe that to some extent the human visual system treats those two groups of problems separately. First, people's ability to generalize recognition of inverted faces across viewpoint is significantly more limited that their performance in the same task involving upright faces: 85% compared to 97% (Moses et al., 1996). This suggests that universal invariance mechanisms (such as a sophisticated general-purpose measurement space, which is supposed to work for any kind of object equally well) provide a pedestal of performance. This, in turn, is complemented by class-based mechanisms, of which Chorus is an example (Duvdevani-Bar et al., 1998). The second piece of evidence for dissociation, this time between two mechanisms having to do with translation invariance, is described in Dill and Edelman (1997; see section 6.6.2).

*You listed the detection of primitives (edges etc.) as a challenging problem when you discussed obstacles that hamper the implementation of structural approaches. At the same time, your implementation of Chorus was only tested on pre-segmented objects. Wasn't that taking too much for granted?*

The need for prior segmentation is a difficult problem for Chorus, as it is for any approach that starts with applying filters indiscriminately to the input image. Entire subfields in computer vision have been devoted to techniques developed in response to that problem. One of these is edge detection, which was seen traditionally as a step towards turning the image into an easily segmentable line drawing. The classical approaches to recognition, starting with the work of Roberts and culminating in the Marr-Nishihara theory, all used edge detection as their foundation, with all the ensuing calamities (edge-detected images do tend to look like shredded wheat at medium magnification). The advent of pictorial alignment (Lowe, 1986; Ullman, 1989) brought about a change: model-based recognition by alignment works fine with raw edge-detected images.

Alignment relies on the coordinates of fiducial geometric features such as object corners. A hypothesis concerning the potential presence of an object in the image can be verified by testing for the presence of the proper geometric features in the proper image locations, determined by the shape and the orientation of the object. It is important to realize that if the precise geometric model of the object is not available, or if the task itself calls for rough categorization rather than exact identification, the system can no longer look for the right feature in the right place. At the very least, a range of locations of the feature is to be scanned, reintroducing the segmentation problem via the back door.

It seems therefore that at least part of the problem of figure-ground segmentation in recognition is inherent in the nature of some of the recognition tasks, particularly of categorization. The current re-emergence of pattern recognition approaches (of which the histogram-based methods and Chorus are two examples) reiterates the need to deal with segmentation, which is also a central problem for pattern theory (Mumford, 1994).

*So, what do you think should be done about it?*

Several things: (1) combine multiple low-level cues (Poggio et al., 1988; Nitzberg and Mumford, 1990; Wang and Adelson, 1994), as the human visual system may well be doing (Grill-Spector et al., 1997), (2) enhance the resulting contour and surface information by "middle-vision" methods (Grossberg and Mingolla, 1985; Ullman, 1984; Kalocsai and Biederman, 1997), and (3) use high-level knowledge to guide segmentation (Mumford, 1994; Geman, 1996).

*Structural methods explicitly aim at representing a huge variety of shapes with the same small and fixed repertoire of shape primitives. How does Chorus fare in this respect? Would its performance scale nicely as the number of test objects is increased?*

This is an empirical issue (as it is, by the way, with the structural methods, where the experience so far has not been very encouraging). Data presented in chapter 5 (figure 5.8) allow only a limited insight into the scaling behavior of Chorus, because of the relatively small size of the database of objects. One conclusion, however, does suggest itself: *within* categories, the ability of Chorus to represent novel instances and support analogy-like tasks is considerable. For example, the processing of new views of a new car on the basis of interpolation among view spaces of several familiar cars (figures 5.12 and 5.13) is very robust, compared to the performance in the same tasks based on interpolation among view spaces of unconstrained reference shapes. The appropriate strategy for a Chorus-based system, then, would be to acquire new prototypes (reference shapes) as it goes along. From the computational standpoint, this is as easy as learning a new RBF module from examples. The real practical issues are the availability of examples for new classes of shapes, and the number of such classes that a system in a given setting has to deal with.

## 7.6 Dialogue 6: On Representation and Recognition in Biological Vision

*Your list of the properties of receptive fields found in the primate visual cortex does not include anything that may correspond to the histograms of features, such as those used in the recognition algorithms of Mel and Schiele.*

It is tempting to assume that the visual system would put such a powerful recognition method to use. Finding cells whose output is proportional to the histogram of some feature over a large portion of the visual field should be very difficult. However, nobody so far seems to have actually looked for such cells; there are certainly enough blanks in the current conceptual maps of the visual pathway where they could fit.

*Is the veridicality you found in the psychophysical experiments on parametric shape-space perception really a kind of rapport between the subject and the experimenter who designed the stimuli?*

Control experiments showed the subjects' visual system to be too selective for that kind of explanation to be plausible: veridicality was found for animal-like objects, but not for nonsense shapes such as "scrambled" animals (Cutzu and Edelman, 1998).

*Could it, then, actually be language-mediated (e.g., due to the use of parts that have agreed-upon names, such as limbs and heads of the animal-like objects)?*

That too is implausible in view of the finding of parametric veridicality in similar experiments in the monkey (Sugihara et al., 1998).

*Doesn't your finding of metric veridicality clash with the well-known reports of asymmetries in similarity judgments? It just seems to be too good (i.e., clean, unconditional) to be true.*

The metric-space definition of internal similarity corroborated by our results does seem to fall short of explaining such prominent phenomena in the perception of similarity as subjectivity, task dependence, and asymmetry (Tversky, 1977; Tversky and Gati, 1978; Nosofsky, 1991a; Medin et al., 1993). I would argue, however, that these shortcomings are only superficial. The importance of the metric-space model lies in its formal treatment of veridicality. On top of that, the perceptual system of the observer can warp the objective similarity space (Harnad, 1987; Goldstone, 1994). In particular, similarity need not remain restricted by the symmetry that it inherits from the underlying distance function; the metric-space model can be considered a starting point for a more realistic definition (Edelman et al., 1996b), which is OK, as long as the basic theoretical framework remains intact.

*You allotted a mere chapter to the survey of neurobiological and psychophysical data on shape representation and recognition. This probably means that many findings that should have been discussed were not.*

True. In the discussion of the neurobiology of recognition, some of the more glaring omissions are the conspicuous neuroanatomical structures that are likely to be functionally important (in particular, lateral and descending connections), data on multiple-cell responses (correlations, oscillation and synchronicity, synfire chains), and the effects of task and context on response properties of cortical receptive fields (RFs). In the sections dealing with the psychophysics of recognition, I did not mention experiments utilizing the ideal observer paradigm, data on the role of visual cues other than shape in recognition, explorations of low-level processes possibly relevant to recognition (such as filling-in and medial axis extraction), and issues connected with depth and surface perception. Although the major reason for leaving all these topics out of the discussion was their lower priority in judging the viability of the SiC theory, there was also another consideration: my hope was that the present treatment of shape representation and recognition would help the neurobiologists and the psychologists themselves to make sense of their data, and perhaps challenge them to disprove SiC.

*What would it take to disprove SiC?*

In physiology, it would take a failure to recover the distal shape similarities from the firings of small groups of cells in the IT cortex, combined with selective responses from those same cells to the test objects. Ironically, I expect the first experimental returns concerning this issue to come not from monkey data but from fMRI studies with human subjects, in which the recovery of a rough map of shape similarities from voxel activation data in area LO has been demonstrated (Edelman et al., 1998). Some relevant physiological experiments were reported in Sakai and Miyashita (1994). That study examined the effects of transformation (rotation) and parametric deformation on the responses of cells in anterior IT to 2D Fourier descriptor images, using the paired associates paradigm pioneered by Miyashita. Unfortunately, that article showed no plot of the response of the cells vs. the deformation of their preferred stimuli, only a histogram of relative effects of rotation and deformation. At about the same time, the Logothetis group reported that IT cells tuned to particular 3D paperclip-like objects also responded to paperclips that differed from their optimal stimuli (Logothetis et al., 1995), again without quantifying the reduction of the response as a function of shape dissimilarity. In this context, I would like to see an experiment that would systematically map the effects of transformation and deformation, using realistic parameterized 3D objects and the same data analysis techniques employed in the psychophysical studies that first demonstrated quantitative veridicality (Cutzu and Edelman, 1998). At some stage, it would also be interesting to try and influence the monkey's categorization performance by injecting current into IT, as it was done for motion perception in MT (Salzman et al., 1990). Area IT has all it takes to justify such an experiment: columnar organization and selectivity to the relevant stimuli.

As far as disproving SiC psychophysically goes, one must distinguish between the prediction of parametric veridicality (that is, $\mathcal{S}$-isomorphism) and the prediction of the particular method of its implementation (Chorus). There is really no question of disproving the former: $\mathcal{S}$-isomorphism has been already demonstrated psychophysically in several cases. Consequently, the next step could be to derive predictions concerning the theoretical conditions for veridicality (i.e., whether or not to expect veridical representation in a given situation) and to test them experimentally, just as the conditions for viewpoint invariance were derived from the various theories and tested to compare them (Biederman and Gerhardstein, 1993; Edelman, 1995a; Tarr et al., 1997). As to the details of the mechanism of veridicality (Chorus): this can be tested by using it to predict the distortion of one parameter-space pattern (measured relative to the ideal which the inter-stimulus similarities are forced to obey) from the distortion of another configuration in the same subject. Specifically, one could try to pinpoint the prototypes (reference shapes purportedly used by Chorus) in the shape space, and use them to derive detailed predictions about the subject's performance in tasks defined over the same portion of the shape space.[5]

A further step in testing Chorus could involve examining its predictions concerning categorization performance for a controlled set of stimuli, something that was not done in (Cutzu and Edelman, 1998). Such an experiment could be patterned after the work of Nosofsky (1991b), which looked into the possibility of accounting for recognition performance in several tasks by an exemplar-based representation model. Nosofsky first derived an MDS solution from the subjects' similarity ratings of thirty-four schematic faces. He then used the resulting face-space configuration to predict classification (categorization) and recognition (old/new) performance, under the assumption that the former is based on comparison of distances in the MDS space to exemplars of the two classes, and the latter on summed similarity to all stored exemplars. Despite the low correlation between classification and recognition performance (which was expected, because different decision criteria are presumably used in these two tasks), the correlation between the prediction of the model and the actual human performance was good. Nosofsky's model (of which Chorus may be considered an extension) also predicted increased weight in the decisions of exemplars that appeared more frequently than others, allowing it to account for asymmetries in performance—a second-order effect that any metric-space similarity model must mimic to gain psychophysical credibility.

*What about testing Chorus indirectly, for example by looking for evidence supporting alternative theories such as RBC?*

So far, RBC did not fare too well in that respect, as I argued in chapter 6. For example, its prediction of viewpoint-invariant performance on geon-level difference among the stimuli was not entirely consistent with human data. One aspect of RBC that I would like to see tested more extensively is the predicted reliance of categorization performance on part structure of the stimuli (Biederman, 1987), because RBC is first and foremost a theory of basic-level (Rosch et al., 1976) processing. Although basic-level categories are thought to be definable via part-related differences (Tversky and Hemenway, 1984), it is not clear that subjects actually form such definitions, as parts seem to be neither necessary nor sufficient to establish a basic-level structure (Murphy, 1991), with other dimensions of shape (e.g., the global outline) coming in their stead.

A rare exploration of the role of parts and of their spatial relationships on the identification of line drawings of common objects was reported in Cave and Kosslyn (1993). Performance was evaluated with intact stimuli and with objects degraded by separation into parts in various manners, as well as with cut-and-paste scrambled objects. There were two main results: first, the way the stimulus was sectioned into parts did not have a significant effect under normal circumstances; second, the proper spatial relations among image-based parts were necessary for easy identification. Scrambling increased naming times and error rates. Breaking an object into unnatural parts had an effect only when the presentation time was very short, and the parts were misoriented. These results are consistent with the idea that the global shape is encoded first (cf. Navon, 1977). Cave and Kosslyn (1993, 247) point out that this suggests an interpretation for Biederman and Cooper's (1991) results concerning priming of contour-deleted objects: the priming contour may have acted on a global representation of the entire object, rather than on representations of geons, as Biederman and Cooper argue.

*How is your view of shape representation space related to Shepard's notion of a psychological space, which figures in his "law of generalization"?*

Shepard's "first law of psychology" (1987) states that points corresponding to a set of stimuli can be embedded in a metric space in such a manner that the likelihood of generalization between two stimuli is inversely monotonically related to their distances. I consider what I called the internal shape space $\mathcal{R}$ (see chapter 3) to be analogous to Shepard's metric representation space.

Note, however, that Shepard's law deals with purely psychological entities, namely, the internal representations of various observable quantities. Nothing is said there about psychophysics: the relationship between the stimuli on the one hand, and their representations and the actions they evoke, on the other hand. If the notion of $\mathcal{S}$-isomorphism is brought to bear on the psychophysical aspect of shape perception, additional hypothetical "laws" may be suggested. For example, one may conjecture that in a system that fulfills the preconditions for $\mathcal{S}$-isomorphism (i.e., a proper measurement space, etc), it will be found that:

- The degree of invariance (under viewpoint or other transformation) for a stimulus is inversely monotonic in its summed distance to familiar shapes (cf. appendix H).
- The degree of shape-space veridicality for a set of stimuli is monotonic in their mean viewpoint invariance and is inversely related to the compactness of the region occupied by the stimuli in the internal representation space (provided that all the stimuli are discriminable).

Obviously, these conjectures must be formulated in a quantitative fashion and subjected to the kind of extensive testing called for in similar cases

(Ashby and Perrin, 1988; Nosofsky, 1991b), before they can assume any status in the theory of perception.

## 7.7 Dialogue 7: On What Has Been Left Out of This Book

*The evidence from human performance seems to me too scarce and too patchy to conclude that part decomposition is irrelevant as a computational model of representation. You must also agree that the failure of the attempts to implement part-based recognition algorithms in the past cannot be taken as an indication of a theoretical flaw. From a theoretical standpoint, parts certainly provide the basis for the most parsimonious and most powerful approaches to representation. How do you propose to deal with situations that clearly call for a part-based analysis?*

The problem you raised is related to compositionality (Bienenstock, 1995), a common label that refers to a number of issues in cognitive science. The neglect of compositionality on the part of the Chorus implementation of $\mathcal{S}$-isomorphism is a sign of a predicament shared by all feature-space methods of shape representation: the lack of explicit treatment of object structure. I mentioned this problem briefly at the end of chapter 2, then proposed to forgo attempts to represent structure explicitly, because this was not needed for tasks such as object identification, discrimination, categorization, and even perceptual analogy. I agree that it is now time to reexamine the need to treat object structure explicitly, if only because people are able to do so when necessary. This would require relaxing the holistic outlook of Chorus.

*Isn't Chorus* necessarily *holistic in its treatment of shape? Worse, I don't even see how it can separate dimensions of shape from those of texture or color in the processing of complex objects. For example, there is no way to know whether a giraffe—presumably represented by similarity to a camel and a leopard—is an ungulate with spots or a predator with a hump.*[6]

Chorus can be adapted to attend selectively to different dimensions of variation of the stimuli, in several ways. First, the input space of the prototype modules can be "skewed" and some of its dimensions stressed (this is a standard technique in pattern recognition). Second, the imposition of class labels on a set of stimuli can steer the system towards the formation of a low-dimensional space in which some of the directions of variation are downplayed and others accentuated. In this manner, the system can be made to treat different views of the same object or its different parametrically related versions equivalently, while maintaining discriminability along other dimensions (Intrator and Edelman, 1997b). Third, selective association between prototype modules can make some dimensions more important in certain situations.

The action of such an association mechanism can be illustrated on the giraffe example. If I see, for the first time, a thing that resembles a spotted camel or a deformed leopard, I *cannot* tell whether it is going to try to tear out my throat or start grazing. One of these acts, however, would immediately suggest the strengthening of an association between the representation of the novel animal and that of its proper class.[7]

Any of these approaches effectively creates a stimulus bias in the similarity space (Shepard, 1964; Nosofsky, 1991a), whose action resembles that of assigning a larger weight to some dimensions (i.e., to similarities to some of the prototypes), at the expense of others. Such adjustment, which may be task-specific (Schyns et al., 1998), should be combined with an effort to make the underlying representation reflect as many as possible stimulus dimensions, because different subsets of these dimensions will be relevant in different situations. The result of selecting a few dimensions out of many in each given task is a *sparse code*, advocated by Barlow (1959). The underlying multidimensional space can be constructed in two ways: by combining abstract features such as "red," or by measuring similarities to concrete prototypes, in which case the corresponding feature could be "similar to a cherry," as in Chorus.

*"Red" seems to be a much better feature than "similar to a cherry".*

I disagree. There is no reason why it should be a priori preferable. Abstract features are a poor basis for categorization and generalization: what else do we learn about the nature of an object by being told only that it is red? It is interesting to note that infants at the peak of the concept acquisition period around the age 2 exhibit a tendency to attribute labels (words) to shapes of entire objects, rather to their color, or to the shapes of their parts (Markman, 1989; Smith et al., 1997), and so do perceptual novices in general (Tanaka and Gauthier, 1997). Only upon receiving a different label for an already encountered object do they associate it with properties other than holistic shape, such as the object's color, material, or local features.

*Are there any computational reasons for having entire concrete objects as reference shapes?*
Possibly. Consider the famous example used by Quine to argue for the indeterminacy of radical translation (Quine, 1969). You walk in the jungle, accompanied by a person familiar with the local fauna but with whom you share no language. A rabbit goes by, eliciting an exclamation "gavagai" from your companion; how do you decide whether this label refers to the rabbit, or to its right hind leg, or to its color, or to any number of spatiotemporal features contained in this kind of stimulus? According to the holistic bias strategy that I just mentioned, your first choice should be to attribute the local-language label "gavagai" to your concept of "rabbit-shaped thing" (it could be, after all, a stuffed rabbit mounted on a small robotic vehicle). The reason for opting for such holistic bias is clear: it disambiguates the choice of associating the label with visual features. This, in turn, makes it easier to learn language from examples, by a process which Quine (1969) calls learning by ostension (as in "this is a cherry," pointing to a cherry).
*You promised to consider non-holistic alternatives to Chorus, but instead you slipped back into defending shape holism.*
Just temporarily. What I would like to claim now is that holistic representation is a sensible opening strategy, which can serve as the basis for the development of more sophisticated analytical approaches. The tricky part is to steer a middle way between the holistic feature-space extreme, justly criticized as being counter-intuitive and falling short of replicating human performance in many tasks (cf. figure 7.3), and the structural extreme, which has remained science fiction (despite its intellectual appeal) since its introduction more than two decades ago. I think the middle way can be found by following a couple of general principles when "upgrading" Chorus to deal with parts and compositionality: (1) the parts should be image-based, not object-based; (2) the parts should be exemplars, not generic shapes.

The goal, then, is to use prototypical shapes as "parts" that are statistically defined rather than generic, and spatially anchored rather than floating. The latter condition is necessary to avoid the need for temporal binding of parts—a traditional handicap of the structural approaches. "Most theories [of invariant representation] assume that invariance is

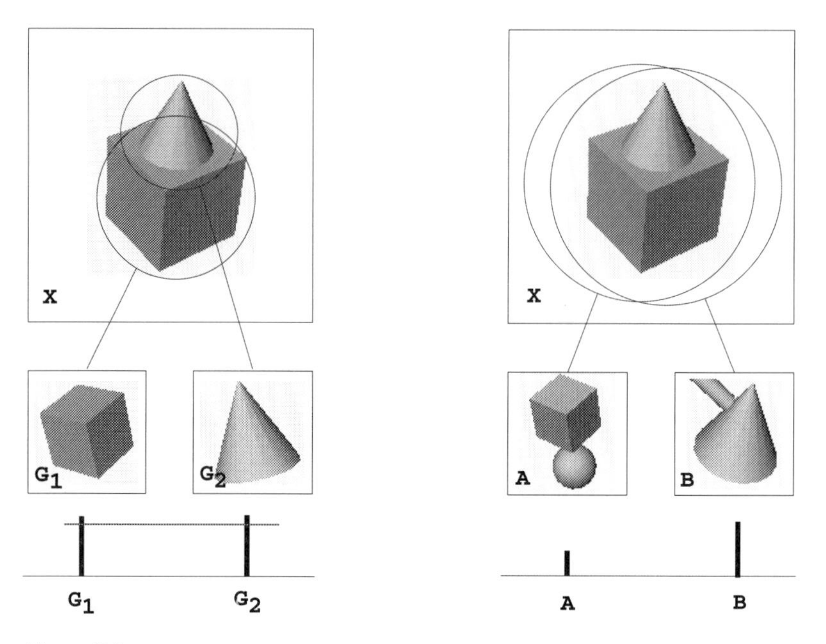


**Figure 7.2**
An illustration of the conceptual difference between part-based and holistic approaches to the representation of structure. *(Left)* Part-based models such as RBC would describe this object as a cone on top of a block; here, modules $G_1$ and $G_2$ tuned to the shape of the parts signal their presence (in an all-or-none fashion), from which the structure of the entire object is determined (a "module" responsible for the detection of the "on top" relationship is not shown in this illustration). *(Right)* Holistic models such as Chorus describe the entire object in terms of its similarity to some reference shapes, $A$ and $B$. This only works with graded-response modules, whose relative activation levels convey information about the structure of the object.

achieved with the help of a decomposition of sensory patterns into elementary features. . . . From this principle, a binding problem arises" (von der Malsburg, 1995). To my mind, the temporal binding problem is largely artificial: choosing to decompose the image into an abstract collection of parts, forgetting about their relative placement in the image, and then wondering how to put the object together again is a bit like shooting yourself in the foot and then complaining that it hurts.[8]

To get around the pitfalls associated with temporal binding, a system can use binding by retinotopy (Edelman, 1994). The line of reasoning leading to this idea is illustrated in figures 7.2 through 7.5. In this ap-

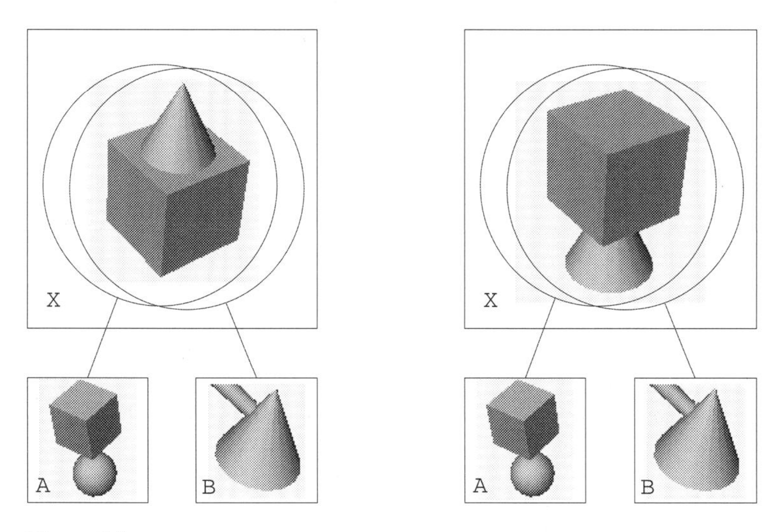


**Figure 7.3**
The holistic approach is limited in its ability to make explicit the similarities and the differences between complex objects which human observers would describe as composed of similar parts arranged in different configurations (cf. section 2.3.4). Consider, for example, the two objects shown here: a cone on top of a cube (*left*) and a cube on top of a cone (*right*). On the one hand, these objects are clearly different and Chorus would indeed easily label them as such. On the other hand, the objects do share some rather conspicuous features, a fact that needs to be represented explicitly in any system that aims at mimicking human competence in visual shape analysis.

proach, structure is represented explicitly, but in an image-based rather than object-centered manner. From the standpoint of functionality, keeping representations image-based (as they are in the original version of Chorus) is only a small concession: although image-based structure is aspect-specific, so is a full-blown structural description, which in any case must be extracted anew for each distinct aspect of the object (Biederman and Gerhardstein, 1993). Computationally, however, image-based structure is much more tractable, especially if the primitives in terms of which structure is represented are encoded by Chorus-like modules. The only modification required for that purpose in the original (holistic) Chorus scheme is control over the location and the size of the retinal receptive field of each module. This can be done in a hard-wired fashion, as depicted in figure 7.4, turning the Chorus of prototypes into a Chorus of fragments.

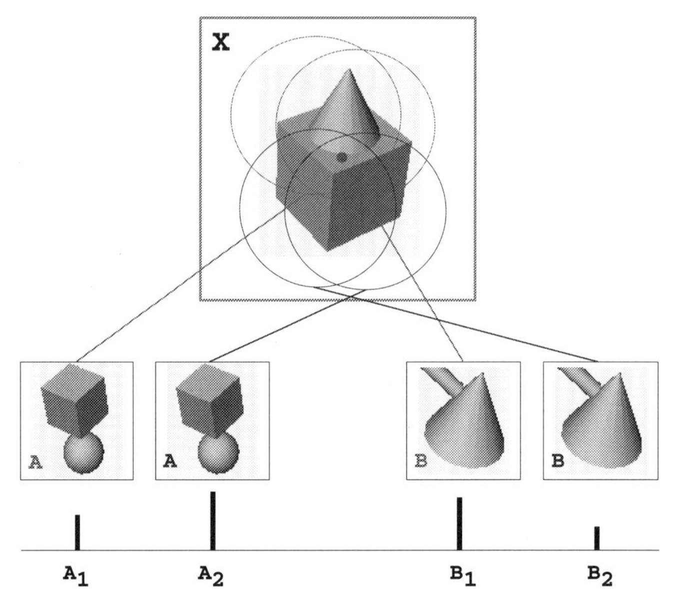
X
A
A
B
B
$A_1$
$A_2$
$B_1$
$B_2$

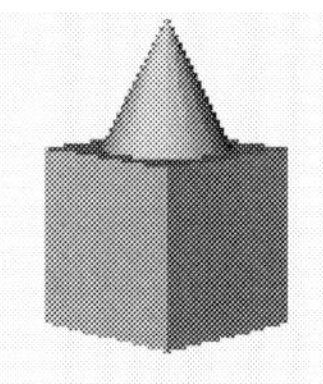

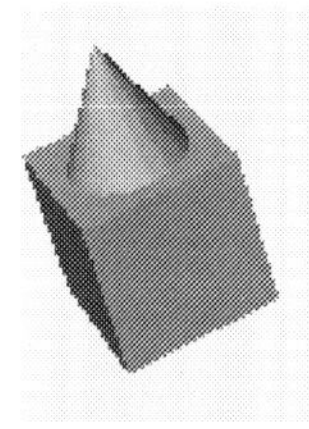

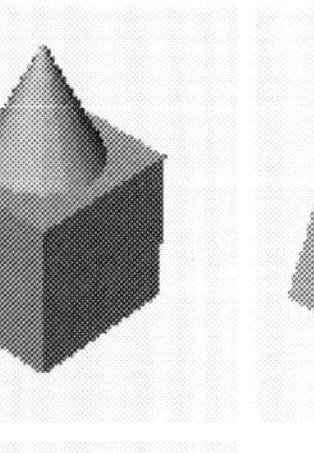

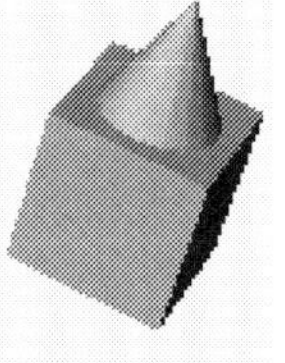

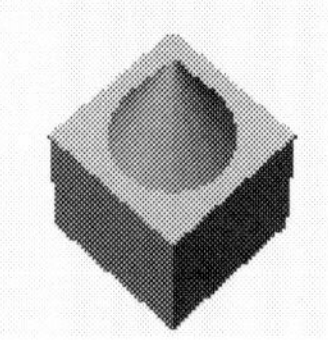

*How can this scheme be learned? The holistic bias you described earlier would work against it.*

Consider a system that is already familiarized with an extensive collection of entire objects, for which some dedicated modules are allocated. Suppose now that a familiar object is being presented to the system, but the label that accompanies it does not match the original label. Human infants in this situation assign the new label to some salient attribute of the object other than its shape. This can be the object's color, or texture, or an image-defined part. Let's concentrate on the latter possibility. Initially (that is, before a label is produced in conjunction with its appearance), the part may be represented in a distributed fashion, by the activation of a small number of Chorus modules (constrained to the appropriate scale, and directed to focus on the proper location in the image, relative to the normal fixation point for the object in question). When the importance of the part is signaled to the system by the new externally supplied label, a new module is allocated (with the proper scale and receptive field already built-in).

*Is there any biological support for this idea?*

Attentional control over the response of a cell has been found in visual area V4 (which precedes IT in the shape processing pathway) in the monkey (Moran and Desimone, 1985). In area IT, similar switching on and off of cells has been reported (Chelazzi et al., 1993). In this

**Figure 7.4**
It may be possible to circumvent the problem illustrated in figure 7.3 using modules tuned to image fragments, in conjunction with binding by retinotopy. *(Top)* In such a scheme, which may be called the Chorus of prototypical fragments, each object-specific module would come in several varieties, distinguished by the location of the module's receptive field relative to the fixation point (indicated by the thick dot). Here, module $A_1$ responds optimally when the fixation is above and slightly to the left of a stimulus resembling object `A`. Likewise, module $A_2$ prefers the object to be below the fixation point. As in the Chorus of prototypes, a new object `X` is represented by the pattern of activities across object-specific modules. This scheme resembles Barsalou's (1998) perceptual symbol system idea. *(Bottom)* Because different aspects (Koenderink and van Doorn, 1979) of solid shapes need to be treated separately in any case, view-specific image-based fragments can be used instead of object-centered parts (which are difficult to detect reliably). The original Chorus scheme can be easily adapted for this purpose; its operation is illustrated in figure 7.5.

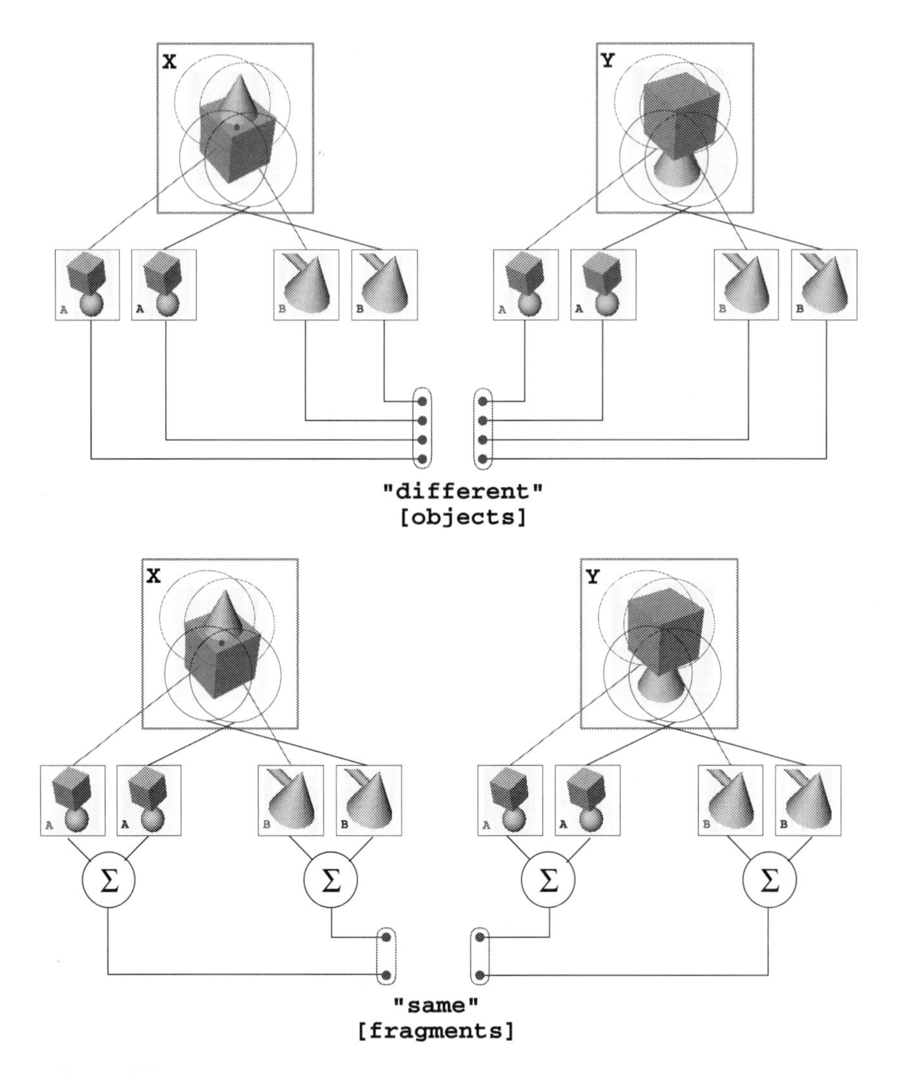


Figure 7.5
If the receptive fields of Chorus modules are confined to retinally-defined fragments of the entire image, their activities can be made to carry additional information concerning the structure of the stimulus, without recourse either to generic parts, or to any kind of binding mechanisms (beyond co-activation and retinotopy). *(Top)* A Chorus system (shown here with duplicated modules differing in their receptive field locations) can easily discriminate between objects X and Y, which consist of the same parts in different configurations. *(Bottom)* If the responses of each group of modules tuned to the same shape are pooled, the resulting representation will reflect the fragment-level similarity between objects X

latter study, digitized images from magazines were used to stimulate IT cells. After an effective and a less effective stimulus were found, the monkey was cued with a stimulus. Following a delay, the animal had to make a saccade to the stimulus presented along with other images. About 100 *msec* before the onset of the saccade, responses to nontargets were suppressed, and the dominant responding cells were those selective for the target. This mechanism can in principle support the learning of fragment-tuned modules, as I suggested above. There is also evidence for the existence in IT of eccentrically positioned receptive fields required by this model. For example, a map of the placement of dozens of receptive fields with respect to the fixation point appears in figure 9 in Kobatake and Tanaka (1994); (see also Ito et al., 1995). A schematic view of the shape processing pathway in primate vision, inspired by these ideas is illustrated in figure 7.6.

The idea of fragments as features is also compatible with the results of the "scrambling" experiments involving fMRI scans of human subjects (Edelman et al., 1998). As I mentioned in chapter 6, that study showed that cutting images of common objects into sixteen parts and rearranging the fragments had little effect on the response of area LO (the human counterpart of V4/IT). In comparison, fragmentation into smaller parts effectively abolished the response of LO. This suggests that the "units" of representation in LO are not entire objects (e.g., faces), but rather object fragments (e.g., eye or mouth images).

The association between units responding to such fragments requires a mechanism that is distinct from the process that supports individual fragment recognition. This distinction may explain the pattern of translation invariance results reported by Dill and Edelman (1997), who found that subjects could generalize *same/different* discrimination across retinal location if the two stimuli differed locally (i.e., in fragment shapes),

**Figure 7.5** ***(continued)***
and Y [note the relationship between this idea and the feature histogram methods for object recognition (Schiele and Crowley, 1996; Mel, 1997), discussed in section 2.3.4]. Top-down connections can then be used to trace back the source of the different contributions to the pooled response, which would amount to the ability to address and describe separately the various retinotopically defined fragments of the stimulus.

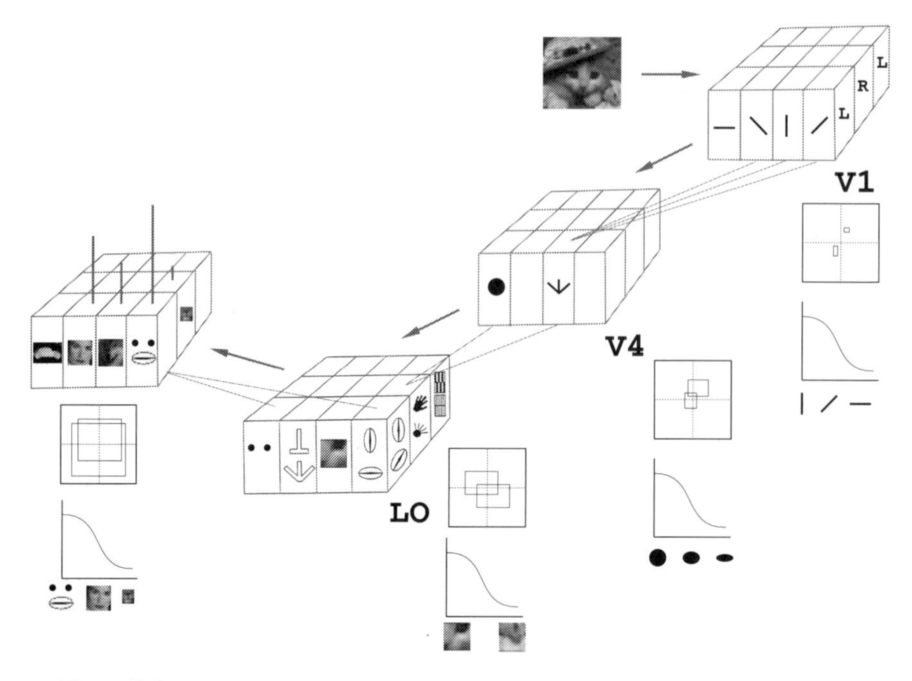


Figure 7.6
A schematic illustration of a model of the shape processing pathway in the primate visual system, based on the biological evidence surveyed in chapter 6 (especially K. Tanaka's description of the functional architecture of the inferotemporal cortex in the monkey) and on the computational ideas derived from the Chorus framework. The principles illustrated here are: (1) the distributed nature of the representation at every stage, made possible by the graded and monotonic response of each "module" to inputs that differ progressively from its optimal stimulus, (2) binding by retinotopy, which supports the emergence of more and more complex features as one progresses from area V1 to area LO and beyond, and (3) low dimensionality. The stimulus here is shown as represented by the responses of only four modules at the top of the hierarchy.

but not if the stimuli were different arrangements of the same fragment shapes. A possible explanation here would consist of two parts. According to the first part, individual fragment processing is invariant under translation, because the fragment-tuned units are replicated over the visual field, and their outputs are pooled, as called for by the histogram-based feature-space object recognition methods (Schiele and Crowley, 1996; Mel, 1997). Invariant processing of individual fragments is also compatible with the idea that the receptive fields of fragment-units cover the entire (central) visual field. This alternative, however, fails to explain how fragments are combined into wholes—an operation that requires the representation of the relative locations of the fragments; it also contradicts the electrophysiological findings of Kobatake and Tanaka (1994) and Ito et al. (1995), which I have mentioned earlier. An intriguing possibility is that the receptive fields of the fragment units have both a considerable extent and a graded structure, so that both the identity of the fragment and its approximate location are signalled in the unit's output. This would constitute a kind of channel coding for those two attributes, which could result in their highly precise representation, based on the hyperacuity principle (Snippe and Koenderink, 1992).

The observation central to the second part of the explanation is that relating the outputs of several fragment-tuned units, unlike the processing of individual fragments, is not invariant to translation. Presumably, this happens because relational information is not made explicit (i.e., does not lead to the establishment of a long-term memory trace) automatically, in an uncontrolled bottom-up fashion, which is why relational structure discrimination does not generalize across translation on the basis of mere exposure to the stimuli (Dill and Edelman, 1997). In this connection, it is also interesting to note that experiments explicitly pitching holistic object similarity against relational similarity—the study of structural alignment of drawings of scenes and rug-like patterns reported in Markman and Gentner (1993)—suggest that subjects do respond to relational cues, yet rely on holistic object similarity if the relational information is weak.

*Structural alignment is related to analogical reasoning and other techniques borrowed from Artificial Intelligence. Is the Chorus of Fragments likewise related to AI similarity models?*

Computational attempts to define similarity within the AI tradition (Aisbett and Gibbon, 1994; Basri et al., 1995) seem to me rather ad hoc in their choice of the primitives (the "fragments"), the possible relationships, and especially the weights assigned to the dimensions of the resulting similarity space. A better strategy, I believe, is to start with a biologically realistic architecture. For example, a measurement space spanned by outputs of some filters spread over the image automatically solves the feature selection problem (at least at the first processing stage) in a manner that makes biological sense. Two models that follow this approach which may be compared to the Chorus of Fragments are described in Bricolo et al. (1996) and Gauthier et al. (1998). In the former model, which has been tested on paperclip-like shapes, views of the objects are represented as lists of local features, which are image snippets (in other words, outputs of filters tuned to fragments of images of objects). Unlike in Chorus, these fragments can be located anywhere in the image; their placement relative to the fixation point is not specified. The second model, which has not been actually implemented, proposes to encode the relative locations of these features as well. In computer vision, a recognition algorithm using this principle has been described in Amit and Geman (1997).

*The representation of structure is obviously very important in language. Now that you concede that object structure should be represented explicitly, would you care to speculate about possible relationships between the direction your theory of visual object recognition seems to be taking on the one hand, and natural language processing on the other?*

As I mentioned in chapter 2, there have been previous attempts to link language and visual shape processing, ranging from grammar-like formalisms for describing shape in computer vision (Fu, 1976) to the drawing of parallels between the phonological structure of spoken words and the geometrical structure of shapes in the psychology of visual recognition (Biederman, 1987). Although I do not agree with the particular approaches that have been taken in the past in the area of theoretical unification of vision and language, I think the idea itself is fascinating, and should not really be presented as an afterthought to a monograph on visual recognition. There are indications that the interest in this idea is reviving: a vision-like approach to linguistic-conceptual structures has been advocated in an exciting recent paper on perceptual symbol systems (Barsalou, 1998). That paper reviews extensive psychological data on visual structure representation, concept formation, reasoning, and many other topics at the interface between language, reason, and vision, and proposes a common theory for all these aspects of cognitive function, based on anchoring concepts and percepts in an image-like reference frame that resembles the "retinotopic" frame postulated by the Chorus of fragments. This work strengthens my belief in the feasibility of finding a common theoretical ground for some aspects of human vision and language (*adventavit asinus . . .* ). Whether or not this belief is to be substantiated, time will tell.

## Notes

1. That is, a theory that postulates a multitude of mechanisms (perhaps specific to the different problems), rather than a single unified mechanism that solves the core problem in the field. According to Marr, the amenability of an information-processing task to a uniform approach is a part of a computational (abstract) characterization of the task itself. Indeed, he suspected that some vision tasks (such as figure-ground segmentation) do not afford a unified treatment in the form of a Type I theory.

2. Good similes for the "grounding" function are found in the molecular biology of the immune system, which needs to link processes inside cells with events outside them. For example, T-cell receptor molecules span the membrane of a lymphocyte, being partly outside the cell and partly inside. When an antigen binds to the outer part, the molecule undergoes a change, which makes this event known on the inside. The cell membrane in this example can be likened to the gap separating the inside of the visual system from the distal objects, and the receptor molecules are the "symbols with strings" that span the gap.

3. Alarming signs of corner-cutting by the visual system have been present all along, of course. One anecdote, which dates back to the era of analog watches, is the widespread inability of people to recall whether their watch has Roman or Arabic numerals.

4. Shape-preserving transformations are the rigid motions and uniform scaling; stretching and bending, which could bring a plasticine plum into congruence with a toy lawn-mower, are disallowed.

5. This approach would be analogous to the methods used in the study of biological motor control, in which competing theories can be distinguished on the basis of small-scale "quirks" of hand trajectories in simple reaching movements.

6. I thank P. Földiák for this example.

7. This is another echo of the famous discussion of induction, found in Hume (1748, 23ff), which I mentioned in an earlier chapter: "Let an object be presented to a man of ever so strong natural reason and abilities; if that object be entirely new to him, he will not be able, by the most accurate examination of its sensible qualities, to discover any of its causes or effects."

8. The widely publicized neurobiological evidence for temporal binding (see Stryker, 1989, for references and comments) seems to be counterbalanced by more recent findings. For example, while experiments on temporal hyperacuity show that humans can reliably discriminate temporal offsets as small as three to five *msec* (Fahle, 1993), delays that are ten times larger fail to disrupt the

ability of the visual system to combine different parts of an image into a whole. Specifically, spatial displacement "barely above the two-point acuity of about one *arcmin*" suffices to induce symmetry breaking in a bistable Kanisza display, but temporal offsets of up to thirty-three *msec* have a very small effect (Fahle and Koch, 1995). This finding speaks against the idea of timing of external events being translated into precisely synchronized neural responses (although the possibility that the internal code used in the brain relies on temporal correlations of cell responses is not ruled out). Electrophysiological evidence against the idea of binding by synchronized oscillations was reported in Young et al. (1992); an alternative account for the oscillations that *are* found in some cases is offered in Kirschfeld (1995).

# Appendix A

# The Measurement Space and the Distal to Proximal Mapping

The concept of a measurement space, introduced towards the end of chapter 3, plays a central role in the theory of representation that is developed in the subsequent chapters. This appendix illustrates the structure of a generic measurement space $\mathcal{M}$ spanned by activities of receptive fields (RFs). This is done by plotting the changes in the representation of an object in this space, caused by its rotation or deformation.

In the simulations described below, successive 2D snapshots of 3D objects rotating in space were rendered using the Silicon Graphics Inventor software toolkit. These were then transduced—mapped into the measurement space $\mathcal{M}$—using a set of 200 filters with radially elongated Gaussian receptive fields randomly positioned over the image. To visualize the arrangement of views of an object in the 200-dimensional measurement space, pairwise distances were calculated among vectors of RF activities corresponding to views that differed by 10° rotation steps around a fixed axis. Those distances were then submitted to nonmetric multidimensional scaling analysis (Kruskal and Wish, 1978; SAS, 1989), which embedded the views (originally, points in 200 dimensions) into a 2D space suitable for visualization (figure A.1; see appendix F for an explanation of the embedding procedure). The basic constraint on $\mathcal{M}$, smooth transduction, is seen to be fulfilled in this example: the smooth and gradual change in object orientation has been mapped into a smooth and gradual change in the location of the point corresponding to the object in the measurement space $\mathcal{M}$.

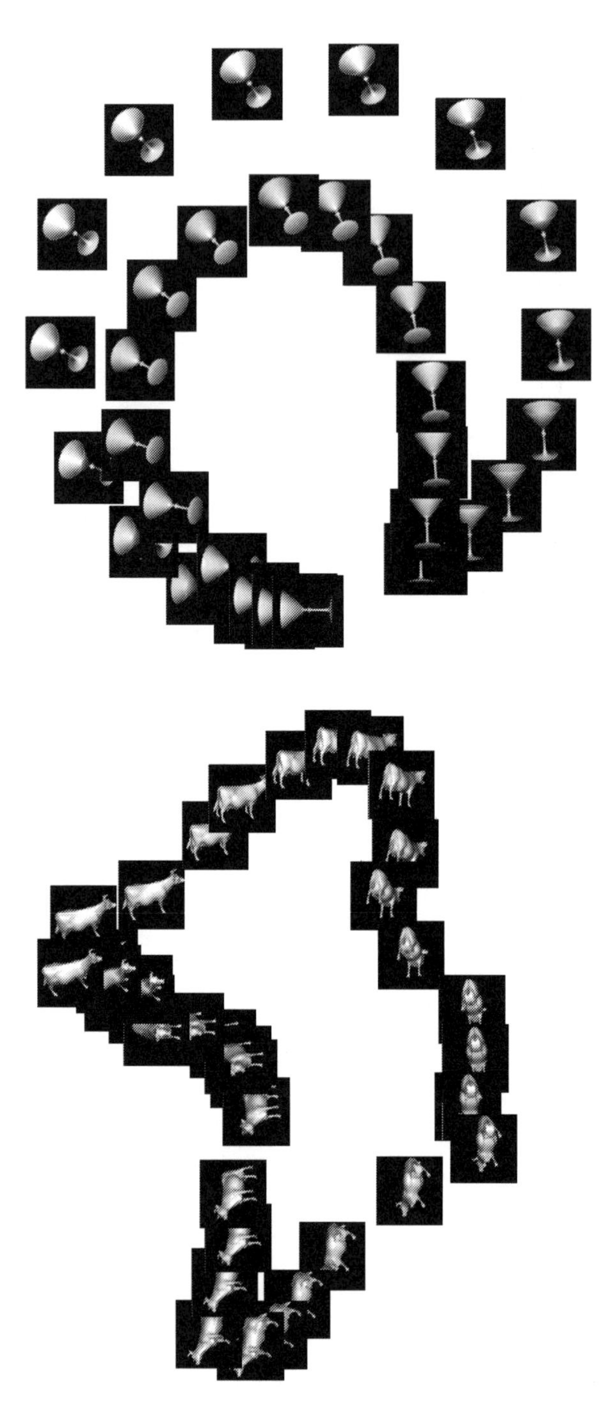

**Figure A.1**
A two-dimensional map of the measurement-space arrangement of points corresponding to successive views of two objects, a cow (*left*), and a martini glass (*right*). In this illustration, the 200-dimensional measurement space has been embedded into 2D for visualization purposes, using multidimensional scaling, or MDS (Kruskal, 1964). The residual stress (discrepancy between the interpoint distances in the original 200-dimensional space and the target 2D space) is 0.08 and 0.03, respectively, in the two examples. Note that gradual rotation of an object (10° at a time) leads to a gradual shift of the measurement-space point corresponding to it. The objects in this and the other illustrations are available from Viewpoint Datalabs, Inc. (http://www.viewpoint.com/).

## A.1 The View Space

The smoothness of the transduction process should result in the preservation of the structure of the object's *view space* (section 3.4.3). More concretely, this means that distance between object views measured in $\mathcal{M}$ must covary monotonically with objective distance between those views. The latter distance can be defined as the shortest-path angular rotation transforming one view into the other.[1] Figure A.2 indicates that up to a certain extent of rotation, $\mathcal{M}$-space distances are indeed monotonic with the rotation distances. On the average, the first deviation from monotonicity for seventy-five objects was found to occur at an angular rotation distance of $\theta = 126.4°$ (the canonical view of each objects was used as its reference orientation).

## A.2 The Shape Space

In addition to the structure of the view space, smooth transduction should also preserve the structure of the *shape space* of an object (section 3.4.3). This prediction has been tested by quantifying the agreement between the $\mathcal{M}$-space distances and deformation distances, defined in an objective parametric shape space. The seven shapes used in this illustration were encoded by vectors of seventy parameters; the Euclidean distance between two points in the parameter space is a natural measure of dissimilarity between the corresponding shapes (Cutzu and Edelman, 1998). Figure A.3 shows the extent to which the $\mathcal{M}$-space distance indeed covaried monotonically with the parameter-space distance between the shapes.

## Notes

1. The angular rotation distance is the angle $\alpha$ for which $1 + 2\cos\alpha = \mathrm{trace}(M)$, where $M$ is the rotation matrix transforming one view into the other (see Kanatani, 1990, 205).

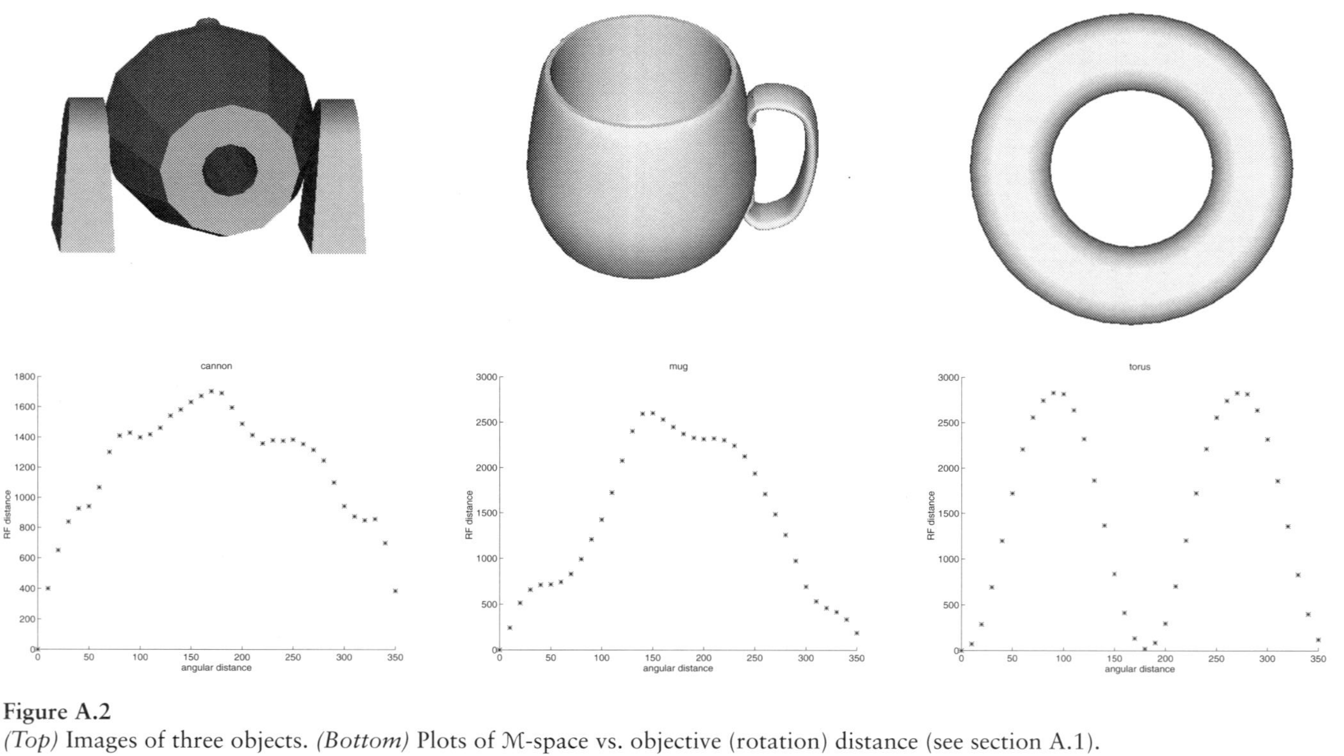

**Figure A.2**
*(Top)* Images of three objects. *(Bottom)* Plots of $\mathcal{M}$-space vs. objective (rotation) distance (see section A.1).

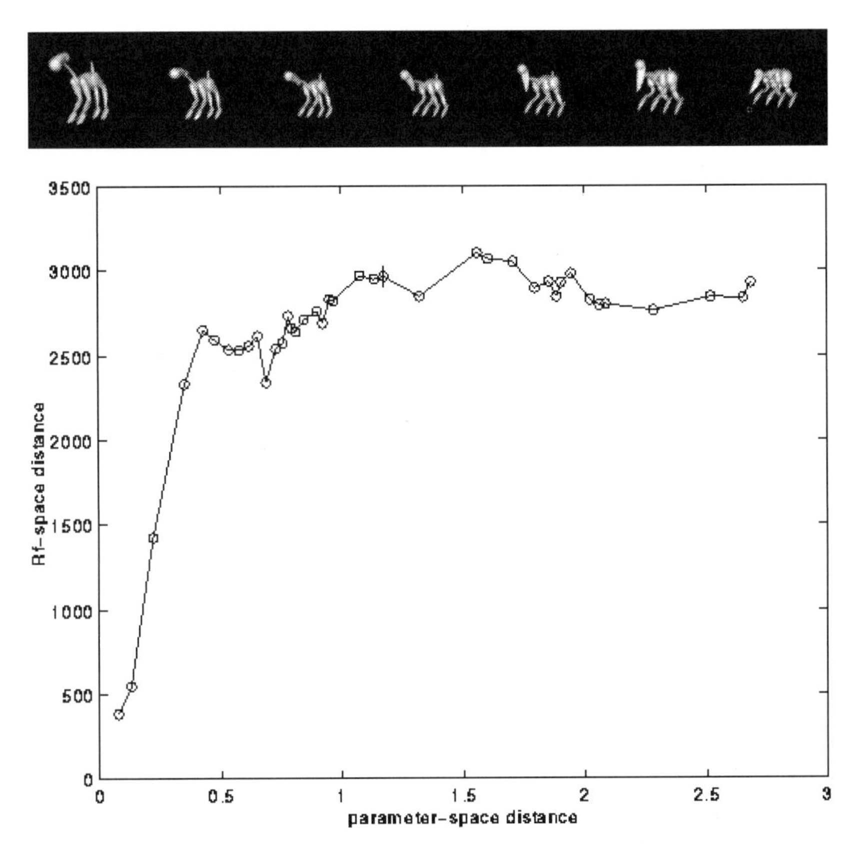


**Figure A.3**
*(Top)* Seven animal-like objects generated from parametric descriptions forming a straight line in a common seventy-dimensional parameter space (Cutzu and Edelman, 1998). The parameter vectors corresponding to the different shapes were constructed from the vectors corresponding to the extremes of the parameter-space segment, $A$ and $B$, using linear interpolation: $M = \alpha A + (1 - \alpha)B$, $0 \leq \alpha \leq 1$. *(Bottom)* $\mathcal{M}$-space distance between pairs of shapes, plotted against objective distance between the corresponding points in the parameter space (see section A.2). The error bar denotes the mean standard error of the mean, calculated for twenty-five randomly chosen pairs of shapes.

# Appendix B

# Representation by Distances to Prototypes

The simplest form of such representation can be obtained by mapping the input vector into the vector of its distances to an ordered set of prototypes. Let us call this mapping the Chorus Transform ($CT$).

## B.1 The Chorus Transform

Let $\mathbf{p}_1, \ldots, \mathbf{p}_n$ be $n$ prototypes and let $\mathbf{x}$ be an input vector, $\mathbf{p}_k, \mathbf{x} \in R^d$. The Chorus Transform ($CT$) is defined as follows:

$$CT(\mathbf{x}) = \frac{1}{\sqrt{n}} \begin{pmatrix} \|\mathbf{x} - \mathbf{p}_1\| \\ \vdots \\ \|\mathbf{x} - \mathbf{p}_n\| \end{pmatrix} \tag{B.1}$$

The application of this transform $CT : R^d \longrightarrow R^n$ results in dimensionality reduction, if the number of prototypical objects, $n$, is smaller than the dimensionality of the measurement space $d$.

### B.1.1 Distance Rank Preservation by $CT$

$CT$ can reduce the dimensionality of the input space in a manner that preserves its similarity structure, as illustrated by calculating the correlation between distances among twenty-five randomly chosen points in $R^{1000}$, and the distances between their $CT$-transformed versions, in $R^n$, for a varying number of prototypes $n$.[1] Figure B.1 shows Pearson correlation and Spearman rank order correlation coefficients between original and transformed distances, plotted against $n$. The application of $CT$ with five prototypes (equivalent to a 200-fold dimensionality

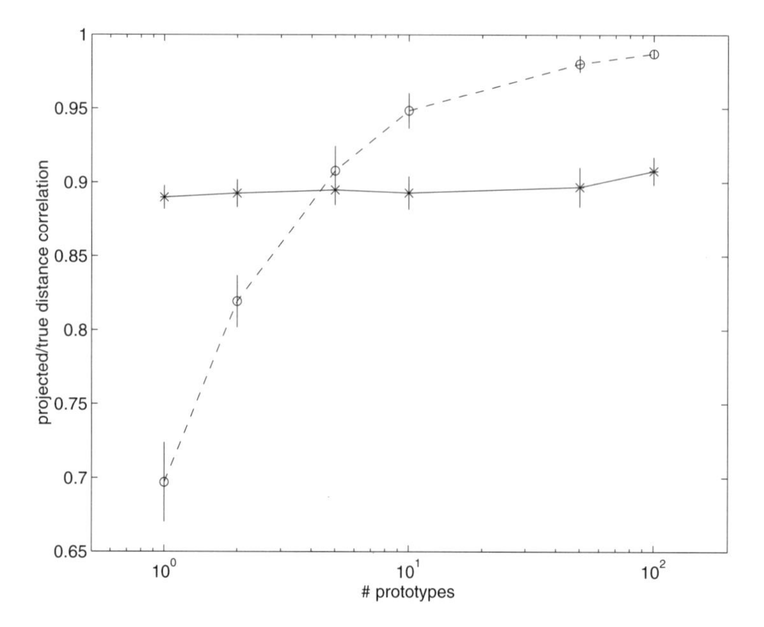


**Figure B.1**
Preservation of distance ranks by the Chorus Transform ($CT$). The plot shows Pearson product-moment correlation (dotted line) and Spearman rank correlation (solid line) between the original and the $CT$-transformed distances among twenty-five points in a space of dimensionality 1000, plotted against the number of prototypes employed by $CT$. Error bars represent the mean standard error of the mean, calculated over ten independent runs.

reduction with respect to the original 1000-dimensional space) yields a distance correlation of about 0.9. This shows how close the distances in the $CT$ space are to the distances in the original high-dimensional space.

### B.1.2 Bounds on Dimensionality Reduction: The Embedding Theorems

To understand why it is possible to reduce dimensionality while preserving certain aspects of the metric structure of the original space, we may consider some recent analytical results on near-isometric embedding of metric spaces. A typical theorem from this field (Johnson and Lindenstrauss, 1984) states that given $n$ points $\{v_1, v_2, \ldots, v_n\}$ in an

Euclidean space $\mathcal{S}$ with distances $d_{ij} = d(v_i, v_j)$, it is possible to find $n$ points $\{w_1, w_2, \ldots, w_n\}$ in $\mathcal{R}^t$ where $t = O(\frac{\log n}{\epsilon^2})$, such that $\forall i, j$ the distance $\delta_{ij} = d(w_i, w_j)$ satisfies $(1+\epsilon)\delta_{ij} > d_{ij} > \delta_{ij}$.[2] In other words, the $n$ points can be embedded in an $l_2$ space of $\frac{\log n}{\epsilon^2}$ dimensions with distortion $\leq (1+\epsilon)$ in the distances. Such nearly isometric embedding of the original space into another space of much lower dimensionality is a highly desirable goal in obtaining a representation that is both efficient and faithful.

Note that the simulations described in figure B.1 dealt with something other than isometry, namely with the correlation between distances in the between the original space and its image under $CT$. In the absence of a theory of correlation-preserving embeddings we must rely on the Johnson-Lindenstrauss theorem to guide the choice of the main parameter of $CT$: the number of prototypes. Simulations illustrated in figure B.2 were designed to study the relevance of the Johnson-Lindenstrauss result to the design of $CT$. To preserve the distances among $n$ points faithfully (i.e., with $0 < \epsilon \ll 1$), one must have $d \gg O(\log n)$, where $d$ is the dimensionality of the original space. Figure B.2 shows the dependence of the dimensionality of the target space obtained with $n = 100$ points on the allowed distortion $\epsilon$; the dimensionality reduction expected from the Johnson-Lindenstrauss embedding is $O(\frac{\log n}{\epsilon^2})$. A set of $n = 100$ points was $CT$-embedded into a space of lower dimensionality (calculated from the J-L formula), for varying values of $\epsilon$, $0 < \epsilon \ll 1$. The quality of the embedding was then measured by calculating correlations between original and $CT$-transformed pairwise distances among the $n$ points. The degree of distance preservation is plotted in figure B.2.

### B.1.3 *CT* As an Implementation of Bourgain's Method

The work of Johnson and Lindenstrauss (1984) provides not only bounds on possible dimensionality reduction, but also an algorithm for carrying it out: it has been shown that any orthogonal projection of an $n$-dimensional space onto a random $t$-dimensional subspace is likely to produce a mapping with the desired embedding properties. The embedding method implemented by $CT$ is different in that the target space is far

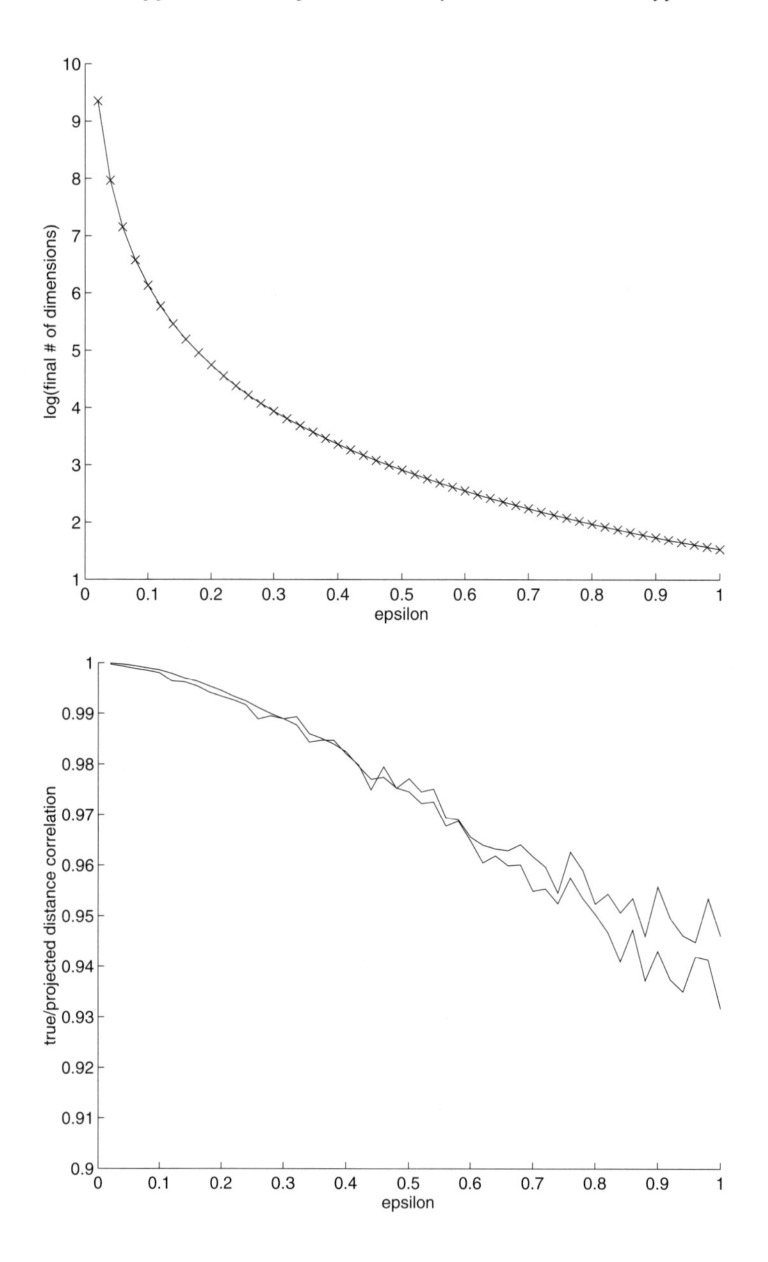
log(final # of dimensions)
10
9
8
7
6
5
4
3
2
1
0
0.1
0.2
0.3
0.4
0.5
0.6
0.7
0.8
0.9
1
epsilon
true/projected distance correlation
1
0.99
0.98
0.97
0.96
0.95
0.94
0.93
0.92
0.91
0.9
0
0.1
0.2
0.3
0.4
0.5
0.6
0.7
0.8
0.9
1
epsilon

from being a *random* subspace of the original space. To realize this, note first that a finite metric space with $n$ points can be isometrically embedded into $l_{\infty}^{n}$, simply by setting the coordinates of a point to the vector of its distances to all other points in the set. As shown by Bourgain (1985), a variation on this embedding method can result in logarithmic dimensionality reduction, if for each point, distances to randomly picked subsets of the $(n-1)$ remaining points (in $CT$, distances to a few prototypes) are retained instead of the distances to all $(n-1)$ other points. Using this method, an $n$-point metric space can be embedded into an $O(\log n)$-dimensional Euclidean space with distortion $\leq O(\log n)$ (Bourgain, 1985; Linial et al., 1994).

### B.1.4 Non-expansion of Distances by $CT$

$CT$ as defined in eq. B.1 is non-expansive, in that it does not inflate distances (Goebel and Kirk, 1990). This property, proved next, will be useful in characterizing the action of $CT$ on neighborhoods of points in the original space.

**Claim 1:** $CT$ is non-expansive, i.e., $\rho_n(CT(\mathbf{x}), CT(\mathbf{y})) \leq \rho_d(\mathbf{x}, \mathbf{y})$, where $\rho_{d,n}$ are the metrics induced by the Euclidean norm in $R^d$ and $R^n$, respectively.

***Proof:*** To prove non-expansion, use the appropriate Euclidean norms and show that

$$\|CT(\mathbf{x}) - CT(\mathbf{y})\| \leq \|\mathbf{x} - \mathbf{y}\|, \quad \forall \mathbf{x}, \mathbf{y} \in R^d.$$

**Figure B.2**
A comparison between the dimensionality-reducing property of $CT$ and the prediction of the Johnson-Lindenstrauss (1984) embedding theorem. The quality of the embedding was examined for varying values of the distance distortion index $\epsilon$, $0 < \epsilon \ll 1$. *(Top)* Dimensionality reduction for a set of $n = 100$ points, afforded by the various values of $\epsilon$ (the theoretical prediction is $O(\frac{\log n}{\epsilon^2})$). *(Bottom)* High Pearson and Spearman (rank) correlation between the original and $CT$-transformed pairwise distances among 100 points (picked at random from the unit hypercube in $R^{10000}$) indicates how well the distances are preserved. For example, a distortion of $\epsilon = 1$, which allows an embedding into five dimensions, results in Pearson and Spearman rank correlations of 0.9316 and 0.9460, respectively.

Let $\{\mathbf{p}_i\}_{i=1}^n \in R^d$ be the set of prototypes and let $\mathbf{x} \in R^d$ be an arbitrary input vector.

$$\begin{aligned}
&\|CT(\mathbf{x}) - CT(\mathbf{y})\| \\
&= \left\| \frac{1}{\sqrt{n}} \begin{pmatrix} \|\mathbf{x} - \mathbf{p}_1\| \\ \vdots \\ \|\mathbf{x} - \mathbf{p}_n\| \end{pmatrix} - \frac{1}{\sqrt{n}} \begin{pmatrix} \|\mathbf{y} - \mathbf{p}_1\| \\ \vdots \\ \|\mathbf{y} - \mathbf{p}_n\| \end{pmatrix} \right\| \\
&= \left\| \frac{1}{\sqrt{n}} \begin{pmatrix} \|\mathbf{x} - \mathbf{p}_1\| - \|\mathbf{y} - \mathbf{p}_1\| \\ \vdots \\ \|\mathbf{x} - \mathbf{p}_n\| - \|\mathbf{y} - \mathbf{p}_n\| \end{pmatrix} \right\| \doteq \left\| \frac{1}{\sqrt{n}} \bar{V} \right\| .
\end{aligned} \tag{B.2}$$

Without loss of generality, consider the $i$'th component of the vector $\bar{V}$. Because $\rho(\mathbf{a}, \mathbf{b}) \doteq \|\mathbf{a} - \mathbf{b}\|$ is a metric, it satisfies the triangle inequality, that is,

$$\rho(\mathbf{x}, \mathbf{p}_i) \leq \rho(\mathbf{x}, \mathbf{y}) + \rho(\mathbf{y}, \mathbf{p}_i).$$

Hence,

$$\bar{V}_i = \|\mathbf{x} - \mathbf{p}_i\| - \|\mathbf{y} - \mathbf{p}_i\| \leq \|\mathbf{x} - \mathbf{y}\|. \tag{B.3}$$

This is true for all $i$, therefore,

$$\begin{aligned}
\|CT(\mathbf{x}) - CT(\mathbf{y})\| &= \left\| \frac{1}{\sqrt{n}} \bar{V} \right\| = \sqrt{\sum_{i=1}^{n} (\frac{1}{\sqrt{n}} V_i)^2} \leq \sqrt{n \frac{1}{n} \|\mathbf{x} - \mathbf{y}\|^2} \\
&= \|\mathbf{x} - \mathbf{y}\|,
\end{aligned} \tag{B.4}$$

as claimed.

### B.1.5 Preservation of Voronoi Structure by $CT$

The non-expansion property of $CT$ can now be used to demonstrate that $CT$ preserves the Voronoi diagram (Preparata and Shamos, 1985) of a set of points in the input space.

#### Voronoi Diagram

For a finite set of points $\mathcal{S} = \{\mathbf{p}_i\}_{i=1}^n$ in an input space $R^d$, the Voronoi diagram is a sequence $\text{Vor}(\mathcal{S}) = \{V(\mathbf{p}_i)\}_{i=1}^n$ of convex polyhedra covering $R^d$, where $V(\mathbf{p}_i) = \{\mathbf{x} \in R^d : d(\mathbf{x}, \mathbf{p}_i) \leq d(\mathbf{x}, \mathbf{p}_j) \ \forall j \neq i\}$, and $d(\mathbf{x}, \mathbf{p}_i)$ denotes the Euclidean distance between the points $\mathbf{x}$ and $\mathbf{p}_i$. In other words, the Voronoi tessellation of $\mathcal{S}$ is a partitioning of the input space into convex regions $V(\mathbf{p}_i)$, such that $V(\mathbf{p}_i)$ contains all the points that are closer to $\mathbf{p}_i$ than to any other $\mathbf{p}_j$ in $\mathcal{S}$ (note the relevance to nearest-neighbor classification schemes). The Voronoi tessellation is an important tool in data coding schemes such as vector quantization (discussed below).

**Claim 2:** The Voronoi diagram is preserved by $CT$.

***Proof:*** Let $V(\mathbf{p}_i)$ be the *i'th* cell within a Voronoi diagram. For every $i$, one can show that $CT$ preserves $V(\mathbf{p}_i)$, that is,

$$\mathbf{x} \in V(\mathbf{p}_i) \Longrightarrow CT(\mathbf{x}) \in V(CT(\mathbf{p}_i)). \tag{B.5}$$

For $\mathbf{x} \in V(\mathbf{p}_i)$, we have by definition $\|\mathbf{x} - \mathbf{p}_i\| \leq \|\mathbf{x} - \mathbf{p}_j\|, \ \ \forall j \neq i$. To show that $CT(\mathbf{x}) \in V(CT(\mathbf{p}_i))$, we must prove that $\|CT(\mathbf{x}) - CT(\mathbf{p}_i)\| \leq \|CT(\mathbf{x}) - CT(\mathbf{p}_j)\|, \ \ \forall j \neq i$. Suppose, by contradiction, that there exists some $j_0 \neq i$ for which

$$\|CT(\mathbf{x}) - CT(\mathbf{p}_{j_o})\| < \|CT(\mathbf{x}) - CT(\mathbf{p}_i)\|.$$

Because $CT$ is non-expansive, we have, in addition,

$$\|CT(\mathbf{x}) - CT(\mathbf{p}_i)\| \leq \|\mathbf{x} - \mathbf{p}_i\|.$$

Hence,

$$\|CT(\mathbf{x}) - CT(\mathbf{p}_{j_0})\| < \|\mathbf{x} - \mathbf{p}_i\|. \tag{B.6}$$

Bearing in mind that this should be true for any $\mathbf{x} \in V(\mathbf{p}_i)$, and in particular for $\mathbf{x} = \mathbf{p}_i$, eq. B.6 consequently becomes

$$\|CT(\mathbf{p}_i) - CT(\mathbf{p}_{j_0})\| < 0,$$

which is a contradiction because $\| \cdot \|$ is a metric.

## B.2 Representation by Rank Order of Distances to Prototypes

A representation based on distances to a set of points (prototypes), as provided by Chorus, suggests a relationship to *vector quantization*—a technique originally developed for signal coding in communications and signal processing (Linde et al., 1980). A vector quantizer $Q$ is a mapping from a $d$-dimensional Euclidean space, $\mathcal{S}$, into a finite set $\mathcal{C}$ of *code vectors*, $Q : \mathcal{S} \rightarrow \mathcal{C}$, $\mathcal{C} = (p_1, p_2, \ldots, p_n)$, $p_i \in \mathcal{S}, i = 1, 2, \ldots, n$. Every

$n$-point vector quantizer partitions $\mathcal{S}$ into $n$ regions, $R_i = \{x \in \mathcal{S} : Q(x) = p_i\}$; the Voronoi diagram is an example of such a partition.

Whereas vector quantization encodes each input pattern in terms of *one* of the code vectors chosen by the nearest-neighbor principle (Cover and Hart, 1967), Chorus does so in terms of similarities to *several* prototypes. This parallel suggests that a discretized representation of the input space, related to the Voronoi diagram, can be obtained by considering ranks of distances to prototypes, instead of the distances themselves.

Let $\mathbf{p}_1, \ldots, \mathbf{p}_n$ be $n$ prototypes, and consider a representation that associates with each input stimulus the *R*ank *O*rder of its *D*istances to the prototypes ($ROD$). That is, an input $\mathbf{x}$ is represented by an ordered list of indices $ROD(\mathbf{x}) = (i_1, i_2, \ldots, i_n)$, meaning that among all prototypes $\mathbf{p}_i$, $\mathbf{x}$ is the most similar to $\mathbf{p}_{i_1}$, then to $\mathbf{p}_{i_2}$, and so on. Note that the index $i$ always heads the list $ROD(\mathbf{p}_i)$ corresponding to the prototype $\mathbf{p}_i$ (a prototype is most similar to itself). The total number of distinct representations under the $ROD$ scheme is $n!$ (the number of permutations of the $n$ indices).

To compare two representations, one may use Spearman rank order correlation of the index lists. A short form of Spearman rank correlation formula (which can be reliably employed when the total number of tied measurements is not large relative to $n$) is $r_s = 1 - \frac{6\Sigma d_i^2}{n(n^2-1)}$, where $d_i$ stand for the rank differences of the $i$'th component of the vectors to be correlated (Mendenhall and Sincich, 1988). In that formula, only the number of mismatches in ranks and their magnitude enter the calculation. In our case, however, we must also take into account the positions of the mismatches. This can be done using the following variant of Spearman's formula: $r_s = 1 - \frac{6\Sigma(n-i+1)d_i^2}{\frac{1}{2}n(n+1)(n^2-1)}$, or, $r_s = 1 - \frac{6\Sigma w_i d_i^2}{(n^2-1)}$, where $w_i = \frac{(n-i+1)}{\frac{1}{2}n(n+1)}$, $\Sigma_{i=1}^n w_i = 1$, and $d_i$ are as before.[3]

$ROD$ is obviously a less informative version of representation by prototypes than Chorus. To see how it is related to the Voronoi diagram, note that the leading component $i_1$ of $ROD(\mathbf{x})$ determines the Voronoi cell $V(\mathbf{p}_{i_1})$ to which the vector $\mathbf{x}$ belongs. $i_1$ combined with $i_2$ define sub-regions within the Voronoi cell $V(\mathbf{p}_{i_1})$ closer to prototype $\mathbf{p}_{i_2}$ than to any other $\mathbf{p}_{i_j}$, $j \neq 1, 2$. Formally, this finer subdivision of the Voronoi cell $V(\mathbf{p}_{i_1})$ is defined by $\mathrm{Vor}(\mathcal{S} - \{\mathbf{p}_i\}) \bigcap V(\mathbf{p}_i)$, where $\mathcal{S} = \{\mathbf{p}_i\}_{i=1}^n$, as in section B.1.5. Each of the $(n-1)$ components $i_1, \ldots, i_{(n-1)}$ of $ROD(\mathbf{x})$ adds more information regarding the location of $\mathbf{x}$ with respect to the prototypes, resulting in a finer subdivision of the Voronoi cell $V(\mathbf{p}_{i_1})$.

## Notes

1. In a finite set of points, rank correlation between original and transformed distances is an appropriate measure of veridicality of representation because it describes the degree to which the original neighborhood of each point is preserved. A perfect correlation in the limiting case, when the number of points goes to infinity, corresponds to an isometric representation in which all the distances are preserved.

2. I thank Nathan Linial of the Hebrew University for bringing this result to my attention.

3. Consider, for example, the following three rank order vectors: $q_1 = (1, 2, 3)$, $q_2 = (2, 1, 3)$ and $q_3 = (1, 3, 2)$. The difference between $q_1$ and $q_2$ is in their first and second largest rank order components (one position difference), whereas $q_1$ and $q_3$ have the same largest rank order component, but differ in their second and third components (one position difference as well). The difference vectors are: $d(q_1, q_2) = (1, 1, 0)$, $d(q_1, q_3) = (0, 1, 1)$, therefore, their Spearman rank correlation is the same. In comparison, the modified formula yields $r_s(q_1, q_2) = 0.375$, whereas $r_s(q_1, q_3) = 0.625$. Thus, a shift in the first two components is given more weight than the same shift in two lower-order components.

# Appendix C
# Quasiconformal Mappings and Deformable Shapes

In some cases, it may be desirable to define shape up to a group of transformations that is less restrictive than the orthogonal group, or, in other words, to allow *deformation* (see figure C.1). Consider Dali's *Persistence of Memory*: our perception of the thing suspended from the tree branch as a deformed clock rather than an uninterpretable shape attests to the perceptual equivalence of some shapes related by deformations rather than transformations. In that case, a suitable framework for the definition of a shape space can be provided by the theory of Riemann surfaces (Krushkal', 1979). Consider surfaces (shapes) of a given genus, that is, simply-connected (one-part) surfaces with the same number of holes in them (a sphere and all its "rubber" deformations are surfaces of genus zero; the doughnut and the cup are surfaces of genus one, etc.). Two such shapes related by a *conformal* mapping can be considered equivalent (belonging to the same class), with a *quasiconformal* mapping taking one shape class into another. The resulting shape space (known as the Teichmüller space) possesses a natural Riemannian metric, in which distance between two shapes is defined by the deviation from conformality of the quasiconformal mapping by which they are related (Krushkal', 1979). The Teichmüller space can be parameterized by a small set of real numbers, which provide a possible coordinate system for the resulting shape space (Sundararaman, 1980).

In Teichmüller theory, the parameterization of Riemann surfaces in a given equivalence class of (conformal) deformations is unique. This follows from the solution to the famous Problem of Moduli in algebraic geometry (Sundararaman, 1980).

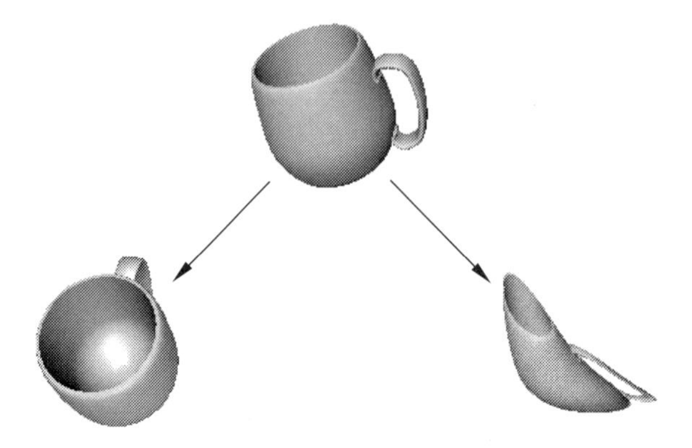

**Figure C.1**
Transformation and deformation. Although the object on the right certainly looks deformed, it is still easily recognized as related to the object on the left. In some sense, therefore, its shape is preserved.

# Appendix D

# RBF Modules for Object Representation

## D.1 Radial Basis Function (RBF) Approximation

An RBF approximation module effectively constructs its target manifold by computing its "height" over the input measurement space as a linear combination of the contributions of the data points (see figure 4.2). The contributions are determined by placing a kernel (that is, a basis function) at selected points $\{\mathbf{x}_i\}$, so that

$$f(\mathbf{x}) = \sum_i c_i K(\mathbf{x}; \mathbf{x}_i) \tag{D.1}$$

and by computing the weights $c_i$ that minimize the approximation error $\sum_n (y - f(\mathbf{x}))^2$ accumulated over all the data $\{\mathbf{x}_n, y_n\}$. A good choice for the shape of the kernel $K(\mathbf{x}; \mathbf{x}_i)$ is the Gaussian $G(\mathbf{x}; \mathbf{x}_i) = e^{-\|\mathbf{x}-\mathbf{x}_i\|^2/\sigma}$, because of the universal approximation properties of linear superpositions of Gaussians (Hartman et al., 1990), and because it can be derived from a regularized solution to the approximation problem, as well as for other reasons (Poggio and Girosi, 1990). The Gaussian kernel is especially relevant in the context of visual modeling, because it makes it possible to interpret equation (D.1) as a linear combination of *products* of activities of 2D image-based Gaussian RFs. In other words, 2D RFs can be combined multiplicatively to form the multidimensional Gaussians that serve as the basis functions in the expansion (Poggio and Edelman, 1990).

## D.2 Theoretical Aspects of RBF Module Design

This section addresses the theoretical underpinnings of the ability of an RBF module to overcome the variability induced by pose changes. As we shall see, once an RBF module is trained on a collection of object views, its response to views that differ from the training examples in a small displacement within the view space spanned by the examples is always higher than its response to views that are displaced away from this view space.

### D.2.1 The Infinitesimal Displacement Case

Consider the following situation, depicted in figure D.1:

- $\mathbf{x}_1$ is a training view, $\mathbf{x}_i$ is another, arbitrary, training view, $i = 1, \ldots, k$.
- $\Delta\mathbf{x}$ is a unit vector, $(\Delta\mathbf{x})^T \Delta\mathbf{x} = 1$.
- $t > 0$, a parameter controlling the extent of the displacement in the direction of $\Delta\mathbf{x}$.

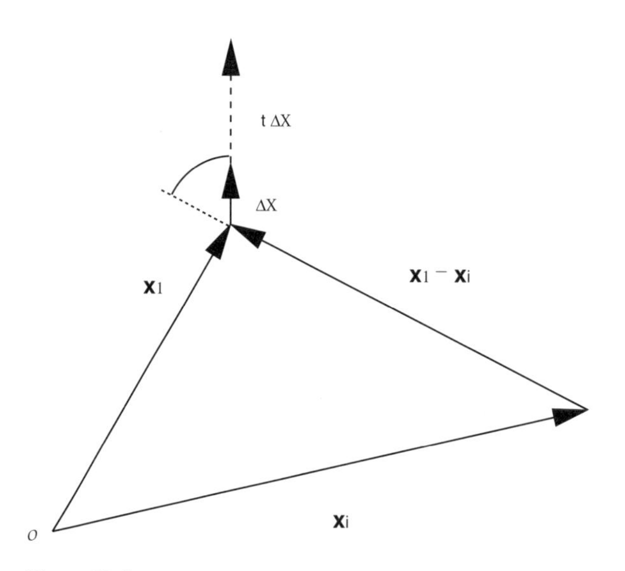


**Figure D.1**
A diagram illustrating the notation used in section D.2; $\mathbf{x}_1$, $\mathbf{x}_i$ are training views of a specific object shape, $i = 1, \ldots, k$. $t\Delta\mathbf{x}$ is a vector representing a displacement from the view space spanned by the training vectors. The angle between $t\Delta\mathbf{x}$ and $\mathbf{x}_1 - \mathbf{x}_i$ indicates the direction of displacement. When all such angles are acute, the displacement is away from the view space, whereas when at least one such angle is obtuse, the displacement is towards one of the $\mathbf{x}_i$'s, and therefore towards the view space.

Train a Gaussian RBF network on a set of pairs $\{\mathbf{x}_i, y_i\}_{i=1}^{k}$, where $\mathbf{X} = \{\mathbf{x}_i\}_{i=1}^{k}$ is a set of views, and the target output is a constant: $\mathbf{y} = \{y_i = 1\}_{i=1}^{k}$. For an input vector $\mathbf{x}$, the corresponding output activity $RBF(\mathbf{x})$ is:

$$RBF(\mathbf{x}) = \sum_{i=1}^{k} c_i G(\|\mathbf{x} - \mathbf{x}_i\|)$$

$$= \sum_{i=1}^{k} c_i \, e^{-\left[(\mathbf{x}-\mathbf{x}_i)^T(\mathbf{x}-\mathbf{x}_i)\right]^2/\sigma^2}. \tag{D.2}$$

Let $\mathbf{A} = (a_i)$, $\mathbf{B} = (b_j)$; define $\mathbf{G}(\mathbf{A}; \mathbf{B})$ to be a matrix whose entry $(i, j)$ is the Gaussian $e^{\frac{-\|a_i - b_j\|^2}{\sigma^2}}$. Training in its simplest form means solving the equation

$$y = \mathbf{G}(\mathbf{x}; \mathbf{X}) \cdot \mathbf{c},$$

for the value of $\mathbf{c}$. The solution is:

$$\mathbf{c} = \mathbf{G}^{+}(\mathbf{X}; \mathbf{X}) \cdot \mathbf{y}, \tag{D.3}$$

where $\mathbf{G}^{+}$ denotes the pseudoinverse (Albert, 1972) of $\mathbf{G}$.

Thus, equation (D.2) takes the form

$$RBF(\mathbf{x}) = \mathbf{G}(\mathbf{x}; \mathbf{X}) \cdot \mathbf{G}^{+}(\mathbf{X}; \mathbf{X}) \cdot \mathbf{y}. \tag{D.4}$$

Upon successful training, $RBF(\mathbf{x}_1) = 1 - \epsilon$, $\epsilon \ll 1$. Now, compute the change in the RBF output resulting from an infinitesimal displacement of the input from a training vector $\mathbf{x}_1$, in an arbitrary direction:

$$\left.\frac{\partial RBF(\mathbf{x} + t\Delta\mathbf{x})}{\partial t}\right|_{\substack{\mathbf{x}=\mathbf{x}_1 \\ t>0,\, t\to 0}}$$

$$= \frac{\partial}{\partial t}\left[\sum_{i=1}^{k} c_i \, e^{-\left[(\mathbf{x}_1 + t\Delta\mathbf{x} - \mathbf{x}_i)^T(\mathbf{x}_1 + t\Delta\mathbf{x} - \mathbf{x}_i)\right]^2/\sigma^2}\right] \tag{D.5}$$

$$= \sum_{i=1}^{k} c_i \, e^{-\left[(\mathbf{x}_1 + t\Delta\mathbf{x} - \mathbf{x}_i)^T(\mathbf{x}_1 + t\Delta\mathbf{x} - \mathbf{x}_i)\right]^2/\sigma^2}$$

$$\cdot \frac{\partial}{\partial t}\{-\left[(\mathbf{x}_1 + t\Delta\mathbf{x} - \mathbf{x}_i)^T(\mathbf{x}_1 + t\Delta\mathbf{x} - \mathbf{x}_i)\right]^2/\sigma^2\}.$$

Denote

$$D \triangleq \frac{\partial}{\partial t}\Big[-(\mathbf{x}_1 + t\Delta\mathbf{x} - \mathbf{x}_i)^T(\mathbf{x}_1 + t\Delta\mathbf{x} - \mathbf{x}_i)\Big]^2/\sigma^2$$

$$D = -\frac{2}{\sigma^2}(\mathbf{x}_1 + t\Delta\mathbf{x} - \mathbf{x}_i)^T(\mathbf{x}_1 + t\Delta\mathbf{x} - \mathbf{x}_i)$$
$$\cdot\frac{\partial}{\partial t}\Big[(\mathbf{x}_1 + t\Delta\mathbf{x} - \mathbf{x}_i)^T(\mathbf{x}_1 + t\Delta\mathbf{x} - \mathbf{x}_i)\Big].$$

Because $\Delta\mathbf{x}$ is a unit vector, we have, by the commutativity of the inner product,

$$(\mathbf{x}_1 + t\Delta\mathbf{x} - \mathbf{x}_i)^T(\mathbf{x}_1 + t\Delta\mathbf{x} - \mathbf{x}_i)$$
$$= (\mathbf{x}_1 - \mathbf{x}_i)^T(\mathbf{x}_1 - \mathbf{x}_i) + 2t(\Delta\mathbf{x})^T(\mathbf{x}_1 - \mathbf{x}_i),$$

and,

$$\frac{\partial}{\partial t}\Big[(\mathbf{x}_1 + t\Delta\mathbf{x} - \mathbf{x}_i)^T(\mathbf{x}_1 + t\Delta\mathbf{x} - \mathbf{x}_i)\Big] = 2(\Delta\mathbf{x})^T(\mathbf{x}_1 - \mathbf{x}_i) + 2t.$$

Thus,

$$D = -\frac{2}{\sigma^2}\Big[\|\mathbf{x}_1 - \mathbf{x}_i\| + 2t(\Delta\mathbf{x})^T(\mathbf{x}_1 - \mathbf{x}_i)\Big] \cdot\Big[2(\Delta\mathbf{x})^T(\mathbf{x}_1 - \mathbf{x}_i) + 2t\Big]. \tag{D.6}$$

Consider the following two possible cases:

*(A)* $\forall i\ (\Delta\mathbf{x})^T(\mathbf{x}_1 - \mathbf{x}_i) \geq 0,$

*(B)* $\exists i\ (\Delta\mathbf{x})^T(\mathbf{x}_1 - \mathbf{x}_i) < 0.$

Note that case *(B)* means that the direction of change, determined by the vector $\Delta\mathbf{x}$, is within the view space spanned by the $\mathbf{x}_i,\ i = 1, \ldots k$, whereas in case *(A)*, the direction of the displacement is away from the view space (see figure D.1). Denote, $d_i \triangleq \|\mathbf{x}_1 - \mathbf{x}_i\|$, $\Delta_i \triangleq (\Delta\mathbf{x})^T(\mathbf{x}_1 - \mathbf{x}_i)$, and note that $d_i \geq 0$. With the new notation, equation (D.6) becomes,

$$D = -\frac{2}{\sigma^2}(d_i + 2t\Delta_i)(2\Delta_i + 2t)$$
$$= -\frac{4}{\sigma^2}(d_i\Delta_i + d_i t + 2t\Delta_i^2 + 2t^2\Delta_i),$$

and when $t$ goes to zero, this yields,

$$D \underset{t \to 0}{\longrightarrow} -\frac{4}{\sigma^2} d_i \Delta_i.$$

Consequently, in the limit for $t \to 0$, from equation (D.2.1) we have,

$$\left.\frac{\partial RBF(\mathbf{x} + t\Delta\mathbf{x})}{\partial t}\right|_{\substack{\mathbf{x}=\mathbf{x}_1 \\ t>0, t\to 0}} \underset{t \to 0}{\longrightarrow} \sum_{i=1}^{k} c_i \, e^{-\frac{d_i^2}{\Delta_i^2}} \cdot \left(-\frac{4}{\sigma^2} d_i \Delta_i\right). \tag{D.7}$$

Denote this limit by $L$, $L = -\frac{4}{\sigma^2} \sum_{i=1}^{k} c_i d_i \Delta_i \, e^{-\frac{d_i^2}{\Delta_i^2}}$.

For case *(A)*, $\Delta_i \geq 0, \ \forall i$. Therefore, if all $c_i > 0$, we would have $L_A \leq 0$, $L_A < L_B$, for $L_A, L_B$ the values of the limit $L$, for cases *(A)* and *(B)*, respectively. This means that an infinitesimal displacement within the view space results in a smaller change of the corresponding RBF activity compared to the change caused by a displacement that is away from the view space. This establishes the desired property of an RBF module: an approximately constant output for different views of the target object, with the response falling off for views of other objects in the infinitesimal view change case.

**Claim D.2.1** $c_i > 0, \ \forall i = 1, \ldots, k$.

***Proof:*** From equation (D.3) we have $c_i = \sum_j (\mathbf{G}^+)_{ij} y_j$, the sum of elements in the $i^{th}$ row of the matrix $\mathbf{G}^+$, where $y_j$ are the targets, $y_j = 1, \ j = 1, \ldots k$, and $\mathbf{G}^+$ is the (pseudo) inverse of $\mathbf{G}$ whose elements are $\mathbf{G}_{ij} = e^{-d_{ij}^2/\sigma^2}$, for $d_{ij} \triangleq \|\mathbf{x}_i - \mathbf{x}_j\|$. Note that $\mathbf{G} = I + A$, where $I$ is a unit matrix,[1] and $A$ is a matrix whose elements are $\ll 1$, under a proper bound on $\sigma$ (see below). Thus, by Taylor expansion for the matrix $\mathbf{G}$, we have,

$$\mathbf{G}^+ = \frac{1}{I + A} \approx I - A + O(A^2).$$

To complete the proof, let

$$\sigma < (\ln k)^{-1/2} \min_{\substack{i,j \\ i<j}} d_{ij}, \quad \text{for } k \text{ - the number of training vectors.}$$

Thus, for all $i$ and $j$, $d_{ij} > \sigma (\ln k)^{1/2}$, $d_{ij}^2 > \sigma^2 \ln k$, and $-\frac{d_{ij}^2}{\sigma^2} < -\ln k = \ln \frac{1}{k}$. Taking the exponent of both terms, we obtain

$$e^{-\frac{d_{ij}^2}{\sigma^2}} < e^{\ln \frac{1}{k}} = \frac{1}{k}.$$

As a result, the sum of elements in any row of $\mathbf{G}^{+}$ is equal to 1 (the element on the diagonal, contributed by the unit matrix) minus $k-1$ elements, each smaller than $\frac{1}{k}$. Thus, we finally have,

$$c_i = 1 - \sum_{j=1}^{k-1} e^{-\frac{d_{ij}^2}{\sigma^2}} y_j > 1 - \sum_{j=1}^{k-1} \frac{1}{k} = 1 - \frac{k-1}{k} > 0 \quad \forall i = 1, \ldots, k.$$

### D.2.2 The Finite Displacement Case

The preceding proof can be extended to a finite input-space displacement of the stimulus. As before, consider a change in object appearance due to (a) the extrinsic effect of pose, or a change along view space direction (object rotation), and (b) an intrinsic shape change, that is, a change away from the view space (shape deformation). First, observe that the effects of two factors determining the appearance of an object, shape and pose, are approximately orthogonal (see figure D.2). Now, let $\mathbf{x}_1$ be, as before, an arbitrary training view of the object, and let $\Delta v$, $\Delta p$, be finite displacements along and in perpendicular to the view space, respectively. Because Gaussians are factorizable, and because the view-space and the shape-space changes in the appearance of a point-cloud object are orthogonal, we have

$$G(\|\mathbf{x}-\mathbf{t}\|) = e^{\frac{-\|\mathbf{x}-\mathbf{t}\|^2}{\sigma^2}} = e^{\frac{-\|\mathbf{x}^p-\mathbf{t}^p\|^2}{\sigma^2}} e^{\frac{-\|\mathbf{x}^v-\mathbf{t}^v\|^2}{\sigma^2}}. \tag{D.8}$$

Consider now a displacement within an object view space. This change in the object's (two-dimensional) appearance results from a (three-dimensional) rotation of the object away from some reference view. The upper bound on this kind of change is therefore finite. To see that, recall that both $\{\mathbf{x}_i\}_{i=1}^N$ and $\mathbf{x}$ are different two-dimensional views of the same object, resulting from projection of the corresponding three-dimensional "views," $\mathcal{X}_i$, $i = 1 \ldots, k$, and $\mathcal{X}$, respectively. That is, $\mathbf{x} = \mathcal{P}\mathcal{X}$, $\mathbf{x}_i = \mathcal{P}\mathcal{X}_i$, where $\mathcal{P}$ is a $3D \longrightarrow 2D$ projection. Any three-dimensional view can be described by a rotation $R_{\mathbf{n}}(\omega)$ away from some "canonical" orientation of the object, say $\mathcal{X}_c$, in the three-dimensional space. Thus,

$$\|\mathbf{x}-\mathbf{x}_i\| = \|\mathcal{P}\mathcal{X} - \mathcal{P}\mathcal{X}_i\| = \|\mathcal{P}R_{\mathbf{n}_1}(\omega_1)\mathcal{X}_c - \mathcal{P}R_{\mathbf{n}_i}(\omega_i)\mathcal{X}_c\|.$$

Under orthographic projection, the difference between projected vectors is the projection of their difference, and the norm, which can only be

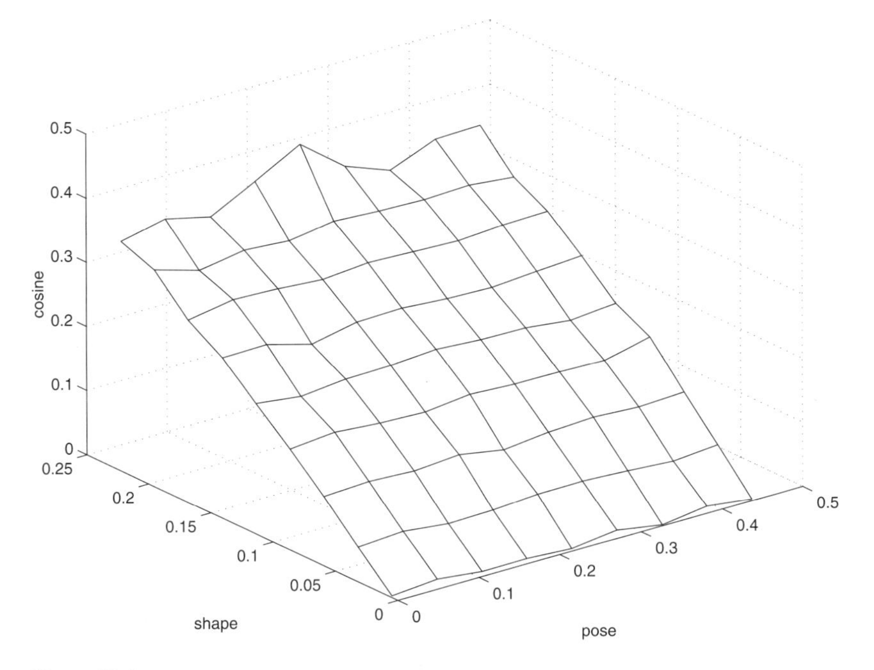


**Figure D.2**
Orthogonality of the effects of shape and pose. The angle between displacements due to variations in pose and shape was measured for 2D orthographic projections of a 3D ten-point cloud object. The plot shows the average value of the cosine of this angle, calculated for 20, 000 randomly chosen values of pose variation (an arbitrary rotation of the cloud's points), and shape variation (a random deformation of the cloud). Data were gathered into a small number of bins, sorted by the angle of rotation (shown in radians along the *pose* axis), and by the amount of shape deformation, measured as the fraction of cloud size (*shape* axis). For sufficiently small deformations, the cosine of the angle is small, indicating approximate orthogonality.

reduced by projection, is preserved by the rotation mapping (Kanatani, 1990). Thus,

$$\begin{aligned}
&\|\mathcal{P}\left[R_{\mathbf{n}_1}(\omega_1)\mathcal{X}_c - R_{\mathbf{n}_i}(\omega_i)\mathcal{X}_c\right]\| \\
&\quad \le \|R_{\mathbf{n}_1}(\omega_1)\mathcal{X}_c - R_{\mathbf{n}_i}(\omega_i)\mathcal{X}_c\| \\
&\quad \le \|R_{\mathbf{n}_1}(\omega_1)\mathcal{X}_c\| + \|R_{\mathbf{n}_i}(\omega_i)\mathcal{X}_c\| \\
&\quad = \|\mathcal{X}_c\| + \|\mathcal{X}_c\| = 2\|\mathcal{X}_c\|.
\end{aligned}$$

Thus, an upper bound on the extent of the view space displacement is easily established. Denote this bound by $D$ and let $\mathbf{x} = \mathbf{x}_1 + \Delta v$. From the above, $\|\Delta v\| \leq D$. By triangle inequality,

$$\begin{aligned}\|\mathbf{x} - \mathbf{x}_i\| &= \|(\mathbf{x}_1 + \Delta v) - \mathbf{x}_i\| \\ &\leq \|(\mathbf{x}_1 + \Delta v) - \mathbf{x}_1\| + \|\mathbf{x}_1 - \mathbf{x}_i\| = \|\Delta v\| + \|\mathbf{x}_1 - \mathbf{x}_i\|.\end{aligned}$$

Hence,

$$-\|\mathbf{x} - \mathbf{x}_i\|^2 \geq -\left[\|\Delta v\|^2 + 2\|\Delta v\| \cdot \|\mathbf{x}_1 - \mathbf{x}_i\| + \|\mathbf{x}_1 - \mathbf{x}_i\|^2\right].$$

As a consequence, because all $c_i$ are positive (Claim D.2.1),

$$\begin{aligned}RBF(\mathbf{x}) &= \sum_{i=1}^{k} c_i \, e^{-\|\mathbf{x}-\mathbf{x}_i\|^2/\sigma^2} \\ &\geq \sum_{i=1}^{k} c_i \, e^{-\|\Delta v\|^2/\sigma^2} \cdot e^{-2\|\Delta v\| \cdot \|\mathbf{x}_1 - \mathbf{x}_i\|/\sigma^2} \cdot e^{-\|\mathbf{x}_1-\mathbf{x}_i\|^2/\sigma^2}.\end{aligned}$$

Now, let

$$\sigma < 2 \min_{\substack{i,j \\ i<j}} d_{ij}, \qquad \text{for } d_{ij} \triangleq \|\mathbf{x}_i - \mathbf{x}_j\|.$$

Thus, $\|\mathbf{x}_1 - \mathbf{x}_i\| \geq \frac{\sigma}{2}$. Because $\|\Delta v\| \leq D$, and $-2\|\Delta v\| \geq -2D$, we have,

$$\frac{-2\|\Delta v\| \|\mathbf{x}_1 - \mathbf{x}_i\|}{\sigma^2} \geq -\frac{D}{\sigma}.$$

Finally,

$$RBF(\mathbf{x}) \geq \sum_{i=1}^{k} c_i \, e^{-\|\mathbf{x}_1-\mathbf{x}_i\|^2/\sigma^2} \cdot e^{-\frac{D^2}{\sigma^2}} \cdot e^{-\frac{D}{\sigma}},$$

or,

$$RBF(\mathbf{x}) \geq e^{-\frac{D}{\sigma}(1+\frac{D}{\sigma})} \cdot RBF(\mathbf{x}_1),$$

for

$$D \ll \sigma, \quad F \triangleq \frac{D}{\sigma} \ll 1,$$

and,

$$e^{-F(1+F)} \gg 0.$$

Now, for a finite displacement in perpendicular to the view space, $\mathbf{x} = \mathbf{x}_1 + \Delta p$, we have by orthogonality (equation (D.8)),

$$RBF(\mathbf{x}) = \sum_{i=1}^{k} c_i \, e^{-\|(\mathbf{x}_1+\Delta p)-\mathbf{x}_i\|^2/\sigma^2}$$

$$= \sum_{i=1}^{k} c_i \, e^{-\|\mathbf{x}_1-\mathbf{x}_i\|^2/\sigma^2} \cdot e^{-\|\Delta p\|^2/\sigma^2} = RBF(\mathbf{x}_1) \cdot e^{-\|\Delta p\|^2/\sigma^2}.$$

For an arbitrary amount of shape-space displacement, say, $\|\Delta p\| \gg 0$, $e^{-\|\Delta p\|^2/\sigma^2} \ll 1$ can become arbitrarily small, since $-\|\Delta p\|^2 \ll 0 \Longrightarrow e^{-\|\Delta p\|^2/\sigma^2} \ll 1$.

Hence we finally have, for a shape displacement,

$RBF(\mathbf{x}) \leq e^{-\|\Delta p\|^2/\sigma^2} RBF(\mathbf{x}_1) \ll RBF(\mathbf{x}_1)$.

From the above arguments, we may conclude that (1) any displacement *within* the view space of the target object results in an RBF activity that cannot be less than some positive, not too small, fraction of its activity on the training examples, and (2) for a displacement *perpendicular* to the view space, the corresponding RBF activity is always below the output obtained in training, and decreases for increasing shape differences.

## D.3 Practical Aspects of RBF Module Training

To train an RBF module, one needs to place the basis functions optimally so as to cover the input space (i.e., determine the basis-function centers), calculate the output weights associated with each center, and tune the basis-function width.

### D.3.1 Finding the Optimal Placement for Each Basis Function

Whereas the computation of the weight assigned to each basis function is a linear optimization problem, finding the optimal placement for each basis in the input space is much more difficult (Poggio and Girosi, 1990). The method described here considers a simplified version of this problem, which assumes that a small optimal subset of examples to be used in training is chosen out of a larger set of available data, consisting of views of the shape on which the module is trained.

Defining the optimal subset of views as the one that minimizes the nearest-neighbor classification error for that object amounts to performing vector quantization (VQ; see appendix E) in the input space (Moody and Darken, 1989; Poggio and Girosi, 1989). Here, the measurement-space representations (see appendix A) are used as the input to the RBF module.

A quantization is said to be optimal if it minimizes the expected distortion. Simple measures of the latter, such as squared Euclidean distance, while widely used in vector quantization applications (Gersho and Gray, 1992), do not correlate well with the intuitive notion of distance appropriate for object recognition. Specifically, Euclidean distances in image space do not reflect object identities if the illumination conditions are allowed to vary (Adini et al., 1997). Likewise, in the measurement space $\mathcal{M}$, representations of similar objects tend to cluster together by orientation, not by shape, if objects are allowed to rotate (Duvdevani-Bar and Edelman, 1995; Lando and Edelman, 1995). This implies that a different measure of quantization distortion is needed.

The measure incorporated in the present implementation of Chorus is *canonical distortion*, proposed by Baxter (1997). The notion of canonical distortion is based on the observation that in any given classification task, there exists a natural environment of functions, or classifiers, that allow for a faithful representation of distance in the input space. The property shared by all such classifiers is that their output varies little across instances of the same entity (class). Ideally, the output of a particular classifier is close to one if the input is an instance of its target class, and if it is close to zero otherwise. Thus, in the space of classifier *outputs* instances of the same class are closer together, and instances of different classes are farther apart, than in the input space. According to Baxter, the distortion measurement induced by the classifier space is the desired canonical distortion measure.[2]

Following Baxter's ideas, the view space of an object was sampled (see figure D.3), and subjected to canonical quantization. The representative views, subsequently used to train the object-specific modules, were chosen in accordance with the following three criteria. First, a classifier (i.e., module) output should be approximately constant for different views of its selected object. Second, views of the same object should be tightly clus-

**Figure D.3**
A set of forty-nine views of one of the figure-like test objects (`A1`), taken at grid points along an imaginary viewing sphere centered around the object. Views differ in the azimuth and the elevation of the camera, both ranging between $-60°$ and $60°$ at $20°$ increments. The Canonical Vector Quantization (CVQ) procedure was used to select the most representative views for the purpose of training the object representation system (see section D.3.1; the selected views of `A1` are marked by frames).

tered in the module output space. Third, clusters corresponding to views of different objects should be separated as widely as possible.

These three criteria were incorporated into a modified version of the Generalized Lloyd algorithm (GLA) for vector quantization (Linde et al., 1980). In contrast to the conventional GLA, which carries out quantization in the *input* vector space, this algorithm concentrated on the module *output* space. Training an RBF network on the centers of clusters resulting from the optimal partition of the module output space addressed the first of the three requirements—an approximately constant output across views of an object. The other two requirements were addressed by a simultaneous minimization of the ratio of between-objects to within-object view scatter (a cluster compactness criterion; see Duda and Hart, 1973).

Increasing the number of examples on which a module is trained always improves both its performance and the view-space compactness criterion (see figure D.4). The present version of Baxter's Canonical Vector Quantization (CVQ) relied on this observation by taking the so-called "greedy" algorithmic approach. The algorithm was initialized with an empty set of views and added new views iteratively. At each iteration, the new view was chosen so as to minimize the compactness criterion, and the entire process followed the gradient of improvement in module performance (see appendix E.1, for details).

### D.3.2 Tuning the Basis-Function Width

A complete specification of an RBF module consists of the choice of basis function centers, the output weights associated with each center,

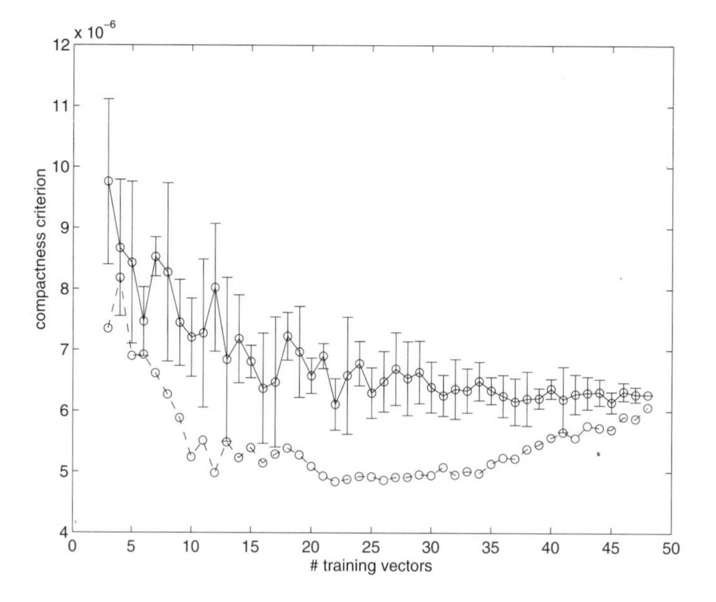

and the spread constant, or the width, of the basis functions. The width parameter has a direct influence on the performance of an RBF classifier (i.e., its ability to accept instances of the class on which it is trained, and to reject other input). Optimally, the width parameter should be set to a value that yields equal miss and false-alarm error rates (see figure D.5). Following the rule of thumb according to which the width parameter

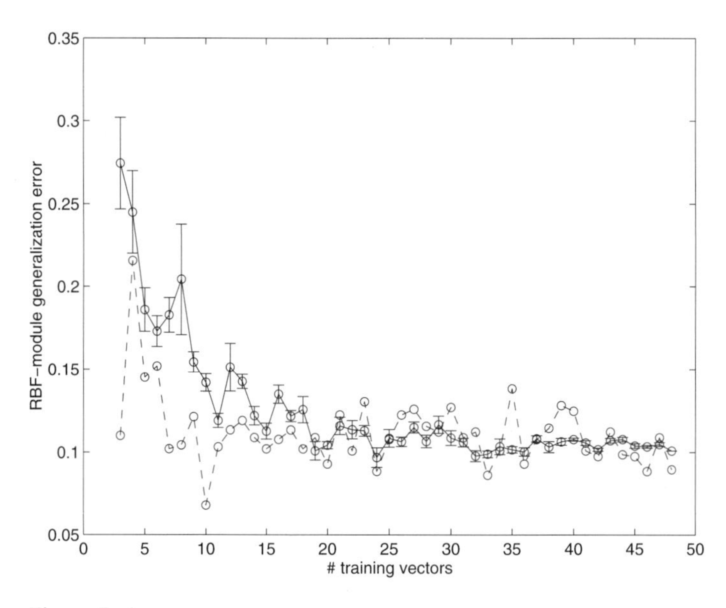


**Figure D.4**
The effect of training-set size on the performance of an RBF module trained under the compactness criterion. *(Top)* The recognition error obtained for the Nissan module, trained as a part of a network consisting of ten object modules (see figure 5.2). For each object, training involved a set of $N = 49$ views, taken as described in figure D.3. The abscissa is the number $t$ of the training vectors (examples). For $t < 15$ or so, the performance of the module trained on the CVQ-derived *code vectors* (dashed line) is better than the error obtained with the same number of randomly chosen training vectors (solid line). When $t$ is large, the resulting error is low in any case. *(Opposite)* The compactness criterion (the ordinate), defined as the ratio of between-cluster to within-cluster scatter (Duda and Hart, 1973), plotted against the size of the training set. Note that the values of the compactness criterion obtained for the CVQ code vectors (dashed line) are significantly better (lower) than the values obtained for a module trained on the same number of randomly chosen vectors (solid line). In both plots, error bars represent the standard error of the mean, calculated over twenty-five independent random choices of the training vectors.

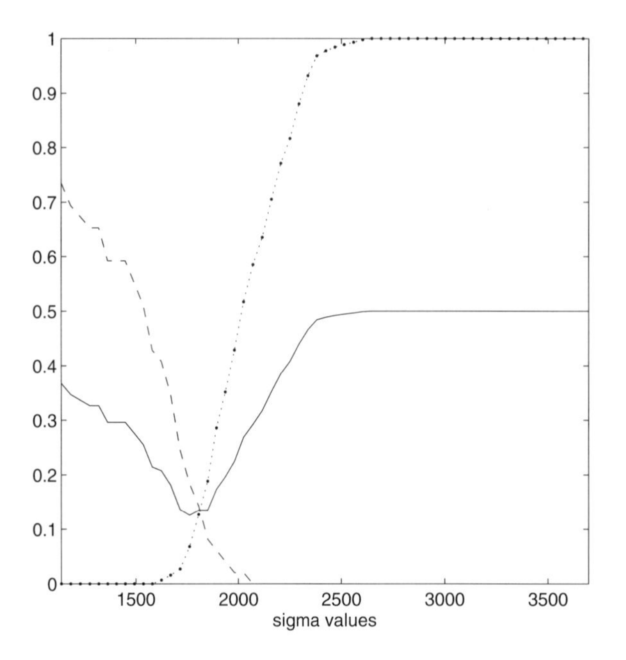


**Figure D.5**
The effect of the basis function width ($\sigma$) on the performance of an RBF module. RBF-module miss rate (dashed line), false-alarm rate (dotted line), and their mean (solid line) are plotted against $\sigma$. The values of $\sigma$ shown on the abscissa range from half the minimal distance up to the maximal distance among RBF-module "centers" (training views) in the input space.

should be much larger than the minimum distance and much smaller than the maximum distance among the basis centers, a straightforward binary search was used to optimize its value.

## Notes

1. $\forall i, d_{ii} = 0$, thus, $e^{-d_{ii}^2/\sigma^2} = 1$ are the diagonal elements.

2. Consider an *environment* of functions $f \in \mathcal{F}$, mapping a probability space $(X, P, \sigma_X)$ into a space $(Y, \sigma)$, with $\sigma : Y \times Y \rightarrow R$. A natural distortion measure on $X$ induced by the environment is $\rho(x, y) = \int_{\mathcal{F}} \sigma(f(x), f(y))dQ(f)$, for $x, y \in X$, and $Q$ an environmental probability measure on $\mathcal{F}$.

# Appendix E
# Vector Quantization

*Vector quantization* (VQ) is a technique that has been originally developed for signal coding in communications and signal processing. It is used in a variety of tasks, including speech and image compression, speech recognition and signal processing (Gersho and Gray, 1992).

A vector quantizer $Q$ is a mapping from a $d$-dimensional Euclidean space, $\mathcal{S}$, into a finite set $\mathcal{C}$ of *code vectors*, $Q: \mathcal{S} \rightarrow \mathcal{C}$, $\mathcal{C} = (p_1, p_2, \ldots, p_n)$, $p_i \in \mathcal{S}$, $i = 1, 2, \ldots, n$. Associated with every $n$-point vector quantizer is a partition of $\mathcal{S}$ into $n$ regions, $R_i = \{x \in \mathcal{S} : Q(x) = p_i\}$.

Vector quantizer performance is measured by distortion $d(\mathbf{x}, \hat{\mathbf{x}})$—a cost associated with representing an input vector $\mathbf{x}$ by a quantized vector $\hat{\mathbf{x}}$. The goal in designing an optimal vector quantization set is to minimize the expected distortion. The most convenient and widely used measure of distortion is the squared Euclidean distance.

## E.1 The Generalized Lloyd (K-means) Algorithm

The generalized Lloyd algorithm (GLA) for vector quantizer design (Linde et al., 1980) is known also as the $k$-means method (MacQueen, 1967). According to the algorithm, an optimal vector quantizer is designed via iterative codebook modifications to satisfy two conditions: nearest neighbor (NN) and centroid condition (CC). The former is equivalent to constructing the Voronoi cell of each code vector, whereas the application of the latter is aimed to adjust each code vector to be the center of gravity of its domination region. The means of the ($k$) initial clusters are found, and each input point is examined to see if it is closer to the mean of another cluster than it is to the mean of its current cluster. In that case, the point is transferred and the cluster means (centers) are recalculated. This procedure is repeated until the chosen measure of distortion is sufficiently small.

## E.2 Canonical Vector Quantization

The adaptation of GLA for the canonical vector quantization (CVQ) is described below:

1. Initialization: Set $N = 2$, an initial codebook size. Set $E_N = \infty$. Set $\mathcal{C}^N$ to be an initial codebook of size $N$. The codebook is randomly chosen from the input set.
2. Find an input vector for which the compactness is optimal, and add it to $\mathcal{C}^N$ to create a codebook $\mathcal{C}^{N+1}$ of size $N + 1$.
a. Set iteration $m = 1$, $D_m = \infty$.
b. Given the codebook $\mathcal{C}_m^N$, perform the modified Lloyd Iteration on the module output space to generate the improved codebook $\mathcal{C}_{m+1}^N$: the set of *input* vectors, whose module *outputs* are the closest to the code-vectors constituting the improved output codebook (see below).
c. Compute the sum-of-squared-error $D_m$. If $\frac{D_m - D_{m+1}}{D_m} < \epsilon$ for a suitable threshold $\epsilon$, go to step (3). Otherwise, set $m \leftarrow m + 1$, go to step (b).
3. Calculate the module generalization error $E_N$. If the criterion $\frac{E_N - E_{N+1}}{E_N} \leq \epsilon$ is satisfied, finish. Otherwise, set $N \leftarrow N + 1$, go to step (2).

The Modified Lloyd Iteration:

1. Compute module activity over the input set, denote this set by $\mathcal{O}$. Denote the set of module outputs on the codebook $\mathcal{C}_m^N$, the *output codebook*.
2. Partition the set $\mathcal{O}$ into clusters using the *Nearest Neighbor Condition*, for the output-codebook vectors being the cluster centers.
3. Using the *Centroid Condition*, compute the centroids for the clusters just found, to obtain a new output codebook.

# Appendix F
# Multidimensional Scaling

Multidimensional scaling, or MDS, is a data processing tool that proved to be exceptionally useful in psychology (Shepard, 1980). This technique is derived from the observation that the knowledge of distances among several points constrains the possible locations of the points (relative to each other) to a sufficient degree to allow the recovery of the locations (i.e., the coordinates of the points) by a numerical procedure (Young and Householder, 1938). MDS-related tools are found in several modern statistical analysis software packages, such as SAS or SPSS.

Assuming that the perceived similarities (that is, inverse distances or proximities) among stimuli determine the responses made to those stimuli (Shepard, 1987), one can process the responses by MDS, and examine the dimensionality of the resulting configuration of the points and the relative locations of the points. The assumption of the orderly relationship between the measured proximities and those derived from the resulting configuration is verified in the process, by the success of the MDS procedure, as manifested in the low stress, which is the cumulative residual discrepancy between those two quantities, computed over all the points.

The ability of the so-called nonmetric version of MDS (Shepard, 1980) to recover the configuration of a set of points from the *ranks* of the interpoint distances is illustrated in figure F.1. Although the result is usually judged on the basis of the residual stress, in psychophysical data analysis MDS is most useful when invoked in a confirmatory mode (Borg and Lingoes, 1987), in which case the configuration it produces is compared to the pattern formed by the stimuli in some underlying parameter space (cf. section 6.5.2).

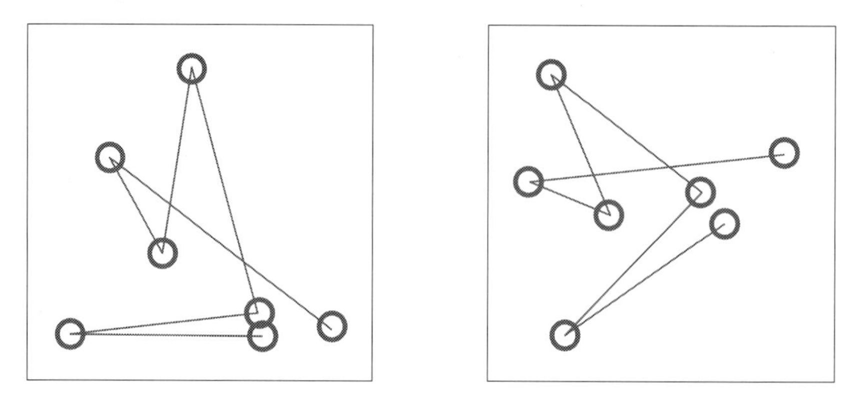

**Figure F.1**
An illustration of the power of MDS to recover a 2D configuration from the distance ranks of as few as seven points. *(Left)* The original configuration. *(Right)* The configuration recovered by MDS. In the experiment illustrated here, the mean correlation between true and recovered segment lengths over 100 trials involving random configurations of seven points was 0.87 (significant at $p < 0.0001$). The mean MDS stress was $0.11 \pm 0.03$.

# Appendix G

# Performance of the Chorus System—Additional Tables

This appendix provides additional information concerning the performance of the implementation of Chorus, described in chapter 5.

Table G.1
RBF module activities (averaged over all 169 test views) evoked by the ten reference objects

| | cow1 | cat | Al | gene | tuna | Lrov | Niss | F16 | fly | TRex |
|---|---|---|---|---|---|---|---|---|---|---|
| cow1 | **4.04** | 1.86 | 0.42 | 1.62 | 0.91 | 1.22 | 1.79 | 1.21 | 0.71 | 0.53 |
| cat2 | 1.69 | **3.55** | 0.26 | 1.02 | 1.10 | 1.20 | 2.10 | 1.04 | 0.61 | 0.53 |
| Al | 0.08 | 0.06 | **1.63** | 0.46 | 0.03 | 0.12 | 0.06 | 0.09 | 0.19 | 0.06 |
| gene | 0.61 | 0.43 | 0.44 | **5.24** | 0.14 | 0.11 | 0.26 | 0.48 | 0.55 | 0.25 |
| tuna | 1.57 | 2.00 | 0.40 | 1.11 | **4.22** | 1.41 | 3.05 | 1.77 | 0.72 | 1.02 |
| Lrov | 0.57 | 0.56 | 0.17 | 0.20 | 0.23 | **3.36** | 1.38 | 0.36 | 0.16 | 0.11 |
| Niss | 0.67 | 0.86 | 0.06 | 0.34 | 0.82 | 0.97 | **3.24** | 0.88 | 0.21 | 0.25 |
| F16 | 0.50 | 0.44 | 0.11 | 0.65 | 0.58 | 0.27 | 0.94 | **2.14** | 0.24 | 0.25 |
| fly | 1.03 | 1.08 | 0.88 | 2.30 | 0.60 | 0.70 | 0.95 | 0.84 | **3.71** | 0.99 |
| TRex | 0.28 | 0.34 | 0.09 | 0.60 | 0.32 | 0.14 | 0.44 | 0.36 | 0.29 | **3.67** |

*Note:* Each row shows the average activation pattern induced by views of one of the objects over the ten RBF modules; boldface indicates the largest entry (see section 5.2.1).

**Table G.2**
Categorization results for the forty-three test objects shown in figure 5.4, for the $k$-NN method of section 5.2.2, with $k = 3$

| | obj | cow1 | cat2 | Al | gene | tuna | Lrov | Niss | F16 | fly | TRex |
|---|---|---|---|---|---|---|---|---|---|---|---|
| QUAD | cow2 | 0.69 | 0.30 | | | | 0.01 | | | | |
| | ox | 0.93 | 0.04 | 0.02 | 0.02 | | | | | | |
| | calf | 0.86 | 0.06 | | | 0.06 | | 0.01 | 0.02 | | |
| | deer | 0.34 | 0.62 | | | 0.03 | | 0.01 | | | |
| | Babe | 0.88 | 0.05 | | | | 0.04 | | | 0.03 | |
| | PigMa | 0.83 | 0.12 | | | | | 0.02 | | 0.04 | |
| | dog | 0.33 | 0.64 | | | 0.01 | | 0.01 | 0.01 | | |
| | goat | 0.20 | 0.69 | 0.04 | 0.06 | | | | | 0.02 | |
| | buff | 0.72 | 0.17 | | 0.03 | 0.01 | 0.03 | | | 0.05 | |
| | rhino | 0.69 | 0.15 | | | 0.01 | 0.02 | 0.11 | 0.01 | | |
| FIGS | pengu | 0.30 | 0.11 | | 0.28 | | | 0.01 | 0.01 | 0.29 | |
| | ape | 0.11 | 0.11 | 0.31 | | | | | | 0.47 | |
| | bear | 0.08 | 0.07 | | 0.75 | | | 0.01 | | 0.10 | |
| | cands | | 0.16 | 0.74 | | | | | | 0.10 | |
| | king | | | 0.67 | 0.09 | | | | | 0.24 | |
| | pawn | | | 0.73 | | | | | | 0.27 | |
| | venus | | | 0.86 | 0.01 | | | | | 0.13 | |
| | lamp | 0.04 | | 0.64 | | | 0.04 | | | 0.28 | |
| | lamp2 | 0.03 | | 0.70 | | | | | | 0.27 | |
| | lamp3 | | | 0.70 | 0.14 | | | | | 0.17 | |
| FISH | whale | 0.08 | 0.11 | | | 0.80 | | | 0.01 | | |
| | whalK | 0.04 | 0.04 | | | 0.91 | | | | 0.01 | |
| | shark | 0.03 | 0.07 | | | 0.89 | | | | | 0.01 |
| | Marln | | 0.01 | | | 0.98 | | 0.01 | | | |
| | whalH | 0.10 | 0.20 | | | 0.70 | | | | | |

Table G.2 (continued)

| | obj | cow1 | cat2 | Al | gene | tuna | Lrov | Niss | F16 | fly | TRex |
|---|---|---|---|---|---|---|---|---|---|---|---|
| AIR | F15 | 0.12 | 0.08 | | | 0.02 | | 0.02 | 0.72 | | 0.03 |
| | F18 | 0.09 | 0.07 | | | 0.06 | | 0.01 | 0.78 | | |
| | Mig27 | 0.05 | 0.37 | 0.14 | | 0.12 | | | 0.31 | | |
| | shutl | 0.24 | 0.31 | | | 0.30 | | | 0.13 | | 0.02 |
| | Ta4 | 0.11 | 0.17 | | | 0.10 | | 0.02 | 0.55 | | 0.05 |
| CARS | Isuzu | 0.07 | 0.07 | | | | 0.04 | 0.83 | | | |
| | Mazda | 0.04 | 0.07 | | | | 0.01 | 0.88 | | | |
| | Mrcds | 0.04 | 0.04 | | | | | 0.92 | | | |
| | Mitsb | 0.04 | 0.07 | | | | 0.01 | 0.89 | | | |
| | NissQ | 0.07 | 0.08 | | | | 0.01 | 0.83 | | 0.01 | |
| | Subru | 0.04 | 0.04 | | | | | 0.92 | | | |
| | SuzuS | 0.13 | 0.17 | | | 0.08 | 0.30 | 0.33 | | | |
| | ToyoC | 0.09 | 0.07 | | | | 0.05 | 0.79 | | | |
| | Beetl | 0.03 | 0.09 | | | | | 0.87 | | 0.01 | |
| | truck | 0.07 | 0.05 | | | | | 0.89 | | | |
| DINO | Paras | 0.01 | 0.05 | | | 0.01 | | | | | 0.93 |
| | Veloc | | 0.03 | | | 0.24 | | | 0.02 | | 0.71 |
| | Allos | | 0.21 | | | 0.36 | | 0.04 | 0.02 | | 0.36 |

*Note:* Each row corresponds to one of the test objects. The proportion of the 169 test views of that object attributed to each of the categories present in the training set appears in the appropriate column. Note that the misclassification rate depends on the definition of category labels. Here, mean misclassification rate, over all 169 views of all objects, was 22% for the first set of category labels (i.e., the seven categories illustrated in figure 5.2), 16% for the second set of labels (according to which the fly and the FIGURES have the same label), and 14% for the third set of labels (where in addition the tuna and the F16 have the same category label).

**Table G.3**
RBF module activities (averaged over all 169 test views) for the twenty test objects shown in figure 5.7

| | cow1 | cat2 | Al | Gene | tuna | Lrov | Niss | F16 | fly | TRex |
|---|---|---|---|---|---|---|---|---|---|---|
| frog | 0.38 | 0.28 | 0.29 | 0.18 | 0.35 | 0.20 | 0.11 | 0.09 | **0.99** | 0.16 |
| turtle | **0.53** | 0.32 | 0.38 | **0.64** | 0.39 | 0.13 | 0.09 | 0.13 | **0.93** | 0.17 |
| shoe | 0.51 | **0.63** | 0.06 | 0.12 | **1.09** | 0.46 | 0.54 | 0.33 | **0.59** | 0.16 |
| pump | **1.33** | **1.44** | 0.01 | 0.17 | **2.37** | 0.32 | 1.02 | 0.40 | 0.83 | 0.19 |
| Beetho | 0.09 | 0.05 | 0.10 | 0.02 | 0.07 | 0.05 | 0.01 | 0.01 | **0.38** | 0.01 |
| girl | **2.66** | **1.78** | 0.13 | **3.27** | **2.55** | 0.20 | 0.73 | 1.07 | **2.03** | 0.86 |
| lamp | 0.72 | 0.48 | 0.71 | 0.70 | 0.41 | 0.36 | 0.09 | 0.09 | **1.53** | 0.09 |
| manate | **1.49** | 0.98 | 0.09 | 0.36 | **2.47** | 0.35 | **1.45** | 0.68 | 0.84 | 0.24 |
| dolphi | **1.14** | 0.98 | 0.04 | 0.34 | **2.20** | 0.23 | 0.68 | 0.51 | 0.72 | 0.13 |
| Fiat | 1.51 | 1.77 | 0.01 | 0.12 | **3.76** | 0.46 | **2.27** | 0.87 | 0.79 | 0.27 |
| Toyota | **2.16** | **2.13** | 0.10 | 0.25 | **2.50** | **2.00** | **2.29** | 0.69 | 0.83 | 0.30 |
| tank | **1.85** | **1.91** | 0.09 | 0.51 | **2.50** | 1.04 | **2.36** | **1.46** | 1.08 | 0.56 |
| Stego | **2.04** | **2.13** | 0.06 | 0.67 | **3.61** | 0.67 | **2.45** | 1.46 | 1.58 | 0.98 |
| camel | **2.20** | **1.34** | 0.04 | 0.77 | **1.75** | 0.30 | 0.65 | 0.54 | 1.02 | 0.23 |
| giraff | **1.87** | **1.93** | 0.03 | 0.54 | **3.24** | 0.19 | 1.04 | 1.21 | **1.63** | **1.72** |
| Gchair | **1.75** | **1.69** | 0.00 | 0.09 | **3.04** | 0.29 | 1.40 | 0.76 | 0.86 | 0.19 |
| chair | **2.64** | **2.65** | 0.02 | 0.44 | **4.05** | 0.82 | 2.39 | 1.06 | 1.78 | 0.51 |
| shell | **1.89** | **1.09** | 0.25 | **1.56** | **0.95** | 0.44 | 0.40 | 0.49 | **1.66** | 0.35 |
| bunny | **1.07** | **1.24** | 0.23 | 0.22 | **1.10** | **1.47** | 0.53 | 0.28 | **0.95** | 0.30 |
| lion | **0.55** | **0.59** | 0.09 | 0.13 | **0.54** | **0.61** | 0.20 | 0.09 | **0.60** | 0.13 |

*Note:* In each row (corresponding to a different test object), entries within 50% of the maximum for that row are marked by boldface. These entries constitute a low-dimensional representation of the test object whose label appears at the head of the row, in terms of similarities to some of the ten reference objects. For instance, the manatee (an aquatic mammal known as the sea cow) turns out to be like (in decreasing order of similarity), a tuna, a cow, and, perhaps not surprisingly, a Nissan wagon.

**Table G.4**
The error rate obtained for the discrimination task vs. the number of test and reference objects (see section 5.2.3)

| | # Reference Objects | | | | |
|---|---|---|---|---|---|
| # Test Objects | 1 | 5 | 10 | 15 | 20 |
| 2 | 0 | 0 | 0 | 0 | 0 |
| 5 | 0.077 | 0.011 | 0.006 | 0.008 | 0.006 |
| 10 | 0.140 | 0.024 | 0.009 | 0.008 | 0.007 |
| 25 | 0.183 | 0.026 | 0.009 | 0.005 | 0.005 |
| 50 | 0.055 | 0.022 | 0.012 | 0.008 | 0.007 |

*Note:* These data are also plotted in figure 5.8. The error rate in entry $(Np, Nt)$ is the mean error rate obtained for the discrimination task using the activities of $Np$ reference objects, and tested on twenty-five views of each of the $Nt$ test objects, employing the 3-NN procedure of section 5.2.2. The mean is taken over ten independent choices of $Np$ objects out of twenty available reference objects, and ten random selections of $Nt$ objects out of a set consisting of fifty test objects [total of $(5 \cdot 10)(5 \cdot 10) = 2500$ independent trials].

# Appendix H

# Trade-Off Between Diagnosticity and Invariance

Ahissar and Hochstein (1997) found that the easier a perceptual learning task is, the easier it is to generalize across orientation and retinal position. Noting that in perception literature one encounters findings that range from complete lack of generalization to nearly complete generalization, they invoke an elaborate model to explain this presumably surprising phenomenon. This phenomenon—which is relevant to all information-processing fields related to pattern recognition—is, however, generic, and may be a consequence of the system's basing the categorization decision on discriminant analysis in an internal feature space (Shepard, 1987), a concept used widely in this book.

In a two-class discrimination task the decision process is based ultimately on a comparison of the distances between the stimulus and points belonging to the two clusters in the representation space (Duda and Hart, 1973). This characterization of the problem does not care whether the representation on which the decision is based takes the form of stored exemplars or prototypes, or a discriminant surface abstracted from the data (an issue currently disputed by Maddox and Ashby, 1993). Under the former model, such generalization suffers from the noise introduced by adding irrelevant feature dimensions into the process of comparing distances between the stimulus and the two clusters (cf. figure H.1). Likewise, under the latter model, generalization across a dimension not related to the originally learned discriminant direction (i.e., to the line connecting the centers of the two data clusters) requires a computationally less reliable extension of the decision surface orthogonally to that direction.

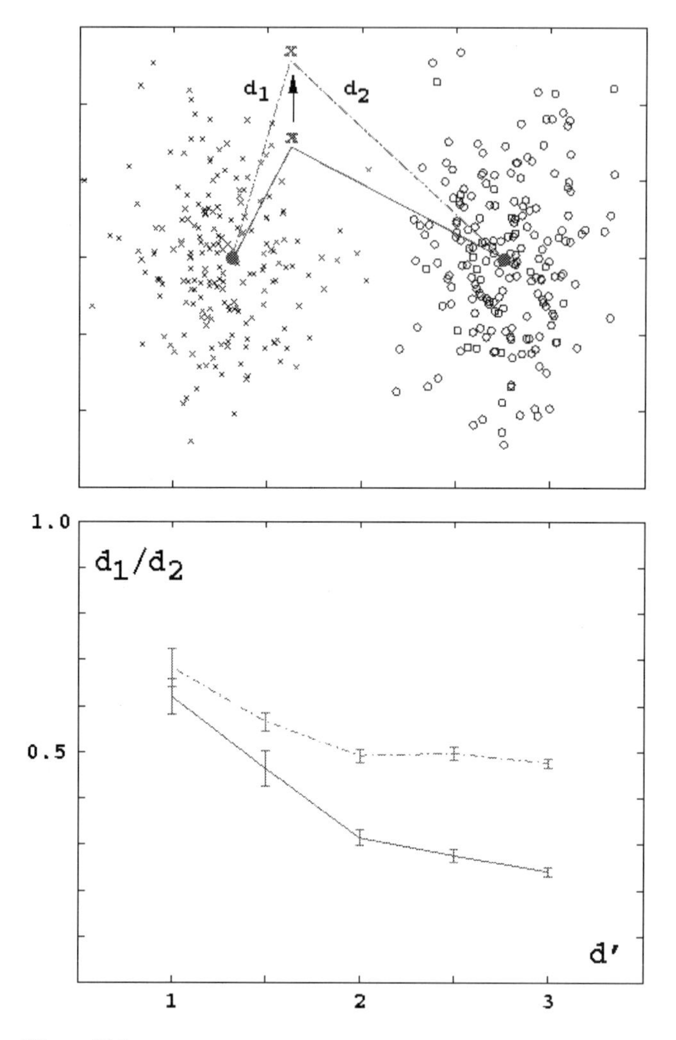


**Figure H.1**
*(Top)* A simple illustration of the problem of two-way classification in a feature space, and its generalization in a direction orthogonal to the distinction between the classes. The clusters of examples are modeled by Gaussian distributions; decision is based on the criterion $\mathcal{C} = d(\mathbf{x}, \mathbf{c}_1)/d(\mathbf{x}, \mathbf{c}_2)$, where $\mathbf{x}$ is the stimulus representation, $\mathbf{c}_{1,2}$ are the cluster centers (marked by solid dots), and $d$ is Euclidean distance. Distances to the centers are shown for two points, one (the lower $\mathbf{x}$) belonging to the original task, and the other—to its generalization. *(Bottom)* Values of the criterion $\mathcal{C}$ for the generalization (upper curve) and the original task, for points from cluster #1 (lower values of $\mathcal{C}$ are better), plotted against cluster separation (in $d'$ units (Green and Swets, 1966); bars denote $\pm SEM$, computed over the 200 points in cluster #1). Note the better generalization for larger cluster separation.

Indeed, Ahissar and Hochstein report that such extension is less reliable if the clusters are closer to each other to begin with, in other words, when the originally learned discrimination task is more difficult [others have made this observation before in various areas related to pattern recognition (Califano and Mohan, 1994; Edelman, 1995a)]. This phenomenon is readily explained within the feature-space framework: whereas the easy case may induce the system to form a linear decision surface (which then affords ideal generalization under a shift of both clusters in parallel to that surface), the difficult case may require more conservative learning, which naturally suffers from impaired generalization. A direct demonstration of this behavior can be found in Edelman et al. (1996a).

# References


Abbott, L. F., Rolls, E. T., and Tovee, M. J. (1996). Representational capacity of face coding in monkeys. *Cerebral Cortex* 6:498–505.

Adini, Y., Moses, Y., and Ullman, S. (1997). Face recognition: The problem of compensating for illumination changes. *IEEE Transactions on Pattern Analysis and Machine Intelligence* 19:721–732.

Ahissar, M. and Hochstein, S. (1997). Task difficulty and the specificity of perceptual learning. *Nature* 387:401–406.

Aho, A. V., Hopcroft, J. E., and Ullman, J. D. (1974). *The design and analysis of computer algorithms*. Reading, MA: Addison-Wesley.

Aisbett, J. and Gibbon, G. (1994). A tunable distance measure for coloured solid models. *Artificial Intelligence* 65:143–164.

Albert, A. (1972). *Regression and the Moore-Penrose pseudoinverse*. New York: Academic Press.

Albright, T. D. (1991). Motion perception and the mind-body problem. *Current Biology* 1:391–393.

Alfeld, P. (1989). Scattered data interpolation in three or more variables. In *Mathematical methods in computer aided geometric design*. Edited by Lyche, T. and Schumaker, L. New York: Academic Press. 1–33.

Aloimonos, J. Y. and Shulman, D. (1989). *Integration of visual modules: An extension of the Marr paradigm*. Boston: Academic Press.

Amaral, D. G. and Witter, M. P. (1989). The three-dimensional organization of the hippocampal formation: A review of anatomical data. *Neuroscience* 31:571–591.

Amari, S. (1978). Feature spaces which admit and detect invariant signal transformations. *Proc. 4th Intl. Conf. Pattern Recognition* 452–456.

Amit, Y. and Geman, D. (1997). Shape quantization and recognition with randomized trees. *Neural Computation* 9:1545–1588.

Ashby, F. G. and Perrin, N. A. (1988). Toward a unified theory of similarity and recognition. *Psychological Review* 95(1):124–150.

Ballard, D. H. (1987). Interpolation coding: A representation for numbers in neural models. *Biological Cybernetics* 57:389–402.

Bar, M. and Biederman, I. (1995). One-shot viewpoint invariance in matching novel objects. Unpublished manuscript.

Bar, M. and Ullman, S. (1996). Spatial context in recognition. *Perception* 25:343–352.

Barlow, H. B. (1959). Sensory mechanisms, the reduction of redundancy, and intelligence. In *The mechanisation of thought processes*. London: H.M.S.O. 535–539.

Barlow, H. B. (1972). Single units and sensation: A neuron doctrine for perceptual psychology. *Perception* 1:371–394.

Barlow, H. B. (1979). Reconstructing the visual image in space and time. *Nature* 279:189–190.

Barlow, H. B. (1990). Conditions for versatile learning, Helmholtz's unconscious inference, and the task of perception. *Vision Research* 30:1561–1571.

Barlow, H. B. (1994). What is the computational goal of the neocortex? In *Large-scale neuronal theories of the brain*. Edited by Koch, C. and Davis, J. L. Cambridge, MA: MIT Press. 1–22.

Barrow, H. G. and Tenenbaum, J. M. (1978). Recovering intrinsic scene characteristics from images. In *Computer vision systems*. Edited by Hanson, A. R. and Riseman, E. M. New York: Academic Press. 3–26.

Barrow, H. G. and Tenenbaum, J. M. (1981). Interpreting line drawings as three-dimensional surfaces. *Artificial Intelligence* 17:75–116.

Barrow, H. G. and Tenenbaum, J. M. (1993). Retrospective on "Interpreting line drawings as three-dimensional surfaces." *Artificial Intelligence* 59:71–80.

Barsalou, L. W. (1987). The instability of graded structure: Implications for the nature of concepts. In *Concepts and conceptual development*. Edited by Neisser, U. Cambridge: Cambridge Univ. Press. 101–140.

Barsalou, L. W. (1991). Deriving categories to achieve goals. In *The psychology of learning and motivation: Advances in research and theory*. Edited by Bower, G. H. Volume 27. New York: Academic Press.

Barsalou, L. W. (1998). Perceptual symbol systems. *Behavioral and Brain Sciences*, in press.

Bartram, D. J. (1976). Levels of coding in picture-picture comparison tasks. *Memory and Cognition* 4:593–602.

Basri, R. (1996). Recognition by prototypes. *International Journal of Computer Vision* 19:147–168.

Basri, R., Costa, L., Geiger, D., and Jacobs, D. (1995). Determining the similarity of deformable shapes. *Proc. IEEE workshop on physics-based modeling in computer vision*. 135–143.

Basri, R. and Jacobs, D. W. (1996). Recognition using region correspondences. *International Journal of Computer Vision* 25:141–162.

Baxter, J. (1997). The canonical distortion measure for vector quantization and function approximation. *Proc. 14th Intl. Conf. on Machine Learning*. Edited by D. H. Fisher, J. Nashville, TN.

Beck, J. (1972). *Surface color perception*. Ithaca, NY: Cornell University Press.

Bellman, R. E. (1961). *Adaptive control processes*. Princeton, NJ: Princeton University Press.

Berkeley, G. [1996 (original edition 1710)]. *A treatise concerning the principles of human knowledge*. Oxford: Oxford University Press.

Bertero, M., Poggio, T., and Torre, V. (1988). Ill-posed problems in early vision. *Proceedings of the IEEE* 76:869–889.

Beymer, D. and Poggio, T. (1996). Image representations for visual learning. *Science* 272:1905–1909.

Biederman, I. (1985). Human image understanding: Recent research and a theory. *Computer Vision, Graphics, and Image Processing* 32:29–73.

Biederman, I. (1987). Recognition by components: A theory of human image understanding. *Psychol. Review* 94:115–147.

Biederman, I. and Cooper, E. E. (1991a). Evidence for complete translational and reflectional invariance in visual object priming. *Perception* 20:585–593.

Biederman, I. and Cooper, E. E. (1991b). Priming contour-deleted images: Evidence for intermediate representations in visual object recognition. *Cognitive Psychology* 23:393–419.

Biederman, I. and Gerhardstein, P. C. (1993). Recognizing depth-rotated objects: Evidence and conditions for 3D viewpoint invariance. *Journal of Experimental Psychology: Human Perception and Performance* 19:1162–1182.

Biederman, I. and Gerhardstein, P. C. (1995). Viewpoint-dependent mechanisms in visual object recognition: Reply to Tarr and Bülthoff. *Journal of Experimental Psychology: Human Perception and Performance* 21:1506–1514.

Biederman, I. and Ju, G. (1988). Surface versus edge-based determinants of visual recognition. *Cognitive Psychology* 20:38–64.

Biederman, I., Rabinowitz, J. C., Glass, A. L., and Stacy, E. W. (1974). On the information extracted from a glance at a scene. *Journal of Experimental Psychology* 103:597–600.

Bienenstock, E. (1995). A model of neocortex. *Network* 6:179–224.

Bienenstock, E. and Geman, S. (1995). Compositionality in neural systems. In *The handbook of brain theory and neural networks*. Edited by Arbib, M. A. Cambridge, MA: MIT Press. 223–226.

Bienenstock, E., Geman, S., and Potter, D. (1997). Compositionality, MDL priors, and object recognition. In *Neural information processing systems*. Edited by

Mozer, M. C., Jordan, M. I., and Petsche, T. Volume 9. Cambridge, MA: MIT Press.

Binford, T. O. (1971). Visual perception by computer. *IEEE Conference on Systems and Control*. Miami Beach, FL.

Bishop, C. (1995). *Neural networks for pattern recognition*. Oxford: Oxford University Press.

Bishop, P. O., Coombs, J. S., and Henry, G. H. (1973). Receptive fields of simple cells in the cat striate cortex. *Journal of Physiology (London)* 231:31–60.

Blake, A. and Zisserman, A. (1988). *Visual reconstruction*. Cambridge, MA: MIT Press.

Blanz, V., Tarr, M. J., Bülthoff, H., and Vetter, T. (1996). What object attributes determine canonical views? MPIK TR 42, Max Planck Institut für biologische Kybernetik. Tübingen, Germany.

Blickle, T. W. (1989). *Recognition of contour-deleted images*. PhD thesis. SUNY at Buffalo.

Bolles, R. C. and Cain, R. A. (1982). Recognizing and locating partially visible objects: The local feature focus method. *International Journal of Robotics Research* 1:57–82.

Bookstein, F. L. (1991). *Morphometric tools for landmark data: Geometry and biology*. New York: Cambridge University Press.

Bookstein, F. L. (1996). Biometrics, biomathematics and the morphometric synthesis. *Bulletin of Mathematical Biology* 58:313–365.

Borg, I. and Lingoes, J. (1987). *Multidimensional similarity structure analysis*. Berlin: Springer.

Borges, J. L. (1956). *Ficciones*. English translation by A. Kerrigan, A. Bonner, A. Reed, H. Temple, and R. Todd. New York: Knopf.

Bourgain, J. (1985). On Lipschitz embedding of finite metric spaces in Hilbert space. *Israel J. Math*. 52:46–52.

Boynton, R. M. (1978). Color, hue, and wavelength. In *Handbook of perception*. Edited by Carterette, E. C. and Friedman, M. P. Volume 5. New York: Academic Press. 301–347.

Breuel, T. M. (1992). *Geometric aspects of visual object recognition*. PhD thesis. Cambridge, MA: MIT.

Bricolo, E., Poggio, T., and Logothetis, E. (1996). 3D object recognition: A model of view-tuned units. In *Advances in neural information processing systems*. Edited by Touretzky, D. S., Mozer, M. C., and Hasselmo, M. E. Volume 8. Cambridge, MA: MIT Press.

Brigham, J. C. (1986). The influence of race on face recognition. In *Aspects of face processing*. Edited by Ellis, H. D., Jeeves, M. A., and Newcombe, F. Dordrecht: Martinus Nijhoff. 170–177.

Brooks, L. R. (1987). Decentralized control of categorization: The role of prior processing episodes. In *Concepts and conceptual development*. Edited by Neisser, U. Cambridge: Cambridge University Press. 141–174.

Brooks, R. A. (1981). Symbolic reasoning among 3D models and 2D images. *Artificial Intelligence* 17:285–348.

Brooks, R. A. (1983). Model-based three-dimensional interpretations of two-dimensional images. *IEEE Transactions on Pattern Analysis and Machine Intelligence* 5:140–149.

Brooks, R. A. (1991). Intelligence without representation. *Artificial Intelligence* 47:139–160.

Broomhead, D. S. and Lowe, D. (1988). Multivariable functional interpolation and adaptive networks. *Complex Systems* 2:321–355.

Brown, J. M., Weisstein, N., and May, J. G. (1992). Visual search for simple volumetric shapes. *Perception and Psychophysics* 51:40–48.

Bülthoff, H. H. and Edelman, S. (1992). Psychophysical support for a 2-D view interpolation theory of object recognition. *Proceedings of the National Academy of Science* 89:60–64.

Bülthoff, H. H., Edelman, S., and Tarr, M. J. (1995). How are three-dimensional objects represented in the brain? *Cerebral Cortex* 5:247–260.

Bülthoff, H. H. and Mallot, H. A. (1990). Integration of stereo, shading and texture. In *AI and the eye*. Edited by Blake, A. and Trasciano, T. London: Wiley.

Califano, A. and Mohan, R. (1994). Multidimensional indexing for recognizing visual shapes. *IEEE Transactions on Pattern Analysis and Machine Intelligence* 16:373–392.

Carne, T. K. (1990). The geometry of shape spaces. *Proc. Lond. Math. Soc.* 61:407–432.

Carpenter, G. A. and Grossberg, S. (1990). Adaptive resonance theory: Neural network architectures for self-organizing pattern recognition. In *Parallel processing in neural systems and computers*. Edited by Eckmiller, R., Hartmann, G., and Hauske, G. Amsterdam: North-Holland. 383–389.

Carroll, J. D. and Chang, J. J. (1970). Analysis of individual differences in multidimensional scaling via an N-way generalization of the Eckart-Young decomposition. *Psychometrika* 35:283–319.

Cave, C. B. and Kosslyn, S. M. (1993). The role of parts and spatial relations in object identification. *Perception* 22:229–248.

Cerella, J. (1987). Pigeons and perceptrons. *Pattern Recognition* 19:431–438.

Chelazzi, L., Miller, E., Duncan, J., and Desimone, R. (1993). A neural basis for visual search in inferior temporal cortex. *Nature* 363:345–347.

Chen, S. and Donoho, D. L. (1994). Basis pursuit. *Proceedings of 1994 28th Asilomar Conference on Signals, Systems and Computers*. Volume 1. Pacific Grove, CA: IEEE Comput. Soc. Press. 41–44.

Churchland, P. S. (1987). *Neurophilosophy*. Cambridge, MA: MIT Press.

Clark, A. (1993). *Sensory qualities*. Oxford: Clarendon Press.

Cohen, J. (1964). Dependency of the spectral reflectance curves of the Munsell color chips. *Psychonomic Sciences* 1:369–370.

Cohn, H. (1967). *Conformal mappings on Riemann surfaces*. New York: McGraw-Hill.

Connell, J. H. (1985). Learning shape descriptions: Generating and generalizing models of visual objects. A.I. TR No. 853. Artificial Intelligence Laboratory. MIT.

Cooper, E. E. and Biederman, I. (1993). Metric versus viewpoint invariant shape differences in visual object recognition. *Invest. Ophthalm. Vis. Sci. Suppl. (Proc. ARVO)* 34:S223.

Cooper, E. E., Biederman, I., and Hummel, J. E. (1992). Metric invariance in object recognition: a review and further evidence. *Canadian J. Psychol.* 46:119–214.

Cooper, L. (1976). Demonstration of a mental analog of an external rotation. *Perception and Psychophysics* 19:296–302.

Cortes, C. and Vapnik, V. (1995). Support-vector networks. *Machine Learning* 20:273–297.

Cortese, J. M. and Dyre, B. P. (1996). Perceptual similarity of shapes generated from Fourier Descriptors. *Journal of Experimental Psychology: Human Perception and Performance* 22:133–143.

Cover, T. and Hart, P. (1967). Nearest neighbor pattern classification. *IEEE Trans. on Information Theory* IT-13:21–27.

Crick, F. H. C., Marr, D. C., and Poggio, T. (1981). An information-processing approach to understanding the visual cortex. In *The organization of the cerebral cortex*. Edited by Schmitt, F. Cambridge, MA: MIT Press.

Cummins, R. (1989). *Meaning and mental representation*. Cambridge, MA: MIT Press.

Cummins, R. (1996). *Representations, targets, and attitudes*. Cambridge, MA: MIT Press.

Cutzu, F. and Edelman, S. (1994). Canonical views in object representation and recognition. *Vision Research* 34:3037–3056.

Cutzu, F. and Edelman, S. (1996). Faithful representation of similarities among three-dimensional shapes in human vision. *Proceedings of the National Academy of Science* 93:12046–12050.

Cutzu, F. and Edelman, S. (1998). Representation of object similarity in human vision: Psychophysics and a computational model. *Vision Research* 38:2227–2257.

De Valois, R. L. and De Valois, K. K. (1978). Neural coding of color. In *Handbook of perception*. Edited by Carterette, E. C. and Friedman, M. P. Volume 5. New York: Academic Press. 117–166.

Desimone, R., Albright, T. D., Gross, C. G., and Bruce, C. J. (1984). Stimulus-selective properties of inferior temporal neurons in the macaque. *Journal of Neuroscience* 4:2051–2062.

Dill, M. and Edelman, S. (1997). Translation invariance in object recognition, and its relation to other visual transformations. A. I. Memo No. 1610. MIT.

Dill, M. and Fahle, M. (1997a). Limited translation invariance of human visual pattern recognition. *Perception & Psychophysics* 60:65–81.

Dill, M. and Fahle, M. (1997b). The role of visual field position in pattern-discrimination learning. *Proceedings of the Royal Society of London B* 264: 1031–1036.

Dill, M. and Heisenberg, M. (1993). Visual pattern memory without shape recognition. *Proceedings of the Royal Society of London B* 349:143–152.

Dill, M., Wolf, R., and Heisenberg, M. (1993). Visual pattern recognition in Drosophila involves retinotopic matching. *Nature* 365:751–753.

Dretske, F. (1995). *Naturalizing the mind*. The Jean Nicod Lectures. Cambridge, MA: MIT Press.

Duda, R. O. and Hart, P. E. (1973). *Pattern classification and scene analysis*. New York: Wiley.

Duvdevani-Bar, S. (1997). *Similarity to prototypes in 3D shape representation*. PhD thesis. Weizmann Institute of Science.

Duvdevani-Bar, S. and Edelman, S. (1995). On similarity to prototypes in 3D object representation. CS-TR 95-11. Weizmann Institute of Science.

Duvdevani-Bar, S., Edelman, S., Howell, A. J., and Buxton, H. (1998). A similarity-based method for the generalization of face recognition over pose and expression. In *Proc. 3rd Intl. Symposium on Face and Gesture Recognition (FG98)*. Edited by Akamatsu, S. and Mase, K. Washington, DC: IEEE. 118–123.

D'Zmura, M. and Iverson, G. (1997). A formal approach to color constancy: The recovery of surface and light source spectral properties using bilinear models. In *Recent progress in mathematical psychology*. Edited by Dowling, C., Roberts, F., and Theuns, P. Hillsdale, NJ: Erlbaum.

Edelman, S. (1991). A network model of object recognition in human vision. In *Neural networks for perception*. Edited by Wechsler, H. Volume 1. New York: Academic Press. 25–40.

Edelman, S. (1994). Biological constraints and the representation of structure in vision and language. *Psycoloquy*, 5(57). FTP host: ftp.princeton.edu; FTP directory: /pub/harnad/Psycoloquy/1994.volume.5/; file name: psyc.94.5.57.language-network.3.edelman.

Edelman, S. (1995a). Class similarity and viewpoint invariance in the recognition of 3D objects. *Biological Cybernetics* 72:207–220.

Edelman, S. (1995b). Representation of similarity in 3D object discrimination. *Neural Computation* 7:407–422.

Edelman, S. (1995c). Representation, similarity, and the chorus of prototypes. *Minds and Machines* 5:45–68.

Edelman, S. (1998). Representation is representation of similarity. *Behavioral and Brain Sciences* 21:449–498.

Edelman, S. and Bülthoff, H. H. (1992a). Modeling human visual object recognition. *Proc. IJCNN-92*. Volume 4. 37–42.

Edelman, S. and Bülthoff, H. H. (1992b). Orientation dependence in the recognition of familiar and novel views of 3D objects. *Vision Research* 32: 2385–2400.

Edelman, S., Bülthoff, H. H., and Bülthoff, I. (1996a). Features of the representation space for 3D objects. MPIK-TR 40. Max Planck Institute for Biological Cybernetics.

Edelman, S., Cutzu, F., and Duvdevani-Bar, S. (1996b). Similarity to reference shapes as a basis for shape representation. *Proceedings of 18th Annual Conf. of the Cognitive Science Society*. Edited by Cottrell, G. W. San Diego. 260–265.

Edelman, S. and Duvdevani-Bar, S. (1997a). A model of visual recognition and categorization. *Phil. Trans. R. Soc. Lond. (B)* 352(1358):1191–1202.

Edelman, S. and Duvdevani-Bar, S. (1997b). Similarity-based viewspace interpolation and the categorization of 3D objects. *Proc. Similarity and Categorization Workshop*. Dept. of AI, University of Edinburgh. 75–81.

Edelman, S. and Duvdevani-Bar, S. (1997c). Similarity, connectionism, and the problem of representation in vision. *Neural Computation* 9:701–720.

Edelman, S. and Duvdevani-Bar, S. (1997d). Visual recognition and categorization on the basis of similarities to multiple class prototypes. A.I. Memo No. 1615. Artificial Intelligence Laboratory. MIT.

Edelman, S., Grill-Spector, K., Kushnir, T., and Malach, R. (1998). Towards direct visualization of the internal shape representation space by fMRI. *Psychobiology* in press.

Edelman, S. and Intrator, N. (1997). Learning as extraction of low-dimensional representations. In *Mechanisms of perceptual learning*. Edited by Medin, D., Goldstone, R., and Schyns, P. New York: Academic Press. 353–380.

Edelman, S., Reisfeld, D., and Yeshurun, Y. (1992). Learning to recognize faces from examples. In *Proc. 2nd European Conf. on Computer Vision, Lecture Notes in Computer Science*. Edited by Sandini, G. Volume 588. Berlin: Springer Verlag. 787–791.

Edelman, S. and Weinshall, D. (1991). A self-organizing multiple-view representation of 3D objects. *Biological Cybernetics* 64:209–219.

Edelman, S. and Weinshall, D. (1998). Computational approaches to shape constancy. In *Perceptual constancies: Why things look as they do*. Edited by Walsh, V. and Kulikowski, J. Cambridge: Cambridge University Press. Chapter 4.

Efron, B. and Tibshirani, R. (1993). *An introduction to the bootstrap*. London: Chapman and Hall.

Eley, M. G. (1982). Identifying rotated letter-like symbols. *Memory & Cognition* 10:25–32.

Ellis, R., Allport, D. A., Humphreys, G. W., and Collis, J. (1989). Varieties of object constancy. *Q. Journal Exp. Psychol.* 41A:775–796.

Fahle, M. (1993). Figure-ground discrimination from temporal information. *Proceedings of the Royal Society of London B* 254:199–203.

Fahle, M. and Koch, C. (1995). Spatial displacement, but not temporal asynchrony, destroys figural binding. *Vision Research* 35:491–494.

Farah, M. J., Rochlin, R., and Klein, K. L. (1994). Orientation invariance and geometric primitives in shape recognition. *Cognitive Science* 18:325–344.

Farmer, J. D., Packard, N. H., and Perelson, A. S. (1986). The immune system, adaptation, and machine learning. *Physica D* 22:187–204.

Field, D. J. (1994). What is the goal of sensory coding? *Neural Computation* 6:559–601.

Fillenbaum, S. and Rapoport, A. (1979). *Structures in the subjective lexicon.* New York: Academic Press.

Fischler, M. A. and Firschein, O., editors (1987). *Readings in computer vision: Issues, problems, principles and paradigms.* Los Altos, CA: Morgan Kaufmann.

Fiser, J., Biederman, I., and Cooper, E. E. (1997). To what extent can matching algorithms based on direct outputs of spatial filters account for human shape recognition? *Spatial Vision* 10:237–271.

Fodor, J. and Pylyshyn, Z. (1988). Connectionism and cognitive architecture: A critical analysis. *Cognition* 28:3–71.

Foldiak, P. (1991). Learning invariance from transformation sequences. *Neural Computation* 3:194–200.

Foster, D. H. and Kahn, J. I. (1985). Internal representations and operations in the visual comparison of transformed patterns: Effects of pattern point-inversion, positional symmetry, and separation. *Biological Cybernetics* 51:305–312.

Freyd, J. J. (1983). The mental representation of movement when static stimuli are viewed. *Perception and Psychophysics* 33:575–581.

Freyd, J. J. (1993). Five hunches about perceptual processes and dynamic representations. In *Attention and performance.* Edited by Meyer, D. E. and Kornblum, S. Volume 14. Cambridge, MA: MIT Press. 99–119.

Fu, K. S. (1976). Tree languages and syntactic pattern recognition. In *Pattern recognition and artificial intelligence.* Edited by Chen, C. H. New York: Academic Press. 257–291.

Fujita, I., Tanaka, K., Ito, M., and Cheng, K. (1992). Columns for visual features of objects in monkey inferotemporal cortex. *Nature* 360:343–346.

Gallistel, C. R. (1990). *The organization of learning.* Cambridge, MA: MIT Press.

Garbin, C. P. (1990). Visual-touch perceptual equivalence for shape information in children and adults. *Perception and Psychophysics* 48:271–279.

Garey, M. R. and Johnson, D. S. (1979). *Computers and intractability: A guide to the theory of NP-completeness*. San Francisco: W. H. Freeman.

Gauthier, I. and Tarr, M. J. (1997). Orientation priming of novel shapes in the context of viewpoint-dependent recognition. *Perception* 26:51–73.

Gauthier, I., Williams, P., Tarr, M. J., and Tanaka, J. (1998). Training "greeble" experts: A framework for studying expert object recognition processes. *Vision Research* 38:2401–2428.

Geman, S. (1996). Minimum Description Length priors for object recognition. *Challenging the frontiers of knowledge using statistical science (Proc. JSM'96)*. Paper delivered at the Joint Statistical Meetings '96 Conference. (abstract at www.amstat.org/meetings/jsm/1996/abstracts/S160P02.txt)

Gerhardstein, P. C. and Biederman, I. (1991). 3D orientation invariance in visual object recognition. *Invest. Ophthalm. Vis. Science Suppl.* 32:338.

Gersho, A. and Gray, R. M. (1992). *Vector quantization and signal compression*. Boston: Kluwer Academic Publishers.

Gibson, B. S. and Peterson, M. A. (1994). Does orientation-independent object recognition precede orientation-dependent recognition? Evidence from a cuing paradigm. *Journal of Experimental Psychology: Human Perception and Performance* 20:299–316.

Gibson, J. J. (1933). Adaptation, after-effect, and contrast in the perception of curved lines. *J. Exp. Psychol.* 16:1–31.

Gibson, J. J. (1979). *The ecological approach to visual perception*. Boston: Houghton Mifflin.

Gilbert, C. D. (1994). Neuronal dynamics and perceptual learning. *Current Biology* 4:627–629.

Girosi, F., Jones, M., and Poggio, T. (1995). Regularization theory and neural networks architectures. *Neural Computation* 7:219–269.

Goebel, K. and Kirk, W. A. (1990). *Topics in metric fixed point theory*. Number 28 in Cambridge studies in advanced mathematics. Cambridge: Cambridge University Press.

Goldstone, R. L. (1994). The role of similarity in categorization: Providing a groundwork. *Cognition* 52:125–157.

Goodman, N. (1972). *Seven Strictures on Similarity*. Indianapolis: Bobbs Merill.

Gordon, W. J. and Wixom, J. A. (1978). Shepard's method of "Metric Interpolation" to bivariate and multivariate interpolation. *Mathematics of Computation* 32:253–264.

Green, D. M. and Swets, J. A. (1966). *Signal detection theory and psychophysics*. New York: Wiley.

Gregory, R. L. (1978). Illusions and hallucinations. In *Handbook of perception.* Edited by Carterette, E. C. and Friedman, M. P. Volume 9. New York: Academic Press. 337–357.

Gregson, R. A. M. (1975). *Psychometrics of similarity.* New York: Academic Press.

Gregson, R. A. M. and Britton, L. A. (1990). The size-weight illusion in 2D nonlinear psychophysics. *Perception and Psychophysics* 48:343–356.

Grill-Spector, K., Kushnir, T., Edelman, S., Itzchak, Y., and Malach, R. (1997). Convergence of visual cues in object-related areas of the human occipital lobe. *Neuron* 21:191–202.

Grill-Spector, K., Kushnir, T., Hendler, T., Edelman, S., Itzchak, Y., and Malach, R. (1998). A sequence of early object processing stages revealed by fMRI in human occipital lobe. *Human Brain Mapping* 6:316–328.

Grimes, J. (1995). On the failure to detect changes in scenes across saccades. In *Perception: Vancouver studies in cognitive science.* Edited by Akins, K. Vol. 5, Chp. 4. New York: Oxford University Press.

Grimson, W. E. L. (1981). *From images to surfaces.* Cambridge, MA: MIT Press.

Grimson, W. E. L. (1990). *Model-based vision.* Cambridge, MA: MIT Press.

Gross, C. G., Rocha-Miranda, C. E., and Bender, D. B. (1972). Visual properties of cells in inferotemporal cortex of the macaque. *Journal of Neurophysiology* 35:96–111.

Grossberg, S. and Mingolla, E. (1985). Neural dynamics of form perception: Boundary completion, illusory figures and neon color spreading. *Psychological Review* 92:173–211.

Hadamard, J. (1923). *Lectures on the Cauchy problem in linear partial differential equations.* New Haven, CT: Yale University Press.

Harnad, S., editor (1987). *Categorical perception: The groundwork of cognition.* New York: Cambridge University Press.

Harnad, S. (1990). The symbol grounding problem. *Physica D* 42:335–346.

Hartman, E. J., Keeler, J. D., and Kowalski, J. M. (1990). Layered neural networks with Gaussian hidden units as universal approximations. *Neural Computation* 2:210–215.

Hasselmo, M. E., Schnell, E., and Barkai, E. (1995). Dynamics of learning and recall at excitatory recurrent synapses and cholinergic modulation in hippocampal region CA3. *Journal of Neuroscience* 15:5249–5262.

Haussler, D. (1992). Decision theoretic generalizations of the PAC model for neural net and other learning applications. *Information and Computation* 100:78–150.

Hayward, W. G. (1998). Effects of outline shape in object recognition. *Journal of Experimental Psychology: Human Perception and Performance* 24: 427–440.

Hayward, W. G. and Tarr, M. J. (1997). Testing conditions for viewpoint invariance in object recognition. *Journal of Experimental Psychology: Human Perception and Performance* 23:1511–1521.

Hel-Or, Y. and Edelman, S. (1994). A new approach to qualitative stereo. *Proc. 12th ICPR*. Edited by Ullman, S. and Peleg, S. Jerusalem: IEEE Press. 316–320.

Henderson, L., editor (1984). *Orthographies and reading: Perspectives from cognitive psychology, neuropsychology and linguistics*. Hillsdale, NJ: Erlbaum.

Hinton, G. E. (1984). Distributed representations. Technical Report CMU-CS 84-157. Department of Computer Science. Carnegie-Mellon University. Pittsburgh, PA.

Hoffman, D. D. and Richards, W. A. (1984). Parts of recognition. *Cognition* 18:65–96.

Holland, J. H., Holyoak, K. J., Nisbett, R. E., and Thagard, P. R. (1986). *Induction: Processes of inference, learning, and discovery*. Cambridge, MA: MIT Press.

Hubel, D. H. and Wiesel, T. N. (1968). Receptive fields and functional architecture of monkey striate cortex. *Journal of Physiology (London)* 195: 215–243.

Hume, D. (1748). *An enquiry concerning human understanding*. The Internet. Available electronically at URL: http://coombs.anu.edu.au/Depts/RSSS/Philosophy/Texts/EnquiryTOC.html.

Hummel, J. E. (1998). Where view-based theories of human object recognition break down: The role of structure in human shape perception. In *Cognitive dynamics: Conceptual change in humans and machines*. Edited by Dietrich, E. and Markman, A. Cambridge, MA: MIT Press.

Hummel, J. E. and Biederman, I. (1992). Dynamic binding in a neural network for shape recognition. *Psychological Review* 99:480–517.

Humphrey, G. K. and Khan, S. C. (1992). Recognizing novel views of three-dimensional objects. *Canadian Journal of Psychology* 46:170–190.

Intrator, N. and Cooper, L. N. (1992). Objective function formulation of the BCM theory of visual cortical plasticity: Statistical connections, stability conditions. *Neural Networks* 5:3–17.

Intrator, N. and Edelman, S. (1997a). Competitive learning in biological and artificial neural computation. *Trends in Cognitive Science* 1:268–272.

Intrator, N. and Edelman, S. (1997b). Learning low dimensional representations of visual objects with extensive use of prior knowledge. *Network* 8:259–281.

Ito, M., Fujita, I., Tamura, H., and Tanaka, K. (1994). Processing of contrast polarity of visual images in inferotemporal cortex of the macaque monkey. *Cerebral Cortex* 4:499–508.

Ito, M., Tamura, H., Fujita, I., and Tanaka, K. (1995). Size and position invariance of neuronal responses in monkey inferotemporal cortex. *Journal of Neurophysiology* 73:218–226.

Jacobs, D. W. (1996). The space requirements of indexing under perspective projections. *IEEE Transactions on Pattern Analysis and Machine Intelligence* 18:330–333.

Johnson, W. B. and Lindenstrauss, J. (1984). Extensions of Lipschitz mappings into a Hilbert space. *Contemporary Mathematics* 26:189–206.

Jolicoeur, P. (1985). The time to name disoriented objects. *Memory and Cognition* 13:289–303.

Jolicoeur, P. (1990). Identification of disoriented objects: A dual-systems theory. *Mind and Language* 5:387–410.

Jolicoeur, P., Gluck, M., and Kosslyn, S. M. (1984). Pictures and names: Making the connection. *Cognitive Psychology* 16:243–275.

Jolicoeur, P. and Humphrey, G. K. (1998). Perception of rotated two-dimensional and three-dimensional objects and visual shapes. In *Perceptual constancies.* Edited by Walsh, V. and Kulikowski, J. Chapter 10. Cambridge: Cambridge University Press.

Jolicoeur, P. and Kosslyn, S. M. (1983). Coordinate systems in the long-term memory representation of three-dimensional shapes. *Cognitive Psychology* 15: 301–345.

Jolicoeur, P. and Landau, M. J. (1984). Effects of orientation on the identification of simple visual patterns. *Canadian Journal of Psychology* 38:80–93.

Joliffe, I. T. (1986). *Principal component analysis.* New York: Springer-Verlag.

Jöreskog, K. and Wold, H. (1982). *Systems under indirect observation: Causality, structure, prediction.* Amsterdam: North-Holland.

Judd, D. B., MacAdam, D. L., and Wyszecki, G. (1964). Spectral distribution of typical daylight as a function of correlated color temperature. *Journal of the Optical Society of America* 54:1031–1040.

Kalocsai, P. and Biederman, I. (1997). Recognition model with narrow and broad extension fields. *Proceedings of the 19th Annual Conference of the Cognitive Science Society.* Edited by Shafto, M. G. and Langley, P. Hillsdale, NJ: Lawrence Erlbaum Associates. 364–369.

Kanatani, K. (1990). *Group-theoretical methods in image understanding.* Berlin: Springer.

Kanwisher, N., Chun, M. M., McDermott, J., and Ledden, P. J. (1996). Functional imaging of human visual recognition. *Cognitive Brain Research* 5:55–67.

Kanwisher, N., McDermott, J., and Chun, M. M. (1997). The fusiform face area: A module in human extrastriate cortex specialized for face perception. *Journal of Neuroscience* 17:4302–4311.

Kendall, D. G. (1984). Shape manifolds, Procrustean metrics, and complex projective spaces. *Bull. Lond. Math. Soc.* 16:81–121.

Kendall, D. G. (1989). A survey of the statistical theory of shape. *Statistical Science* 4:87–120.

Kirschfeld, K. (1995). Neuronal oscillations and synchronized activity in the central nervous system: Functional aspects. *Psycoloquy* 6(36). Available electronically as: ftp://ftp.princeton.edu/pub/harnad/Psycoloquy/1995.volume.6/psyc.95.6.36.brain-rhythms.11.kirschfeld.

Kobatake, E. and Tanaka, K. (1994). Neuronal selectivities to complex object features in the ventral visual pathway of the macaque cerebral cortex. *Journal of Neurophysiology* 71:856–867.

Kobatake, E., Tanaka, K., and Tamori, Y. (1992). Long-term learning changes the stimulus selectivity of cells in the inferotemporal cortex of adult monkeys. *Neuroscience Research* S17:237.

Koenderink, J. J. and van Doorn, A. J. (1979). The internal representation of solid shape with respect to vision. *Biological Cybernetics* 32:211–217.

Koenderink, J. J. and van Doorn, A. (1991). Affine structure from motion. *Journal of the Optical Society of America* 8:377–385.

Koenderink, J. J., van Doorn, A. J., and Kappers, A. M. L. (1996). Pictorial surface attitude and local depth comparisons. *Perception and Psychophysics* 58:163–173.

Koriat, A. and Norman, J. (1984). What is rotated in mental rotation? *Journal of Experimental Psychology: Learning, Memory and Cognition* 10:421–434.

Koriat, A. and Norman, J. (1985). Mental rotation and visual familiarity. *Perception and Psychophysics* 37:429–439.

Kosslyn, S. M., Pinker, S., Smith, G. E., and Shwartz, S. P. (1979). On the demystification of mental imagery. *Behavioral and Brain Sciences* 2:535–581.

Kourtzi, Z. and Shiffrar, M. (1997). One-shot view invariance in a moving world. *Psychological Science* 8:461–466.

Krumhansl, C. L. (1978). Concerning the applicability of geometric models to similarity data: The interrelationship between similarity and spatial density. *Psychological Review* 85:445–463.

Krushkal', S. L. (1979). *Quasiconformal mappings and Riemann surfaces.* New York: Wiley.

Kruskal, J. B. (1964). Multidimensional scaling by optimizing goodness of fit to a nonmetric hypothesis. *Psychometrika* 29(1):1–27.

Kruskal, J. B. and Wish, M. (1978). *Multidimensional scaling.* Beverly Hills: Sage Publications.

Kubovy, M. (1983). Mental imagery majestically transforming cognitive psychology [review of "Mental images and their transformations"]. *Contemporary Psychology* 28:661–663.

Kuffler, S. W. and Nicholls, J. G. (1976). *From neuron to brain.* Sunderland, MA: Sinauer.

Kurbat, M. A. (1994). Is RBC/JIM a general-purpose theory of human entry-level object recognition? *Perception* 23:1339–1368.

Lamdan, Y. and Wolfson, H. (1988). Geometric hashing: A general and efficient recognition scheme. *Proceedings of the 2nd International Conference on Computer Vision*. Tarpon Springs, FL: IEEE. 238–251.

Lando, M. and Edelman, S. (1995). Receptive field spaces and class-based generalization from a single view in face recognition. *Network* 6:551–576.

Lawson, R., Humphreys, G., and Watson, D. G. (1994). Object recognition under sequential viewing conditions: Evidence for viewpoint-specific recognition procedures. *Perception* 23:595–614.

Lawson, R. and Humphreys, G. W. (1996). View specificity in object processing: Evidence from picture matching. *Journal of Experimental Psychology: Human Perception and Performance* 22:395–416.

Le, H. (1991). On geodesics in Euclidean shape spaces. *Journal of the London Mathematical Society* 44:360–372.

Le, H. and Kendall, D. G. (1993). The Riemannian structure of Euclidean shape spaces: a novel environment for statistics. *The Annals of Statistics* 21:1225–1271.

LeCun, Y. and Bengio, Y. (1995). Convolutional networks for images, speech, and time series. In *The handbook of brain theory and neural networks*. Edited by Arbib, M. A. Cambridge, MA: MIT Press. 255–258.

Leen, T. K. and Kambhatla, N. (1994). Fast non-linear dimension reduction. In *Advances in neural information processing systems*. Edited by Cowan, J. D., Tesauro, G., and Alspector, J. Volume 6. San Francisco: Morgan Kauffman. 152–159.

Lettvin, J. Y., Maturana, H. R., McCulloch, W. S., and Pitts, W. H. (1959). What the frog's eye tells the frog's brain. *Proc. IRE* 47:1940–1959.

Li, L., Miller, E. K., and Desimone, R. (1993). The representation of stimulus familiarity in anterior inferior temporal cortex. *Journal of Neurophysiology* 69:1918–1929.

Linde, Y., Buzo, A., and Gray, R. (1980). An algorithm for vector quantizer design. *IEEE Transactions on Communications* COM-28:84–95.

Lindsay, P. H. and Norman, D. A. (1977). *Human information processing: An introduction to psychology*. New York: Academic Press.

Linial, N., London, E., and Rabinovich, Y. (1994). The geometry of graphs and some of its algorithmic applications. *FOCS* 35:577–591.

Little, J. J., Poggio, T., and Gamble Jr., E. B. (1988). Seeing in parallel: The vision machine. *International Journal of Supercomputing Applications* 2:13–28.

Liu, Z., Knill, D. C., and Kersten, D. (1995). Object classification for human and ideal observers. *Vision Research* 35:549–568.

Locke, J. [1994 (original edition 1690)]. *An essay concerning human understanding*. New York: Modern Library.

Logothetis, N. and Pauls, J. (1995). Psychophysical and physiological evidence for viewer-centered object representations in the primate. *Cerebral Cortex* 3:270–288.

Logothetis, N. K., Pauls, J., and Poggio, T. (1995). Shape recognition in the inferior temporal cortex of monkeys. *Current Biology* 5:552–563.

Logothetis, N. K., Pauls, J., Poggio, T., and Bülthoff, H. H. (1994). View dependent object recognition by monkeys. *Current Biology* 4:404–41.

Logothetis, N. K. and Scheinberg, D. L. (1996). Visual object recognition. *Annual Review of Neuroscience* 19:577–621.

Lowe, D. G. (1986). *Perceptual organization and visual recognition.* Boston: Kluwer Academic Publishers.

Lowe, D. G. (1987a). Three-dimensional object recognition from single two-dimensional images. *Artificial Intelligence* 31:355–395.

Lowe, D. G. (1987b). The viewpoint consistency constraint. *International Journal of Computer Vision* 1:57–72.

Lowe, D. G. and Binford, T. O. (1985). The recovery of three-dimensional structure from image curves. *IEEE Transactions on Pattern Analysis and Machine Intelligence* 7(3):320–326.

Mackintosh, N. J. (1995). Categorization by people and pigeons: The twenty-second Bartlett memorial lecture. *Quarterly Journal of Experimental Psychology* 48B:193–210.

Mackworth, A. K. (1972). How to see a simple world: An exegesis of some computer programs for scene analysis. In *Machine intelligence.* Edited by Elcock, E. W. and Michie, D. Vol. 8. New York: Wiley. 510–537.

MacQueen, J. (1967). Some methods for classification and analysis of multivariate observations. *Proc. 5th Berkeley Symposium* 1:281–297.

Maddox, W. T. and Ashby, F. G. (1993). Comparing decision bound and exemplar models of categorization. *Perception and Psychophysics* 53:49–70.

Malach, R., Reppas, J. B., Benson, R. R., Kwong, K. K., Jiang, J., Kennedy, W. A., Ledden, P. J., Brady, T. J., Rosen, B. R., and Tootell, R. B. H. (1995). Object-related activity revealed by functional magnetic resonance imaging in human occipital cortex. *Proceedings of the National Academy of Science* 92:8135–8139.

Markman, A. and Gentner, D. (1993). Structural alignment during similarity comparisons. *Cognitive Psychology* 25:431–467.

Markman, E. (1989). *Categorization and naming in children.* Cambridge, MA: MIT Press.

Marks, L. E. (1992). The slippery context effect in psychophysics: Intensive, extensive, and qualitative continua. *Perception and Psychophysics* 51:187–198.

Marr, D. (1969). A theory of cerebellar cortex. *Journal of Physiology* 202: 437–470.

Marr, D. (1971). Simple memory: A theory for archicortex. *Philosophical Transactions of the Royal Society of London* 262:23–81.

Marr, D. (1976). Early processing of visual information. *Philosophical Transactions of the Royal Society of London B* 275:483–524.

Marr, D. (1981). Artificial intelligence: A personal view. In *Mind design*. Edited by Haugeland, J. Cambridge, MA: MIT Press. 129–142.

Marr, D. (1982). *Vision*. San Francisco: W. H. Freeman.

Marr, D. and Nishihara, H. K. (1978). Representation and recognition of the spatial organization of three dimensional structure. *Proceedings of the Royal Society of London B* 200:269–294.

Marr, D. and Poggio, T. (1977). From understanding computation to understanding neural circuitry. *Neurosciences Res. Prog. Bull.* 15:470–488.

Marr, D. and Poggio, T. (1979). A computational theory of human stereo vision. *Proceedings of the Royal Society of London B* 204:301–328.

McCulloch, W. S. (1965). *Embodiments of mind*. Cambridge, MA: MIT Press.

McMullen, P. A., Hamm, J., and Jolicoeur, P. (1995). Rotated object identification with and without orientation cues. *Canadian Journal of Experimental Psychology* 49:133–149.

Medin, D. L., Goldstone, R. L., and Gentner, D. (1993). Respects for similarity. *Psychological Review* 100:254–278.

Medin, D. L. and Schaffer, M. M. (1978). Context theory of classification learning. *Psychological Review* 85:207–238.

Mel, B. (1997). SEEMORE: Combining color, shape, and texture histogramming in a neurally-inspired approach to visual object recognition. *Neural Computation* 9:777–804.

Mendenhall, W. and Sincich, T. (1988). *Statistics for the engineering and computer sciences*. London: Macmillan.

Miller, E. K., Li, L., and Desimone, R. (1993). Activity of neurons in anterior inferior temporal cortex during a short-term memory task. *Journal of Neuroscience* 13:1460–1478.

Millikan, R. (1995). *White Queen Psychology and other essays for Alice*. Cambridge, MA: MIT Press.

Minsky, M. and Papert, S. (1969). *Perceptrons*. Cambridge, MA: MIT Press.

Mitchison, G. J. and Westheimer, G. (1990). Viewing geometry and gradients of horizontal disparity. In *Vision: Coding and efficiency*. Edited by Blakemore, C. Cambridge: Cambridge University Press. 302–309.

Miyashita, Y., Date, A., and Okuno, H. (1993). Configuration encoding of complex visual forms by single neurons of monkey temporal cortex. *Neuropsychologia* 31:1119–1132.

Moody, J. and Darken, C. (1989). Fast learning in networks of locally tuned processing units. *Neural Computation* 1:281–289.

Moran, J. and Desimone, R. (1985). Selective attention gates visual processing in the extrastriate cortex. *Science* 229:782–784.

Moses, Y. (1993). *Computational approaches in face recognition*. PhD thesis. Feinberg Graduate School of the Weizmann Institute of Science.

Moses, Y., Ullman, S., and Edelman, S. (1996). Generalization to novel images in upright and inverted faces. *Perception* 25:443–462.

Mumford, D. (1991). Mathematical theories of shape: Do they model perception? In *Geometric methods in computer vision*. Volume 1570. Bellingham, WA: SPIE. 2–10.

Mumford, D. (1994). Neuronal architectures for pattern-theoretic problems. In *Large-scale neuronal theories of the brain*. Edited by Koch, C. and Davis, J. L. Cambridge, MA: MIT Press. 125–152.

Murase, H. and Nayar, S. (1995). Visual learning and recognition of 3D objects from appearance. *International Journal of Computer Vision* 14:5–24.

Murphy, G. L. (1991). Parts in object concepts: Experiments with artificial categories. *Memory & Cognition* 19:423–438.

Murphy, G. L. and Medin, D. L. (1985). The role of theories in conceptual coherence. *Psychological Review* 92:289–316.

Navon, D. (1977). Forest before trees: The precedence of global features in visual perception. *Cognitive Psychology* 9:353–383.

Nazir, T. and O'Regan, J. K. (1990). Some results on translation invariance in the human visual system. *Spatial vision* 5:81–100.

Newsome, W. T. and Paré, E. B. (1988). A selective impairment of motion perception following lesions of the middle temporal visual area (MT). *Journal of Neuroscience* 8:2201–2211.

Nicod, J. (1930). *Foundations of geometry and induction*. London: Routledge & Kegan Paul.

Nitzberg, M. and Mumford, D. (1990). The 2.1-D sketch. *Proceedings of the 3rd International Conference on Computer Vision*. 138–144.

Nosofsky, R. M. (1988). Exemplar-based accounts of relations between classification, recognition, and typicality. *Journal of Experimental Psychology: Learning, Memory, and Cognition* 14:700–708.

Nosofsky, R. M. (1991a). Stimulus bias, asymmetric similarity, and classification. *Cognitive Psychology* 23:94–140.

Nosofsky, R. M. (1991b). Tests of an exemplar model for relating perceptual classification and recognition memory. *Journal of Experimental Psychology: Human Perception and Performance* 17:3–27.

Nosofsky, R. M. (1992). Similarity scaling and cognitive process models. *Annual Review of Psychology* 43:25–53.

O'Regan, J. K. (1992). Solving the real mysteries of visual perception: The world as an outside memory. *Canadian J. of Psychology* 46:461–488.

O'Reilly, R. C. and Johnson, M. H. (1994). Object recognition and sensitive periods: A computational analysis of visual imprinting. *Neural Computation* 6:357–389.

Palmer, S. E. (1978). Fundamental aspects of cognitive representation. In *Cognition and categorization*. Edited by Rosch, E. and Lloyd, B. B. Hillsdale, NJ: Erlbaum. 259–303.

Palmer, S. E., Rosch, E., and Chase, P. (1981). Canonical perspective and the perception of objects. In *Attention and performance*. Edited by Long, J. and Baddeley, A. Volume 9. Hillsdale, NJ: Erlbaum. 135–151.

Peirce, C. S. (1868). Questions concerning certain faculties claimed for man. *Journal of Speculative Philosophy* 2:103–114.

Pentland, A. P. (1986). Shading into texture. *Artificial Intelligence* 29:147–170.

Perrett, D. I. and Harries, M. H. (1988). Characteristic views and the visual inspection of simple faceted and smooth objects: Tetrahedra and potatoes. *Perception* 17:703–720.

Perrett, D. I., Mistlin, A. J., and Chitty, A. J. (1987). Visual neurones responsive to faces. *Trends in Neurosciences* 10:358–364.

Perrett, D. I., Oram, M. W., Harries, M. H., Bevan, R., Hietanen, J. K., Benson, P. J., and Thomas, S. (1991). Viewer-centred and object-centred coding of heads in the macaque temporal cortex. *Exp. Brain Research* 86:159–173.

Perrett, D. I., Smith, P. A. J., Potter, D. D., Mistlin, A. J., Head, A. S., Milner, A. D., and Jeeves, M. A. (1985). Visual cells in the temporal cortex sensitive to face view and gaze direction. *Proceedings of the Royal Society of London B* 223:293–317.

Phillips, F. and Todd, J. T. (1996). Perception of local three-dimensional shape. *Journal of Experimental Psychology: HPP* 22:230–244.

Pitts, W. and McCulloch, W. S. (1947/1965). How we know universals: The perception of auditory and visual forms. In *Embodiments of mind*. Cambridge, MA: MIT Press. 46–66.

Pizlo, Z., Rosenfeld, A., and Weiss, I. (1997). Visual space: Mathematics, engineering, and science. *Computer Vision, Graphics, and Image Processing: Image Understanding* 65:450–454.

Poggio, T. (1990). A theory of how the brain might work. *Cold Spring Harbor Symposia on Quantitative Biology* LV:899–910.

Poggio, T. and Edelman, S. (1990). A network that learns to recognize three-dimensional objects. *Nature* 343:263–266.

Poggio, T., Edelman, S., and Fahle, M. (1992). Learning of visual modules from examples: A framework for understanding adaptive visual performance. *Computer Vision, Graphics, and Image Processing: Image Understanding* 56:22–30.

Poggio, T., Gamble, E. B., and Little, J. J. (1988). Parallel integration of vision modules. *Science* 242:436–440.

Poggio, T. and Girosi, F. (1989). A theory of networks for approximation and learning. A.I. Memo No. 1140. Artificial Intelligence Laboratory. Massachusetts Institute of Technology.

Poggio, T. and Girosi, F. (1990). Regularization algorithms for learning that are equivalent to multilayer networks. *Science* 247:978–982.

Poggio, T. and Hurlbert, A. (1994). Observations on cortical mechanisms for object recognition and learning. In *Large-scale neuronal theories of the brain.* Edited by Koch, C. and Davis, J. Cambridge, MA: MIT Press. 153–182.

Poggio, T., Torre, V., and Koch, C. (1985). Computational vision and regularization theory. *Nature* 317:314–319.

Poggio, T. and Vetter, T. (1992). Recognition and structure from one 2D model view: Observations on prototypes, object classes, and symmetries. A.I. Memo No. 1347. Artificial Intelligence Laboratory. Massachusetts Institute of Technology.

Poincaré, H. (1913/1963). *Mathematics and science: Last essays.* Translated by J. W. Bolduc. New York: Dover.

Posner, M. I. (1978). *Chronometric explorations of mind.* Hillsdale, NJ: Erlbaum.

Preparata, F. P. and Shamos, M. I. (1985). *Computational geometry.* New York: Springer Verlag.

Price, C. J. and Humphreys, G. W. (1989). The effects of surface detail on object categorization and naming. *Quarterly Journal of Experimental Psychology A* 41:797–828.

Putnam, H. (1988). *Representation and reality.* Cambridge, MA: MIT Press.

Pylyshyn, Z. (1973). What the mind's eye tells the mind's brain: A critique of mental imagery. *Psychological Bulletin* 80:1–24.

Quine, W. V. O. (1969). Natural kinds. In *Ontological relativity and other essays.* New York: Columbia University Press. 114–138.

Ratliff, F. and Sirovich, L. (1978). Equivalence classes of visual stimuli. *Vision Research* 18:845–851.

Reshetnyak, Y. G. (1989). *Space mappings with bounded distortion, Translations of mathematical monographs.* Volume 73. Providence: American Math. Soc.

Rhodes, G. (1988). Looking at faces: First-order and second-order features as determinants of facial appearance. *Perception* 17:43–63.

Richards, W., Jepson, A., and Feldman, J. (1996). Priors, preferences, and categorical percepts. In *Perception as Bayesian inference.* Edited by Knill, D. and Richards, W. Cambridge: Cambridge University Press. 93–122.

Rock, I. (1973). *Orientation and form.* Cambridge, MA: MIT Press.

Rock, I. (1974). The perception of disoriented figures. *Scientific American* 230: 78–85.

Rock, I. and DiVita, J. (1987). A case of viewer-centered object perception. *Cognitive Psychology* 19:280–293.

Rock, I., Schreiber, C., and Ro, T. (1994). The dependence of two-dimensional shape perception on orientation. *Perception* 23:1409–1426.

Rock, I., Wheeler, D., and Tudor, L. (1989). Can we imagine how objects look from other viewpoints? *Cognitive Psychology* 21:185–210.

Rolls, E. T. (1996). Visual processing in the temporal lobe for invariant object recognition. In *Neurobiology*. Edited by Torre, V. and Conti, T. New York: Plenum Press. 325–353.

Rolls, E. T., Baylis, G. C., Hasselmo, M. E., and Nalwa, V. (1989). The effect of learning on the face selective responses of neurons in the cortex in the superior temporal sulcus of the monkey. *Experimental Brain Research* 76:153–164.

Rolls, E. T. and Tovee, M. J. (1994). Processing speed in the cerebral cortex and the neurophysiology of visual masking. *Proceedings of the Royal Society of London B* 257:9–15.

Rolls, E. T. and Tovee, M. J. (1995a). The responses of single neurons in the temporal visual cortical areas of the macaque when more than one stimulus is present in the receptive field. *Experimental Brain Research* 103:409–420.

Rolls, E. T. and Tovee, M. J. (1995b). Sparseness of the neuronal representation of stimuli in the primate temporal visual cortex. *Journal of Neurophysiology* 73:713–726.

Rolls, E. T., Tovee, M. J., Purcell, D. G., Stewart, A. L., and Azzopardi, P. (1994). The responses of neurons in the temporal cortex of primates, and face identification and detection. *Experimental Brain Research* 101:473–484.

Rolls, E. T., Tovee, M. J., and Ramachandran, V. S. (1993). Visual learning reflected in the responses of neurons in the temporal visual cortex of the macaque. *Society for Neuroscience Abstracts* 19:27.

Rosch, E. (1978). Principles of categorization. In *Cognition and categorization*. Edited by Rosch, E. and Lloyd, B. Hillsdale, NJ: Erlbaum. 27–48.

Rosch, E., Mervis, C. B., Gray, W. D., Johnson, D. M., and Boyes-Braem, P. (1976). Basic objects in natural categories. *Cognitive Psychology* 8:382–439.

Rose, D. (1996). Some reflections on (or by?) grandmother cells. *Perception* 25:881–884.

Russell, B. (1921). *Analysis of mind*. London: Allen and Unwin.

Sakai, K. and Miyashita, Y. (1991). Neural organization for the long-term memory of paired associates. *Nature* 354:152–155.

Sakai, K. and Miyashita, Y. (1994). Neuronal tuning to learned complex forms in vision. *NeuroReport* 5:829–832.

Sakai, K., Naya, Y., and Miyashita, Y. (1994). Neuronal tuning and associative mechanisms in form representation. *Learning and Memory* 1:83–105.

Salzman, C. D., Britten, K. H., and Newsome, W. T. (1990). Cortical microstimulation influences perceptual judgements of motion direction. *Nature* 346:174–177.

SAS (1989). *SAS/STAT User's Guide, Version* 6. Cary, NC: SAS Institute Inc.

Schiele, B. and Crowley, J. L. (1996). Object recognition using multidimensional receptive field histograms. In *Proc. ECCV'96, Lecture Notes in Computer Science*. Edited by Buxton, B. and Cipolla, R. Volume 1. Berlin: Springer. 610–619.

Schiffer, S. (1987). *Remnants of meaning*. Cambridge, MA: MIT Press.

Schyns, P. G. (1998). Diagnostic recognition: Task constraints, object information, and their interactions. *Cognition* in press.

Schyns, P. G., Goldstone, R. L., and Thibaut, J.-P. (1998). The development of features in object concepts. *Behavioral and Brain Sciences* 21:1–54.

Seibert, M. and Waxman, A. M. (1990). Learning aspect graph representations from view sequences. In *Neural information processing systems*. Edited by Touretzky, D. Volume 2. San Mateo, CA: Morgan Kaufmann. 258–265.

Seibert, M. and Waxman, A. M. (1992). Adaptive 3D object recognition from multiple views. *IEEE Transactions on Pattern Analysis and Machine Intelligence* 14:107–124.

Selfridge, O. G. (1959). Pandemonium: A paradigm for learning. *The mechanisation of thought processes*. London: H.M.S.O.

Shapira, Y. and Ullman, S. (1991). A pictorial approach to object classification. *Proceedings IJCAI*. 1257–1263.

Shapley, R. and Victor, J. (1986). Hyperacuity in cat retinal ganglion cells. *Science* 231:999–1002.

Shashua, A. (1995). Algebraic functions for recognition. *IEEE Transactions on Pattern Analysis and Machine Intelligence* 17:779–789.

Shashua, A. and Ullman, S. (1988). Structural saliency: The detection of globally salient structures using a locally connected network. *Proceedings of the 2nd International Conference on Computer Vision*. Tarpon Springs, FL: IEEE. 321–327.

Shepard, D. (1968a). A two-dimensional interpolation function for irregularly spaced data. In *Proc. 23rd National Conference ACM* 517–524.

Shepard, R. N. (1962). The analysis of proximities: Multidimensional scaling with unknown distance function. *Psychometrika* 27(2):125–140.

Shepard, R. N. (1964). Attention and the metric structure of the stimulus space. *Journal of Mathematical Psychology* 1:54–87.

Shepard, R. N. (1966). Metric structures in ordinal data. *J. Math. Psychology* 3:287–315.

Shepard, R. N. (1968b). Cognitive psychology: A review of the book by U. Neisser. *Amer. J. Psychol.* 81:285–289.

Shepard, R. N. (1975). Form, formation, and transformation of internal representations. In *Information processing and cognition: The Loyola symposium*. Edited by Solso, R. L. Hillsdale, NJ: Erlbaum. 87–122.

Shepard, R. N. (1980). Multidimensional scaling, tree-fitting, and clustering. *Science* 210:390–397.

Shepard, R. N. (1984). Ecological constraints on internal representation: resonant kinematics of perceiving, imagining, thinking, and dreaming. *Psychological Review* 91:417–447.

Shepard, R. N. (1987). Toward a universal law of generalization for psychological science. *Science* 237:1317–1323.

Shepard, R. N. and Cermak, G. W. (1973). Perceptual-cognitive explorations of a toroidal set of free-form stimuli. *Cognitive Psychology* 4:351–377.

Shepard, R. N. and Chipman, S. (1970). Second-order isomorphism of internal representations: Shapes of states. *Cognitive Psychology* 1:1–17.

Shepard, R. N. and Cooper, L. A. (1982). *Mental images and their transformations*. Cambridge, MA: MIT Press.

Shepard, R. N. and Kannappan, S. (1993). Connectionist implementation of a theory of generalization. In *Advances in neural information processing systems 5*. Edited by Hanson, S. J., Cowan, J. D., and Giles, C. L. Los Alamitos, CA: Morgan Kaufmann. 665–672.

Shepard, R. N. and Metzler, J. (1971). Mental rotation of three-dimensional objects. *Science* 171:701–703.

Simons, D. J. and Levin, D. T. (1997). Change blindness. *Trends in Cognitive Science* 1:261–267.

Singer, W. and Gray, C. M. (1995). Visual feature integration and the temporal correlation hypothesis. *Annual Review of Neuroscience* 18:555–586.

Sinha, P. and Poggio, T. (1996). Role of learning in three-dimensional form perception. *Nature* 384:460–463.

Smith, L. B., Gasser, M., and Sandhofer, C. M. (1997). Learning to talk about the properties of objects: a network model of the development of dimensions. In *Mechanisms of perceptual learning*. Edited by Medin, D., Goldstone, R., and Schyns, P. New York: Academic Press. 220–256.

Smith, W., Dunn, J., Kirsner, K., and Randell, M. (1995). Colour in map displays: Issues for task-specific display design. *Interacting with Computers* 7:151–165.

Snippe, H. P. and Koenderink, J. J. (1992). Discrimination thresholds for channel-coded systems. *Biological Cybernetics* 66:543–551.

Snodgrass, J. G. and Vanderwart, M. (1980). A standardized set of 260 pictures: Norms for name agreement, image agreement, familiarity, and visual complexity. *Journal of Experimental Psychology: Human Learning and Memory* 6:174–215.

Srinivas, K. (1993). Perceptual specificity in nonverbal priming. *Journal of Experimental Psychology: Learning, Memory and Cognition* 19:582–602.

Stankiewicz, B. and Hummel, J. (1996). MetriCat: A representation for basic and subordinate-level classification. *Proceedings of 18th Annual Conf. of the Cognitive Science Society*. Edited by Cottrell, G. W. San Diego: Erlbaum. 254–259.

Stone, C. J. (1982). Optimal global rates of convergence for nonparametric regression. *Annals of statistics* 10:1040–1053.

Stone, J. V. (1996a). A canonical microfunction for learning perceptual invariances. *Perception* 25:207–220.

Stone, J. V. (1996b). Learning perceptually salient visual parameters using spatiotemporal smoothness constraints. *Neural Computation* 8:1463–1492.

Stoner, G. R., Albright, T. D., and Ramachandran, V. S. (1990). Transparency and coherence in human motion perception. *Nature* 344:153–155.

Stryker, M. P. (1989). Cortical physiology: Is grandmother an oscillation? *Nature* 338:297–298.

Sugihara, T., Edelman, S., and Tanaka, K. (1998). Representation of objective similarity among three-dimensional shapes in the monkey. *Biological Cybernetics* 78:1–7.

Sundararaman, D. (1980). *Moduli, deformations and classifications of compact complex manifolds*. Lanham, MD: Pitman.

Suppes, P., Pavel, M., and Falmagne, J. (1994). Representations and models in psychology. *Annual Review of Psychology* 45:517–544.

Swain, M. J. and Ballard, D. H. (1991). Color indexing. *International Journal of Computer Vision* 7:11–32.

Tanaka, J. and Gauthier, I. (1997). Expertise in object and face recognition. In *Mechanisms of perceptual learning*. Edited by Medin, D., Goldstone, R., and Schyns, P. New York: Academic Press. 85–125.

Tanaka, K. (1992). Inferotemporal cortex and higher visual functions. *Current Opinion in Neurobiology* 2:502–505.

Tanaka, K. (1993a). Column structure of inferotemporal cortex: "Visual alphabet" or "differential amplifiers"? *Proc. IJCNN-93*. Nagoya. 2:1095–1099.

Tanaka, K. (1993b). Neuronal mechanisms of object recognition. *Science* 262: 685–688.

Tanaka, K. (1996). Inferotemporal cortex and object vision. *Annual Review of Neuroscience* 19:109–139.

Tanaka, K., Saito, H., Fukada, Y., and Moriya, M. (1991). Coding visual images of objects in the inferotemporal cortex of the macaque monkey. *Journal of Neurophysiology* 66:170–189.

Tarr, M. J. (1995). Rotating objects to recognize them: A case study on the role of viewpoint dependency in the recognition of three-dimensional objects. *Psychonomic Bulletin & Review* 2:55–82.

Tarr, M. J. and Bülthoff, H. H. (1995). Is human object recognition better described by geon-structural-descriptions or by multiple-views? *Journal of Experimental Psychology: Human Perception and Performance* 21:1494–1505.

Tarr, M. J., Bülthoff, H. H., Zabinski, M., and Blanz, V. (1997). To what extent do unique parts influence recognition across changes in viewpoint? *Psychological Science* 8:282–289.

Tarr, M. J. and Gauthier, I. (1998). Do viewpoint-dependent mechanisms generalize across members of a class? *Cognition* 67:71–108.

Tarr, M. J. and Pinker, S. (1989). Mental rotation and orientation-dependence in shape recognition. *Cognitive Psychology* 21:233–282.

Tenenbaum, J. M., Fischler, M. A., and Barrow, H. G. (1981). Scene modeling: A structural basis for image description. In *Image modeling*. Edited by Rosenfeld, A. New York: Academic Press. 371–389.

Thompson, P. (1980). Margaret Thatcher: A new illusion. *Perception* 9:483–484.

Thorpe, S., Fize, D., and Marlot, C. (1996). Speed of processing in the human visual system. *Nature* 381:520–522.

Tikhonov, A. N. and Arsenin, V. Y. (1977). *Solutions of ill-posed problems.* Washington, D.C.: W. H. Winston.

Tomasi, C. and Kanade, T. (1992). Shape and motion from image streams under orthography: A factorization method. *International Journal of Computer Vision* 9:137–154.

Tovee, M. J., Rolls, E. T., and Azzopardi, P. (1994). Translation invariance in the responses to faces of single neurons in the temporal visual cortical areas of the alert monkey. *Journal of Neurophysiology* 72:1049–1060.

Tversky, A. (1977). Features of similarity. *Psychological Review* 84:327–352.

Tversky, A. and Gati, I. (1978). Studies of similarity. In *Cognition and categorization*. Edited by Rosch, E. and Lloyd, B. Hillsdale, NJ: Erlbaum. 79–98.

Tversky, B. and Hemenway, K. (1984). Objects, parts and categories. *Journal of Experimental Psychology: General* 113:169–193.

Ullman, S. (1979). *The interpretation of visual motion.* Cambridge, MA: MIT Press.

Ullman, S. (1984). Visual routines. *Cognition* 18:97–159.

Ullman, S. (1989). Aligning pictorial descriptions: An approach to object recognition. *Cognition* 32:193–254.

Ullman, S. (1996). *High-level vision.* Cambridge, MA: MIT Press.

Ullman, S. and Basri, R. (1991). Recognition by linear combinations of models. *IEEE Transactions on Pattern Analysis and Machine Intelligence* 13:992–1005.

Väisälä, J. (1992). Domains and maps. In *Quasiconformal space mappings.* Edited by Vuorinen, M. Number 1508 in Lecture Notes in Mathematics. Berlin: Springer-Verlag. 119–131.

van Gelder, T. (1990). Compositionality: A connectionist variation on a theme. *Cognitive Science* 14:355–384.

Vapnik, V. (1995). *The nature of statistical learning theory*. Berlin: Springer-Verlag.

Vetter, T., Jones, M. J., and Poggio, T. (1997). A bootstrapping algorithm for learning linear models of object classes. *Proceedings IEEE Conf. on Computer Vision and Pattern Recognition*. Puerto Rico. 40–46.

von Békésy, G. (1929). Zur theorie des Hörens. *Physikalische Zeitschrift* 30:115–125. [See K. R. Boff, L. Kaufman and J. P. Thomas, eds. (1986). Handbook of perception and human performance. Vol. 1. Ch. 15. New York: Wiley.]

von der Malsburg, C. (1981). The correlation theory of brain function. Internal report 81-2. Max-Planck-Institut für Biophysikalische Chemie. Postfach 2841, 3400 Göttingen, Germany. Reprinted in Domany, E., van Hemmen, J. L., and Schulten, K., editors. (1994). Models of Neural Networks II. Chapter 2. Berlin: Springer. 95–119.

von der Malsburg, C. (1995). Binding in models of perception and brain function. *Current Opinion in Neurobiology* 5:520–526.

Wallis, G. and Rolls, E. T. (1997). A model of invariant object recognition in the visual system. *Progress in Neurobiology* 51:167–194.

Wang, G., Tanaka, K., and Tanifuji, M. (1996). Optical imaging of functional organization in the monkey inferotemporal cortex. *Science* 272:1665–1668.

Wang, J. Y. A. and Adelson, E. H. (1994). Representing moving images with layers. *IEEE Trans. on Image Processing* 3:625–638.

Watanabe, S. (1985). *Pattern recognition: Human and mechanical*. New York: Wiley.

Weinshall, D. (1990). Qualitative depth from stereo, with applications. *Computer Vision, Graphics, and Image Processing* 49:222–241.

Weiss, Y. and Edelman, S. (1995). Representation of similarity as a goal of early visual processing. *Network* 6:19–41.

Weiss, Y., Edelman, S., and Fahle, M. (1993). Models of perceptual learning in vernier hyperacuity. *Neural Computation* 5:695–718.

Westheimer, G. (1981). Visual hyperacuity. *Progress in Sensory Physiology* 1:1–37.

Willshaw, D. J., Buneman, O. P., and Longuet-Higgins, H. C. (1969). Non-holographic associative memory. *Nature* 222:960–962.

Wirth, N. (1976). *Algorithms + data structures = programs*. New York: Prentice Hall.

Witkin, A. P. (1981). Recovering surface shape and orientation from texture. *Artificial Intelligence* 17:17–45.

Wittgenstein, L. (1973). *Philosophical investigations*. London: Blackwell.

Young, G. and Householder, A. S. (1938). Discussion of a set of points in terms of their mutual distances. *Psychometrika* 3:19–22.

Young, M. P., Tanaka, K., and Yamane, S. (1992). On oscillating neuronal responses in the visual cortex of the monkey. *Journal of Neurophysiology* 67:1464–1474.

Young, M. P. and Yamane, S. (1992). Sparse population coding of faces in the inferotemporal cortex. *Science* 256:1327–1331.

Yuille, A. L. and Grzywacz, N. M. (1988). A computational theory for the perception of coherent visual motion. *Nature* 333:71–74.

Zemel, R. S. and Hinton, G. E. (1991). Discovering viewpoint-invariant relationships that characterize objects. In *Neural information processing systems*. Edited by Touretzky, D. Volume 3. San Mateo: Morgan Kaufmann.

Zhu, S. C. and Yuille, A. L. (1996). FORMS: A flexible object recognition and modeling system. *International Journal of Computer Vision* 20:187–212.

Zorich, V. A. (1992). The global homeomorphism theorem for space quasiconformal mappings. In *Quasiconformal space mappings*. Edited by Vuorinen, M. Number 1508 in Lecture Notes in Mathematics. Berlin: Springer-Verlag. 132–148.

# Index